# HANDS OF STONE

*The Life and Legend of Roberto Duran*

Christian Giudice

D0166896

MILO BOOKS

First published in October 2006 by Milo Books

This paperback edition published in 2009

ISBN 978 1 903854 75 4

Typeset by e-type

Printed in Great Britain by
CPI Group (UK) Ltd, Croydon, CR0 4YY

Distributed in the USA and Canada by Consortium
www.cbsd.com

MILO BOOKS LTD
The Old Weighbridge
Station Road
Wrea Green
Lancs PR4 2PH
United Kingdom
www.milobooks.com

# HANDS OF STONE

## Worldwide Praise for HANDS OF STONE

"In the age of the tabloid we know more about many of our sporting heroes than we ever cared to know, but from the time he blasted his way into our consciousness with a punch to the scrotum almost four decades ago, Roberto Duran had been an elusive and enigmatic figure. With *Hands of Stone*, Christian Giudice has separated the wheat from the chaff in the most illuminating deconstruction of a mythic ring legend since John Lardner went toe-to-toe with the ghost of Stanley Ketchel."

George Kimball, author of *Four Kings*

"My favourite book."

Ricky Hatton, former three-time world champion

"Christian Giudice has succeeded brilliantly in separating the myth from the legend and produced a book that serves only to enhance further the reputation of an already astonishing fighter...*Hands of Stone* is the dazzling account of a breathtaking fighter and a remarkable man."

*The Independent*

"A cracking book."

*Daily Star*

"The first – and definitive – account of Duran's extraordinary life both in and out of the ring."

*Boxing Digest*

"Duran's 120-bout career is vividly chronicled."

*The Independent On Sunday*

"Compelling."

*The Sun*

"A must for all fight fans."

*Liverpool Echo*

"A gripping biography. Every page will keep readers enthralled."

*Dublin Evening Herald*

"A profoundly detailed reconstruction of Duran's world."

Gerald Early, *Belles Lettres, A Literary Review*

"What a story!"

*Scotland on Sunday*

"If you buy only one boxing book this year, *Hands of Stone* should be it."

*Boxing Monthly*

*I am not God but something very similar.*

Roberto Duran

To my mother – who faced down a deadly disease – and beat it.

To my father, a fighter, a man, my hero – who once threw a perfect left hook on Schellenger Ave. (between Atlantic and Pacific Aves.) on a summer night in Wildwood.

Thank you for protecting us all of these years.
I wrote this book for you, Pop.

# Contents

# Prologue

*"We mustn't be afraid of violence. Hatred is an element of struggle; relentless hatred of the enemy that impels us over and beyond the natural limitations of man and transforms us into effective, violent, selective and cold-blooded machines."*

Che Guevara

IT IS 26 NOVEMBER 1980 and Roberto Duran Samaniego stands naked in the middle of the ring. His arms sulk by his sides. He feels weak. His body has betrayed him, as he has betrayed himself. His eyes, the twin beacons of his demonic aura, search for the exit.

Always defiant, tonight he bleeds compromise. It is like watching a Ferrari sputtering to the closest gas station. With sixteen seconds remaining in the eighth round in the Louisiana Superdome, his mocking, face-pulling, showboating challenger, Sugar Ray Leonard, has affronted his dignity and stripped him of his *macho*. And so he breaks the contract that he signed the day he stepped in the boxing ring: To punch till the end. Duran has always boxed like he cursed, in quick, immediate thrusts; now the roughest, toughest, most feared fighter in the world raises his left hand and walks away.

"No quiero pelear con el payaso," says Duran. *I do not want to fight with this clown.* He repeats the words, but a ringside broadcaster claims to hear him say "no más," the Spanish for "no more." The phrase will live in sporting infamy.

After a second, Leonard's brother Roger yells, "He quit on you Ray." Leonard runs over and jumps on the ringpost. The fight is done.

People would later dub the man a coward, a fake, a phony. They said laziness and gluttony had precipitated his downfall; fame had accelerated it.

The first part of Duran's career, his life, was over. Act Two was about to begin.

★ ★ ★

Even before I went to Panama I knew one thing for sure about Roberto Duran: The man was not a quitter. I didn't understand the contradictions of the *no más* fight but also didn't buy into the hype. When I told people that I was headed to his homeland, they joked about the infamous moment when he left the ring seven rounds early. "Tell him 'no más' for me," they said.

With a face that reminded some of Che Guevara, others of Charles Manson, Duran's feral stare never left me. His look was compelling, his image enigmatic, his fighting skills unsurpassed. In the ring, Duran came forward and intimidated; he didn't know any other way. Those who stood up to him paid the price in blood and hurt; those who ran were pursued and hunted down. Sportswriters devoured stories of his wild childhood, told of him swimming across bays with a bag of mangoes held in his mouth to feed his family. His eyes were "dark coals of fire" and anything that he sneered at "froze" in terror. But who was this man? Was he really pure evil lodged in the body of a 135-pound prince, or was it all an act?

Even when his ability to intimidate had waned, the *Doo-ran, Doo-ran* cheers still echoed around sold-out arenas. Even when he was only a quarter of his former self, a sad, overweight Elvis making his last call, he was still Duran. Watching those final years of futility it became clear that legends never die, they just age. So when the thought of finding and telling the Duran story crept into my head, I couldn't resist. With the purpose of finding this man, I decided to leave my job, friends and family and head to Panama City. I had a smattering of Spanish, a laptop and some old Duran fights on tape. I didn't even know if he spoke English, or how well.

I was six years old on that November night in New Orleans in 1980. I wanted to know about the young Duran, the kid whose face came to be plastered all over Panama City, and how someone who had nothing became a symbol for hope in a Third World country that suffered every day. I wanted to see how the mere glimpse of Duran's smile could make a difference. Few people have the influence on a country as Duran does in Panama and the only way I would understand it was to follow him there. The only way I could comprehend the strength, the character of this man was to eat *patacones* and *empanadas* with his people, sip coconut juice straight from the fruit, dance salsa, and listen to the music of Osvaldo Ayala, Los Rabanes or Sandra y Sammy. I had to go to Guarare and the gyms in Chorrillo to let the legend seep into my blood amid the 100-degree heat. All his old managers, promoters, friends and schoolteachers would have something to say and I had to absorb it.

Finding him was another story. Somehow in Panama everyone knows Duran personally. He is everyone's *buen amigo*. So when a taxi dropped me off at Duran's home in the El Cangrejo neighborhood the night I arrived, I knew I was onto him. Duran never showed that night, but I knew deep down that I would find him and learn the secrets that many in Panama claimed already to know. "That's the reason that many people respect him because he never forget where he come from," said Chavo, his oldest son. "He's humble and always told me, 'Remember I'm from El Chorrillo, a poor neighborhood, so you have to be humble.' The people respect that. He's always helping the poor people, especially with the kids. People like that." In a country of less than three million souls where many live on less than a dollar a day, that counts.

The boxing scene in Panama is a story in itself, a gallery of memorable, glittering characters. Every gym tells a tale. One couldn't go into the Papi Mendez Gym without seeing Celso Chavez Sr. in a corner cajoling a fighter while his son Celso Jr. wrapped the hands of another prospect. Look closely and there was the prince of Panamanian boxing, two-time lightweight champ Ismael "El Tigre" Laguna, playing dominoes with friends on a corner, or light-flyweight champ Roberto Vasquez knocking an opponent senseless in an El Maranon Gym. Dozens of boxing lifers greet people at the entrance to Panama's most popular gym Jesus Master Gomez in Barraza, while Yeyo "El Mafia" Cortez and Franklin Bedoya reminisce at the Pedro Alcazar Gym in Curundu. Young fighters mimic two-time world champ Hilario Zapata's squatting defensive style or Eusebio Pedroza's brilliance off the ropes. They listen closely to caustic woman trainer Maria Toto as she barks instructions in a gym in San Miguelito, while others hone their skills in Panama Al Brown Gym in "the cradle of champions," Colon. All the while, the sounds of "yab, yab, yab" filter through the heat. And no one in Panama would even know about boxing if it weren't for the voice of the isthmus, *Lo Mejor de Boxeo*'s Juan Carlos Tapia, a man who spits quick-witted Tapiaisms at a feverish rate. Most of the twenty-three (at the time of writing) living world champs meet for reunions at local cards, while boxing wannabes throw combinations in the corners at amateur bouts. Sit down at fight night, grab a local Atlas beer or a bucket of ice with a bottle of Seco-Herrano, a chorizo meat kabob, and prepare for bedlam. You never know what might happen.

"I am Duran," the man used to say after fights, as if the statement spoke for itself. Pure and simple, nothing more or less, just the exclamation that there was not another human on this earth like him. In the ring, there wasn't. With his blend of skill and ferocity, the greased back hair and sharp beard, the man they called *Cholo* (for his mixed Indian heritage) had the best boxers of his generation against the ropes. Duran in full flow was a curious but riveting combination of in-your-face chaos and relentless beauty. As a person he lived just as freely, without caution.

Roberto Duran knows about pain. He knows what it's like to make an opponent succumb before stepping foot in the ring. He knows, inside in his *corazon*, his heart, what it's like to watch a man feel fear. For he did that with a look, one brazen, cocksure glance that had those same men trembling as they taped their hands or worked up a pre-fight sweat. He did it often, and with aplomb, stole men's hearts without trying. That was Duran.

Roberto Duran knows about torture. He knows what it's like to crowd a man, stick him in the ropes, rake his eyes with his beard, jumble his senses with a short hook, bust him below the belt, thumb him, break his will with a running right hand. He knows what it's like to make a man cringe with every punch, break him down so thoroughly so that he would never return the same again. Some never recovered, and they saw that face, that beard, those eyes, and were reminded of the man every time they threw a punch, feinted, jabbed. It was Duran, that face, that look.

Roberto Duran knows about struggle. He knows what it's like to spend his childhood finding ways to provide for his mother. He knows about living with nothing – and still reaching in his pocket to give to others. He knows about poverty, disease, sorrow – and how to dissolve tears with a smile. That's Roberto Duran.

Roberto Duran knows about ecstasy. He knows the feeling of beating a man, an idea, a creation, a nation, to believe there wasn't another human on earth who could challenge him. He knows what it's like to hang through the ropes with tears rushing down, and hear an entire arena sing an anthem in his honor. He knows what it's like to have an entire country on his back and feel their weight each time he throws a punch. He knows what it's like to deleteriously fall, rise again, and return home to thousands calling his name. He knows what it's like to face a monster, a fear, and vanquish it. That was Duran.

Roberto Duran has felt pain. And he knows about sorrow. He is a man who has felt every human emotion to excess, and expressed his reactions for the world to see. Not since and maybe never again will there be a boxer quite like him. Duran was an entertainer, a brute, a fighter, a lover, a loyal friend, an artist. In his prime he took the top fighters in the world and stripped them of their pride.

But the one time in New Orleans in 1980, he lost his. Unfortunately for many people, that's all that counts.

*Christian Giudice*

# 1

# HUNGER

*Blessed be the Lord my rock*
*Who trains my hands for war*
*And my fingers for battle*

Psalm 144:1

DONA CEFERINA GARCIA was looking for her husband – and she had a good idea where to find him. Rumors in the tough *barrio* of El Chorrillo had him drinking in a bar with another woman. That was bad enough, but their teenage daughter was due to give birth any hour, and Ceferina's services would be required to deliver the baby. It was hardly the best moment for the new child's grandfather to disappear with some *puta*, some whore. Ceferina, eyes blazing, mouth set and fists clenched, was on the warpath.

The bar stood next to a concrete apartment block known as *La Casa de Piedra*, the House of Stone, on North 27th Street; Apartment A, Room 96, to be precise, was where her daughter Clara lived and was already going into labor. Ceferina entered the bar with fists clenched and there was her husband, Jose "Chavelo" Samaniego, in the corner with a local girl. Ceferina took in the scene with a look of fury. Many women in Panama turned their heads from the Latin games their husbands played but she was not one of them. Both poverty and inclination had made her a fighter; she had once been thrown in jail for punching the local mayor.

With one fast right hand, she left Chavelo lying on the sticky bar floor and headed back to her daughter.

Ceferina would bequeath her power to her grandson, born just hours later when her daughter Clara pushed eight-pound Roberto Duran Samaniego into her hands on June 16, 1951. They rushed the bloody boy to the Santo Tomas Hospital in a taxicab. "He was born in a stone house, and fell right in my mother's arms at six o'clock in the afternoon," said Clara years later, squatting to illustrate the trajectory of the baby. She named him Roberto after his uncle, the brother of his father Margarito.

Clara was young, not much more than a girl, but the child was already her fourth. Motherhood started early in Panama. She came not from Chorrillo, a poor area of downtown Panama City, but from Guararé, a small town in the Los Santos province in the interior. It has a central square, a couple of bars, a church, a gas station, a hardware store, a small downtown area with banks and markets, and a field which once held an old bullring. A symbolic guitar greets visitors at the town's entrance and Guararé is chiefly known for its *Feria de la Mejorana*, a folk music festival every September that attracts the country's best dance groups and waves of visitors. The highlight is the simple, classy *La Pajarita* dance. Women wear *pollera*, a dress made of linen and lace decorated by flowers, while men in their best suits drink Seco, a pungent liquor produced in the town of Herrera.

Young, curvaceous and willing, the teenage Clara made men look her way. Though not conventionally beautiful, her allure filtered through her eyes. The young Clara flaunted her flowing brown hair and full figure. Her inviting gaze comforted, made men feel wanted. That was her magic. Instead of prodding, Clara caressed; instead of rushing, she glided. She was tender, soft, gentle and generous with the little she had. People who knew her as a teenage mother remember a sweet girl striving for a better life for her children. "She was very pretty and very elegant," said her sister Mireya. "Many men were interested in her but she had bad luck. She had many children, but had to cope with much."

With one exception, all of her men were strong Latin types who took her to bed then hit the road. First, she had a son to a Puerto Rican and named him Domingo, though everyone called him "Toti." His father did not stick around. "He abandoned me in 1950 because my mother had some problems with him," said Toti. "He wanted to take me but my mother did not agree to this, so I did not see him again." After her Puerto Rican lover left, Clara had a brief fling with a Filipino and bore him a daughter, Marina.

In Panama, marriage was no big deal. Many unions, especially among the poor, were consensual rather than contractual; indeed, a marriage ceremony often marked the culmination of a life together rather than the start of one, and served as a mark of economic success. Sometimes a priest might encourage it for an elderly invalid, as a prerequisite for receiving the rite of the anointing of the sick. In rural areas, where the *campesinos'* livelihood was reasonably secure and the population stable, children suffered little social stigma if their parents were not legally married. If parents split up, the paternal grandparents sometimes took in both mother and children, or a woman might return to her mother's or her parents' household, leaving behind her children so that she could work. There were many female-headed families, particularly in cities and among the poor. Legal marriage tended to be the rule only among the more prosperous farmers, cattle ranchers, the urban middle class and the elite.

The southernmost state of Central America, Panama was for 300 years a part of the Spanish Empire. A land bridge between the continents of North and South America, its status as a vital crossroads would eventually be underscored by two massive transport projects: the Panama Railroad and the Panama Canal. The railroad, linking north with south, was forged through a purgatory of disease and death; legend has it that one man died for every railroad tie on the track. Then, in 1903, the state declared independence from neighboring Colombia and granted rights to the United States to build and administer indefinitely a canal connecting the Atlantic and Pacific oceans. The Canal opened in 1914.

A treaty provided the Americans, or Zonians, with rights to both sides of the Canal, a one-sided deal that would cause tension between both parties for much of the twentieth century. Locals living or working in the Zone could be prosecuted under American law and faced the possibility of extradition to the States for trial. From the outset, the Americans turned the area into their own private quarters in which Panamanians, whose Caribbean-black contingent composed most of the Zone workers, were mere houseguests. The Americans created their own country club atmosphere in the Zone with perfectly coiffed lawns, golf courses, comfortable housing, and bowling alleys.

Margarito Duran Sanchez was a US Army cook, born in Arizona, the second son of Mexican parents, Diego and Esther. At nineteen, he was stationed in the Canal Zone and worked in Mi Pueblito, an area of small villages just north of Chorrillo that housed Zone workers. There he befriended Clara's brother Moises. "On my way to work I used to walk past that area," Clara remembered, "and that is where I met Roberto's father. He used to cook in the villages." Moises thought highly of the Mexican and would often give him a lift over unpaved roads to Guarare to see Clara. According to Garcia, Clara escaped from her Filipino boyfriend late one night with Margarito and they became lovers. "She left with him in the middle of the night," said Moises Samaniego. "He came to get her and she was never allowed to see the Filipino man again."

Margarito was a large man who could look after himself if pushed, though it wasn't his nature to look for trouble. "I don't remember him getting in many fights but he could handle himself," said Moises. "He hit down two guys at once in a fight. He was a very big man."

The lovers soon had a son, Alcibiades. He died at two years old from what was reported as an apparent heart attack, though Clara claims it was due to medical negligence. "My older son died when [doctors] let him fall from the cradle," said Clara. "He was seriously hurt and when I picked him up he was already dead." According to Roberto, the brother he never knew died after an operation went wrong. "He was born sick," said Duran. "My mother took care of him because he was born with a heart condition. That was the child my mom loved the most, because his heart was damaged. He slept on the bed and I slept on the floor because my mother loved him the most. My mother took him to the hospital. If it had been now, they would have paid my mom millions because the doctors performed the operation wrongly and killed my little brother, the other Duran. My brother had to undergo a heart examination but he was operated on at the Children's Hospital and the operation was not done properly. My brother died there. If it had not happened so many years ago, but now, my mother would have been able to start a claim."

Before Alcibiades died, the union of Clara and Margarito also produced little Roberto, and at first the family lived in their small apartment in Chorrillo, a low-income fishing town west of Panama City, bordering the Canal Zone, and one of the country's poorest slums. Almost all of the homes were made of wood. Chorrillo was a place to pass through and not look back.

Like the others, Margarito would not stay to see his surviving son grow. He cut out without a word when his tour of duty in Panama ended. Some say the only thing he left his son was his punch. "His father left us and went to live with another woman," said Clara. "Roberto was a year and five months old. His father was not interested in learning about Roberto. So I worked while Duran grew up. Until he was twelve years old we used to go to work together."

Duran Senior shipped out to California and then Germany and would go on to serve with an infantry battalion in Vietnam. He married a woman from Guatemala and later settled in Flagstaff, Arizona. There was no apology and little regret, just a man trying to make peace with the decisions he'd made in his immature youth. While some ageing fathers use the remaining years of their life to reconstruct all the missed birthdays and graduations, Margarito didn't want to rewind anymore. It just so happened that the kid he left abandoned turned out to be one of the greatest boxers ever.

"I didn't know what he was going to be," said Margarito from his Flagstaff home years later. "I supported him as well as I could. Clara was fifteen at the time, and when we separated … she went on to have ten or twelve kids, something like that. I just couldn't do it. I don't have any regrets. When you are in the Army, you just have to go. No ifs, ands or buts, I just couldn't come back. My family couldn't go but I could. I could only bring Roberto with me if I got his rights and adopted him. She didn't want to give him to me. What could I do? We weren't married. The thing was, I wanted to take him back to the States, but she wouldn't give him to me. In Germany, I adopted my daughter … I adopted all my children. If I had gotten Roberto's permission, it would have been okay.

"Was the life in the States better than the one he had? Better, well, no. Maybe he wouldn't have become a fighter … He looked exactly like my younger brother Roberto. That's who I named him after. I baptized him and recognized him. I gave him everything I could. I recognized him in the hospital. That's what a father is supposed to do." The words came out as if Margarito needed to absolve himself of guilt.

Clara was left to bring up her children with no money and no prospects. She would rely on her own extended family, in particular Ceferina, her mother and her rock. Mireya recalled entering the apartment to the sight of her mother breast feeding Clara's children. She took care of the family until she passed years later. "Do you know what she used to do?" a smiling Mireya said. "Like after having Toti, after giving birth she would leave them in my mother's care in the house of stone. Since there was no milk, my mother would put one to one of her nipples, and the other one on the other, so that they would suckle. Because my mother had also just had a baby, my brother Joaquin."

An individual without kin was adrift in Panama. Family ties were the surest defense against a hostile and uncertain world and blood loyalty was ingrained. This loyalty often outweighed that given to a spouse; indeed, a man frequently gave priority to his parents or siblings over his wife. Relatives relied on each other for help throughout life. Grandparents, uncles, aunts and cousins faithfully gathered to mark birthdays and holidays together. Married children visited their parents frequently, even daily. In some small remote villages and in some classes, such as the elite, generations of intermarriage meant almost everyone was related in some way. Co-residence was the basis for the most enduring ties an individual formed.

Clara remained bitter about her abandonment. "When I met him in Las Vegas [years later] he said he used to send letters with someone, but I was never given any of his letters," she said, "and he never helped me with Roberto. Never." Her sister Mireya added, "He left and never came back again. That is the reason why Roberto never wanted to learn anything about his papa. He resented that he had left him."

Roberto would grow up knowing only what relatives told him, of how his parents met at Mi Pueblito. "My father was a soldier and all the soldiers slept in a church," he said. "There was a private military club and my father worked there as a cook and when they had a day off, he would go to the bar. When I was about two or three, my mom took me there. That was when she told me about him. She was strange … after that she didn't know about him anymore. He left and we wouldn't see him again. My mom later told me that he wanted to take me but she refused."

The father did leave his son at least one thing: his Mexican complexion, the light skin tone contrasting with the jet-black hair of a mixed-breed *cholo*. Indeed "Cholo" or "Cholito" would become young Roberto's nickname. The fierce, kill-or-be-killed boxing style of most Mexican fighters was one Duran would also adopt, unlike the more cultured style of most Panamanian boxers.

The young family suffered. Clara could often be seen with her beloved and barefoot Roberto by her side, whether in her hometown of Guarare or on North 27th and 29th streets in Chorrillo. She worked odd jobs and found various apartments when she wasn't staying with her relatives. When available, rice, beans and meat made a typical meal. "Clara and Roberto would come here on weekends all the time," said an old friend, Lesbia Diaz, from Guarare. "Clara even lived here for a couple years. Roberto was always running without shoes, even riding horses around town."

Three years after Margarito left, Clara hooked up with a young man from Guarare named Victorino Vargas. The seventeen-year-old Vargas played guitar for a band and they met at a ball. All of the passion lost on the man that broke her heart now returned. The union was not without problems and Vargas failed to hold down a steady job, but he would father five children with Clara: girls Anabelle, Isabelle and Justiniano and boys Victor and Armando, or "Pototo." In all she would have nine children but only Roberto would carry the Duran surname.

Whenever Vargas returned home, Roberto would be there waiting for him with a big grin and a cry of "Victorino!" Like other children his age, he thrilled to King Kong, Mexican adventure movies and cartoons. He and Toti loved Cantinflas movies, cowboys like Roy Rogers and acted out moves they learned from the popular television *luchadores*, or Mexican masked wrestlers, like the famous *El Santo* (The Saint), El Vampiro and the Blue Demon, who became icons not just for their ring exploits but for their appearances in schlocky but popular movies and comic books. The boys also aped the style of popular American singers like Elvis Presley and Frankie Lymon. On Sundays, they could be seen at the Iglesia de Don Bosco or the Iglesia de las Mercadas, where young Roberto lit candles to Jesus de Nazareth and the Virgen de Carmen. "We always were in the streets, in an area which was filled with sailors," said Toti, "and they used to listen to Elvis Presley and other singers like him. So Roberto would start to dance, hearing these songs."

Childhood was short for little Roberto. Vargas may have been the man of the house, but almost from the time he could work Roberto needed no one to look after him. Often a regular at El Parque Santa Ana, Duran also danced for coins in the streets and shined shoes for pennies in a neighborhood bar. "When Duran was five years old, he used to be in the street a lot and all the money he would make he would take to his mother," said Vargas. "He was good with his mother. They were living there with his mother, him and his brother, and at the age of eight he started to box.

"I never mistreated Roberto, as a stepfather I never hit him. I do not like to abuse children who are not mine. He never even misbehaved with me in a way he would deserve to be mistreated. I used to advise him not to do the wrong things, but he always used to be out there with Chaflan. We had a very humble room, but we lived there. He would leave the house and be away for a couple of days, and then he would return with food for his mother."

Though Toti was older, Roberto often acted like a guardian to his younger siblings. "When Isabelle was born, Roberto asked me whether the baby had any clothes," said Clara. "So he went to see a woman who sang, Ana Maria de Panama was her name, and she gave him a tub filled with clothes for Isabelle. He was a very curious child and he went over all these things and chose a couple, including a hat, which he brought to the hospital so that we could come out with the baby nicely dressed. After I had my daughters, Roberto was a father for them and for us all."

At the age of seven, he told his mother, "Don't worry mamma. You'll see. When I am older, I will help you." He remembered, "At the time there were three children in my family and I didn't have anything to eat. I had to go out and clean shoes. Me and my other brother had to go out and sell newspapers while my sister Marina stayed home. That's what we had to do to survive." Christmas and New Year were the worst; the children would go to bed early because there was not even enough money to buy candy.

From selling the newspaper *La Estrella de Panama* to cleaning shoes, to cleaning dishes in restaurants, to painting jobs, to dancing and singing in night clubs, Duran skipped childhood: he had no choice. The hunger would never leave him. "He grew up fast," said Toti. "I would stand up for him when he was younger, but soon he could do it on his own."

★ ★ ★

The most important man in Robertito's life, at least until his late teens, was neither his father nor his stepfather but a smiling urban gypsy in colorful, ragged clothes called Candido Natalio Diaz. Known throughout Panama City as "Chaflan," which loosely translates as "punchy," he was an eccentric, a short, well-built, wide-eyed *negrito* in a sailor's cap, exactly the type of poor, shiftless Panamanian that the snooty *rabiblancos*, the light-skinned social elite, despised.

"I used to live in Chorrillo in a house made of stone, near a bar called La Almenecer," said Duran. "I used to polish shoes and a person came in and started to dance. There were dozens of people peeking through the spaces from the wooden walls in the cantina. He would make all of these funny faces. When he was finished dancing, he would collect money."

Chaflan was a kind of Fagin to the children of the slums, finding them work, teaching them to survive. He watched out for them, though many adults questioned his motives and some even hinted that his interest in young boys was suspicious. He took a special liking to Roberto, taking him to dance on street corners or in nightclubs for money. He often arranged fights or wrestling matches between the youngsters, setting up a makeshift ring in some backyards to draw pennies from onlookers – then bought them lunch.

Duran hooked up with Chaflan. He was already a restless child, always on the move. "He hardly had any friends," said Clara. "Only Chaflan was his friend. He put him to sell the newspaper and to clean shoes. Chaflan used to tell him, 'Roberto, from the money you make working you have to give some to your mother.'" He always did.

Roberto was something of a prankster and liked to play jokes. When he was ten years old, he was watching a TV that his grandmother had won in a raffle. Trying to grab the seat from her grandson, she offered young Roberto five cents to chop some wood. "I knew her trick to get the seat," said Duran to a reporter. "So I said to her, 'The program is very good, here is ten cents, you chop the wood!'"

His warmth could quickly turn to fire, however. Anyone who disrespected Chaflan or any of Duran's friends would take a punch, thrown with such venom that they would be left gasping. And wherever Chaflan went, the children followed, with Duran leading the pack. To Duran, the man without a home was heroic. He refused to abandon them when others had. Chaflan couldn't replace Duran's father, but he showed him he could accomplish anything he put his mind to.

On first sight, Chaflan resembled the many other throwaways roaming Panama City trying to get by without taking the same risks that everyone else had. Nobody had ever seen him with a job or any stability. But nobody ever saw him dealing with drugs or alcohol. He wasn't a bum. Despite his lifestyle, he was not necessarily a bad influence. Nobody recalled seeing him drunk and many people knew him by name. He had no home but a ready grin, and would share whatever food he had with his posse of children. To people who had made it without having to stick out their hand for a nickel, Chaflan was a hopeless, lazy figure whose charming nature belied inner weaknesses. To Duran, the man making funny faces was more than a street clown; he was the one man who wouldn't abandon him. "If Duran was selling shoes today, his only friend would be Chaflan," read a newspaper headline at the height of the boxer's fame.

Like all clowns, there was a sad side to Chaflan. Panamanian journalist Emilio Sinclair called him "the man whose heart was broken by deception," and said he "cried in silence in the dark and stink alleys of the poor neighborhood." He could often be found sleeping in dumpsters or parks. He and young Roberto would be seen together before dawn, waiting as the sun lifted to get a heap of the morning papers to sell. Yet both were always smiling and they worked as a team.

"I remember getting up at five a.m., or sleeping under a tree in the park to get the papers," said Duran. "We would leave with Chaflan and would wake up in a newspaper factory. We were seven or eight kids who wouldn't go back home and would stay with Chaflan. There was a little window, they would give us a ticket, the first one would get the papers and would sell the papers fast. But most of the time the older kids got them first. Since we were so young, we couldn't keep up with the bigger kids and we couldn't sell the papers fast enough.

"There was a kid who could not talk and was very hunched over. Chaflan would put him to sell papers. Chaflan would stand in a busy street. I would stand where few people came and the hunched boy would be put in the street with no pedestrians by a building where lots of people lived," said Duran.

"Each had their one song. Roberto would sing, 'La Critica-a-a!' Chaflan would shout, 'La Estrella de Panama!' The hunched boy who couldn't talk would scream, and people would wake at 6 a.m. to buy a paper just to make him stop. The boys would sleep in the market, in the stands where they sold fruits and vegetables, or under a tree in the park. Their money went to their mothers."

It was survival of the fittest. "There were many criminals around there, and we were small children standing in the line to get the newspapers," said Toti. "We would get hit in the head and our newspapers would get stolen. I was older and used to get very angry and hit with real fury. I had to defend my brother and watch they would not take away our newspapers. We would sometimes be left crying and without the papers. But Roberto was born with that gift that it seems God gave him. He had very heavy hands and would fight strongly."

"My mother, who was very strict, always said there were two ways a person could go in that neighborhood – bad or good," said Chorrillo neighbor Nora Mendoza. "Roberto was a good kid, very humble. When my mother fed him rice, he was so hungry he would eat the *concolon* [crust] at the bottom of the pan. He often went to Central

Avenue with Chaflan, who was very influential at the time and good for Duran." Central Avenue was the city's main shopping district, a place where money could be made from the tourists and office workers of Panama City.

Young Roberto was a constant in the Mendoza household. With his charming smile and cute looks, he often traveled from house to house to fill his empty stomach. It was impossible to turn the young child away, and many families would snatch him from their doorstep straight to the dinner table. Nora Mendoza remembered El Chorrillo as a place where "most of the men worked at the Canal and didn't have much money, so they built their houses out of wood. Roberto lived in La Casa de Piedra, which was named that because it was made of concrete. Roberto used to come over and my mother would feed him. Everyone was poor in El Chorrillo, so he would come over and eat whatever we gave him. He'd always want more but we didn't have enough for him. I didn't like Roberto very much because I was just a young girl. But he was always at our home."

When not invited to eat at a neighbor's home, Roberto would go behind La Casa de Piedra to see what Nina, a local woman who had turned her home into a small restaurant, had cooking. Nina's became a haven for Duran and friends. There was also a small market in the town of Caledonia where they could order their favorite dishes. A Number Three was rice with beans and meat, a Number Four was a combo platter of rice, meat, beans and macaroni, and a Number Five was everything and a bowl of soup. Almost fifty years later, Duran would still remember the numbers of those orders, the smell of the food leaving an indelible impression on a ravenous boy.

He seemed to thrive on din and chaos. "The country was too quiet, too much peace," recalled Duran. "I was born in the middle of noise. I remember my mother's bedroom, it had a high door where the buses would go by. Next door there was a canteen, and we were used to the noises there, the buses, the quarrels at the canteen. When I would go to the country, where the people were so quiet, I used to feel badly."

Everywhere in Panama someone has an anecdote about Roberto, many of them about the deprivation of his youth. "We all came up fighting," said fellow boxer and childhood friend Alfonso "Peppermint" Frazer. "It helped make us men. We all had it tough, but we didn't have it like Duran. He would finish our meals after we left the table and come up and take a piece of bread. That's how bad he had it."

Chaflan taught him how to fill his belly. Maybe he would have made it without the gypsy's lessons, but many believe he would eventually have fallen in and out of bars, living day to day. Duran learned from Chaflan that he didn't have to live like that.

"They would put up a show together to collect some *reales*, which they would later share," said Nestor Quinones, Duran's his first boxing trainer. "That is why, since age six, he would seldom be in Chorrillo; most of the time he would be hanging out all over in the city. There were five children in all going around with Chaflan, Duran and four more. Duran told me himself that they would not return to their homes after the shows. They would stay at Casco Viejo [the old compound] to buy newspapers to sell. Once they had finished they would get together again and put on their shows with Chaflan."

However, some people kept a close watch on Chaflan. They said his interest in the children was unhealthy, that he sexually molested them, and that he should be locked up. "I never saw Chaflan do anything they accused him of," said Duran. "Chaflan would do all sorts of pirouettes, tricks with his hands and all the ten- and twelve-year-old kids would follow him. So one day he said that if we would exercise with him he would feed us lunch. So we would do what he told us and walk on our hands, exercise and do flips in the air. Afterwards, he would make us clean off in the ocean. Then, all covered in sand, he would put us to wrestle because at that time a lot of wrestlers would come to Panama." Before boxing became a passion, Duran desired to be like the popular Mexican wrestlers. Chaflan helped funnel that passion and asked for nothing in return.

Young Roberto also skirted back and forth between Panama City and Guarare. It wasn't unusual to see the little child rolled up on a *catre*, a canvas-like covering, on the ground of one of his extended family's small homes. He was always on the go, playing soccer and baseball or learning to punch under the tutelage of his uncle Socrates "El Chinon" Garcia. Socrates' brother Jairo later claimed, "It was my brother who gave him that powerful punch. He was the man who showed him how to box."

Roberto and his sister Marina went to elementary school in Guarare for a while, until Clara moved back with them to the capital when Roberto was in second grade. For a while the family lived in El Mangote, on the Pacific side of the Isthmus. Not yet "Manos de Piedra," Duran often came running home to the call of "patas de abejon," because he was so thin. According to Toti, "The abejon is a wasp, which though being fat has very thin legs."

"He was quite a terrible boy," joked Mireya, Roberto's aunt, who was close to him in age. "He misbehaved always. When he was a little boy, he used to climb trees and liked to swing on the branches once he was up there. This is what I remember, because we were of a similar age. My mother had a sister called Angela Garcia, who lived in the Nuevo Arraijan. She had two dogs, one called Biuty and the other Capitan. Do you want to know what Roberto did? Starting at Chorrillo, he walked all the way with Toti, his brother. They crossed on foot the Puente de las Americas and went to Nueva Real, which is very, very far, and came to where my mother was because they did not have any money. They went on foot. These two dogs attacked Roberto and Toti and if my mother had not got out at that moment, the dogs would have killed them."

Eventually Roberto would immerse himself in boxing and see less of Chaflan and the gang. Unlike his protégé, the sage would never prosper. The mores that he taught Duran, he couldn't apply to his own life and it was the nature of such a friendship to wither. Chaflan had plateaued in life and although Duran loved him, he didn't need him anymore. The young fighter grew out of Chaflan.

"When I started boxing, Chaflan would come over to the El Maranon Gym," recalled Duran. "One day I was training and he came over and he tapped my back. When I turned around they took a picture of us. I have the picture in my house as a remembrance of him. After that I didn't see him much. I wouldn't follow him anymore."

# 2

## FIGHTER

*"His mother used to tell me to go to the gym and see if he was there, and to hit him if I found him there. He would ask me what I was doing there, to which I would answer that I had come to see him training. I never brought him back home. I once told his mother that if the boy likes boxing, maybe tomorrow he would be famous."*

Victorino Vargas, Duran's stepfather

AT TIMES HE would sit in his room, stare out the window and dream. *When will I be a boxer?* He would peek in his brother's boxing bag and see himself draped in the fabulous colors. The boots would be too big and the pants would droop on his skinny frame, but when he wore them he felt like a champion. *I will wear this sparkling uniform one day when I become a boxer.* It wasn't the power and speed of the punches that enticed him, not the quick footwork and fancy moves, nor even the cheers of the crowd and the hope of acclaim. It was the outfit.

"One day my brother Domingo told me he was going down to the gym," he remembered. "Everybody would go over and practice there around noon. At that time there were these little blue bags and the only thing that could fit into the bags was shirt and shorts, nothing else. I liked the way the uniforms looked." Just as he had trailed Chaflan through the dusty streets of the city, so he tagged along with Toti to the Gimnasio Nacional (later Neco de la Guardia) in front of the National Guard headquarters on Avenue A. He knew that boxers could get paid for beating up people in the ring, and money meant the difference between eating and not.

"I was carrying the little bag and we're walking to the gym, which is very close to where we live," said Duran. "When I was carrying the bag people would ask me if I was a boxer, and I said, 'No I'm not.' My brother told me to sit outside and wait for him. There was a banister and I sat there and waited. When he came out of the dressing room, he was wearing his boxing shorts and his boxing shoes. I watched him practice that day."

It was a tough gym, packed with former and future national champions. "A boxer named Adolfo Osses told my brother to help him spar," said Duran. "My brother put on headgear, gloves and a jockstrap. I marveled at my brother's uniform. When he finished sparring, I said, 'Toti, how can I get the same gear that you are wearing?'"

"If you become a boxer they give you all that," replied Toti.

"And that's how I became a boxer."

Toti could punch but he wasn't cut out for the ring. "I knocked Adolfo Osses down because I hit hard," said Toti. "He was a professional boxer and I was an amateur. [But] I had a problem with my nose and my nose used to bleed when I would jump rope; that is why I was not able to fight. Duran also had the same problem, but he got rid of that later. I did not. When I knocked Osses down, Duran got enthusiastic about boxing. Duran was only a boy at that time but he had such a strong hand that even Osses was not able to stand his blows. Grandma [Ceferina Garcia] used to hit hard. In my family we all have a heavy hand."

Barely eight years old, Roberto had to spar with the experienced boxers like all the others. "That is what boxing consists of; you may fear no one," said Toti. "I started fighting first and I taught Roberto how to fight. I did not like to see my brother get hit, so I showed him how to fight. This started many years ago, when he was seven or eight."

It wasn't long before Roberto, already obsessed with wrestling and running, was noticed by Sammy Medina, a former national bantamweight and featherweight champion who had once killed an opponent in the ring. "One day a little kid with a shoeshine box walked into the Neco de La Guardia gymnasium," remembered Medina. "He put on a pair of gloves and started to box with a boy smaller than he was. I was impressed by the way he moved his head to dodge the blows and I called him over. He said he wanted to be a boxer. I began to teach him and I had him for a couple of years, boxing amateur about three times."

It was hard to train when you didn't even have enough food to eat. "The only problem we both had was poverty," said Toti. "We would sometimes go to train and get hungry but had no money for food, so we used to go to sell newspapers to make some money. And the following day we had to start running really early, but we were not strong enough. I remember we once started running, thinking it was five o'clock, but we had made a mistake. It was one o'clock in the morning and the police stopped us. We were coming from the bridge towards this area and the policemen could not believe we had mistaken the hour. Roberto liked boxing so much that he would sometimes skip sleeping and go training on the beach in Chorrillo."

Toti and other jobbing boxers made a mere fifty cents a contest. Even established boxers received only a pittance and he soon gave up the sport. "[Ismael] Laguna and all the others used to fight for very small sums in order to get known and start fighting abroad," he said. "In Panama, fighting was not worthwhile."

Roberto loved it, however, and soon had his first amateur bout under Medina's tutelage. The details have been lost to history but he could have been no more than nine years old, and the result was controversial. "He lost his first fight," said Medina, "but the spectators protested the decision because he had even knocked down his opponent." Toti concurred. "He lost his first fight because the arbiter was the boxer's father. Roberto knocked him down three times but the fight was given to the other one."

His mother, who remembered her sister Gladys initiating her son into boxing, was the last to know of her son's new pursuit. "One night a person came to see me and told me Roberto was going to fight that night in El Maranon Stadium," said Clara. "I then said, 'Oh, my God. This is not what I want for him.' But when I realized this was the sport he liked, I let him stay there. I used to make promises to the Virgen del Carmen but I also cried a lot. This was not what I wanted for him. He was a vivacious kid. I remember when he had a fight at the Maranon. Roberto was winning but when the referee decided to give the fight to his rival, Roberto gave the referee a terrible punch."

Roberto began to leave Chaflan and the old crowd behind and to adopt a discipline beyond anything he had learned in random street brawls. Unlike the streets, boxing demanded dedication, precision and self-sacrifice and was an unforgiving, often brutal master. Battered faces and bruised minds were the lot of ex-boxers, even good ones, and most ended their careers as poor as they had started. The veteran Medina was still intending to box himself and couldn't divide his time equally between his own career and training youngsters. Instead, Roberto found a trainer who would become like family. In boxing, relationships come apart like worn Velcro. Trainers once treated like family become dispensable and loyalty in the corner counts for nothing in the end. Everything in boxing, from the hiring and firing of friends to the hoarding of that last penny, is a transaction and the old adage "It's just business" is as common as a pair of wraps in the fight game. Wads of bills displace family; empty promises dissolve friendships.

But when Duran met Nestor "Plomo" Quinones, a former amateur boxer, a longtime bond was forged. In his signature driver's cap, Plomo (which translates as "lead" or "bullet," a relic of his days as a pistol-toting detective) was becoming one of Panama's best trainers. A man with a warm handshake, expressive eyes and a slow, cautious manner, he filled space …

Some individuals can signify emotion through their reactions without saying a word. By reading Plomo's eyes it is easy to see satisfaction when they dart approvingly eyeing money, or disappointment when they sag with his cheeks when the proposition doesn't fit with him. In both instances, the translations are succinct even to the foreigner. Plomo no longer forges ahead. The man enters space as milk fills a glass, slow and with caution. Plomo slithers around the gym like a lazy snake, his life, health and money have dissolved in accordance with Duran's. With his cap, cocked in a manner that makes him simultaneously appear old, innocuous and totally exasperated by life, Plomo greets people with a nod of the head from across the room.

"There were fights between clubs from Chorrillo, Maranon, and I think I was fighting out of the Club Cincuentenario," recalled Duran. "One day I go to the Maranon Gym and I see Plomo and tell him I want him to be my trainer because at the time I didn't have anyone to train me. Plomo wouldn't pay any attention to me because I was just a kid. He weighed me with clothing and all and I was ninety-five pounds."

Quinones did not want to take on Duran right away, not only because of his age but also because he questioned whether one so young would stick it out. "Medina was the first to have Duran," said Plomo. "Duran was eight years old then. He would receive about one dollar for each fight while Medina would keep the remaining eight or ten dollars. It was a business for him. Duran did not like this situation so he decided he did not want to be trained by Medina anymore and he searched for me. He was nine years old and even though I did not request him to fight then, because he was too young, I could see he had very good attributes. He was a daring fighter and this was a very good characteristic. The rest may be taught but the fighter has to be daring. He cannot be afraid.

"When he was a child, he loved to fight and I saw him fighting a couple of times. He was already working as a shoeshine boy. I saw him fighting against another shoeshine boy, older than him, but Duran hit him really hard and knocked him down. I then told him he should fight as a boxer and not in the streets anymore; for during that fight I realized that Duran could be a professional boxer. He had the character to be one."

Plomo had watched scores of little ruffians come and go, arriving full of bravado but unable to stomach the rigors of endless training in the sweltering blood buckets they called gyms in Panama. "Duran came to the gym and asked me if I could be his trainer. He just wouldn't leave until I gave him an answer," said Plomo. "I told him, 'You're just a kid, but if you demonstrate your boxing skills I will teach you. Then he threw a punch with force and I approved him. I told him to come the next day with a bathing suit and sneakers. He would come every day with the same clothes and shoes."

With uncommon perseverance, Duran would finally get his uniform, a moment that neither the fighter nor his brother would forget. "Roberto did not have any boxing clothes and I had been given some as a present," said Toti. "So I gave him the shoes and the shorts, for I was not going to fight. Roberto had started fighting as an amateur boxer and during these fights the people throw coins to the ringside for both the fighters. Roberto started winning these fights."

Roberto was an unusual child even among the mixed bag that Plomo coached. "After training, Duran's day was only beginning," said Plomo. "Duran would go to the streets after training and then to a local park called Santa Ana, where he shined shoes to gain seven cents to bring home and give to his mom. I had several boys that also fought very well, even one who was really good, but he would always cry when hit. When I saw Duran, I realized he resisted being hit and so I decided to leave all the others and devote my time just to him. Duran really had the quality needed."

That defiant attitude would pay dividends for both men. Plomo took Duran and began to shape him. He began to focus his defiance and funnel his boundless energy.

★ ★ ★

Having started out in the sport in 1956 with his first pupil, Zapatito Molina, Plomo was to witness the original Panamanian boxing boom. The sport first took root there around 1910 when the Canal was finished. Black laborers from Barbados, Jamaica and other islands stayed on and fought each other and visiting U.S. seamen for small purses and side bets in bars and theaters. Though the country's first world champion, a gangling, flamboyantly homosexual bantamweight called Al Brown, reigned back in the Twenties, he fought most of his contests in the United Sates and Europe, and the sport did not take off in Panama until after the Second World War, in particular when the U.S. increased its military presence in the contentious Canal Zone. In the mid-Fifties, Plomo started working with young prospects, often around the ages of nine or ten.

"There were many places in Maranon, not boxing gyms but places where people were starting to box," Plomo recalled. "In the yards of houses, people would set up rings and hold boxing matches. They would set down wooden planks where the canvas would be, and then wrap around the ropes. Then people would come and would stage boxing matches. It wasn't a very big ring, but it was big enough to hold matches. Back in Panama during those times there were many quality boxers. They started fighting in the streets and didn't have to go get a gun or anything. They would fight with their hands and whoever won the fight, that's where the fight ended, nothing more. They wouldn't hold any grudges."

The Maranon Gym, later to be renamed Pascual Cielo Gonzalez, was built in the gallery of an old train station. At the time, athletes had no place to train, so when the station closed, the gallery space was converted and the local mayor agreed to let it be used for boxing. A vast, metal-roofed, concrete building, painted light blue, the gym had a basketball court marked inside and a ring in the centre, barely illuminated by shafts of light from window holes. A variety of spectators invariably gathered there, from local workers in typical white, open-necked shirts to a myriad of children staving off boredom by watching prospects hit the speed bag.

Neco de La Guardia in Chorrillo had previously been the best gym around, while nearly two hours from the capital, in the notorious slums of Colon, were two other boxing gyms: Teofilo Al Brown, named after the country's first champion, and a pokey hole called the Box of Matches, so named because young boxers crowded in there so tightly that they had to rub shoulders to punch the bags. Greats like Luis Ibarra, Ismael Laguna and Eusebio Pedroza would train there. "It was such a small gym and so many trainers worked with fighters there," said Plomo. "It was always full and no matter how many people were there, everybody trained together."

By the age of twelve, Duran was a painter and handyman for Don Jose Manuel Gomez, a hotelier he affectionately called "Viejo." His mother already worked at the Roosevelt Hotel, which was popular with American soldiers and their wives, washing and ironing and cleaning rooms, and she introduced her sons to Gomez, a kindly man who taught Duran about dedication to work and basic moral values. Duran would often refer to him as a father figure. It wasn't unusual for the family to sleep in a room at the hotel.

"Jose Manuel Gomez was in love with my mother, but she never paid any attention to him," said Duran. "He gave my older brother Toti a job in the hotel ... it had like sixty or seventy rooms. Later on he gave me a job there too. I would make three dollars a week. We used to sleep in the maintenance room. He taught me to paint, to polish furniture and bed springs. We used to put a covering on the roof to protect us from the rain. We painted the hotel inside out. We used to use brooms to reach the parts that we couldn't reach. I used to go to school sometimes in the mornings or afternoons and sometimes in the night. This man taught me to work and never to steal, that it was better to ask than steal. My brother and I never stole, never smoked and never tried drugs."

Despite the friendliness of the Americans at the Roosevelt, trouble was in the air. On January 9, 1964, in what became known as the Day of the Martyrs, anti-U.S. rioting broke out in the Canal Zone. It began when a U.S. flag was torn down during conflict between Panamanian students and Zonians over the right of the Panamanian flag to be flown alongside it. The U.S. Army intervened after Canal Zone police were overwhelmed, and after three days of fighting, about twenty-two Panamanians and four U.S. citizens were dead.

"Clara always lived in extreme poverty," said her sister Mireya. "When it was January the Ninth, the students entered the area of the Canal. My sister had moved to a place called Caledonia. She had a room there, next to an ice factory. I had gone there for a visit. There was a terrible gunfire there and we all had to get inside and under the bed – my brother Joaquin, Toti, Roberto, Marina and I. That is where my sister was with her poverty."

Schooling came third behind hustling for a living and boxing. Although it has been documented that Duran stayed in school until he was fourteen years old, some family members don't recall him getting past the third grade. He had no inclination to study and was expelled from several schools. "He got up to fourth grade," insisted Clara. "Something was happening with the teacher. She did not like Roberto, and Roberto, who was a quiet child, did not like her bothering him. Roberto used to say: 'Mama, I will later take a private teacher at home.'"

According to Toti, however, Roberto tried to hit one male teacher, then tried to kiss a female replacement. Duran himself recalled his brief education in *Sports Illustrated*. "I remember in school one day, a kid came over to hit me and I moved. We exchanged positions, so his back was toward the steps. I hit him and he fell backward down the steps. And they threw me out."

Duran's natural grammar was the argot of the streets. But the streets were a dangerous place. Though he steered clear of the late-night haunts he would frequent later in his career, and stayed with his tight circle of friends, he would occasionally go to bars or the annual Mejorana Festival in Guarare. He found his share of trouble, often because he would look out for his friends, and his loyalty never wavered.

The fire inside him ignited one evening at La Pollera bar. Aged just fifteen, he had stayed too late into the hours when corruption and addiction prevailed. As was customary in Panama, the fiesta would end only when the final customer left. Drinkers of Panama had plenty of choice, from the national beers of Atlas, Soberana and Balboa, to the local liquor Seco-Herrerano, mixed with coke or orange juice. Someone would be delegated to fetch the bottle of liquor and the ubiquitous plastic container of ice, and the runs back to the bar never seemed to stop. Within minutes at dances or rodeos, the ice would melt into a fusion of water and liquor, sending someone back to fetch another flimsy bucket. Parties in the country often started late and ended the next morning, when everyone was sated. Wallflowers were not permitted. Everyone danced merengue, salsa, or cumbia, no matter what size or shape; everyone knew how to move.

This particular night, slow in dying down, reeked of violence and bloodshot eyes. By its end, five men would be in a Panama City jail cell connected to the St Tomas Hospital, recovering from an assortment of scrapes, broken noses and bruises. It was obvious they had been in a fight and had been caught severely unprepared. *But what*, asked the police, *had happened?*

The young Duran was charming, athletic and strikingly handsome, with a clean-cut and straight black hair. He had first frequented La Pollera with his mother, and had learned to dance there. Early this evening, he met a pretty girl, and was taking her home when he ran into a truculent group of men. It must have seemed easy to them: Beat up the kid, get the girl and keep partying. "Five guys, about six or seven years older than me, start to follow us," recalled Duran. "They come around me. They said they were going to take my girl and I wasn't going to do anything about it. I told them that they weren't going to take anyone. 'She's going home,' I said. One of them comes toward me and, boom, I hit him and he's knocked out. Now, there were four of them.

"It's rainy and I tell her to go to the side, hit another one, and now there are two knocked out and three left. Three jumped me, and I hit one of them and I break my pinky finger and I can't close it. Two left, and I tell them, 'Now it's fair.' Both come on me and I grab them and I knock one out. I've already knocked out four and I say to the guy, 'It's only me and you left.'"

Those are six words that no one in their right mind would want to hear from the mouth of Roberto Duran. He would utter such threats in the ring countless times, but there are rules between the ropes. There were none that evening. The lone survivor considered the fact that, at fifteen, the kid was merely five-feet-five inches tall and barely over 100 pounds. And if he couldn't knock him out, he could cut him up.

"The guy reaches behind him and he has a knife," said Duran. "The guy cuts me from behind and I was like, damn, he cut me. I turn and knock him out. There were five guys knocked out and the police come and I take off running because I'm a minor at that time. And I heard someone shouting, 'Run away Duran, if not they will put you in jail.' I couldn't escape from them because the guy ran better than I did."

Duran was thrown into a cell with the girl and was detained for several hours while the police tried to piece together what had happened. Five men knocked cold, a fifteen-year-old with a broken finger and a slight bruise, a hysterical girl and no independent witnesses.

"It's about seven or eight in the morning and they open the door to tell me that the lieutenant wants to see me," said Duran. "Five guys were there one after another and the police told me to stand there. I had my hand ready to hit them again. All the five guys are all swollen. The cops ask the men if they know me and each one says, 'No. I do not know what happened. I have no idea. I do not even know who brought us here.'

"Then the cop asks if they know what happened last night and they shake their heads no. Then he asks if they were involved in a fight and they say no. Then the cop asks if they are accusing anybody of anything and they say, 'Who are we going to accuse?'"

Still in disbelief, the police let the five men leave and kept Duran and his girl in the cell, mainly to avoid reprisals from the men. "When I get out, I tell the girl to go before the sergeant regrets it and throws us back in jail. I knocked five guys out with my bare hand, and I've even been shot at. My mother sent me to my aunt's house. While we were talking, a big man came in, and she said he was her husband. 'Your husband?' I asked. 'That was the man who sent me to prison.' 'No, that's not true,' he said. 'I had to take him there as if he was going to jail because there was a fight, and I tried to protect him.' Can you imagine my surprise? It was the man who had married my aunt. After a long time, I celebrated a party for him, for this son of a bitch, at my own house."

Duran's reputation in the streets often landed him with challenges. Yet these fights also solidified the unspoken bond that if you were a friend of Roberto Duran's, he would stand up for you. He was fiercely loyal. "When I was starting my boxing career, there was in Chorrillo the first bar with air-conditioning," he said. "At that time there were only canteens. It was the first time that at a bar in Panama, in the upper section of Chorrillo, they put up a music show. I used to hang out a lot then with the Barraza brothers. I was there with them when a girlfriend of mine arrived. I came in and took off my jacket, placing it on the chair. Then I felt like dancing, so I went to dance. Suddenly I saw a huge guy standing next to my table, and peeing on my jacket. When I walked up to him and asked him what he was doing, he said that if I wanted to fight with him, he was ready to fight with me. He then told me to go outside to fight.

"We both went out, my friends close to me, and his friends surrounding him. The guy tried to get in his car after throwing a punch at me, but after avoiding it, I got him out of the car. Then his friends came to fight, and mine got in their way, and the fight started. All of a sudden I saw that five of his friends were jumping on me. I started hitting them one by one, and knocking them down. I finally was left with only one, but then my friends came and threatened the remaining ones. My friends enjoyed watching me because I was a boxer in the street and also in the ring. So I started punching this huge guy all over his body and knocked him down too. When he stood up in the end, he said he did not want to go on. One of the Barraza brothers told him that he had started the whole thing but he answered that he did not want this to continue; he wanted peace now. We got back to the bar and went on drinking. Then we went to have dinner."

\* \* \*

Duran started to box for the Club Cincuentenario amateur squad, which would face other area boxing squads. The Panamanian Amateur Program was composed of boxers representing various clubs around Panama. Club Cincuetenario had nine, Panama had four, and Club Maranon had just one club. Within Panamanian amateur boxing were fine young boxers such as the Maynard brothers, Enrique Pinder, Cristobal Cordoba, Antonio Vargas, Enrique Warren and many others. Along with many of them, Duran would leave Neco de la Guardia and begin training at the Maranon Gym. In February 1965, fighting in the ninety-pound weight class for the Cincuentenario Club, he scored a unanimous decision victory over Enrique Martinez. All three judges felt Duran did enough to win his first recorded bout.

While Duran's bout with Martinez has been recorded as his amateur debut, Duran recalled another opponent. "The first fight in the amateurs in the Maranon Gym, I beat this guy called Antonio 'La Cabeza' Vargas and I beat him bad. I knocked him down, and they still gave him the fight," said Duran. "The guy never wanted to give me a rematch." In a match held in March 1965 that many Panamanian writers had recorded after the Martinez victory, two of the three judges scored the fight for Vargas. By "coincidence," Vargas was managed by program coordinator Demetrio "Baba" Vasquez.

In the streets Duran was judged by his peers, but now he had to impress boxing judges, who favoured style over naked aggression. He showed exceptional promise in his weight class, which didn't have many skilled boxers. He relied on technique rather than his power, which had yet to grow, and his mind rather than instinct. After eight months boxing for Club Cincuentenario, he was 12-1* by the end of the year, and had moved up to the 106-pound division. After the loss to Vargas, Duran, now under the watchful eye of Plomo, wouldn't lose another bout that season. Fans began to take notice of this up and coming fighter, who they called "Robe," and even future world champ Enrique Pinder refused to fight this restless bull. Realizing his potential, several important figures in the Panamanian sports industry began to invest time in the young fighter's career: engineer Erasto Espino, Duran's first adviser, Juvenal L. Chemenuncie, and Mocho Sam, a roadwork and massage specialist.

On October 4, 1966, Duran met Jorge Maynard in a tournament at the Pascual Cielo Gonzalez Gymnasium. Two fighters from each division were invited and Duran and Maynard fought at light-flyweight, or 106 pounds. Maynard, who was also managed by Baba Vasquez, would become Duran's amateur nemesis. In the first bout he won the unanimous decision, handing Duran his first loss that season. Twenty-five days later, the pair faced off again for the Golden Gloves crown and again Duran lost. "Duran was only beginning then," said Plomo. "He was 100 [pounds] going to 106, so he was not ready yet. It was a rather good fight despite being very difficult. Duran succeeded in hitting him hard at times. It was a very close fight but since Maynard was more experienced, the judges decided for Maynard." According to a boxing writer in *La Aficion*, the rematch in Neco de La Guardia was a replica of the first meeting, with Maynard using his technical skills to offset the *burro tirando golpes*, or bull-throwing punches, of his foe. Maynard was now the light-flyweight champ.

"Two times he beat me in a row, then I found out that the referee in the ring was Maynard's uncle," said Duran. "That was pretty strange. That's why he beat me by decision. Each of the times I fought him I gave him my best punches. Then, after those losses, I did thirteen fights and won them all."

He also still had his run-ins in the street. "Chicha Fuerte Ruiz was a much experienced boxer, he was already a national champion," said Plomo. "There was a quarrel between Ruiz's family and Duran's, and Duran offered Ruiz boxing gloves in the middle of the street. I was

---

* Twelve wins and one loss. Boxers' records are often denoted numerically by win-loss-draw; for example, 30-2-1 would mean thirty wins, two losses and one draw.

only told this story. I was not present. Since Ruiz was a professional by then but Duran was not, it could already be imagined that Duran was going to make it as a professional too.

The brawl, late at night, was chaotic. "Chicha Fuerte's wife had a fight with my mother and insulted her," said Toti. "After my mother insulted her back, Chicha Fuerte's wife went to call her husband. He had just finished a fight in Mexico. That night I was going to fight Chicha Fuerte, but Roberto asked me to let him fight with him. They started fighting and Chicha Fuerte's woman hit Roberto. But there were some bandits who knocked Duran down and Chicha Fuerte was supposed to step on Duran and start hitting him. But I kicked his stomach strongly and succeeded in making him fall. Then Duran got on hitting him, but it was at night and you could see very little. They were many and we did not know who had knives. But Roberto knocked Chicha Fuerte down. That was a famous fight story. When the police came, they found no one. We had all run away by then."

Another witness was Victorino Vargas, Duran's stepfather. "When Duran fought with Chicha Fuerte Ruiz, he made a cut on his face," said Vargas. "I advised him not to go on fighting in the street because he was a boxer already. He could be facing a judicial claim. So he stopped his street fights then."

Along with the resistance Duran felt he was receiving from the sport's bigwigs, a controversy had developed with Plomo. After losing in the Golden Gloves final to Maynard, Duran was scheduled to face one of Panama's most skilled boxers, Catalino Alvarado. Plomo felt his inexperienced fighter could first use a tune-up against a lesser boxer but Duran disagreed, sparking the first rift between the pair. Duran was stubborn as a mule when his mind was made up, so Plomo refused to handle him for the bout.

"I was fighting Catalino Alvarado from Maranon Gym, a very good boxer," said Duran. "Out of all the boxers I was the best and the fight was on, but Plomo didn't want to put me into the ring because he thought Catalino was way too good and would knock me out. "There is a guy named Sammy Medina who comes into the ring [to help me]. The way I beat [Alvarado] is that I could see the punches coming. I would telegraph them and just block them. Medina says to Plomo, 'Look what your guy did in the ring, and you didn't even want to put him in there.' And Plomo tells him that he just didn't want his guy to get hurt. After that there were several months that I wouldn't train with Plomo and went to

Medina. After about four months I returned to Plomo because Medina was never at the gym to train me."

Plomo remembered it differently: "When Roberto was still fighting at 106 pounds, Catalino was a much developed boxer, weighing 112 pounds. Duran once asked me to set a fight with Catalino, but I told him that since he had not been training enough, he could not do it. But he insisted, so we organized the fight, which Duran finally won. Since he was a child, Duran had shown that when he had decided something he would always get it. When he wanted to win a fight, he would do it."

Duran still hadn't shown the aggression and power that would later define him, but that was about to change, as jockey Alfredo "La Seda" Vasquez began to manage his career and help him financially. Vasquez encouraged him to rely less on his ability to move and box, and more on his punch. It worked against an opponent named Buenaventura Riasco. Each boxing club had to send a fighter to represent it in a tournament and from them a selection would represent Panama City and face off against the boxers from various provinces. The winner would be Panama's national amateur champion. After completing the elimination rounds, Duran and Riasco were thrown together to compete in the 118-pound division. Panamanian fans took a keen interest in the amateurs, and this particular match promised fireworks.

"Buenaventura Riasco was a very good amateur," said Duran. "We were about to have a fight, but there was a rumor going around that Carlos Eleta was going to become the manager of Riasco and he was coming to the bout to see how good Riasco really was. I said, 'Let Eleta come, because I'm going to knock you out.'"

Carlos Eleta was Panama's leading business magnate and was expanding his considerable interests into boxing. Unlike Vasquez the jockey, he had vast wealth, political clout and a keen mind for closing a deal. Eleta's presence on fight night often meant that he wanted something and now he had his eye on Riasco, a seasoned amateur. It was rare that Eleta did not get what he wanted.

"Riasco's brother said, 'We're going to knock you out,' and right away there was some turbulence at the weigh-in," said Duran. "Then Plomo tells Riasco, 'You see the corner right there. That's where we are going to knock you out.' When the bell rings, Riasco jumps on me right away, and starts hitting me with everything that he has. The second round he breaks my nose, and I go back and tell Plomo that I can't hit this guy because everything I throw he's dodging it. The guy came from a very good boxing clinic; he could avoid all punches."

Duran had learned a few tricks of his own. "I tell Plomo that I'm going to get him now," said Duran. "He was standing there with his right hand forward and his left hand back. I fake Riasco out and the guy comes in, and opens up a little bit. When he does this, I hit him with a right uppercut. The uppercut had so much strength behind it that he falls over the top rope right in the corner where Plomo said I would knock him out. We were fighting for a club championship that day and you could have counted to a thousand and he wouldn't have gotten up. It was such a good fight that the gym was packed and during that time the amateur fights drew more than the professionals."

It was an unforgettable encounter that made waves among the local reporters. "During this great fight, Buenaventura Riasco was leading at the beginning because Duran was a bit anxious," said Plomo. "Duran was not afraid; it was not fear. As it happens, the very nervous system sometimes fails. At the end, when there was only one round left, I went up to Duran and told him that if he wanted to win he had to use his right hand. So during the third round, Duran hit hard with his right hand and sent Riasco to the corner, at the very corner I had told Riasco he was going to end up.

"It was a great night, as if God had enlightened us. I was really moved. Well, to be a good trainer you also need the capacity to be moved, so as to be able to strengthen your boxer. I believe this is my special gift that I am able to be touched, and to feel that I am also fighting. So, I am able to feel anything that happens to my boxer, to communicate with him with my mind if he fails in any way, and to tell him what to do."

Many who witnessed the bout felt that the Riasco knockout was the defining moment when Duran switched from being a boxer-puncher to an insouciant brawler, throwing punches at anything that moved. Though the businessman Carlos Eleta was nowhere to be seen, Duran had sent a clear message: "When I knocked him out I pointed to the corner, and said, 'There's your shit, where's Eleta now?'"

★ ★ ★

One thing about Duran, he could punch. "I remember when Roberto hit this kid with a shot to the chest and it was thought that he nearly killed the guy," wrote Papi Mendez of *La Critica*. He loved to have confirmation of his *fuerza*, his force, and would even test it on family members. "I would not get into the ring with him, just to prevent my getting hit by him," said his stepfather, Victorino. "Once he was training at El Maranon when I got there. I was standing close to ringside and he got down and while walking past me he gave me a strong blow. And then he asked me, 'Was it a strong blow? Was it strong?'"

Many wondered where the power came from. Some claimed he inherited his thunderous right hand from his uncle Socrates Garcia from Guarare, who could break coconuts with his fists. "Socrates was my cousin," said Clara. "He used to fight a lot. Once we were in Guarare and my cousin was angry. He then saw a horse and decided to hit him. He struck him so hard that the horse was stunned."

Margarito, Duran's father, was another large man with a big punch. Others claimed that his grandfather, Felix Moreno, who was hacked to death by his own cousin, was the toughest family member. And whenever the name of Duran's redoubtable grandmother, Ceferina Garcia, was raised, every family member would exclaim, "She hit very hard!"

"My mother was in jail for eight days for having hit Guarare's mayor," said Duran's aunt Mireya. "She knocked him down. She had problems with a policeman called Celso. She was taken to the town hall and the mayor came to talk to her. She was a woman with a very strong personality and she knocked him down with a strong fist punch. After this the mayor sent her to jail for eight days. At that time there was a sub-lieutenant called Ireni Caballero. He would come to the cell and, pressing a spoon on the bars, would say, 'Bad woman, you knocked the mayor down.' But she had just given birth to Joaquin, and at that time it was forbidden to put in jail women who had to breastfeed. When the mayor discovered this, he set her free. That woman certainly hit very hard.

"Her father was called Felix Moreno and he was also a very strong man. This great-grandfather of Roberto's was killed by a cousin of his. That happened one day when he was returning after having killed a cow. He was carrying the meat, and his cousin waited for him on the road and asked him to have a drink with him. He answered that since it was early in the morning, he did not want to drink. In that very moment he killed him, opening the head of Roberto's great-grandfather with a machete. He fell down injured and crawled to the farm of my grandmother Juana. He only had time to ask for some salt before dying. You may imagine how strong he was to have been able to crawl all the distance. It seems that this resistance is something that runs in the family." Clara agreed: "Roberto inherited his power from his great-grandfather. Felix Moreno was so strong that he could kill a man with one punch."

Wherever his power came from, the win over Riasco confirmed Duran's potential. "They carried me on top of their shoulders and everyone was yelling," said Duran. "All this time, some fag back there is grabbing my ass. The more packed it was inside the gym, the more we got paid for the fight. Sometimes we got paid four or five dollars. Plomo would take his share and whatever I had left I would run home and give it to my mom for food."

His next goal was the Pan-American Games, due to be held in Winnipeg, Canada in July 1967. Duran was almost a guarantee to make the team for the tournament in the fifty-one-kilo division. Wins over Alvarado and Riasco had cemented his position as a top prospect, and in 1967 he represented Club Cincuentenario in an elimination tournament that began outside the city in Penonome. However, amateur boxing was riddled with politics, and forces outside Duran's control conspired against him.

"In that time the military was in control," said Duran. "There was a doctor for the amateur boxers and he took care of all of us. There was a very good boxer and the doctor was his manager. That kid had more shots and vitamins than anything. Already at that time, my mindset – I was too smart – was that of a professional. Three days before a fight, I'm painting at a hotel that I worked at and I go into a restaurant to eat lunch. They gave me this tortilla, which is a traditional food made of corn, but they were spraying this spray for fleas and it had fallen on my food. I ate it and drank Coke, and I got real sick because of it. I was sick and before the fight the doctor would not give me an exam.

"I was sad because I wanted to go to Winnipeg. I had a bad fever, and I was sleeping in the deposit downstairs of the hotel. Plomo found me and had me drink an Alka-Seltzer. I drank it and the next day I woke up like a bull. I go tell Plomo that the fight's on. The doctor thought his fighter was going to knock me out, but I gave the kid so many punches that I almost killed him. I fought the next day and the following day, and after those three days I was happier than shit because I was finally going to go to Winnipeg."

Duran had few influential connections in the sport, relying as he did on Plomo, but had earned the right to compete with his performance during the elimination round of the Panamanian boxing competition, beating Enrique Warren among others. However, Jorge Maynard's brother Roberto stood in his path. "At that time there was a military leader called [Jorge] Arauz, who did not like us because we were from the Cincuentenario Club," recalled Plomo. "He would try to have everything accepted without meetings, just through decrees. Maynard used to fight very well then and was experienced. Arauz sent him and another boxer to fight with Duran so as to rule him out. In the fight against Enrique Warren, Duran destroyed both Warren's eardrums. Then the fight against Maynard was set.

"Maynard did not turn up because of heavy rain, so we set it for the following week. But Maynard failed to come again. He had got frightened. This situation turned Duran into the winner. Once we had got everything ready for the trip, Arauz said Duran had no experience and did not allow his participation. He is a bad guy. And he decided to take Maynard. If it had been Duran, we would have returned with a medal because he was a skilled boxer and had shown his capacity. He had won many titles and was a very good boxer. But because of this man's badness, he was not allowed to win this title. Duran was very hurt because of this."

Duran remembered, "I'm on my way and I'm going to go there and meet people. Then Maynard shows up with Jorge Arauz and I'm there with Plomo. Maynard and them never showed up at the gym to fight. The talks heated up because Arauz says, 'This guy ain't going nowhere.' After an hour of discussions, the lieutenant tells me 'shut up' or he'll throw me in jail. I told him to chill and shut up. The point is that I don't go and they send Maynard instead of me. Maynard gets knocked out in the first round [of the Pan-American Games]. I go home really sad."

As a result of the injustice, the boxing community rallied behind the young fighter. Trainers from several gyms protested the decision and were backed by the director-general of the Department of Physical Education and Sport, to no avail. Duran took out his frustrations on the few amateurs still willing to enter the ring with him. Having grown into a featherweight, he beat Antonio Ballestas by unanimous decision in January 1968, and then Jose Villalba on February 11, knocking him down three times and out in the second round. Villalba was Duran's last amateur opponent. With a 29-3 record (some sources have it as 13-3 or 18-3), he moved on.

"Duran told me he would not go on boxing, for he had won all fights and there was no boxer left he could fight with," said Plomo. "He told me he would devote his time to help his uncle, who lived and worked at the Roosevelt Hotel. Duran said he would help him cleaning and painting, so he would have money to take to his mother. Duran had always helped his mother, since he was a little boy he had liked to get some money for his mother. So I agreed."

The intermission would be brief. One day, Plomo offered him what was then a substantial purse to get into the ring, and the little kid from Chorillo would never go hungry again. "I'm painting the outside of the window," said Duran. "I was making one dollar fifty cents a day painting and Plomo comes running in and says, 'Duran, you want twenty-five dollars to fight, win, lose or draw?' I tell him, 'Who do I have to kill?' He tells me it's a four-round fight in Colon with a guy who never wanted to get in the ring with me before in amateurs or the pros named Carlos Mendoza. I hadn't done any conditioning for the fight, but I said, 'Let's go.'"

Mendoza, from Chiriqui, was no pushover and would go on to have a fine career, culminating in a world title challenge. While the bout has since been listed by some sources as Mendoza's debut, Plomo claimed he had already had three pro fights and this was backed up by newspaper reports. "I heard they needed an opponent," said Plomo. "I knew Mendoza was afraid of Duran, but I told [his manager] that I had a boxer called Roberto Duran. He was painting the day I looked for him. I told him to get down because he was going to be a professional. At the time he wanted to retire from the amateurs and I was offered a fight at his weight. He came down and became a pro at sixteen."

Duran ran into a problem right before fight time when a bad sore on his hand worsened considerably. "You could see the actual bone in my hand," said Duran. "The doctor examines me and sees that I have an open sore, and tells me I can't fight. I tell him, 'Please let me fight, I need the money for my mom so we can eat.' I beat Mendoza real bad, with sore and all. That's how I jumped into the professionals."

Duran signed the contract on a Monday, trained for two days and boxed on the Friday evening, 23 February 1968, in the Arena de Colon. Before his debut, Duran and Plomo met at Galicia Restaurant, where Plomo's friend gave the young boxer his first pre-fight meal. It became a ritual. "At Galicia, I would order a salad and a beefsteak or chicken for Duran. No pasta or rice. This is what Duran would eat every day until the day of the fight," said Plomo. "We received the tickets to go to Colon, traveled there, and got there with 118 pounds. I was very strict on his diet, and whenever I would tell him not to eat or drink something, he would always restrain. This is one of the things that helped us to win. He always did what I told him, so we never failed while he complied with my requests.

"Before the fight they were betting and shouting, 'Mendoza, Mendoza.' Nobody knew Duran then. But when the fight started, Duran did not give him the smallest chance to get close to him. He kept hitting him, down and up and down again. During four rounds, Duran hit him so badly that poor Mendoza was not able to do anything. Duran won by unanimous decision."

Boxing writer Papi Mendez had invited the businessman Carlos Eleta along to "see Duran with his own eyes." Knowing that Colon was *the* hotbed of boxing, Duran was considering moving there. However, first he had to decide who would manage his career. Although Duran had met Eleta through his street friend Chaflan, many claim that Papi Mendez was the real mediator between them. It was not unusual for boxing writers to act as fixers and on several occasions in his newspaper column Mendez would take credit for acquainting the pair. Their partnership would change the course of boxing history.

# 3

## PAPA ELETA

*I do not live here to retrieve or multiply what my father lost or gained.*

Jorge Luis Borges, *Remorse*

STANDING AT A window on his vast estate one day in 1963, Carlos Eleta saw a small boy knocking coconuts from a tree. Roberto Duran, then aged twelve, had perfected the art of stealing fruit and Eleta's compound suited him well. More amused than angered, Eleta went outside and caught him. But instead of scolding the intruder and sending him away, he brought him inside and gave him lunch. He never thought that he would see the boy again. "My first impression of Roberto was this twelve-year-old stealing coconuts," recalled Eleta. "I grab him and he is so funny that I invite him inside. I didn't see him again until two or three years later in Colon."

That "two or three years later" was 23 February 1968, at Duran's pro debut. They met and talked and Eleta was impressed with the young fighter. Duran, for his part, needed financial backing, and knew that the cultivated Eleta was one of the most influential men in Panama. The contrast with the capricious little street urchin could not have been greater.

Carlos Eleta Almarán was born on 16 May 1918, the son of wealthy landowners. He earned his bachelor's degree in Malaga, Spain, and his MBA at Bryant College in Providence, Rhode Island. In May 1941, he married Dora Boyd and would have four children: Carlos, Sandra, Alberto and Raquel del Carmen. Groomed for success, the tall, straight-backed, dignified Eleta stepped into his father's business and eventually found himself as a major player in the importation and distribution of brand names such as Chesterfield cigarettes, 7-Up and Fiat. He set up the first TV channel in Panama, Canal Cuatro, and somehow found time to write a string of popular ballads, the most famous of which, "Historia De Un Amor," became almost a second national anthem. He played tennis to championship standard, bred racehorses and was now looking to manage prizefighters.

In Eleta, Old World gentility met New World vigor. Meticulous in dress and grooming, with neat, receding white hair and a slim, athletic build, he could talk with kings and beggars with equal ease. He was as friendly with contacts like the Kennedy political dynasty and sports stars like Joe DiMaggio as he was with boxing trainers and stable grooms. But his charm and grace hid a ruthless side, especially when it came to business, and like any successful man he made enemies. Some hinted darkly at his ulterior motives and cunning nature. He hated being pressured and was known for his frugality and willingness to end friendships on a whim. What he wanted, he usually got.

"After the Mendoza fight, [Roberto] recognized me from the day at my house and asked me to handle him," said Eleta. "He had another fellow managing him. I talked with Vasquez and told him I didn't want to interfere with him and Duran. He said he would give me Roberto for three hundred dollars."

Duran, however, remembers that Eleta actively pursued him. A skilled boxer named Eugenio Hurtado, the husband of Duran's aunt Gladys, had recently lost a close bout and went to see Eleta to ask for a rematch. He asked Duran to accompany him. "I went with a writer named Papi Mendez to talk to Eleta, but I didn't pay any attention to him. Hurtado asked me for a favor, and said he would give me twenty dollars to go with him. For twenty dollars, I was there. Eleta started talking to me and not Hurtado. I wasn't even paying attention to him. He kept saying over and over that he could help me. I realized he was talking to me, but I played the fool. Hurtado finally signs the contract to fight, and Eleta gives me twenty dollars. Now, twenty dollars and twenty dollars and I have forty dollars."

It says everything about Duran at that time that he was more interested in having forty bucks to spend in a bar than he was in an offer to manage his career by the most influential businessman in the country. He was in good company; Hurtado had a penchant for blowing his boxing purses and never thought about the future. "Once he won a bout and earned $3,000, and was lost for four days with nothing for the house," Duran told a reporter from *La Afición*.

However, Carlos Eleta would not be denied. "The next day, Eleta calls me and tells me that he wants to help me with my career. And Eleta wanted to know if I wanted to sign a contract or just a handshake deal. I was [only sixteen] and I told him, however he wanted to do it. Eleta tells me that real men either sign the contract or shake on it. We shook hands and that's how he became my manager."

The well-connected Eleta could offer far more than the jockey Vasquez. "Vasquez couldn't support me because he was always asking to borrow money," said Duran. "The only reason I started with Eleta was because he would pay media members to try to persuade me to let him become my manager. A lot of people told me not to mix with him because he was a thief."

For all his natural talent, Duran was raw, a volatile mass of energy. "He was a fellow who couldn't read and write," said Eleta. "And he had very little attention. It was very difficult to sit him down. We tried to take him to school and that was impossible for him. He was like a wild animal. Duran never kept anything inside, never. He liked to go see animals but he never had attention for anything.

"Before his wife was in the picture, he never told me about other girls. He was afraid to tell me these things. He was not the type of person who was easy to get to know. Before Roberto ever became a champ, he would tell me he wanted to be like Robin Hood. 'I will give it all to the poor,' he said. Nobody thought he was going to be so great. They knew he would be good, but not that great of a fighter."

Perhaps Eleta's most significant role was as a surrogate father. Referred to by most as Senor Eleta, to Duran he became "Papa." Eleta was someone he felt he could trust, someone stable. As tough as he was, Duran yearned for a man to replace his absentee father and Eleta filled that role.

Local notoriety also began to bring the good-looking *cholo* female attention, but his first girlfriend was not a popular choice with Clara and other family members. She was a black girl, or *champundun* in colloquial parlance. Race and class were inextricably linked in Panama, as in most societies, and blacks were at the bottom of the ladder. "She was a very dark girl," remembered Toti. "But he loved her a lot. He wanted to marry her but my mother did not agree. She thought it was only a game." Every good boxer on the isthmus lived in the spotlight, and by now many Panamanians gossiped daily about Duran. His love life was an instant topic of interest, so Duran went to his step-father, Victorino Vargas, for advice.

"I told him not to marry her, for he was going to become famous, so that in the future he could probably be able to get a prettier woman," said Vargas. "He did not want anyone to know. Because he was young, and like all young people, they do not want others to know. But when I realized about this relationship, I told him he should marry another woman."

The relationship didn't stay a secret for long. During a live TV interview, he explained to the public that he was dating a "black woman" and had plans to marry her one day. But the relationship would fade as Duran turned his attention to boxing. Every one of Duran's family members spoke of the affection that girls had for him. "Oh, the girls loved my brother," said his sister Anna. "They would always ask about him and call the house at all hours of the night. But he was a very good brother to me, very protective." Fighting came first. "Most of his time was for boxing," said Toti. "He enjoyed being with women a lot, even when he was very young, but he did not take them seriously. It was like his sport, but not all the time."

With the wealthy Eleta by his side, and willing to do whatever it took to make his fighter a champion, Duran now had a foundation. Even before his pro debut, he had begun to attract a following. "People saw the revelation when I was about fifteen or sixteen years old," said Duran. "I was going against the best boxers of Panama, and they weren't burnt-out fighters. They had a lot of experience." In the locker room before fights, Plomo and his brother would bet each other which hand Duran was going to knock out an opponent with. "Boom, I would knock out the guy with my right hand, and I'd tell Plomo that I told him it was going to be the right hand."

★ ★ ★

While Duran was learning the arts of both boxing and survival, another Panamanian was already an expert at both. In the early Sixties, Ismael Laguna, the "Tiger from Santa Isabel," was the idol of all impoverished young boxers. Laguna was one of their own. Born on June 28, 1943 in Palmira on the coast of Colon, he too had skipped school, shone shoes and sold newspapers on the streets, and fought to protect his patch and his nine brothers and sisters. "I had eight or nine fights for breakfast," said Laguna. "Even when there wasn't a fight, I would tell someone to put gum in my hair so I could find one. If there wasn't a fight, I would go look for one." Colon made other Panama slums look like Club Med. A mainly black area, it was home to fight fanatics who would shout "olé" at ringside just as they did at bullfights in other countries. To Laguna, it was "the land of champions where the boxing tradition started from the time of Panama Brown."

Laguna moved to Santa Isabel when his father, Generoso Meneses, was elected mayor of the region. Despite being caught up in gangs, and spending time in jail for picking up girls' skirts to see their panties (preferably red), Laguna would avoid the path that derailed many of his friends. One day, when he was twelve, he saw a national boxing champion, Carlos Watson, pulling a big crowd on the beach and inviting people to spar with him. Even though Watson said he wouldn't punch hard, there were no takers – until the fearless little Laguna stepped forward. "I was very skinny like a worm," said Laguna. "I went to spar with Watson and the people were saying, 'Don't do that. He's going to whip you,' but I put the gloves on and we went at it."

At first Watson held back on the youngster, but once he realized he was in a fight he tried to pick up the pace, out of desperation rather than bravado. "I opened a cut that he already had over his eye and the crowd was cheering because they always like the weak one," said Laguna. "At the end I was making him move back and people were screaming because I was making this guy look like horseshit."

Furious, Watson hurled punches at the youngster but Laguna was a shadow, and as the blood flowed the professional called a halt to the bout. "That was how I got started in boxing," said a smiling Laguna. "They used to call me Tigre because I would cut the cow's neck and drink the blood. Before that, Cuerito was a nickname when I was younger, which meant little pieces of meat." One of the young Laguna's jobs was skinning and cleaning cattle skins after they were butchered.

Soon he was in the gym, and after a brief amateur career he turned pro at seventeen. He was a natural, with sleek, supple movements and blur-fast hands. Laguna was a good-looking *negrito* with soft features, a kind soul who rarely disrespected his opponents. Only if something stirred him would he strike back. He would fight through a thicket of lusting women; however, his biggest contingent of groupies was the entire nation of boxers following his example.

Laguna came to epitomize the typical Panamanian boxer: a flashy mover who slid in to throw punches and then slipped out without a scratch. The fans loved his style, and they were a knowledgeable audience. In the Forties, they had followed the widly popular Young Finnigan, while in the Fifties and Sixties stars like Isidro Martinez, Jesus Santamaria, Sammy Medina and Antonio Amaya boxed with grace and panache. But none of these spirited pugilists would ever win a world title. Amaya was called "Campeón Sin Corona" – Champion Without a Crown – after he was robbed on two occasions in title bouts, while Martinez was tabbed as the "most beautiful boxer I'd ever seen" by Laguna.

Yet no one touched the people like Laguna. Tall, lithe and charming, he made boxing hugely popular. He also made it a spectacle, sometimes wearing white gloves to show his opponents' blood stains during fights. "Ismael Laguna was a beautiful natural boxer," said Carlos Eleta. "Just beautiful to watch in the ring." Yet even at the height of his fame, he noticed the little urchin called Roberto.

"The first time that I met Chaflan, I was in a hotel restaurant and this man comes on the table with Duran and starts dancing right on the table," he said. "It was crazy. Then I gave him twenty dollars and you should have seen his face. He thanked me – 'Oooh' – it was like I was his best friend. Back then, Duran was still young and wasn't known yet."

Duran dreamed that one day he'd be like Tigre. One day the Panamanians would chant "Doo-ran" when he landed a punch, the same way they now chanted "Tee-gray," and he would dress in the stylish clothes and shining jewelry of a champion.

In 1965, Laguna stood on the verge of greatness, his path blocked by a formidable world lightweight champion from Puerto Rico, Carlos Ortiz. Dangerous on the inside, sleek and unhittable from the outside, Ortiz had no boxing heroes but himself. "I always wanted to be Carlos Ortiz," he said. "I never wanted to be anyone else." They were due to fight on April 10 in Panama. Ortiz ran into Laguna in a local gym to hype the fight and there saw his challenger flitting in and out like a moth. "You couldn't see him because he was moving so quickly," remembered Ortiz. "I was thinking, 'Oh God, what did I get into?' He was very skinny and he wasn't built like a fighter. He was fast and tall and he had everything. I knew I was going to have a hard time. But I trained for the best and I saw how he was. I wasn't going to be surprised when I got into the ring."

Laguna didn't plod or charge, follow or chase; he glided, juked and jived, offering a free shot and then immediately retracting the offer. His head and body moved as if he were dancing to a João Gilberto bossa nova. "When I stepped into the ring, this kid looked like a flash," said Ortiz. "He was so fast that I couldn't believe it. When he moved, it was the fastest thing I'd ever seen in the ring [but] I thought I was going to have an easy time because he wasn't that tough. He was just a good kid, slim and fast, but he looked like I could knock him out."

There were also the foreign soil, the weather and the fans to contend with. Panama's weather separates into two distinct periods, the dry season or summer (*la seca*) between December and April, and the wet season or winter (*el invierno*), which covers the rest of the year. The normal daily temperature is around 30 degrees Celsius and varies little throughout the year. What strikes outsiders is the humidity, which vacillates widely and can make a stroll down the street feel like a Turkish sauna. Ortiz found the heat came in swathes, stifling breath and sapping energy. Other foreign boxers concurred. The people were also fight mad and vociferous in support of their men.

"It was a big thing in Panama because they never had a championship fight there. I couldn't even walk outside," Ortiz recalled. "Every place I went they were heckling me and saying bad things. 'You're going to get killed,' but I was used to this stuff. I didn't mind. I got a big surprise because he was better than what I thought. The fight started and I started boxing him and looking for ways to counter his moves and do what I wanted him to do. And he wouldn't do it. I was the aggressor [but] he would counter everything that I threw at him."

Meanwhile, a penniless, fourteen-year-old Roberto Duran was trying to hustle his way into the stadium to get among the thousands of red, white and blue flags, having first climbed on a car roof to catch a glimpse of his hero. As the fight progressed, men raised their fists in triumph, women hugged and cried, and people of all sizes screamed for "Tigre." Duran, who eventually coaxed his way past the guards, studied every punch, and saw a master class from his fellow countryman.

"I was worried," said Ortiz. "Every round, I came back and asked my trainers how I was doing. They just told me everything was going well and I was winning the fight. But I didn't see it that way." He was right. Ortiz couldn't find Laguna with his punches, and the Panamanian won a unanimous decision and the title. "I never got tired that night," said Laguna. "My trainer told me I was winning and to keep pressing the action. It was the greatest moment of my career. Even now I can still see myself in the ring. I will never forget."

Panama had its champion. Laguna had taken the soul of Al Panama Brown, the missed opportunities of Antonio Amaya and Isidro Martinez, the sorrow of Sammy Medina, the virgin dreams of Roberto Duran, along with the hopes of every man or boy who'd ever stepped into a Colon gym and threw a jab, and carried them into the ring that April night.

"I was a child then," said Duran. "I was a wrestler at that time, while I sold newspapers and cleaned shoes. The important fights were held in the big stadium, and all the champions would get there to walk around. But that was placed on a very high position, so people used to get up on top to be able to watch over the ringside. I saw the trucks up there and thought how in hell I would get there.

"At round fourteen, they opened the doors, and in the middle of all those running, the piece of wood broke, and I fell down together with all the other people who were standing there. I was the youngest of all those people and they were all falling on top of me. When I finally got up, I saw that all the others were already around the ringside. When I got there, round fifteen was about to start. Then finally when Laguna won, he was given a huge trophy which was like a goblet. I looked at him and thought then that I would be even more important than that man. And this is what really happened. At present, besides God, I am even more important than Laguna."

The teenage Duran sought out the new champion and told him, "Laguna, I will be just as good as you or better." They were meant as the words of an admirer, but Laguna was too busy to hear them. This was Tigre's moment. "When we left, Laguna had his car parked there, a big car, and many people were surrounding his car. I was among them. I then saw Laguna trying to drive slowly because there were so many people around him, but one guy stood in front of the car, defying him and trying to hit him. But Laguna just stared and kept on driving slowly. In the end, people started shouting that we had a new champion. Then I went back home."

From that moment on, for every young boxer it was about being Tigre. Even years later, Duran would still sparkle as he interrupted a young reporter: "For me it was always about Ismael Laguna." He was Duran's idol and still is. "When Duran sees me he still comes up to me and gives me a kiss," said Laguna. "Sometimes he jokingly tells me that I gave birth to him."

Not only did Laguna show how to defend himself in the ring, but also how to conduct himself outside of it. Duran would watch and listen, devouring Laguna's instructions, but would still then do his own thing. "All his life he's been the same and does whatever he wants," said Laguna. "In the ring sometimes I would tell him to throw the jab this way, and he would do it another way. But he's always been like that."

★ ★ ★

Duran's debut win against Carlos Mendoza gave little indication of the cyclone to come. In eight more fights that year, Duran stopped or knocked out seven opponents in the first round and the other in the second. First to fall were Manuel Jimenez and Juan Gondola in Colon, then Edward Morales in Panama City. Enrique Jacobs, Leroy Cargill and Cesar Uche de Leon were all one-round victims in the National Gymnasium in Panama. According to *La Estrella de Panama*, Duran sent De Leon to the emergency room at Santo Tomas Hospital. "He was a very good fighter and had not been beaten," said Plomo. "Duran left his rival in such a poor condition that he had to be taken to hospital." De Leon would never fight again. Juan Gondola made it as far as round two in Colon in November, then Carlos Howard was thumped in one in December to complete an explosive first year.

It was clear that Duran was ready for sterner opposition, and the boxers he faced in 1969 were a step up in class. His six fights that year brought six more victories, but none was inside the first three rounds. In January 1969, Alberto Brand was knocked down three times and stopped in four rounds. A six-round decision over Eduardo Frutos was followed by the stoppages of Jacinto Garcia ("Duran almost killed him," said Plomo), the experienced Adolfo Osses, well-travelled journeyman Serafin Garcia and former Panamanian bantamweight champion Luis Patino. By the end of 1969, Duran was 15-0 and had acquired the nickname "El Dentista" because of his habit of pushing opponents' teeth into their mouthpiece. He had also set up a juicy crosstown rivalry with Ernesto Marcel, the one fellow prospect who had the tools to compete with the eighteen-year-old terror.

It took eight rounds for Duran to dispose of Patino, a crafty veteran, on November 23, but the win showed the people that here was more than just a one-punch phenom and that he could last more than six rounds. "This was a good fighter, an experienced one, who had done a good number of good fights in Panama," said Plomo. "So he was like the true exam for those who were building up their careers as professionals. They had to fight against Patino. Duran's first fight to ten rounds was that one. They got up to the eighth round when Duran, PAH PAH PAH, knocked him down."

One of the most famous knockouts Duran would ever score came after the bout. Like most Panamanian men, he had a sixth sense when it came to searching out a good time, women and liquor. If the party didn't find Roberto, he would find it, and on this night a victory celebration was held in his mother's hometown, Guarare, where family, friends and well-wishers joined in the revelry.

Duran retold the story years later. "I had defeated a boxer that was from Parita, and Guarare never had had good boxers until I beat that boxer from Parita, and so we had a big party. There was a ball, and they were dancing and we were drinking. A young woman started caressing me but I had very little money left. At that time I used to drink whiskey. So a man got up and said, 'I will give you a hundred dollars and two whiskey bottles if you knock out a horse.' I told him to forget about it. And then the woman started caressing me again and asked me what that bet was about. I told her that the man wanted to see if I could topple a horse. Then the man said he was ready to pay, so I accepted.

"I stood in front of the horse and stared at him. I asked where should I hit in order to make it fall and they told me that a punch behind the ear would make him fall. I was very drunk but I hit the horse with all my strength, the horse fell down and I broke this finger. This is the horse story. In exchange for two whiskey bottles and a hundred dollars."

According to another version of the story, Duran and friends had finished a bottle of what one would later describe as Old Parr rum, but could not pay for it. The bar owner offered a compromise, with Duran's uncle Socrates Garcia as witness, that if the boxer could knock down a horse with his fist, the cost of the booze would be covered and the friends would drink for free. "They didn't have the money to pay the tab, so they told Roberto that if he knocked out the horse, the drinks were free for everyone," said Duran's friend, bar owner Ralph Bardayan. "He was told to hit him right below the ear. Then after he did it, all his friends and family drank for free." Duran hit the horse below the ear and it immediately fell to the floor. His right hand was bleeding and his uncle insisted he go to hospital, though due to the booze he'd drunk, Duran felt no pain.

Plomo remembered yet another account. "One day they leave to take a vacation and they stopped in Guarare. By now Duran was pretty developed and was still an amateur. In Guarare, he got on a horse and they told the horse to start stepping, but Duran wanted it to run. The horse didn't want to run because it was a walking horse. He came down from the horse and he was furious. He punched the horse and it fell down. Yes, it was true that he knocked out a horse."

Local boxing analyst Daniel Alonso claims to be a bible of the sport in Panama. "Some myths are very difficult to prove. Duran would go back to Guarare in the province of Los Santos. In this area there are a lot of animals. Maybe, but there is no way to prove it."

Life and legend were already becoming intertwined.

# 4

## STREETFIGHTING MAN

*"No black man can beat me."*

Roberto Duran

ROBERTO DURAN WAS not the only rising star of Panamanian boxing. As the sport entered its boom period in the tiny Central American state, others were hunting for glory with the same hunger and determination. The most notable was Ernest Marcel, known as "ñato" because of his pug nose, which had little cartilage left after years of boxing and was jammed onto his face as if composed of silly putty. Marcel was three years older than Duran and came from Colon. He spent much of his youth playing basketball in local leagues, but was always the smallest player on the court and eventually realized that there wasn't much room in the game for five-foot-seven-inch guards in a sport of six-footers. He turned to boxing.

There was no better place to hone his skills than the hotbed of Colon. The province had a knack for hatching and matching the finest boxers in Panama. Inevitably Ismael Laguna, who lived down the street, was his yardstick. "I liked Laguna's style and started learning his tactics when we sparred together," he said. "He was my inspiration." With help from trainer Felipe Vega and boxer the Manhattan Kid, Marcel would create his own style at the Arena de Colon. Although he eventually left to live and box in Panama City, he firmly maintained his roots back there.

In 1966, after more than seventy amateur contests, Marcel turned professional with a first-round knockout. After a string of wins and one draw, Marcel lost his first in a trilogy with Miguel Riasco – whose brother Rigoberto would later win the world junior featherweight title – in July 1967, and dropped another decision nine months later to

Augustin Cedeno. While some boxers came up with excuses for defeats, Marcel knew he had a lot to learn. Learn he did, and he would lose only twice more in his entire career.

Marcel won his next fifteen fights, recording eleven knockouts. Along with his rise came new managers, Captain Vasquez and Colonel Ruben Paredes, who Marcel entrusted to get him better bouts. The military was heavily involved in the sport and Paredes, an important figure in the National Guard and would later briefly run the country, had been a prime mover in the expansion of boxing under the Omar Torrijos regime. Paredes developed a close relationship with Marcel. "Torrijos gave support to all the sports in Panama and helped lift up the boxing here," said Marcel. "Panama was down before and now it was getting back up with his help. He helped make gyms in Maranon, and got the police to help also."

After a revenge knockout win over Miguel Riasco, the young feather-weight contender with the pug nose was about to embark on the most significant battle of his career. Duran was right around the corner. Who was this kid from Colon trying to take my turf, Duran thought? Many things traveled through Duran's stubborn head, one being that he had something to prove to his people. By kicking Marcel's ass, he could avenge the loss of his friend and stablemate Riasco and stake his own claim. Yet a fight between Duran and Ernesto Marcel was one that the Panamanian Boxing Commission was hesitant to make. Why build one prospect and destroy another? The real concern was with Duran's inexperience. Many believed he was too green to challenge Marcel, but Duran told Carlos Eleta he wanted the fight and would win it. "Marcel was ready to fight for a world championship at that time but the boxing commission in Panama would not approve that fight with me," he added. "Eleta did everything he could to get the fight to go."

It was the fight everyone wanted to see. From the rich businessman loosening his tie in a Panama City nightclub to the *campesino* on his farm in Chiriqui, from Chorrillo to David, the topic of conversation was Duran versus Marcel. The two young stars shared a country, a weight class and a tug-of-war on bragging rights. Both were young, insolent and egotistical in the *macho* way of the *barrio*. Both were also coming of age at the right time. Two years earlier a cocksure lieutenant colonel, Omar Torrijos Herrera, and his accomplices had staged a military coup and had overthrown President Arnulfo Arias. By 1970, Torrijos was entrenched himself as the Leader of the Panamanian Revolution, and would build a legacy that eclipsed all of Panama's military heroes. In the quest for a new social democracy he backed the poor, taxed the rich and increased the power of the military. "In 1972, the military started to support sports in Panama," said Marcel. "Panama was down and Torrijos was making everything better. He made gyms and began to get support from the police." He would make boxing a national sport.

In the early spring of 1970, both Duran and Marcel made their way to Mexico City, part of a group of Panamanian boxers sent by Eleta and others to train there in some of the toughest gyms in the world. Always alive to new experiences, Duran was happy to escape the grimness of Chorrillo. His interest was also piqued by the thought that his father might be in Mexico City. Leaving the Beyreyes Hotel a few hours before a training session, he excitedly roamed the vast city, a $500 stipend from Eleta burning a hole in his pocket, and soon got lost.

"The Mexican arena where I fought was very close, and I asked this Mexican how do I get there and he says, 'Just keep straight and you have to see it.' What a coincidence, and the gym was open. I remembered that arena because I used to watch a lot of Mexican movies. I watched wrestlers like El Santo, Chavo, Blue, all these Mexican wrestlers, so I climb into the ring and make believe the ring is full and I felt like I was a wrestler."

While there he also met a beautiful girl. "I fall in love with this Mexican woman ... and I have to leave for Panama," said Duran. "Eleta had this guy like a second hand named Issac Kresh. He asked me, 'You want to fight right here in this Mexican ring?' And I said, 'Hell, yeah I do.' He told me that the fight would be against a guy named Felipe Torres. He said it would be in about three weeks and I told him, 'Let's get it on.' The real reason I wanted to stay was because of the beautiful Mexican girl I had met."

Torres had just gone the distance with the highly ranked Kuniaki Shibata of Japan and had never been stopped, but Duran knew nothing about his style. It didn't matter to him and rarely would throughout his career. His opponent could do the worrying. Duran fought with the same instinctive aggression as his Mexican counterparts, with little regard for grace or beauty, though his defence was becoming ever more subtle. Fighting in his opponent's home, he couldn't let it go to a decision.

"We go to the movies, and I tell the girl that I am going to stay for a few days because I have a fight," said Duran. "And she said, 'With whom?' I told her Felipe Torres and she was astonished. She knew a lot about boxing, but she didn't want to say anything to me. The day of the fight my girl is there, but I had charisma and had won over the Mexican people."

It was 5 April 1970, and Duran had a girl by his side, the Mexican fans warming to him and a right hand from Hell. He also had a fierce desire to see his opponent destroyed. Winning on points was a frustration; seeing the other man prone on the canvas was the ultimate high. He was so obsessed with the knockout that he wouldn't even allow a photo of Eleta's nephew standing over him in the middle of the ring. The knockout was sacred, not a joke.

Both men went toe-to-toe. "It was a very bloody match and the guy gave me a punch and I ended up way over across the ring, but I never fell," said Duran. "It was back and forth, both of us flying across the ring. The fight's over and we were worried that we were going to get robbed. I had the face like a *tamale*. I was all swollen and so was he. When the unanimous decision came out for me, a big fat guy … picks me up and says, 'You just beat the ninth-ranked featherweight in the world.' Marcel never wanted to fight Torres, and I come in without any notice and beat the guy."

Something else happened on the trip to further the rivalry between Duran and Ernesto Marcel. "I had a sparring session with Duran," said Marcel. "I beat him bad for two rounds and after it he called Eleta and told him that he wanted a match with me. Duran was very upset about the beating I gave him in practice. He said, 'No black man can beat me.' Then he went back to Eleta in Panama and told him to get the fight." According to Duran, the two never sparred.

Leaving his Mexican girl behind, Duran returned to Panama. As they shared the same gym for training, Duran and Marcel crossed paths on occasion, and neither gave any ground. Marcel was out to prove that he wasn't scared of the man who frightened so many opponents, while Duran was just Duran, bold and confrontational. What the public saw, the scowl and stare, was no act. To beat his opponents, he had to hate them.

"When the fight with Marcel was realized, Marcel was training at Neco de La Guardia," said Duran. "I used to train at the same time from twelve to two-thirty every day. After that I would go play basketball. When Marcel was training he would yell to me to get in condition because I'm going to knock you out. I told him that I was going to knock the shit out of him.

"Eleta had a company that sold vitamins and he gave me one called Mighty Tech. He told me to take two each day and I thought, if one vitamin is going to make me strong, if I take two then I'll be strong as a bull. I started taking the vitamins in pairs. But they only got me sick. I got this type of wart on my butt, and I couldn't run and I couldn't jog. I told Eleta they had to stop the fight because I couldn't train. I always remembered that Marcel used to tell me that he didn't want to hear any excuses that I was sick or anything. I was fed up with that."

Duran went to the equivalent of a back-alley doctor, his childhood pal Chaparro Pinzon, nicknamed Shorty. The biggest bout in Panama was riding on his rudimentary medical knowledge. "Three days before the fight, I still couldn't walk," said Duran. "Two days before the fight, I let Chaparro stay at my house because he was really poor and had no place to go. He would run with me in the mornings and go with me to the gym. He says, 'Let's pinch this wart and you'll get cured.' I was sitting on the bed screaming like a little girl because he takes out the roof of the wart on my butt and I'm drawing blood like crazy. About four hours later my fever goes down and the swelling between my legs starts to disappear. The next day I wake up like a bull and say that I'm going to knock the shit out of that bastard and he's going to pay for everything he said." Eleta was kept in the dark about Chaparro's crude surgery. "Nobody knew about anything that happened at my house," said Duran. "I was going to win despite my sickness."

Duran and Marcel met on 16 May 1970, over ten rounds at 128 pounds, at the Nuevo Panama Stadium. The trash talking was over. Both fighters knew what a win would mean to their careers. Duran was undefeated at 25-0, while Marcel was 24-2-1. "Marcel was a helluva fighter," said Eleta, who pulled the strings to make the fight happen. "But I knew that Duran could beat him."

Under different circumstances, Duran and Marcel might have been friends, sharing ring notes at late-night haunts. With help from Old Parr they might have squared up over the pool table, thrown some playful jabs, then hugged each other in the way boxers do: one arm, strong grasp, with a hint of nostalgia. But Roberto Duran Samaniego and Ernesto Marcel grew up on different sides of the tracks. Colon and Panama City were close, but if you were from Colon, then you weren't from the capital and that's what mattered most. "It was the best from Colon against the best from the city. That's why the fight was so big in

Panama," said Marcel. Such sentiment was echoed around the country. Fans took sides, grabbed a beer and settled in.

Inside the arena a swooshing sound, unique to Panama, circled like a wave with every punch landed. It appeared to most that Duran had the edge through the first nine rounds. Certainly he was the aggressor, and stung his opponent more frequently. Even if his punches weren't hurting Marcel that much, they arrived from all angles. But it was close, and Marcel believed he was ahead. Now in the final round, according to Marcel, he was still utilizing the same in-and-out tactics that had held up in the earlier rounds. Marcel agreed it was a close fight, although Duran's pride wouldn't ever allow him to admit such a thing. However, the last ten ticks of the clock would remain embedded in Marcel's head, a lonely reminder that to agree to be a boxer is a contract based on vulnerability in a callous world that grants no freebies.

Then, with ten seconds left in the final round, referee Isaac Herrera waved his hands and decided not to let Marcel finish the fight. He said Marcel had barely thrown a punch in the round and he was stopping the bout because of his inactivity. Others claimed Duran had nailed Marcel, and forced him to run to survive the last round. It was ruled a tenth-round technical knockout to Duran. There was confusion. Neither fighter was hurt or close to being knocked out, but there was concern from the Eleta-appointed referee that Marcel wasn't throwing punches.

"Everybody in Panama wanted to know why he stopped the fight," Marcel recalled. "I asked the referee many times after, why he stopped the fight. And Isaac Herrera, one of the greatest referees in the world, tells me he really didn't know why he stopped the fight. I was winning, so people wanted to know why they stopped the fight. Yes, the fight was narrow. After the fight [Herrera] said that I wasn't fighting."

Duran countered, "All Marcel did was hug me the whole fight and smell the cologne I was wearing. Marcel never made weight, lost by forfeit and I even gave him pounds. He never wanted to get in the ring with me. It was just about the time that my body started to become quick. After the fight, I never saw him again. To this day I ask him to his face why he didn't fight me again."

Although Marcel claims to remember boxing official Juan Carlos Tapia interrogating Herrera about the stoppage, Tapia denies it. "I was a judge in that fight," said Tapia. "Marcel got really scared. He received a punch in the ninth round in the throat and he didn't want to fight anymore. In the tenth round, he ran around until the fight was over. The referee told him that he had to fight, and when Marcel did not fight, they stopped the fight and gave it to Duran by TKO. All three judges had Duran winning. If the fight would have lasted ten rounds, Duran would have won a unanimous decision."

While Marcel claimed he wanted a rematch at 128, Duran's natural growth and excessive eating habits forced him to move to the 135-pound limit. "I asked Duran for the rematch," said Marcel. "And he said he would go his way and for me to go my way. And I went on to be a world champ at this weight." Duran countered: "In a three minute round, for two and a half of those minutes Marcel would dance around and run from me. In the last minute, he would try to stand up to me and impress the judges and the fans, but when we went toe-to-toe, I broke him apart. By the fifth round, I was way ahead of him. [Years later, at an honorary dinner] he came over to me, hit me in the ribs and told me that I was the only man to really beat him. And I said, 'If you really wanted the rematch, then why didn't you come up to the 135-pound limit? You were afraid to fight me at 135 because you were afraid I'd beat your ass again.'"

In August 1972, Ernesto Marcel won the WBA featherweight title to become one of four Panamanian world champions. He would retire from the sport, still champion, two years later.

\* \* \*

For all that the Duran-Marcel fight captured the imagination, there was still only one true boxing hero in Panama. In November 1965, Ismael Laguna had lost his lightweight crown in a rematch with Carlos Ortiz, but in March 1970, he had regained it from Mexican bomber Mando Ramos, traveling to Los Angeles – where Ramos was hugely popular – to do so. "The whole stadium was against me," Laguna recalled. "I looked up and saw them all chanting, 'Mando, Mando.'" But the twenty-year-old Ramos was already traveling a path of drugs, women and deceit, while Laguna was too respectful of his craft to fritter away his talent. He stuck and twisted his jab early and often, draining Ramos's body like a wet towel and stopping him on a bloody ninth-round technical knockout. "I met up with some bad people and I got caught up in methamphetamines and cocaine," said Ramos years later. "I wasn't right at all. Mentally my mind was not in the fight.

"Duran and I were supposed to fight at one point," he added. "If I were to have been right, that would have been a great fight. I would have boxed him, but I never got to show my ability in boxing. I could box; I could punch moving backward. I swear I would have boxed Duran like that, punch and moving back and forth."

Champion once more, the experienced Laguna was regarded as one of the best pound-for-pound boxers in the world. Then the unthinkable happened. In September 1970, he was outmaneuvered by an even better boxer, a skinny, broken-nosed Scot called Ken Buchanan, and lost his cherished title for the second time. It meant he would never get to defend against the rising Duran.

The closest the two Panamanian greats ever came to a box-off was a single sparring session. Though few were in the gym to witness it, the story later grew into the proportions of a mini-epic. Duran's sparring sessions were feral portraits of precision. Even when training with stablemates, he gave and asked no quarter, and the fact that he worshipped Laguna meant nothing when they stepped between the ropes.

"Duran was coming up and he didn't have a sparring partner one day," said Laguna. "I didn't want to spar with him because he was too young. I think I was preparing for a bout. I was too experienced, but he insisted. At first I thought we would take it easy, but Plomo urged Duran to go after me. When Duran came at me, I hit him with three quick hooks and opened a cut under his eye. That's when the sparring session ended."

It is not uncommon for fighters to have a selective memory when they have come off second best, and unsurprisingly Duran's account differs. "I was sparring at Neco de la Guardia with Antonio Amaya," he said. "I was young and I had done two rounds with Amaya. Laguna had no one to spar with. Right before, I had hit Amaya really hard. I was just starting my career, but I had already beaten Amaya badly. Then, I hear someone say that Laguna pays people to spar with him. And I say, 'I'm the one.'

"In the first round I start hitting Laguna left and right, and I even move him a little bit. Laguna starts running around me, and I start hunting him down. When I stopped, he hit me with a left and broke my nose. When I saw the blood, I lost it and jumped on top of him and gave him some punches. Curro Dossman, the manager of Laguna, tells Laguna, 'That Cholito is tough. He'll be a champion one day.' When we're finished sparring, I'm drinking orange juice. I say, 'Champ, give me something so I can go and eat.' And he gives me a dollar-fifty and right then I felt like hitting him again. That's the truth about my sparring with Laguna."

Not far from where the incident occurred in the early Seventies, Plomo sits in a gym in Barrazza and retells his version. "Laguna and Amaya were stars from the same block and Duran wanted to fight with them. First, Duran got in there and was sparring two rounds with Amaya, but Curro Dossman stepped in and said, 'Look, this is only sparring, we are not fighting here. If you want to fight, then fight with Laguna.' And this is the truth, for those who tell otherwise then they are trying to cover Laguna. When Laguna got into the ring, he tried to jab Duran and Duran hit him twice with right hands and Laguna was stumbling."

Didn't Laguna break Duran's nose? "No, mentira, mentira! All lies," said the old sage, still protecting his fighter. "I remember watching Laguna fight Ortiz in the first fight in Panama. Their next two fights [won by Ortiz] were much different than the first one, where Laguna was using his cleverness. Ortiz would beat him in the two fights with the same punch. Laguna was a beautiful fighter with much speed and a good jab but he couldn't change when he fought Ortiz. Compared to Duran, Laguna didn't have intelligence in the ring. When Duran got hit he would move out of the way before the next punch came. Laguna would just stay there and receive punches."

The two men did share a common opponent around this time in Lloyd Marshall, a dangerous American lightweight. Laguna had some problems in outpointing the heavy-handed Marshall, while two months later Duran, who had stopped five more opponents since his grudge match with Ernesto Marcel, beat him inside five rounds, on 29 May 1971.

"Laguna fought Lloyd Marshall, who had a really tough right hand," remembered Duran. "Marshall hits Laguna with a right that knocks him on his ass but Laguna wins by decision, and Eleta gives me the fight with Marshall. The entire country said, 'Now they're really going to knock out Duran.' When we're in the dressing room, a boxer tells me to be careful with the right hand because that's his most dangerous, most powerful punch.

"People were saying Marshall was going to knock me out, he was going to do this and that. Not very many people went to the fight. The guy hits me with the same right hand he hits Laguna with, even harder, and couldn't even move me. The crowd said, 'Awww,' when he hit me, but he hit me twice and didn't even move me. That kind of got to Marshall and that's why I knocked him out.

"[In the States] I once went to a place where there were those coffeemakers that keep the coffee warm. I had never seen one like that in Panama and I told Eleta that I wanted one of those. He told me not to worry, that he was going to give me one of those when I would fight in Panama. When I won the fight with Marshall and got down from the ring, he was holding the coffeemaker in his hands." Duran gave his gloves from the fight to John F. Kennedy Jr., son of the late President, who was at ringside as Eleta's guest.

Laguna and Duran would never box each other again. Eleta did initiate talks about a possible bout between but realized there was little point in eliminating one of Panama's two boxing idols. Both believe they would have handled the other with ease. "There was talk that Laguna was sick and that Eleta wanted me to fight him," said Duran. "But he knew I would have destroyed him." Not so, said Laguna: "I would have destroyed him in one round!"

Duran had a similar rivalry with another world champion, his child-hood friend Alfonso "Peppermint" Frazer (Frazer would win the WBA light-welterweight title in 1972). Eleta managed both, and on a few occasions they sparred together. Neither fighter had moved past the ninth grade, as Frazer left school at fifteen and Duran at fourteen. Three years older and slightly bigger, Frazer remembered Duran and the struggles of his childhood.

"Duran and I had two different trainers, but we were stablemates. I was trained by Federico Plummer, and he had Plomo. When I sparred with Duran in Maranon he was getting great already and I had to put my hand on him. He was coming along good but he wasn't up to me yet. So bang, I hit him, and Eleta came in and said, 'You guys take it easy, you're only practicing.' But he tried to show me up. We only sparred once. Duran comes at you because he was young, strong and famous and he wanted to hurt everybody. He didn't know the difference between sparring and fighting, so every time he got into the ring to spar, he would fight. He'd shoot his best punches and try to hurt everybody he worked with."

As always, Plomo was just outside the ring feeding instructions to Duran. He knew that his fighter had to be that aggressive and fierce every second he was in the ring. Without that all-out intensity, Duran wouldn't have been Duran. "They only had one sparring session together because Frazer was scared to get in the ring with Roberto," said Plomo. "Roberto was just starting off and he didn't have good form. [Frazer] hit him down, but Duran got right back up and started to hit Frazer and then his manager stepped in and said, 'No fighting, no fighting. This is practice.' That was the last time that Frazer would spar with him and always had excuses that he was sick or something like that. Duran had to train like that because he needed to practice against a certain style. For instance, if Roberto was going to fight Amaya, the other person he was sparring with had to have the same technique. That's how he had to practice, according to the other guy's style."

Duran has yet another version of the story. "We were in Juan Demostenes Stadium and we stayed to spar with Peppermint Frazer. Frazer was going to fight with someone at that time, but I don't remember who. The fans were saying to Frazer, 'Wait till you see the punches you give Cholito because he doesn't know nothing.' Here comes the technique versus the brutality. I'll never forget in the corner, Frazer tells me to hit him a little softer because 'you're hitting me too hard.'"

However, another of Duran's sparring mates learned volumes from each three-minute class. "Duran used to hold back all the time because he was a perfect guy in the ring," said former pro Mario Molo. "[He] never tried to knock me out in practice. He tried to learn and I would learn also. We both became better boxers. He tried to teach me while boxing me." Molo, who later fell on hard times, can still be seen at boxing shows in Panama. "Mario Molo was one of the first sparrings we used," said Plomo. "He would last longer [than others]. In general, they were not able to resist Duran's blow during training much of the time. To Duran training time was like real fight time. 'Hit me hard because I will hit you hard back,' he used to say. He did not mind who it was, his brother or anyone. He used to request that the other hit as strong as if it were the real fight. This is what I call to train thoroughly. This is good work."

★ ★ ★

EVERY so often, the streetfighter in Roberto Duran reappeared. He found it hard to stay out of trouble. Even with Carlos Eleta by his side and with his potential unfolding in the ring, Duran wasn't guaranteed a free pass with the law. "When I was still living out of the hotel, there were three big bars: Atlas, Ranchero and Balboa," Duran recalled. "They all played music. My mom's friend worked in a restaurant called El Limite. We used to invite my mom to eat where her friend worked. Once, I went to a dance and my mom's friend was discussing something with another person. I intervened, but they started fighting. I tried to separate them, but I feel somebody's hands on my neck from behind. I got him and I flipped him; he tried to stand up and I hit him. The man tried to get up again and I punched him."

The police arrived as Duran was working the guy over. "Four guards fell on top of me. I was taken to jail that night in front of a judge named Belillo, who adored the policemen. We saw the judge, that son of a bitch, I hope he dies of cancer, and the other guy said that he was stopping the fight and that I hit him. Then he said that he was a policeman and he had tried to show me his badge. The judge wouldn't let me talk. So I was sent to a jail called Cárcel Modelo, where they only sent the most violent criminals."

Cárcel Modelo translates, apparently without irony, as Model Jail. An ugly, four-story block, it was built in 1925 in Panama City to house approximately 250 inmates. When Duran arrived there, it held over 1,000 men in appalling conditions. Cells built for three men now contained up to fifteen and prisoners awaiting trial were often kept for interminable periods. Torture, particularly of political detainess, was widely believed to take place there.

Duran found himself in a cell with men even more intimidating than himself. "There were two people: a Peruvian wrestler and a huge black man who looked like he killed somebody. The jail was called *la preventiva* [a system of remand where prisoners considered a serious risk are incarcerated before trial], where the very bad people went. When someone new arrived, they made all of the inmates line up. There were cells on both sides, and as I was walking inside, the prisoners started shouting, 'Here comes a new one.' They would take all the prisoners out and make them stand on a line. I heard them shouting, 'Here comes fresh meat.' At that time I was already boxing, with Eleta consolidating it. When the inmates saw me, they knew me. They all asked me, 'What are you doing here? What are you doing Duran?'"

Despite his minor celebrity, in jail he was just another face. Duran knew he was in danger every minute he stayed in *la preventiva*. All his life, Duran had fought his way out of problems, and he always hit first. Now he was among desperate people who didn't care who he was, and his fists meant nothing. For the first time he could remember, Duran needed protection. Luckily he found someone who would watch his back.

"We had to sleep on the floor," said Duran. "The inmates gave me cardboard, another gave me a pillow and another one gave me a blanket. Later, some guy started to stare at me, a white guy, and he got closer and he told me he was Taras Bulba, the Peruvian wrestler. He told me he had lots of jewelry and he trafficked jewelry. He said that he had been there for long and that if he ever got out, he would never return to the country again. Then he told this huge black guy that if he tried something against me, he would have his head."

Carlos Eleta could have gotten his prized fighter out with a phone call, but wanted to teach him a lesson. It was left to another influential figure to bail him out. "It was a good friend of mine who helped me in amateur boxing," said Duran. "He was a rich man … a colonel at Cárcel Modelo. One morning I was cleaning the front part of the jail when an officer came up to me. I was sweeping the floor in the jail and he asked me why I was there. I told him what really happened."

"Is it true?" he asked.

"Yes," I replied.

"Then, he asked me for my mother, my uncles, my family, my grandma and everyone. He told me that he had grown up with them. Finally, he investigated what really happened and then they let me go. I went back to my cell to get my stuff. I said, 'Taras Bulba, thank you and I'm gone.'

"People told me, 'Manos de Piedra, remember us if someday we get the chance to see one of your fights.'

"'No problem,' I replied, and I was out of there. I went directly to see Carlos Eleta and told him how I had been freed. I told him he had not behaved well, for he should have tried to help me. He said he wanted me to have a punishment for what I had done. But I was young then and did not understand that."

Plomo, as is so often the case, remembered the event slightly differently. "He once had a problem when he went to a club called Balboa en El Chorrillo. Duran liked dancing very much, and having fun, but he did not drink alcohol. He was there one day when a plainclothes policeman started hitting his wife. Duran walked towards him and told him to stop hitting her, that she was only a woman. The policeman told him to shut up unless he wanted to get beaten too. Duran broke the policeman's jaw from the first blow. The policeman had tried to humiliate him, and though he was not wearing his uniform, being a policeman as he was, he thought he had the same authority as if in uniform. A couple of other policemen turned up and Duran explained to them that he had to hit him because the policeman had threatened to hit him. Yes, he was arrested."

A lengthy prison sojourn could have destroyed Duran's career at the very time it was about to take off. After defeating Lloyd Marshall and the Mexican Fermin Soto in Monterrey, he was booked on his first trip to the United States to fight on the undercard of Ken Buchanan's lightweight title defense against Ismael Laguna, at Madison Square Garden, the most famous venue in world boxing.

# 5

## TWO OLD MEN

*"Those guys, they're older than water."*

Angelo Dundee

FIGHTERS DREAMT OF the Garden from the day they laced on gloves. Madison Square Garden was the Mecca of boxing, steeped in the history of the game's biggest fights. Just six months earlier, Muhammad Ali and Joe Frazier had slugged it out there in the so-called Fight of the Century. To headline there was the ultimate validation. The Garden, which was renovated and moved to four different locations, was originally constructed at 23rd and Madison Avenue, Manhattan, in 1879. Not until the "new" Garden – known as "The House That Tex Built" after promoter Tex Rickard – was built in 1925, however, did it become the sport's centre, graced by the greatest figures in the game. In 1968, it was relocated again to Pennsylvania Plaza, between 32nd and 34th streets and Seventh and Eighth avenues.

Duran's opponent was the experienced Benny Huertas, a former gangbanger who was popular with promoters and fans alike because he always came to fight. Huertas had lost almost as many as he had won and, sandwiched between the great lightweights of his era, would be a bit player in the division. No matter how hard he tried, he couldn't shed the distinction of being an extra in the world's most brutal sport, but he always gave his best and was certainly no patsy.

Back in Bayamon, Puerto Rico, they called Huertas "the Boxer" because he would fight with anybody, though he spent most of his youth not in his native country but in New York City. "I was in a big Puerto Rican gang in Brooklyn called the Apaches," said Huertas, "but I didn't want to do this anymore. I wanted something else." He saw an ad in a newspaper for a Hispanic Golden Gloves Tournament at a place called St. Nick's, and at eighteen found boxing. It "was just something to do."

Not long into his amateur career, tragedy struck. "Something happened in around 1962-63. It is so sad that I can't even talk about it," said Huertas years later, nearly in tears. "I killed a guy in the ring. It was sad because I had a new wife and we didn't have a baby. He had his wife and he had a baby who was six or seven months. I thought about when his boy grows and asks, 'Where's my father?' Suppose that thing happened to me with a baby … a lot of troubles."

Huertas took nearly a year off from the ring but couldn't quit the sport; his future rode on it. "Boxing saved my life. The *barrio* where I lived in Brooklyn was a bad one. A lot of people was killed. I had to do something better than that." At the time, world champs such as Floyd Patterson and Jose Torres fought out of the Cus D'Amato gym where Huertas trained. D'Amato was actually Huertas's co-manager, but wasn't hands-on. He stayed in the background and Huertas never really knew one of the most famous of all boxing managers.

He turned pro in 1965, and by the time he was due to fight Duran his record was 18-14-3. Though Duran was barely known at that stage outside his home country and the boxing *cognoscenti*, to those in the know his match-up with Huertas added intrigue to the Garden bill. Was this killer from Panama any good or was his record built on straw men? No one really knew, but Huertas was expected to give him a test. Fight posters billed their ten-round semi-final as Roberto "Rocky" Duran versus Benny "Bang Bang" Huertas and described one as the "sensational unbeaten Panamanian K.O. artist" while the other was the "slam bang Puerto Rican puncher." They were the opening act for Laguna and Buchanan.

\* \* \*

"Papa what time does the ice cream parlor close?" asked Roberto Duran.

"I think around nine p.m.," said Carlos Eleta. "Why?"

"What time is my fight?"

"I don't know, why Roberto?"

"Well, if I finish my fight in time, then I can make it over in time to get a milkshake."

"I was telling him not to be scared to fight at the Garden for the first time," recalled Eleta later, "and all he could think about was ice cream."

For his part, Huertas was totally ignorant of the opponent he was facing, and in fact was more preoccupied by the recent death of his father. "I knew nothing about Duran," he said. "The manager fooled me because at the time I was making 138-140 pounds. I was happy because I made the 138-pound weight limit. Then the promoter came and told me to make 135. I made the weight, but I killed myself. There was an exhibition a couple days before the fight, and it was all Panama. I saw him spar with someone else that day and I said, 'This is going to be a war,' because we had the same style." Both had little regard for defense. Neither wanted to dance around the ring. They were there to *fight*.

On 13 September 1971, at the Garden, Duran wasted no time introducing himself. First, they scuffled, with neither exacting a decided edge. Then a thudding right to the temple left Huertas sprawled out on the canvas. It was all over in sixty-six seconds and Duran made it back to the ice cream parlor before closing. With his milkshake and his knockout victory, Duran waited to see if Laguna would return the light-weight crown back to Panama.

Benny Huertas would continue to fight anyplace they needed a body. "When you spend a lot of time in one thing and stop, you don't want to leave it alone," he recalled. "I have to stay in the house now and do nothing. I can't work because of the discs in my back and in the garment business you have to work like a horse."

Because of the way Duran knocked out Huertas, those who hadn't seen him fight before were convinced that he was going to accomplish things in the sport. One punch was enough to sell some boxing writers. "The undercard ... produced one fighter of special note, who will have to be watched as a possible future lightweight champion," said the august *Ring* magazine. "I'd seen Huertas and he was a damn good fighter in the gym in Gramercy Park," recalled boxing analyst Bert Sugar. "[Duran] takes him out in one round and it wasn't even a fight. It was a mauling, a mugging. The kid had something. Good looking ... everything."

Panamanian boxing writer Alfonso Castillo, a small, bespectacled ex-jockey, was one of those who witnessed the destruction of Benny Huertas. He immediately coined a new name for the phenomenon: *Manos de Piedra*. Hands of Stone.

In the main event, Ken Buchanan again outpointed Laguna to retain his world title. It would be the Tiger's last fight and Duran promised to avenge his friend's loss. "Duran said that on one occasion that his inspiration to be a boxer was when he saw Ismael Laguna beat Carlos Ortiz," said Panamanian boxing analyst Daniel Alonso. "After the Huertas fight, Duran said that he would beat Buchanan next for Laguna."

Before he would get the chance, he was introduced to two elderly men who many would credit with his ultimate development as a fighter. Ray Arcel and Freddie Brown were American sages who knew more about boxing than anyone else alive.

* * *

Ray Arcel was born in the final months of the Nineteenth Century and began working with boxers in 1917, at the age of seventeen. Growing up a Jew in an Italian section of East Harlem meant he had his share of street fights, but he also had a sharp mind, went to a good school and harbored ambitions to be a doctor. All of that changed when he started to hang out at Grupp's Gymnasium on 116th Street. There he encountered Dai Dollings, a fanatical Welshman whose pedigree went back to the bareknuckle era. Dollings, a strict vegetarian, had coached marathon runners, would walk to the gym in all weathers and complained about the softness of the New World: "You bloody Americans, you're made of tissue paper." When the young Arcel told him he wanted to be a trainer too, Dollings replied, "The hell with a trainer. You want to be an *analyst*."

And that's what Arcel became. He studied fighters like a scholar in the unheated gyms and smoky boxing clubs of New York State and beyond, and learned the black arts of corner work from the legendary Doc Bagley, who could stem a gushing cut with a plug of chewing tobacco. He also loved his fighters. His idol was Benny Leonard, the imperious Jewish-American lightweight who created the template for the modern boxer. Arcel would tell his boxers, "This is your school, where you learn your lessons."

The list of champions he worked with eventually ran well into double figures. He handled Tony Zale during his three epic wars with Rocky Graziano, trained Ezzard Charles for his gory classics with Rocky Marciano, and seconded so many of Joe Louis's victims during the great heavyweight's long reign that sportswriter Jimmy Cannon labeled him "the Pallbearer."

By the mid-Fifties, Arcel was running the popular *Saturday Night Fights*, which appeared every week on the ABC television channel in the US. He was an independent operator, and a successful one, but this did not endear him to the New York hoodlums who then ran the sport. He started having trouble making fights. Main event boxers would cancel at the last minute. He received an anonymous phone call telling him to "get out of the TV racket if you know what's good for you."

In 1953, the fifty-four-year-old Arcel was standing outside a Boston hotel talking to a fellow trainer when a man stepped up behind him, hit him a vicious blow to the head with a length of piping wrapped in a paper bag, dropped the weapon and disappeared into the crowd. Arcel almost died and spent the next nineteen days in hospital. The assault was instrumental in his decision to retire from the sport he loved in 1956 to work in the purchasing department of an alloy company. By the early Seventies he was still in good shape but venerable, with neat gray hair, wise eyes and a dapper sense of dress in a Fifties style. He had been out of boxing for eighteen years and was a man out of time, but his knowledge and analytical skills hadn't waned.

In March 1972, Carlos Eleta's boxer Alfonso "Peppermint" Frazer was due to challenge champion Nicolino Locche for the world title. Eleta had met Arcel twenty years earlier, when the American helped to train a talented Panamanian lightweight called Federico Plummer. "Then, after many, many years, I get Peppermint Frazer and Duran," said Eleta. "I have a chance for Frazer to fight for the championship of the world with a fellow from Argentina. So then I tried to contact Ray. I called Teddy Brenner at Madison Square Garden to get in touch with him.

"Brenner said, 'Forget about it, Ray is retired and having problems with the mafia.' They tried to control him, but they couldn't because Ray was a very honorable person. As soon as I talked to him he said, 'It's been a long time Carlos, what can I do for you?' I told him, 'Well, I have a fighter who is fighting for the championship of the world and I need you for that fight.' Ray told me he would do anything for me, under one condition, that he wouldn't charge me a penny. That was Ray Arcel. I had so much respect for that man. He was a very strong man. The mafia tried to get to him, but they couldn't."

Arcel took the job. It was a tall order. The champion, Locche, was a chain-smoker possessed of uncanny defensive skills, with over 100 wins to his name. Not for nothing was he known as "the Untouchable." About twenty days before the bout, Arcel arrived to bring Frazer to a peak. Though he couldn't speak Spanish, he was fluent in the language of boxing and his mind was sharp as a tack.

With him came Freddie Brown. While the sharp-featured Arcel could have been mistaken for a university don, Brown, a "mere" sixty-seven, was a cornerman straight from central casting, a stocky, flat-nosed, cigar-chomping pug with the "dese, dem and doze" accent of the Lower East Side. A peerless cutman, he combined the patience of long experience with the blunt speaking of a man who knows his trade.

Peppermint Frazer had already received some helpful advice from Ismael Laguna, who was now tragically in the grip of sickle-cell anemia and was fading away from the sport. "I talked to Laguna, who beat up Locche for ten rounds but didn't get the decision," said Frazer. "He told me not to shoot at his head because I'd miss and tire myself out. Instead, I had to shoot at his shoulders and chest and wear him down."

Ray Arcel was also at work. He managed to watch a Locche training session by "dressing like a Panamanian," donning dark glasses and a Panama hat, and drawing on his vast memory bank, immediately spotted that Locche's style was reminiscent of Johnny Dundee, a featherweight from the Twenties. He went back and told Frazer not to follow if the champion retreated and tried to draw him to the ropes: "Just stand there and look at him. Don't do anything." This would negate Locche's counter-punching style.

The plan worked to perfection for fifteen rounds. Not known as a knockout puncher, Frazer disrupted the champ with skill and intelligence. "In, out, in, and out, I just left his head alone and I would just shoot a straight right once in a while," said Frazer, savoring the memories. "I did just what Laguna told me." When the final bell sounded, Panama rejoiced. It was March 10, 1972, and Frazer was champion of the world. "That day was like a carnival," said Frazer. "Oh, they treat you like a king: All the women, the money, everything. So many new friends you didn't know you had. But it depends what type of person that you are. Some people can't live without the fame."

Unfortunately, those same fringe benefits that all champs savor only lasted seven months as Frazer lost his title to the wonderfully skilled Colombian Antonio Cervantes. "I tried to get inside against Cervantes, but he had a long reach and kept me off him," Frazer said. "They said in Panama that he was no good, but I saw him in Venezuela and I knew he was good. I had nothing to be ashamed of." Having made his biggest purse of $50,000, Frazer bought two houses, which he still has to this day.

Eleta wanted Arcel and Brown to look at his other hot prospect, a kid called Duran. They were skeptical, but by chance Arcel was at the

Garden – a friend had told him to check out Ken Buchanan – with his wife Steve when Duran iced Huertas in the first round. Duran bounded over to where the Arcels sat and shook their hands, even though they had never met. When told it was Duran's twenty-second knockout in twenty-five wins, Arcel reportedly said, "Either he's another Jack Dempsey or he's been beating bums." But out of friendship with Eleta, he took a look at this young hotshot. The fact that Eleta deemed him worthy of such elite cornermen was a sign of his talent. Eleta also felt that he had got the most he could from Plomo Quinones and Duran needed something more.

Duran's next opponent was the experienced Hiroshi Kobayashi, who in his previous fight had lost his world junior lightweight title. "Eleta tells me that he's going to get me a fight with this guy who just lost the championship and that's going to be the test for me," said Duran. "If I win that fight, then Eleta assured me of a shot at the lightweight championship of the world. I ask him who it is, and he tells me this Chinese guy. I tell him that this Chinese guy is a dead man and I'm going to kill him." Kobayashi was in fact Japanese, a veteran of seventy-four fights, and had reigned as champion for almost four years. He was Duran's sternest test to date.

They fought on 16 October 1971, in Panama City. Despite a remarkable ability to absorb punishment, Kobayashi wilted under Duran's attack. He landed some clean shots but was stalked, hunted down and overwhelmed. Like a man trapped in a closet with no space to move his arms, yet still trying to block punches, Kobayashi was pummeled into a seventh-round stoppage. A national hero arrived back in the dressing room.

"I'm in the locker room and Freddie Brown comes in with Eleta and I get introduced to him," said Duran. "The gym is so packed. At the time Eleta was friends with John Kennedy Jr., who was young, and Joe DiMaggio, who Eleta had brought to Panama. Carlos Eleta knew all those people. Ray Arcel and Freddie Brown sat next to me and they tell Carlos Eleta, 'This guy is a natural and I'm going to convert him into a champion. And from what I saw, there isn't much he needs to change because from what I saw he knows a lot.'"

While Eleta mingled with elite figures from all stratospheres, Duran rarely bothered to look far past his own circle of friends. "I told Roberto that I wanted him to meet Joe DiMaggio one night, and he said, 'Why, who has he fought?' That was Roberto," laughed Eleta.

Arcel and Brown made a point not to tamper with the kid's bullishness. Passivity was not in Duran's nature and they did nothing to change his aggression; they just upgraded it. Together they provided the polish to Plomo's wax job, so when Duran went into one of his rages, there was purpose behind it. Indeed, Arcel told Brown and the other trainers, "Don't you dare tell him what to do. Leave him alone. He knows what to do. Just condition him. See that he's in shape." The instinctive defensive skills that kept him from absorbing heavy punishment during his first twenty-five fights were also being honed. Most importantly, Arcel saw that Duran knew how to *think* in the ring, not just fight.

"Plomo was a little jealous of Ray and Freddie and would start things," said Eleta. "I always used to tell Duran that his fights were won during training and he would tell me that it didn't matter because he had a right hand like Ingemar Johannsen."

"We had only heard about him," said New York boxing writer Bert Sugar. "Carlos Eleta called me and said, 'You have to see this kid.' He had Ray Arcel and Brown with him, which was a helluva mark. The kid obviously had something. I give Arcel and Brown a lot of credit. Anytime you have a force you have to direct it, and although he also had natural talent, I think you have to harness it. I mean some kids are great street fighters who piss away a career. Now, you had two of the greatest trainers of all-time. Just like Charley Goldman could shape and mold a clumsy Rocky Marciano, who I saw in training once fall over his own feet and knock himself down, if you can shape talent ... and when Eleta brought them in, you knew he thought he had something. And if Arcel and Brown accepted the assignment, you knew they saw something."

Duran returned to his hometown in January 1972 to face the globe-trotting Cuban Angel "Robinson" Garcia. Nicknamed for his likeness to the great Sugar Ray Robinson, Garcia was almost old enough to be Duran's father and had the longest fight record of any boxer then active: 119 wins, fifty-five losses and twenty draws – and they were just the bouts the record compilers knew about. His indefatigability was exceeded only by his appetite for women and booze; he would often enter the ring after a bottle of wine and box none the worse for it. Duran, however, was too much for him.

"He was dangerous," Garcia said in an interview years later, "but I knew how to work the ring. I shuffled back and forth and worked angles and kept him out of range, confusing him ... I caught him with some good shots but he was too young and strong. He won the decision but after the fight he looked at me and said, 'Cuban, you know a lot.'"

The ten-round decision ended Duran's streak of ten straight knockouts. "I made a mistake and took a pill to make weight," said Duran. "I only needed to lose one pound and I ended up losing six pounds against Robinson Garcia. I tried to knock him out but I lost too much weight and I didn't have enough strength. I think if he would have stood up to me and come to fight, I would have knocked him out, but he didn't come to me. I learned something that night. Whenever I fought, I would learn from boxers because I was very smart. I would learn from them and find their defects."

Garcia was too intelligent to brawl with Duran. From the outset, he realized that the young tiger was too strong to stand in front of. Duran took this as an insult. To him, fighters were meant to fight, not hide. "Duran was all the time throwing his punches, but Garcia was blocking him all the time," said Plomo. "Garcia was a good boxer. He had fought twice with Laguna, and had knocked him down twice. After this fight, Garcia was in New York to help us as a sparring partner during the fight with Buchanan, but he only lasted two days. He was not able to continue because Duran hurt him badly during the training."

Soon after the Garcia fight, it was reported that the World Boxing Council would order its junior lightweight champion, Ricardo Arredondo, to defend against Duran, the number one contender. But Duran had outgrown that weight. His sights were set instead on Ken Buchanan, the lightweight champion who had beaten his idol, Laguna. On 10 March 1972, Duran knocked out the little-known Francisco Munoz in the first round. Three months later, he would step into the ring to fight for the championship of the world.

# 6

# THE SCOT

*"I'll never forget you. Every time I take a piss I'll think of you."*

Ken Buchanan to Roberto Duran

AT THE AGE of eight, Ken Buchanan went to the cinema with his father to watch *The Joe Louis Story*, a biopic of the famous heavyweight champion. "I kept thinking throughout the film, I want to be like that guy, champion of the world," he recalled. "That was my inspiration." A short time later, he walked into the Sparta Boxing Club, lied about his age, and within four months was boxing his first three-round bout.

The Buchanans lived on a public housing estate near the Portobello district of Edinburgh, Scotland's capital city. Word traveled through his school that little Kenny was a fighter, and that soon made him a target for bullies wanting to try him out. "I never lost one street fight," he recounted with pride. "Kids used to pick fights with me, not because they didn't like me, but some of these guys, I found out later on, would say, 'That little guy Ken Buchanan in our school, did you know he was a boxer?' So they challenged me. I didn't want to fight; I thought it was stupid. But I beat them all. In fact it was good practice for me. I popped a few..."

Little Kenny admired the then-fading Sugar Ray Robinson as the "ultimate" boxer and harnessed his own skills in a successful amateur career that spanned ten years and took him to the European Championships in Moscow in 1963 and a silver medal at a tournament in Germany in 1965. "All I wanted to be was a world champion, all my life was for this one goal," he said. "Everything after that was secondary." He turned professional at nineteen and, boxing in trademark tartan shorts, won thirty-three straight bouts before a controversial points loss in Italy when challenging for the European lightweight title. By the time he met Laguna, he had won thirty-six out of his thirty-seven bouts, but had never fought outside Europe, at a time when most of the world's best lightweights were from Latin America or Japan.

By Buchanan's definition, a "patsy" was a challenger who had little chance of winning. Outside of Great Britain, a patsy might be categorized as soft or a "pussy," a fighter lacking a hard edge and with a record bloated by weak opponents. Popular opinion outside Europe held that the Scot had built his record against the tea-and-crumpet crowd, and when Laguna's American agent was instructed to "find someone Laguna would be sure to beat," Buchanan seemed to fit the bill. "The people in Laguna's camp thought I was a patsy," said Buchanan. "He was an undisputed champ, both the WBA and WBC champ. But the WBC didn't want to recognize me because they didn't think I was a worthwhile opponent. Ismael was supposed to defend against [Mando] Ramos in a rematch. Ramos was in Panama and he got all cut up in the gyms, so they had to take him back to California. I ended up thanking Ramos. I got my shot and that was it."

Laguna was recognized as world champion by both of the sport's international governing bodies, the US-based World Boxing Association (formerly the National Boxing Association), and the World Boxing Council, formed in 1963 and based in Mexico. When Laguna signed to fight Buchanan instead of Ramos, the WBC and the affiliated British Board withdrew their recognition of him as champion. The WBA, however, sanctioned the bout and it went ahead in San Juan, Puerto Rico.

"A fellow Scotsman of mine fought [light-heavyweight champion] Jose Torres in Puerto Rico some years before that and the heat beat him that night," said Buchanan. "Jose knocked him out and I think Ismael thought it was going to be much the same for himself. We shook hands, said hello. I didn't speak Spanish and he didn't speak English, or Scottish, so we weren't exactly on speaking terms. We went out and fought in the open-air stadium and it was 125 degrees. My manager was putting Vaseline on my face and my dad was putting suntan lotion on my back. I must be the first British boxer to win a world title and get a suntan at the same time."

Buchanan had a plan to neutralize Laguna's famed left jab. "I would throw my jab a split second before he threw his," said Buchanan. "I had to keep on top of him because he knew that this was the first time that

I'd be boxing in this heat and I think he thought it was going to be a lot easier than it was. He was a wee bit surprised that I was taking it to him so much. I don't know exactly when it happened, whether it was the sixth, eighth or tenth round, when Laguna finally realized that it wasn't going to be as easy as he thought it would be.

"I don't know what kept me going that night, I really don't. When we were younger my dad used to take my brother and I to swimming baths because his dad was drowned at sea. I built my strength up with swimming. We used to do underwater swimming. I could hold my breath and swim an Olympic swimming pool underwater. I think that's what helped me with Laguna and the heat. I was used to holding my breath for several minutes."

It wasn't until the late rounds that Buchanan felt he had the edge. "I think it was the eleventh or twelfth round where I thought that I had the faith, not much, but I thought, I have to keep pushing myself. I have to keep on top and tough with my jab. The last two or three rounds got it for me on a split decision. By then, all my hopes and dreams had been answered on that sunny afternoon in Puerto Rico."

Yet not a single British reporter was at ringside for his title win, partly because it was costly to send a writer all the way to Puerto Rico, partly because of indifference about a challenger who had failed to capture the public imagination back home, and partly because the British Board had refused to recognise it as a world title bout. Buchanan's feeling of being a prophet rejected by his own people grew even stronger when he returned home. "When I got back, the British Boxing Board was going to fine me. They said they didn't recognize WBA champions and didn't give me permission to fight Laguna."

In the trade, however, people were taking notice. If the hard-bitten US fight scribes retained any doubts about Buchanan's ability, they disappeared when the wiry Scot took on Donato Paduano, an unbeaten Canadian welterweight who outweighed him by a stone, at Madison Square Garden. Buchanan boxed rings round him, wowed the New York crowd and was voted Fighter of the Year for 1970 by the American Boxing Writers Association, a rare accolade for a European boxer. A magnificent, even-tempered boxer who could brawl when needed, the soft-spoken Scot didn't lose his cool in the face of adversity.

Buchanan was due to make his first defense against Mando Ramos in a bout which the WBC deigned to recognize for the title. However, Ramos pulled out a few days before and instead Buchanan trounced

Ruben Navarro in Los Angeles. Ramos's sorry decline would be not untypical of Latin American champions. "What happened was that he had postponed the fight for a month, so I had been in the camp for six weeks already and I'm worn out," recalled Ramos. "I fucked up. I went out to this jazz bar [and] we're in the back snorting coke and my trainer comes in and everybody leaves the room except for me. This pretty little girl comes in and asks, 'You looking for a party?' We went into a room and we had sex and I caught some disease. Then, I went home and had sex with my wife and gave it to her and she divorced me. So I was going through a lot of mental stuff."

For a short period, Buchanan was the undisputed world lightweight champion, but in June that year he forfeited the WBC belt after a contractual dispute, deepening his bitterness towards the sport's governing bodies. Then came the rematch with Laguna in September 1971 at the Garden, the night that Roberto Duran took out Benny Huertas in one round. "I got cut a couple times in the second fight. Laguna poked me in the eye in the first two rounds," Buchanan recalled. "My left eye was blowing up like a balloon. So my trainer Eddie Thomas took a razor blade and he slit my left eye open at the bottom to let all the blood out and have the swelling go down. Sylvester Stallone owes me money for that because he stole that off me. He bloody well did. Did you ever see that happen?"

In the eleventh round an inadvertent clash of heads opened another cut over Buchanan's right eye. "In those final rounds, the doctor kept coming to my corner to check my eye because there was so much blood, but my manager would stick his thumb in the cut over my right eye and showed the doctor my left eye and it wasn't deep. It was OK. And just as the doctor had turned to go away, my trainer takes some grease from his hand and puts it in the cut. Once they said, 'Seconds out,' he put the grease right in the cut. They couldn't see it. Eddie Thomas was a great cornerman. It saved me, and saved the championship. I know they would have stopped it."

Buchanan wasn't the only one who appreciated his cornerman's magic. "That was a helluva job Eddie Thomas did in Buchanan's corner," said fight publicist Harold Conrad in the book *The Hardest Game*. "I've watched a lot of corners and I've never seen one worked better. Thomas was like an icicle. No matter what was happening in the ring, how much damage was being done to his guy, he never got flustered in there. He watched every move and seemed to hand out the right advice, for he turned his guy over to fighting right when he had to. But during the rounds he kept getting ready for what he had to do during the rest period. That minute really flies by when you've got problems. That man gives the impression of knowing more about all aspects of working a corner than anyone around right now."

The cut that Thomas slit would need ten stitches, eight on the outside and two on the inside, and Buchanan would later need plastic surgery to remove the scar tissue. Laguna, the idol of Panama, never climbed through the ropes again.

The bout between Buchanan and Duran wasn't just about a championship, but revenge. "One day, he came to me and told me about the fight where Laguna fought with Buchanan and Laguna lost," said Duran's mother, Clara. "Roberto did not like this. Then Eleta came to talk to me and told me Roberto wanted to fight with Buchanan. I reminded him my son was only twenty years old, but since he wanted to do this fight, I had to sign some papers giving my authorization; he asked me to do it. At the time, when Duran had to fight I felt sick and was taken to hospital to be operated on. After the operation I learned they wanted to tell Roberto about it, so I asked the doctor to let me travel instead, so that Roberto did not get worried before the fight. I got my permission to leave the hospital. When I arrived home, Roberto called me and asked me whether I was sick. I told him everything was OK. I was holding the scar the operation had left, but calmed him down telling him I was all right."

Buchanan's camp saw nothing complicated in Duran's aggressive style and felt their man would take charge in the later rounds, when they expected the challenger to tire. "Duran didn't have an unorthodox style, he was a complete fighter who could punch to the body and to the head, move good," said Buchanan's American cornerman, Gil Clancy. "There wasn't anything special that we did for the fight except to tell Kenny to use his jab a lot and keep moving. We were going to wait for Duran to get tired." There was nothing illogical about Clancy's plan. Having seen Duran in the States only against Huertas, and knowing his history of quick destruction, he expected the young boxer to "blow up" after a few rounds.

Duran also had his usual pre-fight dramas. "I went to train with Plomo in Chiriqui," said Duran. "I'm at a hotel, the National Hotel and when I'm done training I throw myself in the pool and I'm already hot and sweaty. I get this fever and I feel like I'm going to die. I call Eleta and tell him everything that happened. I started crying because I thought I was going to lose my chance to fight for the world championship. I come back and three or four days later I'm fine. The doctor tells me I'm ready to fight. I'm happy as a ham and they send me to New York."

Before Duran left for New York, he made the plane and hotel reservations for a dear friend. "I was gaining fame in boxing," Duran recalled. "When I was boxing like eight or ten rounds, Chaflan came to me and asked me that if I fought for the championship one day, if I would take him. So I promised him I would. For my world championship fight, I asked Eleta to bring Chaflan. I came a week before the fight to train at Grossinger's [and] Eleta brought Chaflan over. I was in New York staying at the Mayflower Hotel. I was very happy to see him because it was a promise I made to him and I kept it."

Duran wasn't the type of person to ignore those who had helped him when he couldn't afford a meal. It wasn't long before the smiling Chaflan made himself at home. However, this wasn't Panama, where everybody knew his name. To the New Yorkers, he was a crazy guy panhandling in the bars. *Look at this guy's dance. He's fucking crazy.* It would mark the last time he and Duran traveled together.

"Eleta took Chaflan to his room. That night Carlos couldn't find him, but the next morning he found him sleeping in the bathtub," said Duran. "He thought it was a bed. Chaflan would go to the bars and try to make money like he did in Panama. When I realized about it, I told him that if he did it again and the police caught him he wouldn't be able to see the fight and would have to go back to Panama and never come back. So he stopped dancing."

★ ★ ★

On June 13, 1972, Buchanan and Duran signed contracts for the fight at a press conference at Les Champs Restaurant in midtown Manhattan, then sat down to a roast beef lunch. It was the first time they had met. Garden publicity director John Condon did his best to play up the challenger's rough past for the assembled hacks. "Street fighting in Panama is as popular as baseball is in America," he said. Duran, speaking through an interpreter, predicted he would knock out the champion within nine rounds, and added that he thought Ismael Laguna was a better boxer.

Buchanan, six years his senior and playing the elder statesman, responded rather loftily, "Duran is a young lad so I guess he's entitled to boast if he wants to, but I don't believe in predicting and prefer to do my talking in the ring. He hasn't really fought anyone of note. There are probably other lightweights who have worked their way up the ratings who are more deserving of a title shot, but the Garden offered me a $125,000 guarantee for this fight and I took it." Buchanan said a Panamanian promoter had offered him $150,000 for the fight but he turned it down in favour of the Garden, where he had been treated well in the past.

Film of Duran knocking out Hiroshi Kobayashi was shown, then John Condon asked if anyone wanted to see it again in slow motion. "I thought that was slow motion," dead-panned Buchanan. The Scot and his party left immediately after lunch to set up training quarters at the famous Grossingers country club in the Catskill Mountains, 100 miles north of New York City.

Buchanan's sarcastic remark was not lost on Duran. "I had an interview, and they put a video of mine on the television. Ken Buchanan is next to me with some trainer, and I'm watching my own fight. Buchanan had a bread with butter, and this writer asks, 'Why aren't you looking at Duran's video?' He said, 'He's too slow for me,' and I start laughing. He didn't know the surprise I had waiting for him."

Duran trained at the nearby Concord Hotel, but Buchanan didn't take time to study him. Since beating Laguna a second time, he had easily won two non-title bouts and was in great shape. He had heard the reports about how strong this young Panamanian was but felt confident he could handle him. "I didn't even watch when Duran fought Huertas," said Buchanan. "I knew he was winning all of these fights by knockout. He was young and apparently he wanted to emulate Ismael. When we fought he was just too keen at times to get on with it. When the fight goes on, you could see that when he threw a punch and missed, he got real frustrated. If you could say what he felt, he was like, 'Why don't you stand still because I want to hit you?'"

Days before the fight, Duran had to deal with his first set of "groupies," something he attributed to dirty tricks by his opponent's camp. "The week after I was in New York, they got news that I wasn't an easy fight," Duran said. "American girls would call me over the phone at eleven-thirty in the morning, 'Mister Duran, come and spend the weekend with me because you look so good.' I told Plomo that all these girls are calling me and he said, 'Don't pay attention because it's just a trick.' I tell him, 'What the hell am I going to do in New York, I don't even know how to take a bus or anything like that.' Freddie Brown tells me, 'It's just Buchanan's people and because they saw you train they're trying to distract you. They know you're not going to be an easy fight at all.'"

On 26 June 1972, 18,821 fans jammed into the Garden, paying $223,901, a new indoor record for lightweights. Bagpipes played the Scot into the ring, while the Panamanian contingent responded with drums. Duran came in at 132¼ pounds, with Buchanan at 133½. The champion had lost only once in forty-four bouts and was a 13-5 favourite, though many in the crowd hoped that the raw power of the young challenger, who had won twenty-four of his twenty-eight bouts inside the distance, would be enough to upset any odds. He also had Chaflan, whose presence in his eclectic attire screaming at Buchanan to "sacudele la minifalda" or take off the skirt, a reference to the Scottish kilt, was a priceless sight at ringside.

As they faced each other in the middle of the ring, Buchanan knew that this was no speedy, elusive Laguna in front of him. While Buchanan had to time Laguna, throw his jab a second earlier, while not worrying about his power, he had to be aware of Duran every second. Just seconds into the fight, he had his first test of the young man's power. A right cross made him stumble and his glove grazed the canvas, causing referee Johnny LoBianco to rule it a knockdown, though many thought it was a slip. Later in a fierce first round, Buchanan landed a wild left hook that sent an off-balance Duran into the ropes.

The fight quickly became a free flow of elbows, uppercuts, knees and feints. Buchanan wasn't handling the pace with much aplomb over the early rounds and his knees buckled in the fifth round from another Duran right hand. Later, Buchanan's mouthpiece shot out of the ring from another straight right. "Laguna would stick and move and he was a survivor," said Buchanan. "But Roberto was young and strong and was in there to make his mark … to be just like Ismael was when he was young. He would do everything, throw everything, until the referee told him to stop." At times during the fight, as Buchanan later noted, it was almost as if Duran was trying to kick him. Few men would have been capable of withstanding such an onslaught as the challenger built a clear lead on all three cards over the first twelve rounds, but Buchanan stayed calm as Duran rushed in.

The fighters headed out for the thirteenth. Duran continued to charge forward, hurling a blizzard of leather at the beleaguered champion, but Buchanan was made of stern stuff. In the dying seconds of the round, he caught Duran with a decent right hand. As he followed up with a couple more straight punches, the bell rang. Neither fighter seemed to hear it as referee LoBianco moved in and grabbed Duran by the shoulders to pull him back. As he did so, Duran fired a low, almost casual right hand that hit Buchanan squarely on his protective cup.

Buchanan grabbed his groin, his face contorted in pain, then keeled over and rolled on the canvas. Later he would claim the punch was destined to arrive *under* his testicles, in an upward trajectory against which the cup offers less protection. Buchanan's cornermen leapt into the ring and tended to him as the boxer squirmed in agony on the canvas. After about fifteen seconds, he was able to rise, still hunched in distress, and sat down on his corner stool. There, he was visited by referee LoBianco and the ringside doctor. After a few more seconds, LoBianco turned away from the corner and waved his arms in the air, as if to signal the bout was over. But no one seemed sure. As Buchanan's cornermen protested, the Scot, his face battered and weeping blood, rose to his feet and said several times to the referee, "I'm okay, I'm okay," though he was clearly still in pain.

Despite this, as the warning buzzer went off for the start of the fourteenth round, LoBianco walked across the ring to raise Duran's arm in victory. Bedlam ensued, with Duran leaping into Eleta's arms, a huge grin on his baby face, as his supporters skirted the edges of the ring.

The fiesta lit Panama and New York City until the sun rose. Boxing writer Papi Mendez described the scene in Panama as a *mar de enthusiasmo*, a sea of enthusiasm. In *La Critica* the headline read, "Buchanan received a beating like the one you get in the worst slums of New York."

"I felt like I was King of the World," recalled Duran. "I had avenged the loss of my idol Ismael Laguna. I wanted to come right back to Panama because I was in love with my wife and she was pregnant at the time."

Going into that thirteenth round, the scoring was one-sided. Judge Bill Recht had the bout 9-2-1 for Duran, while LoBianco, 8-3-1, and Jack Gordon, 9-3, also gave it to the challenger. Two of the three officials forgot to score the last round. "I felt that I was doing okay going into the thirteenth round," said Buchanan. "I didn't feel I was losing the fight. I remember the commentary saying that I was cut under the left eye, and then when I came out for the fifth round, they changed and said, 'Buchanan isn't cut, the blood is coming from Duran's nose."

"He was an awkward fighter but I didn't even have a bleeding nose; it was his nose that was bleeding. If they had given me a few minutes to recover I could have continued. LoBianco didn't want to know, he just saw a chance to stop the fight and that was it. I didn't know why Duran wasn't disqualified. LoBianco was in the ring, number one man, and he just took it upon himself to do what he did. As far as I was concerned he was paid to do a job and he done it, so he goes for the money. And the proof is in the pudding. He should have went to the judges, and said to them, 'Did you see what happened there?' If LoBianco had went to talk to them, then I would still be champion."

Originally, Clancy wanted Buchanan to pace himself, hoping that Duran would punch himself into exhaustion. The punches kept coming as if Plomo recharged Duran's battery between each round. Some fights can be blamed on a trainer's strategy, but this had nothing to do with Buchanan's corner, and all to do with Duran.

"First of all Duran hit about four times harder than Laguna," said cornerman Gil Clancy. "He was really nailing Kenny with some pretty good shots. It was partially my fault that Kenny lost that fight, because Roberto was knocking everybody out early and I figured if my guy could get him into the last six rounds of the fight that Duran would be tired and Buchanan could take over. I was dead wrong. The guy had so much energy you can't believe. Buchanan's best round was the round before, and then after he got hit low it was all over. Some people thought it was a knee Duran hit him with."

Instead of utilizing Buchanan's strengths, the idea was to wait for Duran's weakness, one that never surfaced. The Buchanan camp thought Duran couldn't go fifteen rounds because he'd never had to. The strategy involved risk, but they had no choice. How else could he have fended off Duran? A trainer had to work with the skills in front of him, and although Buchanan was a slick boxer, he wasn't going to overwhelm Duran with quickness, the type of plan that occasionally gave Duran fits.

After the punch, boxing people had their opinions. Former light-heavy champ Jose Torres revealed his theory. "When you know your man is badly hurt, no matter how many punches you throw, you cannot get tired. Tiredness is mostly psychological, so when you are kicking the shit out of the guy you do not get tired. When you see a fighter get hit low and go down and start screaming, he is losing the fight. If you are winning the fight and you get hit low a hundred times, you don't go down a hundred times. You kick the shit out the guy, but if you are losing you stay down, unconsciously. The cup protects you a hundred percent, you have to be punched from under the leg."

Reality set in for all involved. "He did hit him low and there was no question about that, but LoBianco never called it a low blow or anything else," said Clancy. "No time out or five-minute rest, nothing. The best they could have done, if Kenny did have a protective cup on, was give him a five-minute rest period and let the fight continue. Again, Kenny was way behind in points. The only way he could have won the fight was by a late knockout. There wasn't a big controversy after the fight."

Covering the fight at the time, Bert Sugar concurred with Clancy: "LoBianco caught shit, mostly from the Buchanan followers. [Buchanan] was going nowhere. He was a very slick, good fighter but he was no match for Duran. In the thirteenth round Buchanan got the shit kicked out him. LoBianco didn't see the punch that ended the round. I can still see Buchanan melting on the ropes. I clutched my cojones."

For Buchanan, the pain would never subside as he was holed up in a Scotland hospital for ten days following the bout. "The referee let Duran hit me anywhere he wanted," said Buchanan. "In the thirteenth round, LoBianco has a hold of Duran and a hold of me, and when the referee touches you, you have to stop. But Duran never did. Bang! He hit me. But he never hit me straight on … at one point his hands were like ten inches off the ground. Next thing that happens, he hits me right up there and busts a vein in my right testicle."

LoBianco could have disqualified Duran; he could have declared Buchanan unable to continue and ruled the bout a "no contest"; he could have given the champion time to recover, warned the challenger, then allowed them to continue. Instead he declared Duran the winner because he had not seen the low blow and felt Buchanan was in too bad a state to continue. With a relatively muted protest from Buchanan's corner, LoBianco's ruling stood. "A lot of people who said that if Buchanan had the right corner Duran would have been disqualified," said promoter and matchmaker Don Elbaum. "I know if I had Buchanan, I would have gone nuts. I would have been fighting that."

Others, like Philadelphia promoter J. Russell Peltz, rubbished the various excuses. "I don't understand all the Buchanan stuff that's come up. He was getting his ass kicked when Duran hit him. It was a low blow, but if he got up he would have just got beaten even more."

Most fighters lack impartiality when it comes to analyzing a poor performance. They all got screwed at one point in their careers. It is hard to deny the fact that Buchanan was in dire need of a knockout if he was keeping his crown. Even if Buchanan shook off the pain and continued, he was in there with a fighter not willing to give him a break. While fighters keep a running tab and decide when their lead is big enough to stay away from their opponent in the late rounds, Duran rarely exhibited such reticence. As "cute" as some experts felt he was as a defensive fighter, Duran came forward all the time. While other fighters used their feet to get away from danger, Duran always went toward his foe or cut off the ring, trusting his instincts to steer him clear of trouble. Often he would throw a right hand or a left hook, go with it, then force his way inside, clinching and locking his opponent's arms. That way, nothing would come in return.

No single punch in Duran's career would cause so much animated discussion. No previous Duran punch landed with so much on the line. In fact, the only punches that would place Duran under such scrutiny were ones he didn't throw a decade later in New Orleans.

"We talked one night at his hotel [in England] into the small hours," said Buchanan. "I told him that after I fought him, I became European champ and I was boxing in Italy when I got poked in the eye by the referee. Roberto started laughing. I asked him why. 'Ken hasn't been very lucky in boxing, between the referee sticking his finger in your eye and me punching him up the balls,' Duran said to me.

"I told him, 'I got you! I got you!' Even today the liquid doesn't get up that way and it stops and I still get a pain there every time I go to the bathroom. I'll have that until the day I die. I told Roberto, 'I'll never forget you. Every time I take a piss I'll think of you.' Over the years you mellow, but there are times when I feel a wee bit like, what would have happened? You know, Carlos Eleta bought that fight. It never cost Madison Square Garden to pay me because Eleta put the money up. He was a millionaire. You know the old song, 'Money talks, but it don't sing or dance.' He brought in the referee. I was really annoyed with Madison Square Garden and the referee because he wasn't competent. He shouldn't have been in there, it should have been Arthur Mercante or someone like that."

Eleta appeared to want nothing to do with Buchanan after New York. Few believed that Duran feared any fighter, but he had little say over who his next opponent would be. "Duran never, ever wanted to fight me again," said the Scot. "I tried to get the rematch … but there was no chance, nothing. I think Eleta knew a wee bit more and thought, this Ken Buchanan is better than we thought he was, so let's stay away from him. For years there was an anger because I never got my shot. I would have given him a shot, why didn't he do it for me? But I never blamed Roberto. I tend to think Duran wanted to fight me again, but Eleta didn't want it to happen. He faced Hagler, and fought them all. I think he would have fought me anywhere, anytime."

After the fight, Eleta told a reporter, "We would be willing to give Buchanan a return bout any time." However, he had a way of placating people at the time, then backtracking when he felt pressured. Years later, he claimed, "Omar Torrijos wouldn't allow the rematch with Buchanan. He told me, 'Carlos, don't make that fight. Don't trust another fight with him in the States.' He told me that the first defense had to be in Panama. Buchanan wouldn't fight in Panama, so it was cancelled."

Despite the recriminations and the bitterness that lingers in Buchanan, Roberto Duran no longer haunts him. Late-night pisses bring back memories, but he no longer boils over with frustration. Still, when so many people remember, it's hard to forget. "I was no longer world champion and I was beginning to see how corrupt the sport was. It left a sour taste in my mouth," said Buchanan. "But that was boxing and you take the good with the bad."

New York State Athletic Commission physician Dr A. Harry Klieman reported that his examination of Buchanan showed "fluid on the testicles." Buchanan returned to Scotland and a hospital in Edinburgh, where he was treated for swollen testicles and bruised kidneys, then flew to the Mediterranean island of Majorca for a restorative holiday with his wife and young son. At the same time, he vowed to return to New York and train harder than ever against "real rough and tumble boys" in a bid to regain his crown. "If Duran wants to repeat his kind of fight, then I too will throw the kind of punches that aren't in the book," he promised.

# 7

# THE LEFT HOOK

*"Violence is terribly seductive; all of us, especially males, are trained to gaze upon violence until it becomes beautiful."*

Martín Espada, Puerto Rican poet

THE LIGHTWEIGHT DIVISION has a long and colorful pedigree. It can be traced back to the end of the eighteenth century, to the days of bareknuckle pugilism, when men fought to the finish in illegal or quasi-legal contests held at secret locations. Various boxers from Great Britain and the United States, the two hotbeds of the sport, claimed the "world" title after the adoption of the Queensberry Rules late in the nineteenth century, but the first man who seems to have been recognized as champion on both sides of the Atlantic was one George "Kid" Lavigne after he knocked out England's Dick Burge in seventeen rounds at the National Sporting Club, London, in 1896. At that time the weight limit for the division was 133 pounds, but it would eventually settle at 135 pounds.

The most notable early champion was the wonderful Joe Gans, the "Old Master," who in the pre-First World War period combined form and power, stamina and technique, in a manner rarely seen before or since. His three bouts against Battling Nelson, an imperishable Scandinavian known as the "Durable Dane," were among the most terrible in history; one went forty-two rounds before the bloodied Nelson was disqualified for a low blow. Gans died in 1910, his slender body ravaged by tuberculosis.

The Twenties brought more gifted fighters like Freddie Welsh, Lew Tendler, Charley White and, above all, the peerless Benny Leonard, a New York Jew of matchless guile and execution. Leonard inspired a generation of boxers from the crowded tenements of America's biggest cities and deeply influenced trainers such as Ray Arcel. The Thirties saw a great triumvirate of box-fighters, Tony Canzoneri, Barney Ross and Lou Ambers, and the relentless Henry Armstrong, a one-man army who once held world titles at three weights simultaneously, a feat unlikely to ever be repeated. Ike Williams, Jimmy Carter and Joe Brown, talented black Americans who could box and punch, ruled the Forties and Fifties. Latin fighters then became the dominant force in the division with the arrival of Carlos Ortiz in 1962.

Indeed, by the time of Roberto Durán's ascencion, non-US boxers topped not just the lightweight division. With the exception of Joe Frazier at heavyweight and Bob Foster at light-heavyweight, every single champion was from either Central or South America or the Far East. Great fighters like Argentina's Carlos Monzon and the Cuban-Mexican Jose Napoles were regarded as the best, pound-for-pound, in the sport and, odd as it may seem to those who now look back on the Seventies as a golden time for heavyweights, the bellwether division was moribund. Champion Joe Frazier was much maligned for defending against no-hopers and only the no-longer-youthful Muhammad Ali brought color to the division.

Panamanian boxing not only benefited from this boom, but was about to become an unlikely arbiter in the sport worldwide. It now had two champions, Duran and Alfonso "Peppermint" Frazer, and would soon have two more, bantamweight Enrique Pinder and former Duran conquest Ernesto Marcel. For a country of only 1,600,000 people, fewer than most major cities, this was a remarkable achievement. The most important development had been the political takeover of Omar Herrera Torrijos, an ambitious army officer and keen advocate of the national sport, after a coup in October 1968. Torrijos ousted the right-wing nationalist president, Arnulfo Arias, won an internecine power struggle with his co-conspirators, and emerged as sole dictator. He pitched himself as the first ruler to represent the majority of the people, who were poor, Spanish-speaking and of mixed indigenous, Hispanic and African descent, as opposed to the *rabiblancos* or "white-tails," the light-skinned social elite who lived in Panama City and dominated commercial and political life. He instituted wide-ranging reforms aimed at the middle and lower classes, opened schools and redistributed agricultural land. He also suspended democratic institutions and persecuted the wealthiest families, as well as independent student and labor leaders who opposed his rule. Boxing and physical fitness were encouraged and given state funding.

Sportswriters visited the tiny state at this time to find out its secret. One noted that only the Brazilians' passion for football compared with the Panamanians' for boxing. "The Panamanians not only want to watch, they want to get in there and have a go themselves," he wrote. "One only has to walk through the streets of Panama City's shanty towns, the makeshift slums ... to see evidence of their keenness. Contests are organized by the locals, and young boys, sometimes no older than ten years, stand in an imaginary roped square and slug it out."

Many of the newest buildings were spacious gyms to accommodate the hordes of would-be fighters. Up to fifty boxing contests were held every week – as many as in the UK in a month. "The second oldest trade in Panama City, next to the prostitution, is that of the shoeshine boys," wrote journalist Dave Fletcher. "These youngsters, usually between eight and fifteen years old, have enough foresight to realize that fighting is the only way to make a name for themselves. Many can be seen sparring amongst the bars and shops when custom is at a low ebb. Panama is one of the few places in the world where the term 'hungry fighter' can still be used literally. Although the standard of living is generally low, the average young Panamanian is generally fit, and obesity is considered to be a disease of the 'Gringo.' A Panamanian would think nothing of walking twenty miles in search of employment, or to say hello to friends in one of the neighboring villages.

"Many hundreds are employed in Panama City and take to selling drugs or pornography. It is the theory of some that boxing is a natural safety valve, through which the unemployed can release their depression. However, this theory is soon cast to the wind when one ventures to the more provincial parts of Panama, to the huts and shacks on the banana plantations where giant posters of Ismael Laguna, complete with crown, scorch in the midday sun, and where sacks of sweetcorn and grass are used as punchbags. Even the villagers of the Darien jungle province of Panama know the name Buchanan, which they pronounce 'Bookanar.'"

Buchanan, however, was far from Carlos Eleta's thoughts. Duran's next proposed opponent was not the Scot but veteran former champion Carlos Ortiz. The bout was first intended to be a title defense in Panama but was then switched to a non-title bout – meaning Duran's championship would not be at stake – over ten rounds, on the undercard of the Muhammad Ali–Floyd Patterson fight at Madison Square Garden that September. "Duran and I signed to fight," said Ortiz. "We were supposed to fight in 1972, in Madison Square Garden. I don't know what happened to him, but he ended up going back to Panama. He didn't want to fight me. They saw that I was in good condition. They came down to see me at the Gramercy Park Gym where I was training at the time, and that I was training with middleweights at 138 pounds. It was a problem because I was in condition and then ten days before the bout, no one knew where he went. I found out he checked out of the hotel room and went back to Panama. He gave no excuses. He didn't want to fight. But he was the champ, so he could do it."

According to members of Duran's camp, he had been diagnosed with bronchitis and had to return to Panama. "But he was not sick in reality," admitted Plomo. "This was just to prevent him from fighting with Ortiz, who was a well qualified boxer and much loved as well. So after spending twenty-two days there, they did not let Duran fight, and we came back to Panama."

"I couldn't force him to fight me," said a frustrated Ortiz. "That's why I came back. I had to fight for the championship and prove again to myself that I could do it. I spent eight months training for the fight, fighting here and there, getting in shape. I was going to fight the champion, whether it was a title fight or an over-the-weight bout. As soon as I'd fight for the title, then I'd prove something to myself and quit. I think it was more of a managerial decision because Duran didn't duck nobody. A real fighter doesn't duck anybody. The ones who make decisions about the fights are the managers. They thought I was going to make a fool of Duran, and he'd be in trouble. If he looked bad, he'd have to fight again. They didn't want that.

"I had that feeling inside of me that I could beat him, not that I would look good against him or make a good fight out of it but that I could beat him," said Ortiz decades later. "I wouldn't have signed for the fight if I couldn't beat him. My comeback was that I was going to go as far as I could go. I got Buchanan, but it wasn't my fight. Buchanan was far away from my mind, until they brought him up to me.

"When Duran went to Panama, the Garden was in deep trouble. If I didn't fight, they were going to lose that date and a lot of money. So Teddy Brenner gave me the situation, he said, 'Carlos, this is what's going to happen. This is a problem. He's not going to fight you. We are going to lose a lot of money because we already have publicity and the fight has to go on. I have a few kids that you would want to fight.' I didn't prepare for Buchanan; he meant nothing to me. I wanted to fight Duran. Once Duran left, that was it. When something you love goes away and you don't have it no more, that's how I felt when Duran left. I lost my passion. He didn't have to tell me why he didn't fight because that was his priority."

Eleta was not the first manager to protect his investment. It was announced that Duran had a stomach upset, and Ken Buchanan stepped into his place as a late substitute on the Madison Square Garden bill. The Scot fought Ortiz on nine days' notice, returning from a holiday to get in a few days' sparring before the bout, and beat him easily, forcing the thirty-six-year-old former champion to retire at the end of the sixth round – for good.

Ortiz has an interesting insight into the competing merits of Laguna and Duran. "I think Laguna would have boxed the shit out of him. Laguna would have outboxed him and outpunched him. I don't think he would have caught him because Laguna had a good chin, he was tall and had a good reach."

It was next reported that Duran and Buchanan had signed contracts for a rematch in New York on October 20. However, Duran then claimed the Panamanian Government was insisting he made his first defense in his own country, and sought to put the bout off until the following year. In October 1972, it was reported that Buchanan had signed a new contract to challenge Duran at Madison Square Garden on November 17, and if Duran did not accept, he would be banned from boxing in New York.

* * *

Despite the confusion around the proposed Ortiz and Buchanan bouts, Duran was enjoying the perks of being a champion. Thousands of admirers had been waiting to greet him at the Paitilla airport when he returned with the belt; he was now a national celebrity, and everyone clamored to be near him. After settling back home, he attended a night in his honor in Clara's hometown. "They held an homage here in Guarare for Roberto," said longtime fan and Guarare resident Lesbia Diaz. "Many people came from all the provinces."

Since he was young, he had brought back his purse money to help his mother. Now, he was champion, all his promises were coming true.

No longer did Clara have to cook and clean for the Americans in the Canal Zone.

"Momma, I do not want you to work anymore," Duran told Clara.

"All right papa, I will not go on working then," she responded.

By his side was a beautiful young girlfriend, Claudinette Felicidad Iglesias. She had an angelic face, an addictive smile, and long flowing hair that draped over her shoulders. Acccording to Clara, the couple met in their teens through Felicidad's mother, who sold numbers, an illegal but widely tolerated street lottery. "They were very young," said Toti. "They were still minors. The parents did not want Felicidad to go out with Duran because they were too young. And they did not want Roberto because they knew that he was a boxer and they believed boxers became crazy."

Felicidad came from a relatively wealthy family. She was petite and pretty and Duran was smitten, but she was expected to find a suitor in her own social circle, not a poor boy from Chorrillo. Although Clara adored Felicidad and welcomed her into the family, the feelings were not reciprocated. "Duran lived at that time in Caledonia," said Plomo. "There was a furniture shop called Montemarte. Duran's apartment was right on top of this shop. On the other side of the street there were some shops. When Felicidad used to go past that place after school, Duran used to look at her and say, 'I like that girl very much.'

"So I would tell him to go to her and to tell her something. But in the end, it was as if it had been destiny. One day Duran went downstairs to talk to her, the girl smiled at him, and right away they started talking, and went together walking and talking. That was the beginning of their love. But he had problems, because her parents, once Duran and Felicidad were already in love, opposed this relationship. Duran took Felicidad to where his mother was in Chorrillo, because he wanted to live together with her, but Felicidad's parents accused him of having violated their daughter. They told all kind of stories about Duran. But Felicidad herself said she had agreed to becoming Duran's woman because she was in love with him. Duran was arrested because of this, but he was later set free. Later on they got married, but they lived together before their marriage.

"After meeting her, Felicidad became his most important woman. Being a Panamanian man, as he was, he had several women, but always his home was with Felicidad."

Although Duran had many girlfriends, none affected him like

Felicidad or "Fula" as she was known. In 1972, after much coercion, she moved into his apartment in Caledonia. Their first son, Chavo, or Roberto Jr. was due to arrive later that year.

Instead of defending his title, in September and October of 1972 Duran took on two relatively easy opponents, Greg Potter and Lupe Ramirez, in non-title bouts. Potter, from Joplin, Missouri, was a college graduate and former US Navy champion, a stand-up boxer who had turned pro only a year before but had already gone the distance with both Carlos Ortiz – "a master," said Potter – and the highly ranked Ruben Navarro. He was relaxing at home after the Navarro bout when his trainer called to say they'd been offered a short-notice, non-title fight against the new champion, whose scheduled opponent had pulled out. Potter trekked to Panama, where he suffered from diarrhea and was weakened when he climbed into the ring.

"It was a slugfest," he remembered. "I went out and slugged with him and you don't do that with Roberto Duran. As a young man he grew up on the streets and he shined shoes and had to fight from a young age to keep the money he made, and he had a lot of ... the word that comes to mind is *hate*, built up in him. He was a vicious fighter. He was fighting when he came out of the corner."

Potter was no match for the fired-up champion and was knocked out in the first round. He later gained a Masters in psychology and a PhD in counseling, and runs a practice counseling on personal performance and goal-achieving. He still recalls his opponent with rueful admiration. "I don't remember a whole lot about his punch because he knocked me out in the first round. But I think he could hit pretty good."

Lupe Ramirez, who had previously gone the distance with both the brilliant Antonio Cervantes and the hard-hitting Chango Carmona, was also blasted out in a single round.

Duran's next opponent was a much stiffer test. Twenty-two-year-old Esteban DeJesus, from Puerto Rico, belonged with the best that his proud country had to offer. He came from the rowdy town of Carolina on the Atlantic coast, otherwise known as "El Pueblo de Las Tumbas Brazos," or the Arm Hackers' Town, for the natives' predilection for violence, often involving machetes. It was also called "La Tierra de Gigantes," Land of Giants, because it was home to a seven-foot-eleven-inch goliath called Don Felipe Birriel. Baseball hero Roberto Clemente was another celebrated Carolinan. Having survived such a dangerous place, DeJesus learned his trade in the rings of San Juan. An all-rounder who could box, move and punch, he went on to win the Puerto Rican lightweight title in New York's Felt Forum. He had already boxed in the Garden and his last win had come just three weeks before the Duran bout. He boasted a 29-1 record, with eighteen knockouts to his credit, his only loss coming against WBA featherweight champion Antonio Gomez. DeJesus was the third-ranked lightweight in the world and he was sharp and ready.

Throughout his career, Duran would badmouth Puerto Ricans about how they couldn't take a punch, and they would respond in kind. Both he and they seemed to enjoy the jingoistic rivalry between two small but proud Latin-American states, both of which lay in the long shadow of the USA. Added to that was the special intensity when Latin fighters face off with their countrymen at their back. "If a Latino man fights a non-Latino you can bet we'll be rooting for the man who speaks Spanish," said former world champion Jose Torres, himself a Puerto Rican. "But the rivalry doesn't stop there. The competition between Latinos is even more exciting. You see, we know each other. We know how to intimidate each other. And we know how to resist it. But we are very dramatic in the process. Some of us even get violent, a luxury we seldom get off the gringo." Added to that was Duran's chilling intensity. "When I went up into the ring, I would look at them hard so they knew that I wasn't just coming to play," he said. "That's why I would go out to kill them fast. My deal was always to win by knockout."

But still enjoying his emotional championship victory over Buchanan, Duran had been criticized in the local press for over-celebrating and constant partying. He also had a complicated personal life. Despite his relationship with Felicidad, he had another gilfriend, Silvia, who would bear him a daughter called Dalia. She lived in the town of Puerto Armuelles, though she would later move to Miami, and Duran would drive over every weekend to see her. Two months before the DeJesus bout, he was driving his Volkwagen through the hills of Chiriqui when a rainstorm came down.

"I couldn't see the road and either way there are hills," remembered Duran. "I'm going really slow in the car, and I'm scared as hell. All of a sudden the lights come on and I step on the brakes. I'm going downhill. I picked up a hitchhiker on the way, going downhill and the car hits something, and I hit the steering wheel and I split my lip in two parts. The other guy hit the windshield. I get out of the car, I'm dizzy and my lip is open in two pieces.

"When I look up, I told the guy we have to get out of here, and I look down and I have a hole in my elbow. So I have a hole in my elbow and a split lip, and it takes five minutes to walk up the hill. When we get to the top of the hill, it stops raining. A car is coming, and it stops to ask me, 'Duran what happened?' I tell him what happened, and we go to a town called San Felix. And the doctor checks me and gives me stitches. His hand is shaking as he gives me stitches. I say, 'Why is your hand shaking?' And he said, 'I'm afraid that you're going to die here on me.' By that time, people had heard that I had an accident and the hospital was full. He sews my elbow up. A friend of mine who was a major in David comes and picks me up. The doctor said I could have a couple drinks. When I get the drink, all the stitches break open again. I cover it up, and I went to New York to go fight with Esteban DeJesus."

"Duran Injured in Car Mishap" announced the headline of an Associated Press report on September 15, 1972. "World lightweight champ Roberto Duran escaped serious injury in an automobile accident," read the report. "Duran's Volkswagen overturned. He was forced to brake suddenly when the car ahead of him slowed down without warning. Duran suffered a slight cut on his right elbow and lacerations of the face." The report named Mariano Ramirez as the passenger.

"After the accident I go to New York because we took the fight with DeJesus," said Duran. "I still have my open wound on my elbow. Carlos Eleta shouldn't have sent me. He sent me up there to train for a month. If you really look at the fight the only thing that DeJesus did was knock me down in the first round. The only thing he did was hit me with that left hook. He never beat me. I saw the fight; he didn't beat me. Remember he's Puerto Rican, and lived between New York and Puerto Rico. Remember he's always there, so to the Americans it was always more convenient to have him win there than a Panamanian who's in Panama."

Featherweight legends Willie Pep and Sandy Saddler were introduced before the fight, a premonitory meeting of two of the great rivals in boxing. As they stood toe-to-toe for the introductions, DeJesus, 138, in blue trunks and white stripes, settled in at eye level to the five-foot-seven, 137½lb Duran. They were to compete over ten rounds, without the title at stake, on November 17, 1972.

Neither Duran nor DeJesus was willing to look at the other for more than a split second; their eyes focused on the canvas until they touched eight-ounce gloves to initiate battle. Puerto Rico had a history of great boxers and DeJesus wouldn't always get the respect he deserved for his skills. "I was very surprised at the trouble that DeJesus gave Duran because I didn't think he was a great fighter," said fellow countryman Carlos Ortiz. "But when he fought Duran, he did a great job. He would hit Duran with that left hook."

The punch would live in infamy. "That" left hook thrown by DeJesus would be the first punch to expose a chink in Duran's style. The perfectly placed shot put Duran on his backside early in the first round. Never before in a pro bout had Duran felt the canvas against his back. Stunned more than hurt, he rose at the count of six, shaking his head as if to say, *okay, I felt that, now I'm awake and you will pay.* Duran's gut reaction was immediately to attack, but wading in without caution against DeJesus was regrettable, as he absorbed more punishment before returning to his corner. All three men in Duran's corner were in constant motion at the bell, sponging, massaging, exhorting, cajoling.

With confidence rising, the polished DeJesus opened the second with a right to Duran's chest followed by a left hook to his head. He began to control the flow of the fight, breaking through Duran's defense with another jaw-numbing left hook in round four that made Duran stumble and nearly fall. He struck again a round later as an off-balance Duran stumbled into another powerful hook and had to clinch. Not only was DeJesus out-muscling the Panamanian, but he was using one of his own signature moves against him: a faked left followed by a quick, hard right.

Through the shouting of the largely pro-DeJesus crowd, Duran's mother Clara, a rare sight at ringside, could be heard shrieking, "Throw the hook to the liver!" But the champion continued to get picked off. DeJesus stayed in a crouch and sprung from his toes with every punch as Duran pawed, frustrated at his impotence. Ringside broadcasters speculated that the champion's lackluster performance might have something to do with him being five pounds heavier than for Buchanan.

With the bout slipping away, Duran was active enough to win round five, dancing, picking his angles and landing a solid uppercut, but it was a shortlived rally. An energized DeJesus danced in the sixth and seventh, overcame a low blow and jolted back Duran's head with two left hooks, a punch he couldn't miss with. Pawing at air with his little-used jab as a range-finder in the eighth round, Duran finally connected with some quality right hands that DeJesus would quickly shake off. In desperation, Duran landed punches after the bell, his blood boiling at the prospect of a loss. He would not get another opening.

The voice of Luis Henriquez could be heard between rounds urging Duran to come alive. It was too late. Although Duran was energized in the ninth round, he lost his way in the tenth, fruitlessly chasing his elusive opponent. To drive home his supremacy, DeJesus nailed Duran with a final clean hook. Even while Duran's handlers took off his gloves, he pawed at DeJesus with his right hand. Reluctantly he then shook his opponent's hand.

In the non-title affair, judges Harold Lederman had it 6-3-1, Bill Recht 6-2-2 and Arthur Mercante 5-4-1, all to DeJesus. The Puerto Rican from the Town of the Arm Hackers jumped up and down in his corner with his hands to the sky. Few in the 9,144 crowd could argue that Duran deserved his first defeat in thirty-two pro outings.

The Panamanian media, already developing a love-hate relationship with Duran, quickly picked up on stories that he had been enjoying the nightclub scene a little too exuberantly. On November 21, reporter Macume Argote wrote a piece entitled, "Duran needs to learn how to box." Another local reporter, Tomy Cupas, added, "Duran had his mind on other things in Madison Square Garden." It had been noted in the Panamanian press that "before the trip the Duran camp denied the rumors of the little Hercules having relations with certain lunatics that he had been seen with on the isthmus."

If former world champ Jose Torres was right in his assessment that all fighters know when they have not done enough conditioning, then Duran couldn't fool himself. He left the ring in his shiny green robe and took out his frustration on the bathroom walls of his hotel. His bloodied hands reminded him of his dispassionate performance.

"After that fight, we went with Ray Arcel to a restaurant and Duran was crying," said Eleta. "I told him that you don't win the fight in the ring, but in training. I said, 'Always remember that. Never forget that I say this.' He wanted the rematch immediately, but I postponed that fight … so that he would get out of this feeling. I wait until he is ready and then I tell him that he would fight DeJesus again."

Two and a half weeks later, Ken Buchanan stopped Oriental junior welterweight champion Chang Kil Lee in less than two rounds and then took a blast at Duran. "He's doing everything he can think of to get away from me," said the embittered Scot. "If he beat me as easily as he claimed, why is he waiting so long to give me a return?"

Despite the defeat, and his continued avoidance of Buchanan, in November 1972 the British trade magazine *Boxing News*, which had the most reliable ratings in the sport, rated Duran as the true champion of the division, and listed the top ten contenders:

1. Rodolfo Gonzalez (US), WBC champion
2. Ken Buchanan (Britain)
3. Esteban DeJesus (Puerto Rico)
4. Chango Carmona (Mexico)
5. Mando Ramos (US)
6. Pedro Carrasco (Spain)
7. Ruben Navarro (US)
8. Antonio Puddu (Italy)
9. Javier Ayala (US)
10. Jimmy Robertson (US)

Two months later, the World Boxing Council dropped Panamanian boxers from its rankings following a dispute with the Panamanian Boxing Commission. The commission had broken off relations after WBC President Ramon Velasquez stripped Enrique Pinder of his bantamweight title for refusing to fight the top contender, a Mexican. Bizarrely, according to Velazquez the Panamanian Commission had never been a member of the WBC anyway. It forced the Panamanians to side decisively with the rival WBA, something that would have far-reaching consequences for world boxing.

# 8

## REVENGE

*"Ads, commercials and, indeed, all the media itself, are dedicated to identifying – and hyping – male machismo. So much so that boxing crowds in Latin countries immediately boo if a defensive fighter is successful in preventing his opponent from connecting solidly while not doing much himself in return ... There is not much fun in winning unless you can show evidence of machismo."*

Jose Torres, *The Ring*, May 1981.

IT WAS THE middle of the day in Panama in January 1973 and Roberto Duran was walking around with a gun sticking out of his jeans. It was not an accessory he needed, but it certainly enhanced his bad-ass persona. If the promise of his fists wasn't intimidating enough, the shine of a pistol indicated in simple terms the man's invincibility. In a couple days, he was due to defend his title for the first time against Jimmy Robertson, who was white, durable and willing. Robertson, from Los Angeles, reportedly wasn't keen on the fight, but couldn't turn down a title shot.

Robertson had come over with the LA-based promoter Don Chargin, and neither of them were under any illusions. "Then, that guy was hard as a rock," Chargin said of Duran. "He'd wear Levis and a tight, tight T-shirt. The first time I saw him he was at a hotel talking to people by a pool. He would walk around with a gun in his waistband. Nobody would do anything to Duran and he could get by doing anything."

A few years earlier, Chargin had taken a phone call from his friend Andy Russell, a Latino singer out of LA. Russell was in Panama and had seen Duran fight. "He said, 'You won't believe this kid. You've got to come see this kid.' So I wrote the name down, but I just never got a chance to get down there and I missed out."

Robertson went into the bout with a reasonable 24-6-1 record, though he had lost three of his previous four fights. Duran, meanwhile, had been complaining about having to train over the Christmas season. On January 20, 1973, they climbed into the ring at the Nuevo Panama Gymnasium. "We knew [Jimmy] wanted a chance and he knew how tough it would be," said Chargin. "Duran destroyed him. In fact, he knocked out three [recorded as two] of his teeth in the first round. He took a beating and earned every cent."

Robertson went four more rounds minus his teeth. In the third, he was drawn into a perfect overhand right that left him on one knee, although he gamely bounced back up and managed to survive the follow-up onslaught. Duran would comment on his opponent's bravery after the fight. In Spanish, a fighter of Robertson's mold is referred to as *bastante duro* or very tough. And in the fourth round, as Robertson was bounced along the ropes by triple right hands, it was clear that he deserved the compliment and had earned respect from the partisan crowd. Unfortunately that meant nothing in the middle of the ring.

Robertson rolled along the ropes during the fifth, his body movement disappeared and his face left wide open for a right and left hook. Without warning, his legs gave way like a fast-collapsing table. The young fighter had met another straight right hand. Now, he was on the canvas leaning on his right hand, trying to decide what his next move would be.

"One, two, three, four, five, six ..."

Robertson could hear the count clearly and he would redirect his body weight so he was now on one knee.

"... seven, eight, nine, ten!"

After surveying the scene, Robertson understood the gap between possible gain and permanent injury and elected to fight another day.

The clean-shaven Duran laughed with reporters after the fight, acknowledged that Robertson had the edge in the second round and that he was "feeling weak." Meanwhile a Panamanian journalist practicing his English had wandered over to speak to the loser.

"Jimmy, I am very, very, sorry that you lost the fight. You did a good fight."

"Thank you," said the beaten fighter.

"What is your opinion about Duran? He punch too hard?"

"Yes, he is very strong and hard to fight."

"Duran said you got him in the second round and that he felt weak, did you notice this?" asked the reporter.

"No, I didn't."

"Did you lose teeth, tooth?"

"One tooth."

"OK, Jimmy I am very sorry that you lost today," said the reporter.

Robertson trudged back to the dressing room.

"Now, bring me to Esteban DeJesus," said the champion. Toti remembers that his brother began to be called "El Dentista" for his power punching.

* * *

The WBC lightweight champion, Rodolfo "Gato" Gonzalez, was based on the West Coast, where he was popular among the large Mexican community. With his champion banned from New York, Eleta decided to establish him in California too, and Duran's next two bouts took place in Los Angeles.

First, he stopped southpaw Juan Medina in seven rounds on February 23, 1973, in a non-title fight. For Medina "just going the distance would be a victory," recalled promoter Don Chargin from ringside, and he tried all he could to stay away from his pursuer, but eventually Duran caught up and stopped him in the seventh round. Finding his opponent in the ring strictly to survive was something Duran would have to get used to.

The West Coast trip was more important to Duran for events outside the ring. "I went to train in the Olympic Auditorium with Luis Spada behind the Hotel Alejandria," he said. "I was twenty-one at the time and waiting to fight Medina. Three people came to me and said that I had the same face as Margarito [his father]. They were my aunts and uncles. They said my father was coming to see me and that's also when I met my uncle, Roberto, whose name was given to me because my father loved him so much. I went to the hotel and after a couple of hours my father came to see me. I knew it was him after he told me who he knew in my town in Panama."

Margarito had failed for two decades to even ask about him, and had never even sent money. Suspicious and resentful of his father's timing, Roberto saw someone looking for a handout. "He is a very sensitive person and would always complain about not having lived with his father," said Plomo. "He used to tell me he wanted to find out about him, to know what he was like, and I remember he once said he had left Germany and was living in Arizona. At that time he had already fought in the USA, and had turned world champion, but he still did not know who his father was. We had two fights in Los Angeles, after being world champion, and he repeated the story about his father being a Mexican, and his wish to know whether he was then living in Arizona or not. This interview was broadcast by radio and TV, and in the end, his father did come one day to our hotel in Los Angeles.

"Roberto got very angry, and asked him why was it that he was only now interested in meeting him, now that he was a champion. He added he could not be sure he was really his father. After asking what his name was, to which his father said, 'Margarito,' he inquired about the other people in the family he knew. Margarito answered he knew Uncle Joaquin, with whom he used to spend long hours. I told him not get angry at his father, after all he was his father.

"Roberto left the room for a while, and upon returning he went on with the questions. He asked whether he knew who his grandfather was, to which Margarito answered his grandfather's name was Chavelo. They looked at each other for a while, after which they embraced strongly, and when they finally looked at each other again, they heard the words they had longed for so long: *Father, Son*. That was the beginning of a totally new friendship."

Margarito wasn't after anything except to see his son. "The reason I got in contact with Roberto was because I was in California and I was reading a boxing magazine," he said. "At the time I was visiting my oldest brother. Then I see Roberto Duran in the magazine. I told my oldest brother that he had to be my son. 'I bet it is my son,' I told my brother. Soon enough I saw him when he came here to fight."

Despite the reconciliation, they rarely kept in touch afterwards. Duran would face Javier Ayala less than a month later. Duran weighed 140 for Ayala, and went in at 139 for Medina. "There was a belief that Duran struggled to make weight for some of his fights," said West Coast promoter Don Chargin. "Of course, the fighters don't always let you know if they did have trouble. Duran was very popular with all the Latin fans. His father was Mexican. He would mix around with everybody around the gym and that's what Latin fans liked. You know, he might have been wild in Panama, but when he came to Los Angeles he was always on time at all the press events and was always good with the press."

Ayala proved to be a testing opponent. He came in with a poor 13-7-1 record but was able to fend off Duran; Chargin recalled that Duran made "Ayala fight the best fight of his life." During the bout, at the Los Angeles Sports Arena on March 17, Duran knocked Ayala down in the last round but a bizarre occurrence meant he couldn't finish him off, and left him feeling short-changed by promoter Chargin and the locals. "There was quite a bit of time left, maybe a couple minutes in the round," said Chargin. "Duran knocked Ayala down and his head hit the bell. Back then the bell was a box with a button on it. So everybody stopped because of the confusion. Ayala was hurt, but he cleared and was able to finish the fight. We had a tough time with Duran after because he thought it was something we did on purpose. It took us a week before he finally understood what had happened."

Before he left the West Coast, Duran spent some more time getting to know Margarito's side of the family. "We went to my father's house and we were drinking beer," said Duran. "They gave us food, but we didn't eat it because it was too spicy. I only saw my father maybe four times during my boxing career. Twenty-one years had passed after that first time. I always called him, but only his woman answered. He never did and never returned my calls."

Margarito countered, "I used to see him every time he used to fight. They'd call us beforehand and reserve our seats."

Although people give sundry testimonies on the person Duran really was, from a hard drinker who would enter New York bars and call out the toughest guy, to a party lover, to a legendary womanizer, the people who dealt with him inside boxing painted the same portrait of a maniacal figure. Was he acting out against his father each time he entered the ring?

"It wasn't an act. He used to be a mean little guy when he was younger," said Kronk trainer Emanuel Steward. "But that's what made him who he was, that rage. You couldn't take that away from him. But he mellowed with age. He's such a nice guy and you can just see that in his body language, he just likes to be around people."

The rage hid sensitivity. Duran put up walls that only a select few could get beyond. One of the barriers was a refusal to learn English. The belief was that he didn't want people to misinterpret him. Ironically, the situations in his life that left him damaged were also the easiest to talk about. Duran doesn't clam up about his feelings for his father and refuses to hide his feeling of abandonment. Yet he never received a satisfactory answer for why his father didn't love him enough to look after him, and they would never become close.

"One night I was done fighting once and we all went to have drinks at Caesar's Palace," said Duran. "My dad was drunk and he started dancing. He fell! So he has to go to the room, but I had no clothes so I gave him my boxing robe. Later on, when he wouldn't call back, I thought that he didn't want to talk to me or maybe his wife talked to him so that he didn't contact me. But I don't want to know anything about that family anymore."

After the Ayala fight, Duran knocked out Gerardo Ferrat on April 14 in Panama City in another over-the-weight match. Ferrat, another Mexican, had fought the best in the division but spent a sizeable part of the fight looking into the referee's eyes, as he was dropped three times before succumbing to a straight right hand in the final moments of the second round. "Ferrat came out with the determination of swapping punches, and Rocky didn't hesitate in answering the call," described *Ring* magazine succinctly.

Next came a true test. Duran's second title defense was against Australian aborigine Hector Thompson, who had never boxed outside his native country but who was unbeaten in his last twenty-six contests. "Hector was a legend in Australia," said Eleta. "They didn't believe that anyone could beat him. Supposedly, he killed a man in the ring or something like that. The guy was a killer." In 1970, Rocco Spanja had died in hospital after losing to Thompson.

Born in Kempsey, a river settlement on the Pacific coast midway between Sydney and Brisbane, Thompson was raised in a boys' home after the death of his mother. He was introduced to boxing there at just five years of age, and developed into a skilled and very strong fighter who could box, stay poised in heated exchanges and was adept at beating opponents to the jab. An Australian champion at two weights, he had just won the Commonwealth light-welterweight title and had lost only twice, both early in his career, in forty-three pro bouts.

The bout was held in Nuevo Panama on 2 June 1973. Duran came in at 134 pounds, a pound less than Thompson, who often fought at the slightly heavier light-welterweight. At the weigh-in Duran had predicted a knockout within five rounds but it was soon clear that the rugged Australian was both strong and smart and would be no pushover.

Duran stung him with a right to the ribs and an overhand right to let him know whose turf he was on.

Duran broke down Thompson early in the second round with a left hook to the head, and then landed four straight head shots to end the round. Thompson tried to counter but with no success as a patient Duran ducked and swayed with marvelous economy while maintaining his forward drive. Every move, every punch followed a precise pattern, as if he had orchestrated every second in his mind in training.

The fight wasn't without its oddities. Four times after rounds ended, Duran walked to Thompson's corner instead of his own. Duran seemed stupefied by his own actions. The confusion didn't halt his attack as he knocked down Thompson with seconds remaining in the third round. After a mandatory eight count, Thompson walked into another big left hook before the bell sounded. Using the intermission to clear his head, Thompson boxed well in the fourth and in the fifth he traded with Duran, hustling points and landing two solid uppercuts. As the intensity increased, both men traded body shots and uppercuts in the sixth and seventh round.

A jarring left hook to the neck sent Thompson sprawling in the eighth and blood squirted from his nose like a spigot. He was up quickly but disoriented, and after the second mandatory eight-count Duran landed two more shots and referee Nicasio Drake stepped in to halt it with fifteen seconds left in the round. Thompson was slumped against the ropes and appeared unable to defend himself. The Australian later complained that the stoppage was premature, but Duran was well ahead on points and had clearly outworked him.

That night, Thompson faced an indomitable champion. Some would contend that Duran never fought a more vicious, focused fight. "Thompson, a classical stylist, had gambled on his skill being too much for Duran, but like Ken Buchanan before him he learned the hard way that technique without power is not enough to counter Duran's explosive hitting," concluded *Boxing News*.

"I think the one fight where people realized how great he could be was against Thompson," said Eleta. "You should have seen that fight, they went at each other, tried to kill each other, but not in the way it is translated. It means that they fought very hard in Spanish. It showed that Duran had that something extra.

"Duran didn't like any fighter that he had to fight. After that they got together and were friendly. But that's why Duran was Duran, because he got everybody afraid of him. That's why he would say, 'I am going to kill you' and all that."

Thompson went on to be one of the greatest Australian boxers ever but a world title would elude him. In 1976, another of his opponents, American Chuck Wilburn, died in hospital from injuries sustained during their bout, and Thompson himself was eventually forced to retire after an electro-encephalogram revealed he could suffer permanent brain damage if he continued.

The title had also brought Duran a new home with a pool in Nuevo Reparten, an upscale community in Panama, a place where he could indulge both his generous conviviality and his roughly playful sense of humour. While later taking pictures during a party at Duran's home, a local photographer was standing by the side of Duran's pool. Next thing he knew Duran was telling the people that "it was time to push a photographer in the pool." At the moment it seemed a harmless announcement that Duran made to get some laughs. Minutes later the man and his equipment were in the water, while Duran and his friends basked in the moment.

Duran asked how much for the equipment.

"One thousand dollars," said the dripping photographer.

"I'll give you two thousand dollars," replied Duran.

"I couldn't stay mad any longer," said the photographer, after fishing out his equipment.

A little over two months after the Thompson fight, Duran was surrounded by Puerto Ricans in the Roberto Clemente Coliseum in Hato Rey, Puerto Rico. On DeJesus's turf, he faced Adolphus "Doc" McClendon, who had nine losses in eighteen bouts, in a ten-round non-title bout, and banged out a unanimous decision, with few notable exchanges. "Doc didn't do much after holding his own for the first three rounds," reported *Ring*. "He also managed to land a sneaky right hand. That won the plaudits of the fans, but they were few and far between." After the fight, the generous Duran gave McClendon an expensive gold watch as a gift. Material things meant little to him. It wasn't unusual for him to offer a piece of clothing to a stranger in public just to see their reaction. In an airport one day, he ripped off his T-shirt to give to an admirer, and continued to walk shirt-less through the terminal.

His Nuevo Panama haven was the venue for his third defense against Japan's Ishimatsu "Guts" Suzuki, on a bill that also featured fellow WBA champion Ernesto Marcel defending his featherweight crown. A crowd of 16,000 turned out to watch the two local heroes on September 8, 1973. Suzuki, a flamboyant personality with more courage than skill, was an attention-lover who later became a comedian and actor (*Black Rain, Empire Of The Sun*) and was noted for unintentionally humorous comments, such as, "My life has turned three hundred and eighty degrees because of boxing," and, "I know the human being and the fish can coexist peacefully." He came into the fight with a 25-10-5 record and the intention of unseating the brash young champion, and succeeded in gashing Duran's eye in the third round, but was sent to the canvas five times before the bout was stopped in the tenth round. The champion attacked from the outset, producing some of the best boxing of his career, and by round eight Suzuki's eye was badly swollen. Duran floored him twice in the ninth and a further three times in the tenth before the referee called a halt. Marcel also won in style.

In a post-fight interview, Duran said, "I am a little tired. Suzuki was very good."

"Who was better, Suzuki or Thompson?" asked the reporter.

"Thompson, muy fuerte. Very strong."

From December 1972 to February 1973, Duran only needed eleven rounds to dispatch Tony Garcia in Panama, Leonard Tavarez in Paris, France, and Armando Mendoza in his hometown in three non-title bouts. "Duran had a problem when he traveled to Europe," said Plomo. "He fought against Tavarez who was [French] champion. It is not known whether Duran ate something that made him sick, a beefsteak or something else, or if he was given something in bad condition on purpose, you can never be too sure about what people who love their country may do, the cook perhaps...I was already getting him ready and he asked to go to the bathroom. Then, in the middle of the fight, when they were interchanging blows, all of a sudden, PRUUFF! The excrement went off. He had diarrhea. That happened after he had already knocked Tavarez down and they had put up his hand. He had to go running to the bathroom."

A dramatic photograph of a thunderous Duran right cross appearing to cave in Tavarez's face later appeared in several publications. "The 35-year-old Frenchman was bleeding from the nose as early as the first round and barely escaped a knockout when he was floored at the end of the third, only to be saved by the bell," reported *Boxing News*. "Duran launched another fierce attack in the fourth and Tavarez's manager, Jean Traxel, threw in the towel after one minute of the round."

★ ★ ★

A week before Christmas, 1973, the promotional group Top Rank, headed by the ambitious former attorney Bob Arum, announced that Duran would defend his title against the only man to beat him, Esteban DeJesus, for his biggest ever purse of $125,000. DeJesus, as challenger, would receive $40,000. Arum had promoted most of Muhammad Ali's title defenses in the Sixties and was one of the first to spot the opportunities afforded by closed-circuit cinema broadcasts, foresight that would make him a major player. The fight would have happened sooner but Eleta had deterred previous approaches with his stringent demands, including not leaving Panama to fight. "The trouble started when Duran … reportedly had been assured that he would be too tough for DeJesus," wrote columnist Alberto Montilla, after the first fight. "However, Esteban gave Duran a boxing lesson and Duran, report had it, felt he had been suckered into a bad deal in New York. This was not true."

If there was an ideal mix for a prizefighter, Esteban DeJesus had all the ingredients, just not in sufficient abundance to qualify for greatness. A magnificent counter-puncher, he instinctively understood the nuances of the fight game. DeJesus had not received due credit for beating Duran in their first fight. Many blamed poor conditioning on Duran's part, while Duran had the excuse of his injured elbow. DeJesus was undefeated since beating Duran at the Garden.

Eleta urged Duran to remember the feeling he had in the restaurant after the first loss. Losing was a sign of weakness, and no man could strip him of his virility. He wore gold rings and the Armani suits, but Chorrillo was still inside him. He was fighting for every Panamanian who grew up with nothing. The Duran name would become ingrained in the hearts of the Panamanians for his generosity as well as his accomplishments. Although he earned and spent to excess, money meant nothing to Duran; people did. Money was just something that would arrive after each bout.

Duran fought his best when he had something to prove, never more so than in the return bout with DeJesus. He wanted DeJesus with a passion, while lesser opponents were merely a break in his carousing. DeJesus had to be taken seriously; Duran knew this much. This was the guy who floored him in their first fight, whose left hook was the hot topic in pre-fight interviews, who cursed Duran in public and challenged him during press conferences.

Weeks before the fight Duran told a local reporter, "I wake up with DeJesus. I breakfast with DeJesus. I lunch with DeJesus. And I go to sleep with DeJesus. There is not a moment that I don't think about him. I have no fear. In the first fight, I was not in good physical condition. This time I am in better condition than I was when I massacred Buchanan. I hope that DeJesus doesn't run like a coward." On March 15, a photo in *La Critica* showed Duran holding up six fingers to signify the round he would knock out his opponent.

He further elaborated in a radio interview with journalist Tomy Cupas.

"How do you feel about the fight?" asked Cupas.

"I am in perfect condition and DeJesus is covered in shit," said Duran.

"Listen, champ, we are on air …"

"Excuse me, but I will take him out at all costs."

Ray Arcel arrived on March 9 to train Duran in a gym in the interior in Veraguas, Santiago, while DeJesus stayed in Panama City and trained at Juan Demostenes Arosemena. There were rumors that Duran hurt his hand in sparring, while DeJesus, whose sparring partners were the Puerto Rican Benitez brothers, allegedly suffered a cut days before the fight. Trainer Gregorio Benitez complained about the training conditions and tried to postpone the fight a week, though this may have been because DeJesus was struggling to get down to the weight.

It was also the hot season, when humidity became almost unbearable, hardly the best time for anyone to step into the ring against the local hero.

"Duran didn't have trouble with guys who moved. He had trouble with a guy who was a good fighter," said Gil Clancy. "And DeJesus was a guy who could fight. What you are looking for is to see the effect of when a guy lands a punch, to see how well the other guy stands up."

DeJesus also had one weapon that no mortal man could counter without help: magic. He brought with him his *brujos*, the shamanic wizards or witch doctors in whose magic many black and native Americans believed. *Brujos* are respected and feared from Mexico to Chile. They can cast a spell on enemies, cure ills and stop a straying husband. In Chile they believed that to become a *brujo* one must perform evil acts, even killing a family member to acquire magical powers. According to some legends, *brujos* can fly when wearing a vest made from the skin of a virgin worn inside out.

Newspapers referred to DeJesus as "the sorcerer from Puerto Rico." Clara Samaniego prayed to Virgen del Carmen, patron saint of the *mestizo* population, for her son's safety but also took measures to counter his opponent's dark magic. "Esteban DeJesus did not know me at that time," said Clara. "He came to Panama, and said that anyone who wanted to meet him could go visit him. I went to see him, and I immediately saw the African *brujos*. I sensed this was not going to be a good thing for my son during the fight the following day. So I sent Roberto [a religious object] so that he did not fall on the first round. But Roberto threw away what I had given him.

"When I arrived I said I wanted to talk to a lieutenant, and I asked him to take me to see Roberto, for I was his mother. When Roberto saw me, crying, I told him to hook him up from downwards and upwards, combining them. I then claimed for the help of my late mother, 'Mrs Ceferina Garcia, give Roberto a breath, and help him stand up.' Roberto says he felt her breath after a while, and he stood up. I started shouting at him where to hit his rival, and this was when Roberto finally recovered."

Despite stifling heat and humidity, Duran, resplendent in green trunks with yellow stripes and a Super Malta advertisement, wasn't even sweating as he entered the ring for the showdown at the Nuevo Panama Gymnasium on 16 March 1974. The combatants had nearly identical records with Duran 40-1 (thirty-five KOs) and DeJesus 41-1 (twenty-nine KOs). Sixteen thousand fans had snatched up tickets ranging from $10 to $100 apiece, and Duran was a 2–1 betting favorite. HB soda and Atlas beer flowed as the fans watched local fighter Mario Mendoza ignite proceedings with a seventh-round knockout victory.

Once again, Duran would find himself looking up at DeJesus. DeJesus started strongly and set up the first big left hook with a straight right that landed flush on Duran's jaw. Duran's unruly black locks flew up in the air as he tried to balance himself. Unable to recover, the next left hook flattened him, again. He rose quickly with a disgusted look, took an eight-count and promised to exact revenge.

"I don't agree that he beat me in the first fight," said Duran. "DeJesus fought with Roberto Duran who just had an accident. When I fought the rematch, I was having too many problems making the weight for the fight here in Panama. I get a pimple on my face, I break it and keep messing with it. I burn it and get scarred. When he knocks me down in the rematch, Plomo says to me, 'Hey what happened, he knocked you down with the same hand as before?' I said, 'Take it easy man, I'm about to rip his ass up.'"

Cornermen Arcel and Brown knew their fighter was only temporarily shaken. Between rounds, Duran sat without emotion, no snarl or disdain, just innocence; a surreal snapshot of detachment. Whatever the old men preached, Duran looked through them. He knew what to do. In truth, DeJesus, 134½, had also struggled mightily to shed pounds to reach the 135-pound lightweight limit, and lacked the vim of their first fight.

The old adage that you "don't hook with a hooker" was forgotten as Duran tore into DeJesus in an action-packed second round. In the third, Duran responded with a blizzard of punches. On the inside he shortened his blows, used his shoulders to crowd the Puerto Rican and raked DeJesus with the top of his head. He ended the round with a furious nine-punch barrage. It marked the first clear-cut round for Duran in over thirteen rounds of boxing with the Puerto Rican.

The champion began to move and show his defensive skills in the fourth, landing and avoiding DeJesus' counters at blink speed. He had the ability to "go" with a punch, turning or tilting his head slightly, but decisively on impact to negate the force. Blows that looked solid to spectators and seemed to jolt his head were in fact robbed of power. Rarely did Duran take a clean shot. The challenger was always dangerous, but was clearly bothered by both his opponent's attack and the Panama heat. His blows arrived singly, not in combination, and he began to jab and move to dodge punishment. Brawling with *this* Duran was not an option.

The champion bled first, a gash opening under his left eye after the sixth round. But he ignored it to land a left-right combination and then artfully fall into DeJesus, bringing his elbows up to his chest to grab him in a clinch to prevent any counter. It was a beautiful sequence, executed in rapid succession.

By round seven, the writing was on the wall. The force of Duran's punches could be measured by the swaying of the crowd; with each solid hit they rose in a wave, arms aloft. The roar became deafening when Duran clubbed DeJesus to his knees with a quick right hand halfway through the round. For a few seconds it looked like DeJesus wouldn't get up. He looked all in, yet he couldn't stay down. Being a boxer came with a steep price. Defeat was no shame but any perceived lack of courage was. The life he had chosen gave him only one option:

to fight. DeJesus willed himself to rise, and survived the round on instinct alone.

After the break, Duran continued to ravage his challenger with left hooks to the liver. One eight-punch combination in the middle of the ring put the seal on his dominance. DeJesus had a hopeless look in his eyes as he doubled over from each hook. Each break between rounds was merely a temporary respite from the torture. The sixty-second interval forces a boxer to confront the truth. In these brief periods of introspection, DeJesus had to decide whether to come forward with the same intensity and risk injury, stay away from his opponent or even quit. In what other sport must an athlete answer such profound questions? As promoter J. Russell Peltz said, any fighter who gets in the ring "has stones." DeJesus pondered the eighteen minutes of warfare thus far, he sat with eyes ahead and mouth agape, stare blank, thoughts jumbled, as his handlers tried to revive him and urge him on. They flushed his entire body with water. One massaged his shoulders while another jostled his cheeks like a proud grandmother. DeJesus never changed expression.

By the end of round ten, the Puerto Rican was grimacing at every punch. He again slumped on his stool at the bell and told his manager, "No voy más. I'm finished, I can't go on." Gregorio Benitez, an uncompromising character who always believed he knew best, responded sharply, "You aren't going to quit now. You have come for the title...to fight." He brooked no argument.

Not a minute later DeJesus was back on the canvas from a Duran right to the side of his head. Referee Isaac Herrera crouched close to the fallen fighter's head and counted him out, conscious but spent. As soon as he signaled the end, DeJesus rose and walked back to the corner.

Duran bounced over to Eleta and threw his arms around his manager. With security forgotten, fans flooded the ring. A journalist jabbed a microphone into Duran's face and he smiled, happy amid chaos. Soon he disappeared among back-slapping military brass. A white-haired and angry Ray Arcel tried to fight through the melee to reach his fighter, to no avail. Somewhere else, Eleta was talking to a reporter about a possible return bout with Buchanan. "After Duran hit him in the kidney early in the fight I knew it was over," he said.

"With Heart and Truth Cholo Retains Title," declared the headline in *La Critica*.

# 9

# HANDS OF STONE

*"I almost killed that guy."*

Roberto Duran

FROM JULY 1974 to February 1975, Duran took just twenty rounds to dispose of six opponents. Flash Gallego fell in five in July, while Adalberto Vanegas, Masataka Takayama and Andres Salgado were all blown away in first-round knockouts. Only the bout against Japan's Takayama, who was dropped three times in short order, was a title defense. "I was the matchmaker for that bout with Takayama [in Costa Rica]," said Luis Spada, who worked for Carlos Eleta. "Roberto knocks the guy out in like a hundred seconds, and they are mad at me because it was so quick. I said, 'You told me to make the bout and I did.'"

Puerto Rican Hector Matta was the only one of the six to go the distance, losing a ten-rounder in San Juan. Matta, whose father trained fighting cocks as well as boxers, fought well; Duran was under par, and some of the local boxing writers even called the bout a draw. Esteban DeJesus fought in the co-main event, but a "rubber" between him and Duran was unlikely given that DeJesus now seemed unable to make 135 pounds.

Duran was also forced to pull out of a non-title fight at Madison Square Garden that August. Carlos Eleta was unwilling to sign an agreement to defend against Ken Buchanan within ninety days of the Barreto bout, even though he apparently had a two-year-old contract to give the Scot his chance, and so the New York State Athletic Commission suspended Duran from boxing in the state for more than a year. Commission chairman Edwin Dooley then called off the Barreto bout. Before Duran headed back to Panama, a reporter went to his room at the Mayflower Hotel seeking an interview with the champ. "Duran is in the shower and he is ready to go in a motorcade to a party in Brooklyn where everyone wants to see him," said translator Luis Henriquez. He hinted that there might be "a physical confrontation" if any reporter attempted to interview the champ. "I didn't like being pressured," was Eleta's memory of the ban.

Instead, a lightweight from Portland, Oregon, entered the picture. Ray Lampkin had dreamed of being a fighter since his childhood, but at first lacked the discipline needed to excel in the fight game. He made the Olympic national qualifiers as an amateur but not the finals. "I smoked cigarettes for ten years," Lampkin admitted. "Even though I was winning fights in the amateurs, I wasn't a good fighter. I was in no shape because I was still smoking. All the fights that I had lost, I ran out of gas in the last round."

Lampkin looked to turn pro but had no trainer or manager. While promoter Sam Singleton tried to find him a spot on a local card, the boxer worked three jobs out of necessity. His plea to "just find me someone to fight" was repeated often, until one day in 1972 it was answered. "They found me someone to fight named Gordon 'Newsboy' Johnson," said Lampkin. "I didn't even know who he was, so I just got out there and started to train. I knew some guy who told me, 'You're going to get some newspapers thrown at you.' And I said, 'He might be throwing some newspapers, but I'll be throwing punches.'"

After winning the decision in his pro debut, Lampkin woke up to what was possible. "If I did this well without being in the proper shape, imagine what I could do if I stopped doing the things that were holding me back. I didn't want to wonder how good I could really be." He didn't lose in his first twenty pro fights, the only blemish being a single draw. Lampkin became something of a local attraction in Oregon, but his progress was slow. "I decided if I was going to make a move in the boxing game, then I had to get a manager," he said. "Some guys who have trainers and managers don't even go ten-zero, I thought."

He eventually hooked up with Mike "Motormouth" Morton, a Runyonesque mainstay of the Pacific Northwest boxing scene, and early in 1973 traveled to Puerto Rico to fight Esteban DeJesus for the North American Boxing Federation lightweight title, with only Morton by his side. "I went over there without my trainer Jack Brackey, who was the best teacher of the game that I ever had," said Lampkin. "He taught me how to be a pro, and my manager wouldn't send him over there with me. Since the promoter only provided two plane tickets, he was left out. Fighting DeJesus without my trainer was one of the biggest mistakes of my career."

Not only a trainer and teacher: Brackey was also Lampkin's shadow. When the sun went down and Lampkin didn't want to finish his routine, it was Brackey who prodded him. When the young fighter needed a pick-me-up in the latter rounds of a fight, it was Brackey who put his hands around his waist and urged him back out there. When the left hook was thrown too wide, Brackey was there to shorten it up. When Lampkin got knocked down, Brackey went with him. Now Lampkin, who had never traveled to another country, was alone.

"When I got to San Juan, there were a lot of things I didn't like. People were telling me, 'Don't drink the water.' I was so scared to drink the water and by the time the fight came around I was so weak. My manager should have gotten me bottled water or something."

Fighting in the new Roberto Clemente Coliseum in Rato Hey was also a problem. "It was a brand new ring and it was real slippery," said Lampkin. "Every time I tried to swing or throw a punch, I was slipping. In the first round, DeJesus hit me with a right hand and I went down. He dropped me for the first time in my life. I got up and went twelve rounds with him. I slipped two or three times during the fight. If we had prepared ourselves for this, and checked the ring, we would have known beforehand that there was a rod in the middle and that we needed rubber shoes. I knew that I could have beat him if we were on even ground."

Despite the decision loss, the fight proved that Lampkin could compete with the elite in his division, and several months later he got his wish for "even ground" when he fought DeJesus again at New York Felt Forum. "I had inflamed gallstones in this fight," said Lampkin. "It may sound like excuses, but I shouldn't even have been fighting. I couldn't do any roadwork, but their mindset was that I could wait and see a doctor [when I got back to] Oregon. I was like, 'But I could die now.'"

Lampkin survived the painful disorder, which his doctor would later note as a "miracle." Once again, however, he lost the decision. "I have respect for every fighter because I don't want to disrespect anybody," Lampkin said, "but I still think that I could have beaten Esteban. I was too fast for him, and I could box.

"I was always hoping to meet up with Duran," Lampkin said. "I figured the longer I stayed up there, one day he would have to fight me. When they finally make the fight, they tell me that I'm going to have to go to Panama. He wouldn't fight me anywhere else. I told him that I would go straight to his house and fight."

The match was made for Nuevo Panama, Panama City, on 2 March 1975. Lampkin knew that the man he was facing had more to offer than attack. "People never gave Duran credit for being such a good defensive fighter," said Lampkin. "Boy, he wasn't easy to hit."

To Lampkin, the logic of the fight played out like this: DeJesus beat Duran, Lampkin almost beat DeJesus, therefore Lampkin had a good chance to dethrone Duran. Lampkin didn't regard Duran as an unstoppable force, even though the champion was coming off a trio of first-round knockouts. "They were trying to make Duran out to be this Superman character," said Lampkin. "He was human, and when you cut him, he bled, just like I did. They were acting like he couldn't be beat, and I saw Esteban do it. They tried to intimidate me and tell me that if I beat Duran, I probably wouldn't leave there alive. I told them that if I die, then I would be a dead champion, because if I beat him they were going to have to kill me."

Lampkin and his team arrived in Panama on a Friday before the fight on Sunday. "No fight could prepare me for Duran," Lampkin reminisced. "Duran had his own style, and there wasn't another fighter who had that same style. My sparring partners, well, none of them could really fight like Duran. Duran's always looking to punch, and had pretty good speed and power. He also had a good right hand, a weird style and was very hard to hit. I just trained hoping to make him fight my fight. I didn't worry about his style. I wanted to make him adjust to my style. I figured if I landed everything I wanted to land, he would fall."

Although lack of conditioning would occasionally blight Duran's career, as a lightweight he was young, strong and savvy enough to prevail even when his energy ran low. He knew when to clinch or claw, hit low, take needed breaks, go toward the ropes or plant himself in the middle of the ring. It was usually enough to keep him out of trouble or allow him to catch his breath. Despite being able to hide his flaws from certain boxers, others quickly recognized Duran's mouth agape searching for that second wind, along with a decrease in punches, and then attacked. Duran's power, for a lightweight, was a hot topic. It was a straight right hand often prefaced by a left hook to the body. If the one punched missed, several were fired from every angle. And with the mind of a crafty veteran, Duran knew that his punches might leave him off balance. So Duran perfected the punch-and-hold tactic that threw off all the challengers who expected the staple bum-rush to leave him vulnerable for counters. Those challengers who ran from Duran were caught in the late rounds. On Panama's boisterous street corners over dominoes, many wondered aloud how many rounds it would take for Duran to destroy Lampkin.

"They kept him away from me," Lampkin added. "They knew he would try stuff like that, and they didn't want me and him together. The only time I saw Duran was in the ring. They didn't want us to be at the same weigh-in or nothing. In fact, he weighed in first, and then they got him out of there … before he would act the fool."

Keeping Duran hidden before the bout not only stopped any possible physical or verbal assault, but left the challenger in the dark. "I didn't know who he was," Lampkin remembered. "I really didn't. I kept asking, 'Is that Duran there?' And they said, 'No, that's not him.' I didn't know when I was ever going to see the guy." One thing that Lampkin dreaded was the heat. Duran had spent his life training in veritable tanning-salon gyms; Lampkin hadn't. This was Duran's land.

"The building is hot, there's no air-conditioning at all," said Lampkin. "It's like an oven with the temperature at five hundred degrees … and it was like the summertime back there. When you get there you don't think about that stuff; we never knew. All you do is get in there, go to the dressing room, and come out when it's time to fight. We thought it was like any other arena."

By the time Lampkin was walking down through the aisles of the Nuevo Panama Gym, however, everything was forgotten: the jungle heat, the crowd, the pressure. It was man against man, and the American began well. Duran cut off the ring, using his jab to set up three left hooks to the face, but Lampkin, whose upright style and sculpted body made him seem much the bigger man, responded with a clean straight right that made Duran lose his footing. "When I hit him with a body shot, he would kick his leg up real high, and people thought he was trying to kick me," Lampkin said. "I can't remember what round it was, but I know I hurt him."

There was nothing squeamish about Lampkin. He elbowed Duran in the head during a clinch in the second round, a warning that any dirty stuff would be countered in kind. Clean shots bounced off Duran's devilish beard throughout the round, which Lampkin earned.

Through the early rounds, Duran looked to have a slight edge. Breathing heavily by the fourth, he scored with combinations and stag-

124 HANDS OF STONE

gered Lampkin in the fifth with a clubbing right cross. Legs weazy, but mind intact, Lampkin wobbled around the ring, took another right and instinctively fell into and wrestled Duran to the floor. After the brief delay, Duran refused the head and cracked Lampkin with a left to the ribs that sent him hobbling back to his cornermen.

But always Lampkin fought back. Even inside, a space Duran called his own, Lampkin often ended several close-quarter exchanges with a chopping right and scored on the outside with a left-right-left combination. Few men had hit Duran like that, and several rounds were too close to call. Still, Duran was landing the bigger punches and between the seventh and eighth rounds an issue arose in Lampkin's corner. It was reported in the *New York Times* that Lampkin was forcibly sent out by his handlers for the eighth round, though it wasn't explained why.

The pace was torrid as neither man looked to back down. Even those blinded by bias had to admire the American's persistence. Few lightweights could have taken the punishment Duran gave Lampkin and kept going forward. In the ninth, Lampkin walked through a punishing left hook to the body and a pair of rights to the head; his courage never wavered. Duran concentrated on a huge welt that had formed under Lampkin's left eye, banging the puss out with a vicious uppercut.

Duran forged on and caught his second wind in the late rounds. By the end of round thirteen, both of Lampkin's cheeks were swollen and his step was heavy. He had given his soul, yet still he wouldn't fall. He took solace in the middle of the ring and raged back at Duran.

"He was a guy who would do anything to win," Lampkin said. "He was a dirty guy and I knew that but he was the main guy. I figured I was holding my own. All I wanted … to keep him in the kitchen and hit him with some good shots and knock him out. But it was very hard to do. I was the first one to take him fourteen rounds. What got me was that my corner had defeated me when they ran out of water. It was like amateur night in my corner."

Lampkin plodded out of his corner for round fourteen; he wouldn't return the same fighter. Within the first thirty seconds, Duran had landed a short, glancing left hook that set him up. Lampkin, near the ropes, dropped his guard for a split second. A whipping left hook sent him to the canvas and out on his back, his head bouncing off the floor like a weight dropped on cement. Ringsiders cringed at the sickening force of the fall. Even before the referee had knelt down to count, Lampkin tried to raise his head, but couldn't. He had no chance of beating the count. By that point, ringsiders were more concerned about his health.

As soon as the hook had landed, Duran knew the possibility that something grave had occurred. "I almost killed the guy," he noted later. Handlers, security guards and medics began to crowd around Lampkin, a wounded man lying among strangers. "I remember him taking me down and my head hit the canvas pretty hard and I tried to get up and I have a picture of me on my elbows," said Lampkin. "From the slamming of my head, all of a sudden I tried to raise up real fast and then I just fell back out."

Duran capped the nightmare off with his most infamous quote: "Next time I send him to the morgue." The media ran with it, and it became emblematic of the Panamanian's perceived callousness and brute hostility. However, Duran's camp denied that their fighter was a monster. "No, those are lies," said Plomo. "The guy was half-dead, he did not need to frighten him any further. They took him to hospital on a stretcher because he failed to react."

"I told him that I never had been knocked out in my life and I don't feel that he would have done it if I had water in my corner," said Lampkin. "I sensed that we were both tiring. They weren't expecting me to last, nobody did, especially the Panamanian people. When I went back there they told me that I had beaten Duran, but I didn't win the fight. His daughter and son told me, 'We've never met you Mister Lampkin, but my daddy said you were his toughest fight.'"

The punch, and the quote, would cement Duran's reputation. Society believed that Duran didn't have the capacity to feel compassion, not in the ring. The media blew up his quote on the morgue, thus enhancing Duran's ugliness. "[Lampkin] could have died after that fight," said Duran. "I told him I would kill him next time. I fought him with very little training. I lost too much weight; I was dying. I always have a quality that I would never lose … I have a gesture where you don't know which two hands are coming. It's the moment where you think the right is coming and it's the left, and then you expect the left and I hit you with the right. That's why I had a lot of boxers confused, I was just too smart for them." Duran would call Lampkin his toughest challenger.

WBA President and ringside physician Dr Elias Cordoba originally called Lampkin's condition "delicate but not serious." However, it wasn't until thirty minutes after reaching the local hospital that Lampkin regained consciousness. According to WBA doctor Keith

Arthur, the reason for Lampkin's delayed consciousness was "a severe accumulation of blood in the thorax which diminished the blood flow to the brain." At this point, the number one contender was fighting for his life. A wire story even reported that Lampkin had died.

At the Santo Thomas Hospital, Lampkin went into convulsions. "They took me back to the dressing room or somewhere and everybody was all over me," Lampkin recalled. "'Give him some room,' and then someone said, 'Get this man to a hospital.' I can vaguely remember that, and then I went to the hospital."

Although Duran claims that he, Toti and his mother visited Lampkin at the hospital twice after the fight, Lampkin doesn't recall it. "Sure, Roberto and I went to the hospital together," said Toti Samaniego. "Lampkin was acting crazy and was talking about a rematch and stuff like that." Plomo also remembered the visit, as Duran was worried if "the guy was alive or dead."

Lampkin tested his legs two days after the fight but couldn't walk. Most men would have taken the knockout as a sign to quit boxing, but not Lampkin. "One thing, I did suffer a concussion because I couldn't walk. My left leg was paralyzed," said Lampkin, "from the fall on my head. I was dragging my left leg and I had to go home in a wheelchair." After being cleared to return to Oregon, Lampkin was met at the airport by the mayor. He was immediately taken to the hospital for more tests and to make sure he didn't have blood clots.

"It was a very difficult time," Lampkin recalled. "I had to go to a neurosurgeon. Then I was under treatment for six months. A woman was working with me so I could walk again. First, I could walk; then I could run again. If you didn't know it, you would never think that anything was ever wrong with me. I was just as strong as ever."

Lampkin continued, "Maybe some would call, but he didn't. Duran never called or anything. Maybe twenty-some years later, I saw Duran. He and Sugar Ray Leonard came to Oregon to a casino. I saw it in the paper, so I went down to the casino and I walked up to Duran and said, 'Hey, you remember me, Ray Lampkin? We fought each other.' He looks at me, 'Huh, huh?' But I made him remember. Then we took some pictures together. We got to know each other like good friends. And he had his lawyer call me in Portland to come to Panama as a guest."

Even now, when people look at Ray Lampkin they remember the knockout, the trauma. Some wonder how he survived such a beating to keep fighting. "I didn't get rich or win the championship of the world, because of that fight and the injury that I suffered," said Lampkin. "That was the fight that sent me downhill into retirement. I had seven more fights after the Duran fight and I was never the same. I never recuperated from the injury. I wanted to make myself believe that I did, but I kept getting hurt. I didn't want to die, so I left it alone. After that concussion it got to the point that I couldn't take a good head shot. I didn't want to be crazy or walking around like a vegetable or something. I'd rather be rich, but have some sense with it so I could enjoy it."

Duran, however, felt no remorse. "If I did not do this to him," he told Plomo, "he would have done it to me."

* * *

Roberto Duran reveled in his "killer" image but on occasion he also tired of it. "I do not wish by any motive to have this public image," he told *La Critica*. "I am human and not invincible. When I was in front of the North American Ray Lampkin and I knew that he was in bad condition after the knockout, I prayed to God that he would recover soon."

Yet what he said and what he did were often at odds. After an easy knockout of Jose Peterson in Miami in June, he traveled to the Nicaraguan capital of Managua to face Pedro "El Toro" Mendoza. In Nicaragua, Duran met the despot Anastasio Somoza, who asked him to take it easy on his local opponent. "Somoza, the President of Nicaragua, invited Duran for a fight with another boxer they had at his weight," said Plomo. "But the President asked [Duran] to let him fight a bit, not to hurt him right at the beginning, so that he can show how he fights. This is what Somoza told Duran when he went to visit him at the presidential residency. So Duran told me what Somoza had told him, not to be too hard at the beginning. He liked to hear what I had to say about things. He knew I was right most of the times. And I told him this was not the right thing to do.

"In the end, this boxer, called El Toro, did not last long. After Duran had struck him twice, he fell down. Then a woman came to the ring, and Duran thought she was coming to greet him, for she called out his name. 'Duran,' she said, and suddenly, PAH, a terrible blow. She was a Nicaraguan woman, and when Duran moved away, she received the impact of this blow and fell down as well. At that moment all the Nicaraguan people outside got on the ring ready to beat us.

"They shouted that they wanted to get us because that man had hit a woman. The police were not there yet, and Duran and I were fighting against them, our backs stuck together. We fought there against those fanatics for about ten minutes until the police came. They rescued us and took us to the hotel. But then, while we were there, some two hundred people came and started shouting, 'We are going to kill this Duran, because he hit a woman.' We did not know what to do, we could only think of leaving. We had to leave using the back entrance at the hotel, hiding, towards Costa Rica. There were always flights leaving for Costa Rica. The people stayed there shouting in front of the hotel. They did not know we had left already. It was total madness what happened there. We could have faced a terrible problem."

The story quickly became yet another piece of the Duran legend, like the street fighting, the flattened horse and the "morgue" quote. Don King's publicist, Bobby Goodman, told a version in Alan Goldstein's *Fistful of Sugar*. "He's just an animal in the ring. I remember the time he knocked out Pedro Mendoza in one round. Some woman, I think it was Mendoza's wife, jumped in the ring and made a beeline for Duran. He just whirled around and flattened the broad with a right hand, better than the one he starched Mendoza with."

*La Critica* also had a feature on the melee. One of its correspondents in Managua reported, "The woman threw a punch at Duran…and he threw a punch, effectively knocking out the young woman." Another report named the woman as Eleanora Baca.

Carlos Eleta, however, disputed the adverse press reports. "A woman came running into the ring after the knockout," he said. "She started throwing punches and screaming at Duran. At first, he thought she was going to embrace him, but she kept using abusive language and swinging. Roberto put up his arms to protect himself and in the scuffle she fell down. That's all there was to it and I have the film to prove that Duran didn't throw a punch."

Duran also wouldn't admit it. "I never hit a woman, never in my life," he said. "Just swatted her away with the back of my hand."

★ ★ ★

With controversy dogging the champion, it was perhaps unfortunate that, after next knocking out one of the Acuna boxing family, Alirio, in three rounds in Panama, he had his first run-in with the abrasive Viruet brothers. Born in Areceibo, Puerto Rico, the Viruets had made New

York City their home. As quick with an insult as a jab, the cocky brothers – including Dorman, Edwin and Adolpho – cruised through the Big Apple's amateur scene, using the canvas as their dance floor.

"I dropped out of the school while in the eighth grade because I was impatient to become a boxer," Edwin told *The Ring*. He couldn't punch, but had a great left jab and a highly elusive, showboating style. He was 21-1-2 as a professional when he signed to meet Duran in a non-title fight in Uniondale, New York, on September 30, 1975. The Panama–Puerto Rico rivalry brought a 14,396 crowd to the Nassau Coliseum, breaking a box office record set by Frank Sinatra.

The old adage that styles make fights never held more weight. Tall, rangy and tricky, Viruet went through his full repertoire, dancing an Ali shuffle in the opening moments, tying up Duran and shaking his head after punches to show he wasn't hurt, sticking out his tongue at Duran's cornermen and generally infuriating the short-fused champion. Several times in the middle rounds he took off around the canvas, strutting like a man in a walking race, and in the tenth even jogged a lap of the ring, to wild applause from his supporters. Duran struggled to find a way past Viruet's long jab, but each of his punches was worth three of Viruet's gentle pats, and by the middle rounds he was landing solidly.

The judges were unimpressed with the showboating Puerto Rican and awarded Duran the unanimous decision. *Ring* reported that the bout "was a Sunday stroll for the champ once he changed his style and stopped dignifying Viruet's bag of running tricks by chasing him." Though the largely pro-Viruet crowd lustily booed the verdict for ten minutes, Duran had won hands-down from the sixth round onwards. Both men had words at the final bell, with Viruet telling Duran, "I can't even break an egg with my punches but you couldn't knock me out, and you're supposed to be a knockout puncher." Duran responded with a foul-mouthed tirade.

"Edwin frustrated the shit out of him that night," said Viruet's handler, Al Braverman. "Afterward, in the dressing troom, Duran came up to me and said, 'Why did you put that jumping jack in the ring? He should have stood there and fought me?'" But Braverman and Viruet knew what a fighter called Sugar Ray Leonard would later realize too; there was a way to frustrate Duran in the ring, to make him blow his top – and it might be the only way to beat him.

Duran was not the only person frustrated. A crowd of 7,000 attended the Revolution Stadium in Panama City to watch the bout on closed circuit, but when the picture failed to come through they started to smash up the place and the National Guard had to be summoned.

As the dominant fighter in his weight division, Duran was now regularly mooted for a possible "dream fight" against either junior welterweight champ Antonio "Pambele" Cervantes or WBC welterweight champ Jose Napoles. However, a rift between the two world sanctioning bodies put paid to the Napoles bout, while Cervantes, who had knocked out Duran's friend Peppermint Frazer, was deemed too dangerous by Carlos Eleta, thus ruling out what would have been built up as the greatest Colombia-Panama clash since Panama was liberated in 1903. "I didn't want to put Roberto in with him," admitted Eleta years later in Panama City. "He was a very dangerous fighter." Cervantes was a dark-skinned native of Palenque in Colombia, a village that produced an inordinate number of world champions. He was a masterful and highly experienced technician who had beaten Esteban DeJesus, Nicolino Locche and many other prominent fighters. The closest he came to fighting Duran was a run-in in the street when Cervantes was in Panama to fight Frazer.

"Duran knew he would win this fight, but I do not know why he did not want to fight it," said the ever-loyal Plomo. "It might have been because of the money. But let me tell you a bit about Cervantes. One day, Duran and I were walking in the street when we came across Cervantes. So Duran said he was going to show me Cervantes was afraid of him. 'What's up? When will we be fighting, you and I?' he said. To which Cervantes said they were going to fight when the fight was signed. Duran told him he was ready to fight right then and there, to which Cervantes answered he did not fight just like that, only for money. Duran, believing he was afraid, told him he was a coward. But this fight was never signed."

The Cervantes question surfaced years later in Panama. "Pambele was a very disciplined man," said Duran at a press conference. "To me, he was a slow boxer. Besides he was a boxer who would open up to anyone. And a man who opens up to Roberto, and who is very slow, I get him out quite quickly. I am not going to stand the beating, and I can hit better than Benitez and Frazer [both fought Cervantes]."

Given his oft-repeated antipathy towards Puerto Rican opponents, the Roberto Clemente Coliseum in Hato Rey seemed an odd choice for his next defense, especially against a local opponent. Unlike Edwin Viruet, whose quick feet stifled Duran, Leonico Ortiz suggested resilience through ignorance. His billboard back was wide and hairy, his legs were thick as a linebacker's and his nest beard as bushy as Serpico's. He looked like he'd keep plodding ahead even if you hurled a rock between his eyes.

Ortiz came into the ring on December 14, 1975 with an alleged 24-5-1 fight record. A southpaw and the father of four children, he adopted a peek-a-boo style and decided early that he would fight with his back against the ropes, perhaps in an attempt to tire out Duran. Even the most accomplished of pugilists weren't encouraged to adopt such a claustrophobic style. The ropes were best used as a place to force your opponent to. Only the great ones, most famously Muhammad Ali in his epic "Rumble in the Jungle" with George Foreman, could use them to advantage. As though fighting from the back seat of a car with a seatbelt strapped around his waist, Ortiz trapped himself in Duran's zone. "Occasionally the bewhiskered Ortiz would attempt to fight his way out of his uncomfortable situation," reported *Ring*, "but his spurts were short lived as the champion continued to wear his man down by the steadily exerted pressure and power of his gloves."

A Duran left hook and right uppercut jammed Ortiz's head back in the first round, delivering a message that he would pay for his mistakes. Ortiz landed a big left hand of his own at the end of the second round, but returned to his safety-net, the ropes in the third. For both boxers, many punches landed awkwardly on arms and shoulders. As if chopping down a tree, Duran took out a tiny piece of Ortiz in each round.

Remarkable recuperation bought Ortiz several more rounds, angering Duran in the process. Inside, Duran challenged himself to destroy the man; anything less was inexcusable. Ortiz rarely moved or jabbed. It was his wish to stand and deliver, and as the seconds ticked away in the seventh, a Duran hook along the ropes left Ortiz staring absently at the canvas. Ortiz collapsed and stayed parallel to the canvas, while throwing his hand into the air to locate anything to clinch. Somehow Ortiz survived the round.

At the bell for the tenth round, Freddie Brown held Duran back, then shoved him into the ring as a master would a fighting cock. Blood seeped from Ortiz's mouth as Duran's left hook landed flush. The champ slid away immediately, leaving his opponent's counter to whistle in the breeze. Although Ortiz showed life in the twelfth, and shoved Duran at the end of the following round, he took nearly twenty unanswered blows in the fourteenth.

Few men could withstand such a consistent beating. Trying to last the final three minutes, Ortiz couldn't escape a huge right hook which put him flat on his back. The ropes, no longer his friend, couldn't hold him anymore. He was counted out with only twenty-one seconds left in the fight; twenty-one seconds for Ortiz to explain to his children that one day he faced a monster and stood up to him. He rose to his feet, but too late to stop the ensuing celebration. Plomo extracted Duran's mouthpiece and the crowd surged from each corner as Duran leaned over the top rope to point at someone in the seats.

Some critics suggested that having made very heavy weather of stopping two skillful but relatively harmless men in Viruet and Ortiz, Duran had lost his motivation, and his next opponent was another man it was difficult to look good against. Saoul Mamby was a black Jew of Jamaican-Spanish descent who lived in New York.

Duran and Mamby had run together in Central Park and even sparred on occasion. "We had worked together when he was getting ready for DeJesus. I knew he was a very good fighter. Very strong, very sharp. He could box and he could punch. I remember he hit me with a right hand and the punch – the pain lasted for about three months, in my rib. And I still had to go and fight Antonio Cervantes after that." (Boxing Insider, 2/6/06)

Mamby, who had served as a soldier in Vietnam, cleaned windows and drove a gypsy cab in the Bronx to supplement his boxing income. He was the archetypal have-gloves-will-travel journeyman. With his green duffle bag slung over his shoulder, he turned up for short-notice bouts and drew the wrong end of hometown decisions. His cagey style was strictly for the purists, he was never seen on national television and was never in a position to object to the choice of opponent, or how much he was paid. But he could box, had beaten Benny Huertas and Doc McClendon and drawn with Edwin Viruet, and had never been knocked down. "Mamby boxed the way Sarah Vaughan weaved a melody," said Boxing Illustrated, "economical and exact, without flash."

After thirty-two fights, Mamby was a top-ten junior welterweight, yet he weighed in the lighter, at 138¾ pounds to Duran's 140, suggesting the Pananamian had not trained as he should. Mamby was aware that Duran had already signed to defend his title against Lou Bizzarro three weeks later, and took this as a sign of disrespect, as if Mamby was nothing more than a stepping stone.

They met in a ten-round non-title affair in front of 2,060 on May 4, 1976 in Miami Beach, Florida. Mamby needled him with a strict, decisive jab that annoyed and stung at the same time. Once again, it was persistence versus resistance.

Boxing historian Hank Kaplan had a ringside seat. "The turning point of the fight came in the sixth round," he wrote. "By design, Duran was out to destroy the body. Duran broke through Mamby's defenses and crashed left and right hooks to the body, which must have unsteadied him. Mamby made the battle close up to round six, but Duran showed why he is the most respected champion in the second half. The long distance does not seem to minimize his power, an attribute seldom seen…."

Referee Cy Gottfried scored the bout 48-44, while the judges' scores of 48-45 and 48-42 also saw it one-sided for the champ. Mamby, however, felt he "gave a good account of myself."

"I did that fight," said promoter Don Elbaum. "Even though Saoul might not admit it, he told me after that fight that he'd never been hit that hard in his life. Every punch hurt, he said. Duran could really hit."

Mamby also revealed a rarely seen side to Duran after the fight. "I was supposed to be an opponent and I got paid like one," said Mamby. "Would you believe I got only three thousand dollars for fighting a champion? When Duran heard about it, he chewed out the promoter and apologized to me."

Mamby would go on to win the WBC junior welterweight title and to defend it five times, but ended his long career with little money, partly, he claimed, because of Don King and his stepson Carl, who managed Mamby and for at least one fight managed his opponent too, a clear conflict of interest. US authorities even asked Mamby to participate in phone-tapping King during one of their periodic investigations of the controversial promoter but Mamby refused. He would box until the age of fifty-two and always remained a big Duran fan.

Four days later, twenty-five-year-old Esteban DeJesus became a world champion at his third attempt when he roundly outpointed Guts Ishimatsu of Japan over fifteen rounds in San Juan to take the WBC lightweight title. Ishimatsu had been tempted to Puerto Rico by a purse said to be $160,000 tax free, a record for the lightweight class, and the decision against him was overwhelming. Puerto Rico's boxing boom matched that of Panama. DeJesus was now one of four concurrent Puerto Rican world champions, and his win set up the mouth-watering prospect of a rubber match with Duran to unify the two rival versions of the lightweight championship.

## 10

# "LIKE A MAN WITH NO HEART"

> *Has anybody here seen Roberto Duran?*
> *I met him once yeah I shook his hand*
> *I looked in his eyes and now I understand*
> *The love and the anger in the eyes of Roberto Duran*
>
> Tom Russell, " The Eyes of Roberto Duran"

THE RUST BELT city of Erie, Pennsylvania, was a boxing backwater and so seemed an odd choice for Roberto Duran's first title defense in the United States. His opponent was the Italian-born, American-raised Lou Bizzarro, and their fight was originally set for the wealthy European principality of Monaco, but CBS bought the television rights and moved the fight to Erie, Bizzarro's adopted hometown, to fit its schedules. Duran and his entourage had the hardest time even finding the place.

"We were driving to Pennsylvania and we couldn't find the boxing commission," said Carlos Eleta. "It was three or four days before the fight and the commission disappeared. So I call Ray [Arcel] and tell him what happened. Nobody knows anything. So I call Jose Sulaiman in Mexico and tell him I need some advice because I don't know what is going on. They were going to name their own referee and judges. This wasn't the real commission, but they weren't doing anything because they were planting a lot of money on Bizzarro to go fifteen rounds."

The problem with the state boxing commission arose when co-promoter Don King moved the bout to a Sunday to fit the prime-time TV slot. "Back in those days in Pennsylvania they had the 'blue laws,' where there was no professional boxing on a Sunday," explained Lou Bizzarro. "The fight was supposed to be on Saturday, but King changed it to that Sunday and knew that the fight would be outlawed, and if I won I wouldn't get the belt because the Pennsylvania State Athletic Commission wasn't involved. King was going to do it his way. But what was I going to do? I wanted the fight." The blue laws, a legacy of the state's Puritan past, forbade certain activities on Sundays, such as liquor sales and boxing matches.

Sanctioned or not, the title fight had the city buzzing. "It was the biggest thing ever in Erie," said King's co-promoter, Don Elbaum. "We paid him about $125,000 for him and King. It was either that or Duran got $125,000 and King got $10,000. We thought we could steal the title."

After getting lost in Erie trying to find the commission, the Duran camp was then astonished to see the boxing ring that Elbaum had erected. Bizzarro was a noted "runner" and so the bigger the ring, the better his chances. "The day before the fight, we go to see the ring and it was like one for a bull fighter," said Eleta. "It was huge, so Bizzarro would run all over the ring. They didn't even have any cushion, all they had was a table and the canvas, all so he could run – and he did. The only problem was that because there was no padding, Bizzarro got blisters on his feet." Seeking any advantage for his fighter, Elbaum had apparently found a ring big enough for Bizzarro and all his family. "It was the biggest ring ever made," admitted Elbaum. "I actually had a thirty-foot ring built. When Ray Arcel came in with Duran, he looked at the ring and then looked right at me and said, 'I thought you had class.'"

Eleta joked, "I didn't believe in the mafia until I saw that ring."

Lou Bizzarro, however, dismisses the stories as yet another boxing myth and says he has the evidence next to him every day of his life. "The ring was twenty-four by twenty-four feet," he said. "I know because I still have it sitting in my restaurant."

Born near Naples in 1948, Bizzarro had moved with his family to the USA soon after. His brother Johnny built the family boxing name while facing and losing to lightweight greats like Carlos Ortiz and Flash Elorde, and skinny young Lou followed him into the pro ranks without having a single amateur fight. Sparring with his highly ranked brother and others had already given him a thorough grounding in the game. "Not having any amateur fights actually made my career go faster," he said. "By that time, I had gotten a lot of good ring work and felt I could handle some of the top fighters in the world."

A sometime Sears model, the good-looking Italian prospect went undefeated in his first twenty-four fights. With wins over common Duran opponents Hector Matta and Benny Huertas, Bizzarro used both those fights as a measurement of how he'd fare against the great Duran. "Huertas was a tough kid who hit hard and walked right through you and threw bombs," said Bizzarro. "In fact, he hurt Duran before getting knocked out. Matta was a slick kid and when I beat him it moved me into the top ten."

Lou was a local hero in the small, blue-collar city, and talked up his chances to the press. "I look at it this way," he told reporters. "Duran is only human like anyone else." But having previously visited the notorious Fifth Street Gym in Miami, he knew what he was up against – a twenty-four-year-old terror already considered by some to be the best fighter, pound-for-pound, in the world.

"I knew Roberto because he was the talk of the Miami Beach Gym," said Bizzarro. "He was knocking out middleweights with sixteen-ounce gloves and headgear. He'd just kick them right out of the gym. And he was sparring with the toughest guys from Miami. He was just so vicious that nobody wanted to get in the ring with him anymore. When you got into the ring with him, he was your enemy. It was a fight every time, just a fight to get him off of you."

Most notoriously, Duran flattened Vinnie Curto, a middleweight contender, in the Miami gym. "Sure, he knocked down Curto," said trainer Angelo Dundee, whose brother Chris ran the gym. "Roberto used to always work with bigger guys. I couldn't believe what happened, so when he came down from the ring I checked his gloves. Roberto was wearing these old, old, heavy gloves and they were all water soaked. I changed them immediately and he got back in the ring."

Bizzarro had spoken to Curto about the incident. "Vinny was a real slick boxer. He told me that every time Duran hit him, it hurt. And that was when Curto was a nice, nineteen-year-old prospect. [Duran] couldn't separate between the gym and the ring. It was always a fight. Then, there were the guys called gym fighters who were the toughest guys during sparring, but fell apart when they got in the real bouts."

Stories of Duran's prowess were becoming legendary. There was another one about a middleweight who sparred with him at the Fifth Street Gym and wanted to take it easy because of his greater weight, but Duran insisted they slug it out. "Holy Christ!" said the middleweight. "He hit me on my left arm so hard I couldn't use it for a week. If those punches had landed on my ribs, I would have been knocked out."

Duran was also said to have flattened a highly rated welterweight in a Puerto Rican gym.

A dignified, classy guy who cared about others, Bizzarro had never met anyone quite like Stone Hands. "I brought Duran in a week ahead of time and we had a press conference," Elbaum recalled. "Louie was 24–0 and at the press conference he was all dressed up. He was a good-looking, handsome kid. He got up and he was thanking everybody from the mayor down to the sponsors, me, and then he looked at Roberto and he said, 'Thank you, Mister Duran.' It was so … I get sick, it was too sugary. But this was Louie. Nice, nice, nice.

"Lou sat down, and Duran got up and said ten words in Spanish and sat down. Luis Henriquez, his translator, started shaking his head, and the sportscaster Al Abrams asked what he said. And Henriquez said, 'He said he would send him home in an ambulance.'"

Bizzarro remembered a similar Duran. "I saw him a couple days before the fight at the press conference. Oh, he was vicious. He wanted to kill me before the fight. He didn't say much, but it was more the way he would look at you and stare you down. You have to remember that Duran wasn't a pleasant guy to be around. He was a mean guy."

Unfortunately for the Erie contingent of 4,500 fans who arrived on May 22, 1976 stealing the title was probably the only way they would get it off Duran. Built like a character from a video game, Bizzarro was a spaghetti-thin boxer whose legs moved too fast for his body. His game plan was to lace up his boots and circle that ring until the final bell. Duran didn't like dancers. Anyone willing to move and get out of harm's way affronted Duran's *machismo*, and a man not willing to trade in the middle of the ring, or at least make an effort to fight, was a *payaso*, or clown.

As Duran has admitted on several occasions, he felt nervous in the moments before the fight began. Expectation weighed on him. "Something's wrong if you're a fighter and you're not nervous when you go up to the ring," said Bizzarro. "Before every fight I had butter-flies. But as soon as the bell rings, they go away."

From the first round, Bizzarro took off, and Duran had a weary look as he tried to cut off the ring. How long could Bizzarro run and hide? Shaking his shoulders back and forth, Duran moved in a cool fluency, fully aware that the motor would eventually quit on Bizzarro. "He could go backwards faster than anyone could go forward," Elbaum recalled. "And I felt we had a helluva shot to get a decision, especially in his hometown."

As the bell sounded at the end of the second round, Duran hurt Bizzarro with an uppercut to the chin. Bizzarro stumbled as he located the corner. Whether it was after the bell or just a punch Bizzarro wasn't ready for, the damage was done. "It was a little overwhelming for me, absolutely," said Bizzarro. "It was a dream of mine. I beat him and the money rolls in. But it was all too much for me at the time.

"In the second round, I knew I was hurt when he hit me with a punch after the bell. I made a mistake by dropping my hands. Don [Elbaum] had told me to be ready for anything with this guy and not to drop my hands in the clinch. As soon as I did it for the first time, 'Boom,' he gets me. It took me four rounds to recuperate."

The third man in the ring that evening was Puerto Rican referee Waldemar Schmidt. "In the seventh round, I hit Duran with a right hand and knocked him down, and Schmidt called it a slip," claimed Bizzarro. "It happened again in the eighth with a hook and he called it a slip again. I couldn't believe it when he was talking to Duran in Spanish. Elbaum thought he was going to be German, and that's why he OK'd him. It turns out that the guy is from Puerto Rico."

In the clinches, Duran and Bizzarro held a running dialogue. Duran also raked his gloves across Bizzarro's no longer model face and hit him late. A left-right-left combo dumped Bizzarro for a count of nine in the tenth, and he was on the floor again before the end of the round. Surprisingly Bizzarro came back to have his best round in the eleventh, but it was his last throw of the dice. "I didn't want the referee to stop the fight," he said. "I came back and beat him in the eleventh round."

Heeding his camp's advice, Bizzarro sketched a circle around Duran. It was a strategy implemented in training which made his handlers seem like geniuses for the first ten rounds. However, it was a strategy plagued by inconsistency. When people searched for weaknesses in Duran's repertoire, the holes were so slight that they had to invent their own. Buchanan's trainer Gil Clancy was guilty of this, and Elbaum wasn't far behind. Duran threw so many punches with so much force behind each one that it seemed an impossible feat for any boxer to keep up the pace. Elbaum thought Duran would burn out by the late rounds. Others had made the same mistake. "Don told me that Duran would start fading by the tenth round, but I don't know what he was talking about," said Bizzarro. "If anything, I started to fade. He would never fade the entire fight. Duran hurt me from the second round on."

Duran closed the gap considerably as Bizzarro slowed, and in the fourteenth he finally cornered his man. "Late in the round a savage right uppercut sent Bizzarro reeling onto the ropes and referee Schmidt gave him a standing eight count," reported *Boxing News*. "Another right dropped Bizzarro for six, and Schmidt continued the count to eight before waving Duran in for the finish. A tremendous right to the head made Bizzarro's legs fold under him, and he lay on his back without moving as he was counted out."

Though just one second remained in the round, many spectators believed the fight should have been stopped before the final knockout. Elbaum wasn't one of them. "No, because he was hurt but he wasn't out on his feet," said the promoter, "even though it was a situation where his brother Johnny wanted to stop it, he was running up the steps to stop it and I had to grab him and we were wrestling on the ground outside the ring so he wouldn't stop the fight."

In fact, the end came so suddenly that there was little time for intervention. "I didn't see Johnny running up to the ring," Bizzarro remembered. "All my focus was on Duran. That was just my brother looking out for me. He had been in there before and knew everything that Duran was doing. But I was fine. The only problem was that the new shoes I bought gave me blisters down to the bone. I couldn't walk for weeks after the fight."

Duran eventually made his way over to the fallen fighter, arriving with his hands extended. At that moment, Bizzarro looked anything but a male model. "The challenger fought the first nine rounds with his legs, and the last five with his heart," summed up *Boxing News*.

"The one thing that angered me the most was that they were taking Bizzarro around as if he were the world champion, in a very expensive and fashionable car. And I was given no importance at all," said Duran. "That is why I was so angry that I did not want to win; I wanted to kill him. The referee should have stopped that fight but even the referee was against me. There was the entire Italian colony there, all against me. When I knocked him down [the referee] did nothing so I asked him what was going on, but he refused to act. That was one of my best knockouts."

Duran would find his way back to Erie years later, in his career twilight. Through manager Mike Acri, Bizzarro and Duran still get together. Bizzarro would have an uneventful end to his career but followed Duran's never-ending saga.

* * *

Duran next took on the tough Colombian Emiliano Villa on July 31, 1976. Villa had just given junior welterweight champion Wilfred Benitez a surprisingly hard fight and was 25-3-1 coming into the bout. Duran took two months to prepare.

"Villa was a huge Colombian boxer," said Plomo. "During the fight, Duran hit him and Villa fell down and made a turn on the floor, and stood up again. Everyone was very surprised to see the impact of the blow. He decided to go on fighting, but then Duran hit his liver, and with a cross to the head he knocked him down. But the first fall had been incredible. He was already on the floor, rolled down, and stood up again. That had never been seen before."

Villa appeared to jump like a kangaroo after being hit. Years later, Duran was watching a replay of the bout on his big screen TV in Panama City; he fiddled with the reception so the seventh-round knockout comes in perfectly. As the punch landed, a "Chucha madre," a common Panamanian slang was heard from across the room. Hesitating as if waiting for someone to remind him that he was hurt, Villa stared at Duran for a long second, and then dropped. Villa was down on both knees when the referee stopped the bout. "One of my best knockouts was the Colombian," said Duran. "I gave him a blow like this, pah! The guy fell down, gave a complete turn, and ended up standing up. The referee did not know whether to count or not."

Next stop was the Hollywood Arena in California on October 15, 1976 and title challenger Alvaro Rojas. Nearly 6,100 fans gathered for a fight card billed as "Night of the Knockouts" in which Duran's bout was part of a CBS-TV double-header featuring heavyweight George Foreman in the main event. It was another chance for American television viewers to get a look at this lightweight king who knocked everybody out, and Duran didn't disappoint.

"He had this thing about him," said fight promoter Butch Lewis. "He had that beard, that Manchu thing, and the guy used to look like the devil. He had the black coal eyes and the hair. When Duran walked in the press conference with his chest out, [Rojas] just stepped aside. Al Braverman was like, 'Don't move out of the guy's way, you're letting him know.'" The champion had few doubts about the outcome. "This fight will end," he told one interviewer, "when I connect." *BN* 8.10.76

Rojas, from Costa Rica, was a poor challenger. A press kit distributed to boxing reporters had his win-loss statistics as 26-8, with twenty stoppage wins, but this was questionable. He had certainly beaten one former world champion, Clemente Sanchez, but lost to the few other name boxers he had fought, including former WBC champ Guts Ishimatsu, who had stopped him in the fourteenth round of a title defence in Tokyo. Yet he was conveniently rated tenth in the world by the WBA so he could qualify to fight Duran for the title. *Ring* magazine called it "a gross mismatch."

The champion, clean-shaven for the bout and as handsome as a matinee idol, had trained at Gleason's Gym in Manhattan and looked as big and strong as a welterweight. He hurt Rojas with the first right hand he landed, and thereafter it was only a matter of time. Rojas made the mistake of trying to trade punches, and at 2:17 of the first round was spreadeagled face down on the canvas, like a cartoon figure that had fallen from a high building, after another crushing right to the chin. As the referee counted him out, Duran, standing in a neutral corner, spotted Esteban DeJesus in the crowd and ducked between the ropes to berate him, shouting, "I want you next."

Duran was paid $125,000 or nearly $65,000 per minute of work. With every strand of his slicked-back hair still in place, there was little evidence that Duran had just earned a night's pay. "I was in very good condition. I hit him in the *pecho*," Duran told an interviewer in the ring while Rojas was still lying flat on his back. A guy with a cigarette dangling from the side of his mouth handed Duran a flag, which he waved at the crowd. Another fight, another body in his wake and Duran was off. Carlos Eleta hurried to give Duran an ice cream cone in the dressing room afterwards. "I told Duran not to worry about the title but about the ice cream," said Eleta. "It worked."

The boxing fraternity was impressed. "Duran could be the man American boxing so desperately needs to revive interest in the divisions other than heavyweight," said *Boxing International*.

Duran's next bout was on another Don King show that February, this time at the Fountainbleu Hotel in Miami Beach, on an indoor tennis court in front of just 1,200 spectators. His opponent was Vilomar Fernandez, a short, feisty challenger born in Santo Domingo in the Dominican Republic but fighting out of the Bronx. Fernandez's record was an unimpressive 19-5-1, with only eight knockouts, but he was a good boxer. It was the first defense of Duran's title reign that had not been transmitted to Panama.

Despite his lack of power, Fernandez was deft at pinpointing Duran's head as the champion bulled in. It was no one-sided affair as Fernandez, a water-bug skirting the ring, often moved to his right, paused, then changed direction. His peek-a-boo, in-and-out style kept him out of harm's way as the rounds ticked off.

In round five, however, as Fernandez was once again backpedaling, Panamanian referee Sergio Ley interceded and warned him to start throwing punches. Fernandez fought bravely for the remainder of the fight, as if Ley's warning forced Fernandez to abandon an effective style to stand in front of Duran. Does a referee have the right to tell a fighter that his brand of fighting, although effective, isn't what the fans want to see?

"The doctor who treated me that fight was Doctor Pacheco, who was a good friend of Eleta's," said Duran. "I had a problem with the liver and the spleen and after examining me he said he was going to give me a shot for my liver to prevent damage in the spleen. He gave me the shot and I fell asleep. Then I heard when Pacheco was telling Fernandez, 'Strike underneath, underneath, his liver is in bad condition.' And I thought he was telling this to me, so I kept hitting him in the liver. I then knocked him down with two strong blows."

Although capable of knocking out anyone with his straight right, Duran's opponents also had to be aware of his left hook and right uppercut. In the thirteenth round, Duran came out with hooks to the body. However, most of the round was a demonstration on the clinch-and-hold tactic displayed by the Bronx challenger. Duran finally released a left hook to the liver followed by a token right to the chest that sat a dejected Fernandez down in a corner. Ley counted him out as he sat there with his head slumped. Seconds later, Duran slung his arm around his opponent's shoulder, consoling him like a younger brother.

After the bout was stopped in the thirteenth, a group of reporters huddled around Roberto in the middle of the ring. After telling one reporter that Fernandez was a smart fighter who knew how to move effectively, Duran also explained how he was cold until the eighth round when he started to look for the knockout punch.

Then, in a spontaneous act that Duran rarely showed in fight inter-views, he started speaking English for the reporter. In the middle of the ring, Duran took the microphone when it seemed to everyone that he was clearly done speaking. "Gracias, thank you, thank you," said Duran. Then, came a free-flow of emotion that made more sense to Duran than the befuddled commentator. "Too much jab, too much jab for me. Tired for me, needed rest. Move, move, move, me knock him out." His spontaneity was refreshing. Obviously frustrated with what he wanted to convey to the audience, the fight also elicited similar frustrations.

★ ★ ★

Still looming in Muhammad Ali's shadow, Duran fought Javier Muniz in May at the Civic Centre in Washington, DC. Fighting on the undercard of the Ali-Alfredo Evangelista card, Duran didn't allow the lack of notoriety to get to him.

"I'm not hurt that much anymore," Duran told a *Washington Post* reporter before the non-title affair. "The most important thing is that I perform better than anyone else in the ring." Muniz, a heavy-machine operator, tried to console himself before the showdown. "I know Duran will come at me with a brick in each hand," he said. "It's an eerie feeling, knowing his experience, his reputation, but you can't back out. You tell yourself that he can't hit you with a third arm." Duran won a wide ten-round decision.

Two non-title wins – over Muniz and Bernardo Diaz by one-round knockout in August – set up Duran's eleventh title defense and a true grudge match. He headed back to Philadelphia to take on Edwin Viruet at the Spectrum, on 17 September 1977. Duran – who was 59-1 with fifty KOs – couldn't afford to let Viruet mess with his head again. This was the Puerto Rican who had slapped him outside the ring after his bout with Leoncio Ortiz; Duran vomited street curses whenever he neared. This was more than hype to sell tickets; the disdain was real for both fighters. The fight was co-promoted by J. Russell Peltz and Don King and Duran-Viruet was the main event, while Philly's Matt Franklin-Billy Douglas was the semi-final bout. Viruet, who had lost only two of his twenty-eight bouts but won only eight inside the distance, worked out at Passyunk Gym in South Philadelphia; Duran would train at Joe Frazier's Gym at the corner of Broad and Elmwood in North Philly and did his roadwork with local fighter Youngblood Williams.

"Duran is cold, like a man with no heart," Williams told a Philadelphia reporter. "When we run he says things like, 'I keel that s.o.b.' or just, 'Keel him, keel him.' He says it over and over. Once, a dog was standing down the road and Roberto says to me that if that dog don't move out of the way, we gonna kill him. He wasn't kidding man."

Williams, who served several jail stints, spent time playing dominoes and shooting dice with Duran. He was undefeated at the time and had earned a reputation for inner-city sparring wars with Philly's elite. "Duran runs for one hour, then stops in one place and, for about ten or fifteen minutes, just keeps throwing some of the fastest damn combinations I've ever seen," he said, two days before the bout. "Closest I ever saw in an American was Tyrone Everett. But I believe Duran is quicker with his hands than Tyrone was. He may be the meanest man I ever saw. I really do believe he don't mind hurting people."

More than most, Duran hated to be shown up in the ring. Trainers Paddy Flood and Al Braverman handled Viruet, while Duran had his usual cornermen in Brown and Arcel. Although Viruet had no problem treating Duran with the same contempt with which he treated other opponents, he also was an evasive fighter whose technique drew raves from boxing purists. His skill came not from the blue-collar work of a one-dimensional fighter but from natural instincts, sharpened on city street corners. People either enjoyed or reviled this "cute" style.

The weigh-in heightened the tension. It was held at the Spectrum's Ovations Club, and the weights were recorded the day before the fight, which wasn't common at that time; the weigh-in usually was conducted at noon on the day of the fight, and the switch thoroughly upset Viruet's camp, which was distressed by the fact that Duran would gain his strength back in the hours before the bout. The change was made because the fight was being televised on a Saturday afternoon rather than in the evening. Duran had no problem with the schedule change and weighed in at 134½; Viruet was nowhere to be found. An hour and a half later he supposedly made 135 pounds, dodging a fine by the commission.

"He eventually showed up, but they put him right on and yanked him off the scale," said Peltz. "Al Braverman did. And I don't know if he was with King at the time, but he was definitely with Viruet. He had trouble making weight, I remember."

"Viruet never made the weight," Duran recalled. "He never weighed in. He went to go lose weight and he never came back to weigh in. Both Eleta and Flacco [Duran's interpreter and helper] fell asleep on that one. The important thing was that they wanted me to fight."

Plomo concurred, "He did not get on the scale. Is the champion supposed to get on the scale but not the rival? I believe Carlos Eleta was to blame there. No manager can accept that his own boxer gets on the scale and the other one does not. But Eleta was a terrible guy."

Roberto Duran's mother Clara Samaniego (left) with unidentified female relative.

Victorino Vargas, Duran's step-father.

The young "Cholo," a handsome and cocky streetfighter.

Ismael Laguna, lightweight champion and hero to all Panamanian boxers.

Ken Buchanan slumps against the ropes after being hit below the belt to end their their WBA lightweight title fight in controversial circumstances in 1972. *Photo: Action Images*.

An emotional champion celebrates the Buchanan victory with trainers Plomo Quinones (left) and Freddie Brown (right).

Esteban DeJesus hands Duran his first loss in a non-title ten-rounder in New York. The two would stage a gripping three-fight feud.

Promoter Don King signed Duran at a time when boxing needed a new star. They would work together on some of the biggest fights of the era. *Photo: Empics.*

New York took the young Panamanian firebrand to its hard heart and he packed the famous Gleason's Gym whenever he trained.

The trappings of success: a 680-pound pet lion named Walla (left), and an entourage that included his own interpreter, right-hand man Luis "Flacco Bala" Henriques (above).

Beating Carlos Palomino in one of his greatest performances. Duran (left) was relentless against the tough former welterweight champion at Madison Square Garden in 1979.
*Photo: Associated Press.*

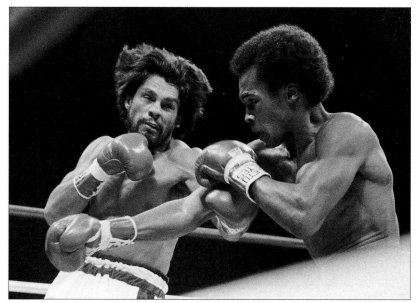

Action from Duran's classic first bout against the brilliant Sugar Ray Leonard for the WBC welterweight title. The smaller man was relentless and took a hotly-disputed decision. Their second bout, however, would end in ignominy. *Photo: Corbis.*

Duran's training routine was a thing of beauty. He turned rope-skipping (right) into an art form, and sometimes even hit the speedball (left) with his head.

With faithful trainer Nestor "Plomo" Quinones, who understood his moods and passions. *Photo: Arturo LeConte.*

While the fight officials dealt with the weigh-in, there was another problem. "The most fun we had with that fight was with King's canvas. He uses the canvas with his big logo," said Peltz. "We had the Spectrum and had a reputation for having a great arena. I didn't want King's logo in the center. So I decided … I told them to put our logo on the canvas. When they sent King's logo on that Thursday we had it shipped over to JFK Stadium, and had some guy scribble his initials on it and hide it somewhere. A day before the fight they couldn't find the canvas and I was like, 'Geez, we might have to use ours.' He sent Richie Giachetti down to my office and he stayed there the whole day trying to locate that canvas. He said I got some paper here, but you couldn't even read the name of the guy who signed for it.

"We finally used our canvas and we got it on national television because that was a touchy subject in those days, what could and couldn't get on TV. When the show was over, I saw King and he was wearing a crème-colored three-piece suit with all these frills on it like George Washington. He pointed at me and said, 'I know you fucked around with the canvas. I can't prove it, but I know.' We uncovered it the next day and got it back to him.

"The good thing about King in those days was that he could only deliver the main event. Anybody else that he put on the show, he would have to pay for. I expected a decent crowd, but I think we sold like 7,500, but 7,000 in advance. I didn't understand it because Duran was big in New York and they would come to Philly for the fight."

The fight was picked up by ABC for home TV broadcast, and King needed a venue. In the early 1970s, Peltz and company had been drawing big crowds at the Spectrum. Peltz would pay King a site fee, and expected to use Duran as the bait. "The day of the fight we thought we'd sell another 7,000 or at least 3 or 4,000 like we were doing," Peltz recalled. "But we only sold five hundred. The problem with the Duran fight was that something happened with the scale and ABC-TV was going to pull the plug the day of the fight. Jay Seidman came up to me before the fight and told me ABC wasn't going to televise the fight. He said, 'They think that there's some kind of shenanigans going on.' It didn't make sense because I didn't understand why they would care if Viruet made the weight or not. We went into a room with Howard Cosell, Alex Wallau and maybe Chet Forte was in the room. There had to be some big shots from ABC and they just wanted to pull the plug. I was pleading with them they just couldn't do that. Alex was telling them how I was an honest guy and everything.

"The first fight started and the people were coming up to me, and Alex came up to me and said, 'We just got it settled.' I was shaking and I couldn't even button my shirt. He fixed my tie and was like dressing me at ringside. The card was anticlimactic. I didn't have Duran losing that fight, but it was a tough fight to get into."

The fight also had its moments of farce. Viruet would dance, stick his face forward and pull it back, laugh at the disdain on Duran's face, pull his version of the Ali Shuffle, and hold his left straight out to keep Duran at arm's length. He seemed to be enjoying himself, but it was the champion who was landing the meaningful punches. "That was the thing with Viruet," said boxing writer J.R. Jowett, who covered the bout. "He would do all these cutesy moves, but he couldn't punch worth shit. It just wasn't a good style to watch and I didn't give him many rounds against Duran." Philly sportswriter Ray Didinger called Viruet's antics the equivalent of a "fly circling a lion's mouth."

Viruet did two things that other boxers tried, but didn't produce the same effects: First, he stood up to Duran following the unwritten Latin code of machismo; then he made him miss. DeJesus did the same thing, but he could also make Duran pay for his mistakes. *He talk too much obscene*, Duran would say about Edwin.

During the fight, as Viruet ridiculed Duran, another problem arose. "The doctors gave Roberto something before that fight that affected him a lot, trying to reduce too much weight," Eleta said. "Because of that medicine, he lost energy." At times it showed. "They gave me this injection to get stronger and faster," said Duran, "an injection that they gave to horses, and I almost died. I turned red and pale at the same time. I had to do fifteen rounds with Viruet that night. My strength and my know-how kept me from being knocked out."

Duran took more risks and landed the harder punches. Although Viruet did open a slight cut under Duran's left eye toward the end of the fight, he was by then a long way behind on points. After taking heavy punishment in the final round, Viruet complained about the decision. Venezuela's Isidro Rodriguez had it 73-68, Panama's Sergio Ley, 73-65, and Pennsylvania judge Frank Adams 71-65, all for Duran.

Felicidad had by now become a steady influence as a boxing wife. While some partners detest the fight game, Felicidad dabbled in promotions, understood the boxer's psyche and knew when to come and when to stay away during training. She often ran in the morning with Roberto and even went into the gym to make sure he was in condition. She also became a loud presence during fights, shrieking encouragement and instructions to her man. "My presence encourages him during the tedious ambience of his rigorous training," she eloquently told one reporter.

Duran himself was at ringside to watch a compatriot fight for a world title in Los Angeles that November. Jorge Lujan was born in Colon four years after Duran and grew up watching the fighters in the teeming gym known as the Box of Matches. "Colon was the cradle of champions," he said. "I think so because of the beach, the ocean, the sun, fighting five or six times a day in the streets." He eventually found himself sparring with the bigger Duran. "Duran would practice like it was the real fight. He was more heavy than me. I told him, 'Don't hit me!' Then, bam, bam, bam, and he hit hard. But I still had to fight against those boxers."

Lujan's life would become a cautionary tale and showed the path Duran could easily have followed. Before facing Alfonso Zamora for the WBA bantamweight title, he was stuck in prison on Coiba Island for forty-five days for a drug offense. They had to get him out of jail so he could fight. "I was a flyweight when I went into jail," he said. "When I left Coiba I had gained weight, so I had a fight at bantamweight." The brash young Panamanian took on Zamora, a pocket rocket, and tamed him, taking his crown in the tenth round. He noticed that the champion was breathing heavily by the eighth round and knocked him down with a left hook that had all his strength behind it. It paved the way for the finish two rounds later. "I believed that I could win that bout because I was a counter-puncher and Zamora, a Mexican, came to me," said Lujan. "The place was filled with Mexicans, but I was cool, not scared of anything. I had faith in myself for that bout. I hit him with a right hand, adios."

People immediately began to treat Lujan differently. "The boxing journalists wouldn't let me sleep," said Lujan. "Everybody wanted to talk to me, champion of the world. I was very happy. Before, when I used to fight and win, it was tranquilo or cool. Now, 'Hey, Lujan, knock, knock, are you home?' I didn't want to talk with anybody. I was very tired. I had trouble dealing with the fame. You don't have any privacy, everyone is like, 'Hey Champ, hey champ.' The drinking, the women, there is no privacy when you are champion. They don't write anything when you are no longer champ."

Ismael Laguna noticed the difference. "He was doing drugs, cocaine, all the time," said the former champ. "He was in and out of jail. One time I bought and was working at a kiosk, and I gave Lujan twenty dollars to get change for me. I turn around and I never saw the guy again. He went to buy drugs.

"Another time I had a table at one of the fights, and we were sitting with President Omar Torrijos and Rafael Ortega came up to ask Torrijos for money. Ortega was always like that, asking people to help him out. Torrijos pulled out a hundred dollars and gave it to him. Ortega started to jump up and down, 'Thank you, thank you.' Lujan had been drinking heavily, and yelled to Torrijos, 'I never asked you for *pinga* [dick].' I was so mad I just walked away from the table. He talked that way to the President."

These were the pitfalls Duran had so far avoided. Now he was heading into his biggest bout, a date with destiny that would decide who was the undisputed champion.

# 11

## ESTEBAN AND THE WITCH DOCTORS

*"Duran said he would KO God if he had to."*

Miguelito Callist, Panamanian boxer

AT THE START of 1978, only two of boxing's thirteen weight divisions had single, undisputed champions. The split between the WBA and the WBC meant each had its own champion at every weight except heavyweight (Muhammad Ali) and middleweight (Rodrigo Valdes). This unsatisfactory state of affairs often saw two talented "champions" avoiding each other, both content to make money against lesser opponents rather than risk all against someone of comparable ability. When two rival champs did clash, the prospect was usually mouth-watering for boxing fans, but politics and money meant it rarely happened.

Few of these confrontations were more eagerly awaited than a rubber between Roberto Duran, the WBA champ, and Esteban DeJesus, the WBC champ. Both held a win over the other, and since winning his title DeJesus had made three defenses and shown fine form. He was the only lightweight left in the world with a realistic prospect of beating Duran.

The parties finally agreed to do it one more time in the desert resort of Las Vegas. The combination of super-casinos, high-rolling gamblers and major boxing promotions was beginning to shift the sport's centre of gravity to the desert town, and over the next two decades many of the biggest bouts would be held there.

Before heading to Vegas, Eleta made plans. He knew that his fighter's worst fault was his occasional lack of training and so duped him into beginning his preparations early. "It was a problem because when he was in Panama, people always wanted to be near him," said Eleta. "My trick was that I told him there was a tune-up in Panama before DeJesus, so that he would start training hard. When I told him that it had been called off, he just looked at me and smiled." Duran, already in trim for the non-existent tune-up, was then sent to training camp in Los Angeles. This was DeJesus, and anything less than full strength wouldn't cut it.

Duran was noted for sparring hard, and he broke the nose of sparring partner Mike "Youngblood" Williams, the undefeated middleweight from Philadelphia. He then decided to break in another young prospect, Jorge "Kid Dynamite" Morales, a DeJesus acolyte. What started out as a training session quickly turned into fisticuffs.

"Well, Dinamita Morales is Puerto Rican," said Plomo. "We started training in Los Angeles, and while we were there at the gym, Dinamita always wanted to train with Duran. He would ask him to fight against him every day, provoking him. One day, when there was no one who could train with Duran, Dinamita was there and started to provoke him again. Dinamita's father was also there and he started saying, 'Can you see, Dinamita, he is afraid, because he knows Puerto Ricans are stronger than Panamanians.' So Duran told me he was going to train with him, if that was okay with me, and I agreed.

"He hit Dinamita so strongly that one felt sorry for him. Even his father came up to the ring, trying to stop the fight. I told him to go away, but since he refused I kicked him and hurt his eyebrow. They claimed it was Duran who had hit him, and put him to trial. In the end, he was made to pay thirty thousand dollars, despite the fact that I had been the one who had injured him. I always take good care of my boxers. If anyone wants to start a problem with one of them, I am ready to defend him."

Promoter Don Chargin had walked into the gym moments after the incident. "They had known each other before and there was a problem with the workouts and there was an argument in the gym. You know how everybody, when they boxed with Duran, would try to work a little harder because he was a mean guy. Even in the gym he was like that. One thing led to another and I think they threw a couple punches after that. His father came up to the ring too, but it wasn't anything real bad," said Chargin.

Though promoting the fight as the "Combat Zone," Don King was not pleased at Duran's involvement in the unscripted spat. "He could have been injured seriously," King told *Sports Illustrated*. "What else can happen before this fight? It was a job just to get the managers of the fighters to even think about a match. They had fought twice and neither wanted to fight a third time. First, I convinced DeJesus. But the hard part was convincing Eleta. Then, when we did agree, trying to find a site that pleased him was impossible. One place was too cold; the next was too hot. A third place, somewhere in Africa, was okay, but then Eleta didn't think he could get Duran's money out. He finally said yes to Las Vegas."

The *Los Angeles Herald-Examiner* profiled Duran the week before the bout. The report would not have made pleasant reading for DeJesus and his camp:

> A speed bag in the Main Street gym, shattered by the lightweight champion's brutality, had to be replaced. So did a sparring partner for much the same reason.
>
> Sylvester Stallone, the Oscar winner who is filming across the street, spends most every lunch break at 318½ So. Main. So do scores of others. Some bring cameras. They have been drawn to the gymnasium by a Panamanian prizefighter who took the nickname of Rocky because guys named Graziano and Marciano made it fashionable.
>
> He is Roberto Duran, the WBA lightweight title holder of five and a half years, who exudes a sort of animalism like perhaps no other fighter. You get an insight into Duran's feral ring style while watching him in the gym. He remains a destroyer because he works at it. Savagery is his business.

The reporter interviewed sparring partner Youngblood, who had been sent for because "he can't hurt me"; Youngblood was two stones heavier than Duran. "The man is one of a kind," he said. "If he sparred with anybody his own size in the gym, he would knock 'em dead. Duran is a nice person outside the ring. But when you work with him, it's like working with an animal. I think one reason he's so vicious in the ring is because he takes fighting so seriously. He's not like any American fighter I've seen. His work is like a crusade."

Duran clearly enjoyed his training sessions and played to the crowd, pummeling Youngblood, cursing and growling at the heavy bag, then punching the speed bag into a blur before battering it with his head – an exercise, he claimed, to strengthen his neck muscles. "He concludes his routine with rope jumping," said the *Examiner*. "It, too, is accentuated by savage sounds. He has the rope going so swiftly at one point it seems he is only rocking back and forth on his feet. The rope somehow passes under."

Duran's friend and longtime aide-de-camp Luis Henriquez related the story of a meeting Duran had had a couple of years before with General Torrijos. The Central American strongman wanted Duran to pose for a joke photograph while stretched on the floor, to look as though the general had kayoed him. Duran politely refused. Lying down was one thing he wouldn't do in jest, even for the dictator. "He seems to look on the arena as a place to kill or be killed," added Henriquez, "and he is not about to get killed." Life had made Duran that way. In classic Duran style, he told a reporter that if DeJesus got up this time, he would send him right back down. He meant it.

First, though, he had to deal with the *brujos* again. Duran's fear of witches and wizards had been instilled by his mother, who would suggest her own counter-measures to evil spells. "We're standing in the ring before the fight trying to choose a corner," said Eleta. "There were lights in the one corner and it would have made Roberto too hot during the fight, so we picked the other one. But that was not good for Roberto because 'the *brujos* told him to change corners.' I told him that I talked with the witches and they said it was okay. He believed in that stuff. That was Roberto."

The Caesar's Palace Sports Pavilion sold out for the fight, which was telecast by CBS. On January 21, 1978, the Hollywood stars came out. In one ringside seat was Sylvester Stallone, while not far away was the Chairman of the Board himself, Frank Sinatra. "Sinatra used to invite him to his suite at the end of the matches," said Plomo. "There were many movie actors that used to invite him. Had Duran been a North American boxer, he would still be a rich man. Americans know how to value what is worth giving value." Sinatra wasn't a Duran favorite; he once gave the legendary crooner a pair of gloves and Sinatra looked at them and just threw them to one side. Olympic gold medalist Sugar Ray Leonard was also at ringside, already assessing Duran as a future opponent.

DeJesus trained until the final day before the fight due to weight problems. Duran made $250,000 to DeJesus's $150,000. For bettors, Duran went from a 2-1 to a 7-5 favorite before the fight. Both fighters struggled to make the lightweight limit, though DeJesus finally came in a full pound under it. They clashed at the weigh-in, with DeJesus jibing in Spanish, "You're too weak at that weight. I'm going to murder you."

Scuffling broke out between their handlers and Don King's frustrations rose to his hair's height.

"With the Puerto Ricans we started a great fight," said Plomo. "An uncle of Duran's, a very heavy man, a logger [fought]. It was a very big fight, and four Puerto Ricans fell down. Esteban tried to deceive Duran, but Duran reacted at once and only touched him, and Esteban fell on a chair. Duran told him he'd rather restrain them, for he was going to get him that night during the fight. The only person who got hurt was Duran's uncle, who was beaten by four of them. Duran told him that he was going to beat him badly that night, and it was not a lie."

In the six years since he lost that first fight to DeJesus, Duran had convinced himself that no one would beat him. Consequently, no one did. "I didn't respect anybody," Duran said. "Boxing to me was a joke, I didn't give a damn about boxing. The third time I fought with DeJesus, I caught him and began to understand his style. I learned it when DeJesus fought Antonio Cervantes. When Pambele boxed DeJesus he didn't know what to do. A lot of Panamanians were in favor of DeJesus and I was even in his corner. When I saw that Pambele started to box him, I said, 'Look, there is DeJesus' defect.' He lost, time goes by and then he wins the title from Ishimatsu.

"I find him in Miami training for a fight and he is putting wraps on his hand. You could tell he was having trouble with the weight, to the point where he didn't even want to talk. He was having a terrible time. When a man's hungry he doesn't have any strength. I tell Plomo that this guy is passing Cain and Abel. When I get the third fight I knew I had to box him. DeJesus gets these witches and they come up to me and ask, 'What's going to happen when DeJesus knocks you out?' I tell the woman that I'm going to knock the hell out of DeJesus. He's not man enough to knock me out. I'm going to knock him out with all of his witchcraft. I told him that I could even knock him out if I was drunk."

They stood across from each other for the last time. They had shared an ongoing dialogue in the argot of the streets but now it was no longer about Puerto Rico and Panama anymore, just two fabulous boxers who dominated a division they were both outgrowing. Duran kept his distance at the opening bell, jabbing and moving away from that familiar left hook. DeJesus also hesitated to engage. Neither fighter wanted to rush to battle.

The fight erupted in round three. Duran pounded DeJesus with his signature right hand to the head, followed him to the ropes but let him off. DeJesus returned fire and pasted Duran with a right of his own. Still, the men couldn't equal the pace of the rematch.

Snarling and sneering, Duran barged DeJesus around and shook him again in the sixth with a barrage of thudding hooks. DeJesus fell into Duran's waiting arms from the force of the punches, the weary look on his face was unforgettable. Bruises loomed on his cheek and on his eye. Duran refused to let up, but DeJesus took his best punches and danced away from any serious damage.

The most telling punch of the night landed in round ten, a magnificent right that sent DeJesus and his *brujos* back into a corner. It was only a matter of time before Duran caught up with his opponent. Going into the eleventh, the judges – one from the WBA, one from the WBC and one from the Nevada commission – had Duran comfortably ahead. DeJesus, however, was brave, and landed his best punch of the night, a left uppercut to the jaw that unbalanced Duran.

The Puerto Rican tried to follow up in the twelfth but a right to the chin – thrown seconds before his own right hand – sent DeJesus down. He began to paw helplessly, trying to grasp a rope, anything. In Panama people would refer to it as *puso a gatear*, pawing like a cat. It seemed DeJesus did not want to go on, but referee Buddy Basilico stared hard at him and felt he could continue.

These two fearless men had engaged in a boxing trilogy so macho and yet so cerebral that it touched the highest peak of the Noble Art. Now the end was nearing. DeJesus regained his feet and seconds later walked into another right hand. Duran's next eleven punches connected as DeJesus lay expressionless along the ropes, as if praying that Basilico would step in. After the first nine punches connected, DeJesus lazily slumped into the ropes. Duran landed two more vicious shots before DeJesus handler Manny Sciaca entered the ring. Surprisingly, Basilico, with back turned, had still not stopped the slaughter. The fight was stopped at 2:32 of the twelfth round. "I cannot erase the loss," said Duran. "But tonight I erased DeJesus."

He was, finally, the undisputed lightweight champion of the world. He had also equalled the record of twelve successful defenses set by the Joe Brown. His jubilation did not stop him engaging in a brief brawl in the ring with DeJesus' brother, which was quickly broken up. "I knew I had the fight in the seventh round when I punched him in the throat," said Duran later. "I could have knocked him out earlier, but I felt that I must fight cautiously because I had not fought for a long time.

DeJesus was best in the early rounds but after that I was able to make him miss a lot."

It marked the end of a three-fight feud steeped in Latin lore, where two men forged mutual respect through bitter conflict. It is the nature for boxers to fight, hug and forget. In forgiveness they form a brotherhood. Though not ranked among the very greatest Puerto Rican fighters, DeJesus was well respected in boxing. "He had a lot of fans," said Jose Torres, the former world champion from Puerto Rico who became a journalist in the USA. "In Puerto Rico, they love all the champions. But when you lose, you also lose that popularity."

Esteban DeJesus' last fight was a losing bid for the junior welterweight title in July 1980. By then, he was in the grip of drug addiction, having graduated from marijuana to shooting up speedballs of cocaine and heroin, sharing needles with his older brother Enrique and friends. "In general, you start first with friends and you get so wrapped up with the drugs that before you know it you're hooked," he later told Puerto Rican TV. "They take you to parties and you start using the stuff. The worst part is when you open your eyes. It's too late. You're already addicted."

On November 27, 1980, DeJesus mainlined coke before getting in his car to drive to a family celebration. On the way, he became embroiled in a traffic dispute with eighteen-year-old Robert Cintron Gonzalez, and leapt from his car brandishing a .25 caliber pistol. DeJesus shot the teenager in the head. He died four days later. DeJesus was subsequently convicted of first-degree murder and jailed for life.

In 1985, his brother Enrique died of AIDS. Having shared needles with him, Esteban took a test and found that he, too, had the dreaded disease. His *brujos* could not save him now; nothing could. As his health deteriorated, his jail sentence was commuted to allow him to receive treatment at the House for the Re-education of Addicts, an old milk factory. There he lay on a bed in a room with eighteen men, all former addicts dying from AIDS. Prayer was their only hope.

Days from the end, DeJesus fell to skin and bone. But before his body and will gave way, DeJesus had one last, face-to-face meeting with his old foe. Duran, who had regularly disparaged – and beaten – Puerto Ricans, was not a popular figure in the country, but when a call came that Esteban was dying, the instinctive generosity of spirit that was as much a part of him as macho bluster quickly emerged.

"There was a man who was always around DeJesus who told me

that he was dying of AIDS," said Duran. "He said, 'I need you to go see him because he could pass away any minute.' We go to a place, the jail is here and DeJesus is staying across the street from it. When I see him there so thin, my tears run out because he used to be a pretty formed, muscular guy. I start crying and I hug him, and I kiss him and I tell my daughter to kiss him. That was when I won over the Puerto Rican public."

Duran did more than win over Puerto Rico with the gesture: a love for Duran was culled through his fearless response to this mysterious disease. Jose Torres used to run into Duran at Victor's Café, a popular Cuban restaurant and Duran's favorite hangout, on fight weekends in New York City. Torres knew firsthand about death in the ring. He was there to see Benny "Kid" Paret when the beating he suffered against Emile Griffith in March 1962 left him in a coma from which he would never awake. Torres would drive Paret's wife back and forth from the hospital to see the fallen fighter before his death ten days after the fight.

Almost two decades on, Torres was caught in death's web again. "When DeJesus was dying in Puerto Rico, I went to see him," Torres recalled. "Duran went that same day. Duran walked to the bed and embraced him in the bed. He was dying and he embraced the man. You knew he was dying of AIDS, so I would not get that close because we didn't know that much about AIDS at the time. We knew that you could get it from anybody. I was very concerned about that. He just walked over to him and just lifted him out of the bed. I will never forget that. That made Duran for me as one of the nicest human beings I've ever met. That attitude there, that move.

"I wrote about DeJesus for the *New York Post*, a piece about that experience. This is the first time I talk about it since then. It's funny because every fighter has that compassion. I think that anybody can be that way; you don't have to be a fighter."

Fight promoter Butch Lewis added, "He went to the hospital and visited the guy when nobody knew about AIDS. At this time it was like the polio scare in the nineteen-fifties. Everyone was like, 'What is AIDS?' He went to the hospital, held his hand and everything. I'll always remember that. I thought, who would be brave enough? As tough as he was, deep down he had an affectionate side to him. It seems all guys who are so violent in the ring have that side to them."

DeJesus succumbed on 13 March 1987. His death was reported briefly in the London *Times*: "Esteban DeJesus, the former world-class boxer, who has died at the age of 37 of AIDS, contracting the disease by using an infected needle to support his drug habit in prison, was the only man to beat Roberto Duran in the 70s."

Even in death, they were linked.

\* \* \*

On 27 April 1978, Duran faced Adolpho Viruet, brother of Edwin, at Madison Square Garden. It was stipulated that Adolpho had to weigh under the agreed 143-pound limit. Duran, at 142, was at his heaviest since Javier Muniz in May 1977. He had not fought at the Garden for almost five and a half years and 17,125 fans, the largest crowd there since Ali beat Frazier in 1974, paid $275,366 to see him. Duran would take home a tax-free purse of $100,000 while Viruet managed $15,000. Viruet, a southpaw, told a New York reporter, "We both came from the same place, the streets. The Bronx, Panama, it's the same thing. You still have to rumble with your hands."

It was Duran who came to rumble. Referee Arthur Mercante warned him for being dangerous with his head and instructed the judges to take the seventh round away from him for hitting low. It made no difference in the result as Duran attacked his southpaw opponent from the opening bell and stayed on top of him for the whole fight, his feet flat on the canvas so he was always set to punch *behind* his full weight. After avoiding Duran for the first five rounds, Viruet became more aggressive but didn't have the firepower to keep him off. He did land a cracking left to the Panamanian's jaw in the seventh, and made him miss hugely with a right uppercut, while Edwin Viruet at ringside led a large Puerto Rican contingent in cheering his brother and abusing Duran in Spanish, but neither Adolpho nor his voluble older sibling could punch hard enough to defeat a fighter of Duran's caliber. The decision was unanimous in Duran's favour. Afterwards Edwin climbed into the ring and Duran calmly walked over and gave him a heavy shove. Edwin squared up before the cornermen intervened and blue-shirted security police got between the two camps.

"Edwin was much tougher," said Duran afterwards. "All Adolpho did tonight was run and complain about my hitting him with low blows. I've fought guys on a bicycle, but this guy was on a motorcycle." Years later, from atop his apartment building in New York City, Adolpho seemed to be delusional about the result. "I don't want to say nothing about ref and judge but to me they all crooks. I beat Duran but Duran's got connections."

Rumors spread of a possible showdown with junior lightweight champ Alexis Arguello, but the negotiations failed. While Arguello was moving up to the lightweight division, Duran was abandoning it. "It was promotions," said Arguello. "They never signed nothing; it was only talking. It would have been a great fight, but we moved to higher weight classes.

"I met him after I won my first title from Ruben Olivares. He's a good person who carries himself really well. There's nothing that I saw that he behaved badly except one time when I was invited by Don King to fight in Vegas. I was in the lobby of Caesar's Palace and he came up to me and I thought he was coming to say hello. Instead he was pushing me and pushing me, telling me to sign the contract or he would kill me. I told Duran, 'I'm a serious person. Don't push me.' That was the only rough encounter I had with Duran. In my heart I think he was one of the greatest lightweights in boxing history."

Arguello, from Nicaragua, was diplomatic but always felt that he had the tools to take Duran. "Latin fighters are tough fighters with big hearts and courage, especially Duran. In Latin America, there has been a variety of styles. For example, Miguel Canto of Mexico was a great boxer; Monzon, from Argentina, was a heavy hitter with a good heart; Duran was short, but a heavy puncher with good movement, good head movement and combinations. I don't want to disrespect a great fighter. What I can tell you is that it would have been a great clash. It would have been a collision where we both don't know … I could say that I would have won and he could say he could beat me. Time catches up to all of us in the sport of boxing. It's something that a friend of mine used to tell me, 'What you do when you enter, they do to you when you go out.' That's life. We're born, we live and we die."

At the end of July 1978, it was reported that Duran had broken two fingers on his right hand in a car accident in Panama and would be out until October. Conflicting reports suggested a thumb injury, others said that Duran was feigning for commercial reasons, presumably so he would not yet have to surrender his lightweight titles, which increased his marquee value while he fought non-title bouts.

Duran went back to Panama after defeating Viruet, gained yet more weight and prepared to fight light-middleweight Ezequiel Obando on September 1, 1978. It would reveal if Duran looked comfortable at the higher weight and if his punches were destructive against a bigger man. Duran came in on the welterweight limit of 147 pounds while Obando was four pounds over at 151.

"Obando was a guy with huge muscles, tall and looked like he was a bodybuilder," said Duran. "Eleta tells me, 'I want you to fight him anyway because I want people to see you.' I said, 'Give me the fight, I don't give a damn.' When the guy comes into the ring he wants to impress me with his physique. He wanted to knock me out, but he didn't know that I could hit that hard. He came in again and my hand was already in the air ready to catch him. I hit him so hard with one punch that you could have counted up to a thousand and he wouldn't have gotten back up." Duran needed only two rounds to dispose of Obando, who was too green to give him a test.

Having cleaned up his division and run out of credible challengers, Duran issued a statement that October from Panama City, possibly at the behest of the publicity-minded Don King, in which he challenged "all the champions in the other divisions, from bantamweight up to middleweight, to fight me." The statement went on, "I'll fight them over the weight, for my title or for theirs. This challenge goes for champions like Carlos Zarate, Wilfredo Gomez, Danny Lopez, Alexis Arguello, Pipino Cuevas, Carlos Palomino, Samuel Serrano, Saensak Muangsurin, Antonio Cervantes and Rocky Mattioli. I'd like to become the first man in history to win four different world titles. The welterweight, junior welterweight and junior middleweight titles are all within my reach."

Don King's grip on the heavyweight crown had loosened and he needed a new global star. Duran was it. King had lost the inside track with heavyweight champion Muhammad Ali after a failed attempt to drive a wedge between Ali and his manager, Herbert Muhammad, and consequently missed out on some of the biggest fight promotions of the late Seventies. At the same time, many of the sport's names now came from outside the United States, including the imperious Carlos Monzon and the classy Alexis Arguello. Duran was probably the most saleable of them all to US TV audiences, provided the right opponents could be found.

On November 4, newspapers reported that Duran had signed a four-fight contract worth $500,000 with Madison Square Garden. His first appearance was due against light-welterweight Monroe Brooks, followed by a defense of his lightweight title aganst leading WBA contender Alfredo Pitalua, then a fight against light-welterweight champion Antonio Cervantes, and finally a challenge to welterweight champion Carlos Palomino. That, at least, was the plan.

\* \* \*

First up was the ranking black boxer Monroe Brooks, at the Garden on December 8. A streetfighter in his youth, Brooks was ready for the challenge. "I had no fear of him," said Brooks. "I didn't care if it was the Hands of Stone, the Hands of Walls or anything. If I could I'd fight him again right now, I would. I love the man. He was good for boxing."

Brooks was born in Midland, Texas, and was introduced to the fight game at the age of nine through a relative. "I had a cousin who lived a house down from me and he used to have a bag hanging from a tree. He would just hit the bag every now and then, and he would go to the park and there would be a bunch of guys who would put the gloves and box. I got to the point to where I wouldn't do what he told me. One day I follow him and he said, 'I'm going to stop your little ass.'" His cousin forced him to box the other neighborhood youths. "I whupped all of them. He made me box every one of them, and he was so shocked because I was so young.

"I heard about a gym that was starting up and I wanted to go see this boxing gym. I snuck away from home, walked in and I told the coach I wanted to box. There must have been a hundred kids in the gym and I pointed them out and said, 'I can whup all these boys.'"

The coach, Sergeant Hamilton, responded the same way Plomo had to an enthusiastic young Duran. He explained that boxing could not be picked up without proper training. Hamilton had seen many youngsters arrive at the gym willing to fight, only to vanish at the first sign of violence. "He just so happened to have three sons who boxed," said Brooks. "So I whipped his three sons, and everyone else they put in front of me. I just realized I was already a fighter. If you hit me I was going to hit you back. I was a fighter on the street."

The meanest cats on the block don't always make the best boxers, but Brooks learned his craft during eight years as an amateur and would go on to win forty-eight fights as a pro, thirty-three by knockout, and to hold a North American Boxing Federation title. He drew inspiration from an unlikely source. "My mom would beat up anybody," he said. "She was a fighter who took nothing from nobody on the streets or off the streets. She raised six kids by herself. My mother always came to my fights. If there was a fight in town my mother was going to be there. That's where I got my fighting from, my mom."

Brooks beat so many Mexican opponents that he was labeled "the Mexican Killer." He remembered, "The hardest puncher was Rudy Barro, a Filipino. Let me put it this way; after that fight I said to myself, 'Damn, you take a good punch.' Every time this guy hit me it felt like a truck running into me. Not just a truck, a Mack truck."

After losing to Adolpho Viruet, Brooks realized he was battling more than his opponents. "I realized that I was anemic. I actually think I lost three fights from being anemic. I know I lost my world title fight for being anemic. I couldn't get off with punches and do things that I could always do. I was shocked to be beat by a boxer like that. I didn't know exactly, but I found out when I fought for the world title. In fact I almost died."

Brooks traveled to the Far East to challenge for the light-welterweight championship. "In Thailand, my blood was so low that they could hardly find a pulse for me. I beat the boy nine rounds straight and they stopped the fight because they said I was too tired to finish," Brooks recalled. "I was going to make that fifteenth round but they didn't want me to come through with that title. I beat that boy pitiful.

"I started losing energy from about the seventh round. Everything started to become blurry to me and it was like I was drunk. I told my trainer that something wasn't right. But he didn't know I was anemic, and there was nothing we could do about it. He was just giving me instructions to fight. I fought like a champion. After that fight I stayed positive all through my boxing career. If a person is going to lose their positive thoughts, they should just quit before they get hurt."

Brooks, who boxed at light-welterweight (junior welterweight), was also stepping up in weight. "I actually had to pick up seven pounds to fight Duran. I didn't feel as if I lost any strength. What I did to mess up my fight with Duran was I pulled a muscle sparring with Wilfred Benitez in New York. I told Jackie McCoy about it at the time. He said, 'Let's go home. Let's get on the plane.' And I said, 'No, Jackie, you pull me out of this fight and there's going to be a fight between me and you.' I didn't have no fear of Duran. He couldn't intimidate me. I was the one who had the mouth." Back at the Garden, his old stomping grounds, Duran weighed in at 147, surprisingly heavier than Brooks at 143, and was even bigger by the time he entered the ring. To many boxing scribes, the Panamanian was too short, too small, and was making a tactical mistake in jumping up two weight categories.

On December 8, 1978 at the Garden, Duran had two things to prove: that he could punch and take a punch in the 147-pound class. He answered accordingly as he nailed the taller, wiry strong Brooks with a left hook as the first round ended. Then, after absorbing some sharp punches from Brooks, he began to methodically chop him down. In the fourth, Duran almost completely submerged his right into Brooks' face, and in the sixth he ferociously spun Brooks' head with a jarring left hook.

After punishing Brooks for the first seven rounds, Duran forced him against the ropes and landed a left hook with the force of a bat hitting a tree. The manner in which he set up Brooks was magnificent, as he perfectly positioned his body to the left of Brooks, assuming that there would be a slight opening under his right arm. There was and Duran delivered the decisive blow to the body. Brooks slumped to the canvas, and Mercante threw up his arms and halted the bout as the fighter reached his feet. The victory was official at 1:59 of round eight.

The damage might have come sooner had Duran not had to suffer mightily to lose twenty-one pounds from his 168-pound frame during training. Even the critics admitted that Duran was a legitimate welter-weight contender. "Something told me that I was watching greatness," said boxing analyst Steve Farhood, who covered the bout. "Basically he kicked the crap out of a world class fighter."

At least Brooks had refused to run, and twenty-five years later could still hold his head high. "You have to box, box, box Duran," he said. "You know Duran was more of a slugger but he had some boxing tech-nique also. I had the boxing skills that were phenomenal and I felt I had enough to do what I had to do. Anemia didn't play any part, not in this fight." Were there any weaknesses in Duran? "The only weakness I felt was in me." Later a security guard at a high school in Los Angeles, Brooks still thinks of Duran. Fighting him was an "honor," but he has one last wish for his Panamanian friend: "Man, Duran better not ever get hit by Rudy Barro."

In April, Duran walked through the game Jimmy Heair, veteran of ninety bouts, to win a unanimous decision in Vegas. The rugged, blond-haired Tennessee native, who had never been knocked down, took an awful beating but somehow stayed on his feet till the end. "I have never seen anything more brutal than that in all of my years," said commen-tator Howard Cosell. Nit-pickers complained that Duran's punch was not as percussive as it had been and that he should have stopped Heair. People held him to the highest standard. He was an all-time great and fans expected him to fight like one every time he got in the ring.

It was clear that, despite the four-fight program mapped out for him, Duran was going to relinquish his lightweight title. Both the WBA and the WBC had ordered him to make his next defense against different contenders – Alfredo Pitalua and Jim Watt respectively. Not only was that impossible, but he had also outgrown the weight. At the zenith of his profession, he abandoned his WBC and WBA titles in January 1979. His future lay with bigger men. No longer would he always be the strongest man in the ring, or punch the hardest, or have the scariest reputation. He was about to head into the toughest division in boxing.

# 12

## "THE MONSTER'S LOOSE"

*"I wanted to graduate, win a world title and retire by thirty."*

Carlos Palomino

EVERY TIME DURAN hit New York he created a spectacle, whether he was playing softball in Central Park or piling into a steak at Victor's Café 52, surrounded by acolytes. He had grown fond of Gotham and the city embraced him. Raucous crowds of Latin well-wishers flocked to his training sessions, while actors, singers and famous athletes sought his company. .

"When I won the world championship, the Yankees invited me to the clubhouse," said Duran. "The pitcher Luis Tiant … gave me passes and shirts and everything from the locker room. The game wasn't started yet, but Reggie Jackson told me he was going to dedicate a home run to me and after the game he would give me the bat. I said, 'Okay,' and he hit the home run. At the end of the game he called me to the locker room and said, 'Remember what I told you? This is the bat and I want to give it to you. But I want you to know something. When I hit that home run I cracked the bat.' He gave it to me and I carried it back to Panama. Someone eventually stole it from me."

In his huge white cap, satin baseball jacket, massive shades and gong-sized medallions, the young prizefighter was every inch the *barrio* star, swaggering into Gleason's Gym to a pounding ghettoblaster or stopping traffic as he signed autographs and posed for photos on the sidewalk. His favorite hangout was Victor's, which would relocate in 1980 from Columbus and 71st Street to West 52nd Street in midtown Manhattan. It was owned by Victor del Corral, who became a great friend of Duran's, and was a popular haunt for budding TV, film and music stars.

Now the most feared fighter, pound for pound, in the world, Duran was reaching the peak of his popularity when he signed to fight former welterweight champion Carlos Palomino. The welterweight division was entering perhaps the most thrilling phase in its history and Duran was about to assault a division full of glamor, danger, intrigue and money. Chance had thrown up four of the most exciting young boxers ever to compete together in one weight class at the same time. The WBA champion, Pipino "the Assassin" Cuevas, was a daunting Mexican puncher of almost criminal ferocity, a butcher of challengers. The WBC champion was Puerto Rican *wunderkind* Wilfred Benitez, a defensive wizard of bewildering virtuosity. And fast rising through the ranks were two prodigious contenders: Olympic gold medallist Sugar Ray Leonard, a showboating genius, and the menacing Detroit knockout artist Thomas Hearns. Amazingly, as of February 1979 Leonard was the oldest of the quartet at twenty-two; Cuevas had just turned twenty-one, while Benitez and Hearns were only twenty. Together, this fearsome foursome promised a decade of ferocious competition.

Not to be forgotten was Palomino, who Benitez had recently deposed. Rugged and experienced, a fierce body puncher with great stamina, he was a formidable obstacle to anyone seeking welterweight glory. Palomino was the second of eleven boys born in a small town in the state of Sonora, Mexico. Life was frugal but his mother drummed ambition into him, and after crossing the border to Los Angeles to find work he took up boxing. His amateur career blossomed after he joined the US Army and he won All-Army and All-Service titles and almost made the 1972 Olympic team before turning pro. In 1976, he accomplished his first goal by knocking out Britain's John Stracey for the WBC welterweight title. In the same year, Palomino walked down the aisle to accept a diploma in recreational administration from Long Beach State University.

Palomino treated boxing as a profession, one he pursued with dedication but never loved. He had three goals: graduate from college, win a world welterweight championship, and retire by age thirty, and with two of them accomplished he was already planning for a career once his ring days were over. He dabbled in acting, including an appearance in the popular TV comedy series *Taxi*.

A stand-still hard-hitter who would go into the trenches, the moustachioed Mexican successfully defended his title seven times but suffered two lengthy layoffs due to bone cracks in his right hand and had been inactive for eight months when he took on Benitez in January 1979. Not only did he face one of the world's finest instinctive fighters but also he was in Benitez's backyard. "No doubt in my mind that going into the Benitez fight that I had to knock this guy out," said Palomino. "I had seen too many times where a Mexican guy came to Puerto Rico and got a bad decision. I didn't even want to go there, but the WBC made me go. The fight was outdoors and there was a canopy over the ring. It was so hot that I lost fourteen pounds of water in that fight. All my fights had been in Vegas and LA inside the auditorium, so I was not used to this weather."

Palomino claims he hurt his opponent several times. "One of my sparring partners told me later that Benitez said he was going to quit in the third round, that Benitez went back to his corner and said, 'This guy hits too hard.'" Minutes later, trainer Gregorio Benitez slapped his son's face as he sent him out at the start of a round. It might have won him the title. "I guess it woke him up because Benitez jabbed and stayed alive for the rest of the fight," said Palomino. "Benitez had no real punching power, but he was the best defensive fighter I ever fought. It was like he had a sixth sense. He knew every punch I would throw before I threw it."

As Palomino sat disconsolately in his dressing room after the bout, promoter Bob Arum came in and promised him a return bout. But the WBC would never honor his rematch clause. Instead, Palomino was offered $250,000 to fight an elimination bout with Duran, with the victor to face Benitez. "I was psyched for Duran and I prepared for a twelve-rounder," said Palomino. "At the time, people were saying that he didn't hit as hard as a welterweight. I knew it would be difficult but I thought I could overcome it with my punching power." In the run-up to the Duran bout, however, Palomino learned that Wilfred Benitez signed to defend his title against Sugar Ray Leonard rather than give him a rematch. "That took the wind out of my sails," said Palomino. "I didn't want to wait around and win a non-title bout."

Ready for the charades Duran often played at press conferences, Palomino was surprised when they actually met. "I told my manager that if Duran tried to start anything at the weigh-in, I was going balls-out on the spot. I was not going to take anything. Before the bout, he comes up to me and shakes my hand. He tells me how much respect he has for me as a fighter. Then he asked me for an autograph for his son. To this day we hug when we see each other."

Asking another boxer for his autograph may have seemed out of character for the Chorrillo wildman, but warmth and generosity were as much a part of him as the myopic brutality he employed in the ring. His close friends were more familiar with the playful Roberto than the beast that surfaced at fight time. Duran's training sessions weren't without the occasional flashes of his darker side, however. Journalist John Garfield was watching in the Howard Albert Gym in the Garment Center when, with admirers crowding into the training area, Duran went into the ring to shadowbox. "Somebody in the back kept yelling in Spanish, 'Pipino Cuevas will kill you.' Duran paid him no mind and continued to shadowbox," wrote Garfield. "But the heckler was relentless. Finally, Duran whirled on the heckler and leaned over the top strand of the ropes, right above where the mothers and children were worshiping him, and he pulled down his trunks and grabbed his nuts and yelled at the heckler in Spanish, 'Pipino Cuevas can suck my cock.'"

Palomino, who was 27-2-3 coming into the bout, doubted that Duran would be as effective at the higher weight and thought he would lose both power and speed. Duran, however, was the 7–5 favourite. The bill-topper was Larry Holmes's heavyweight title defense against Mike Weaver, which would provide its own drama, but for most of the 14,136 crowd Duran was the attraction. As the Garden faithful took their seats on 22 June 1979 and the boxers met in ring center for their instructions, Duran rocked back and forth on his feet while Palomino stood immobile. Duran stared hard at his opponent and received no response. The fighters listened to referee Carlos Padilla's instructions, touched gloves and headed back to their corners.

Duran had come to fight, which had not always been the case in recent contests. Those in attendance could see the difference in the way he moved, as if to the addictively sassy rhythm of a salsa. He knew Palomino was good and that he was a barrier to the millions of dollars with Leonard, and that meant he needed to find his groove straight from the bell. And he did. "Although he didn't have devastating punching power, his quickness really surprised me," said Palomino. "I never really got hurt but he was so shifty, used angles and was in such a defensive mode that it took away from my offensive mode."

Duran deliberately stood with his back to the ropes in the second round. He turned his man into his punches, rested his head beside Palomino's ear to gain leverage, scraped his skull along Palomino's brows, shortened his blows to make maximum use of the space and doubled up with hooks to the head and body – all against the ropes. It was a superb display of in-fighting, and it was only the beginning. One second Palomino had the man ripe for an uppercut, then he was gone. In contrast Duran would lock his opponent's left arm and follow with a right uppercut, an old trick, or *truco* in Spanish, that worked for him throughout the fight.

Duran struck with such speed and power that at times Palomino bent over, wincing in pain. He faked the right hand to set up other punches and had Palomino flinching from these feints like a boy reflexively jumping back from the strength of an older brother. Yet, with his right hand up by his face, he remained both conscious and respectful of Palomino's left hook. In other fights, Duran would hold his guard low, showing contempt.

In the fourth round, the salsa continued. Duran landed a right uppercut, which turned into a left hook, straight right combination, and jolted back Palomino's head. He survived another big right in the middle of the ring in the next round, and in the sixth was set up beautifully when Duran again faked the right, causing him to jerk back his head. When the punch didn't come, Palomino straightened up, only to find the right hand coming *now*. It laid him on his back with a thud.

Palomino quickly pushed himself up. He was stunned but not hurt, and took the mandatory eight-count. While chasing Palomino around the ring, Duran planted a right to the liver, but couldn't stop the former champ. After the bell sounded for the sixth to end the onslaught, a weary Palomino headed to his corner. A broadcaster compared Duran to "Krakatoa about to explode," but Palomino shook off the knockdown and came back strong the next round.

Nobody hid in the final round. It wasn't in either man's nature. Latin fighters fought in a culture where reputation meant everything. "It was a ten-round war," said Palomino. "I came back to my corner in the ninth round and they told me that I had to go out and take it to him. So I went right after Duran in the tenth."

As the final bell sounded, Palomino put his glove into Duran's midsection as a gesture of respect, but Duran was too busy raising his hands to notice. Then he fell to his knees, and still not noticing Palomino's extended glove, turned to the crowd for the acclaim he deserved. The referee and two judges all scored 99-90 to Duran, meaning he had won nine rounds and shared one. It was an utterly comprehensive victory over one of the finest welterweights in the world.

"I was a big Palomino fan and ... he just made Palomino look like a novice," said boxing writer Steve Farhood. "Palomino was flinching when Duran would fake a punch. I had never seen that before. Palomino was never in the fight and maybe he won one round. I don't want to call Palomino a great fighter, but he was almost on that level."

By the end, Duran had Palomino's full respect. "He outboxed me every round and outhustled me the entire fight," said the Mexican. "It was the only fight that I didn't feel mentally or physically ready for. Duran and Benitez were the best defensive fighters I faced. They were notches above anyone else. After that fight, I told them that Duran would be champ of the world again, if he fights Leonard like he did against me. I had respect for him before the bout but so much more after."

It had been a great fight, lacking the changes of fortune of the very best but providing a masterclass in in-fighting, punching and conditioning. *Boxing News* called it "a wonderful fight, a fight of a life-time."

Celebrations were muted, however, when Duran was told the bad news about a friend. He was told in a New York hotel lobby of the death of Chaflan, his gypsy Svengali from the old days, killed by a car. One reporter remembered seeing Chaflan at a store opening in Caledonia. "Candido Diaz was Chaflan, not Superman," remarked one paper. "Because of this he was unable to resist the impact of the vehicle that hit him."

Duran broke down and cried. "They wouldn't tell me until after the Palomino fight," he said. "They said that Chaflan was killed by a car. I cried a lot. He knew me since I was around seven or eight years old. Chaflan built a tree house and we would all sleep up there until four a.m. and then go get a ticket for the newspapers. He was never a mean person to children. With a dollar he would take you to eat or to the movies. Later he was accused of being a pervert and that he would corrupt children but I never saw that and I don't believe it."

Many newspapers now carried planted publicity about Duran challenging the winner of the Wilfred Benitez-Ray Leonard WBC title bout. WBA champ Pipino Cuevas, who many believed was the most dangerous welterweight around, was also heavily touted as a Duran target and reportedly wanted a guarantee of half a million dollars. Don King, who promoted the Palomino fight, sided with the WBC while Bob Arum lined up with the WBA.

Palomino retired from the sport on his thirtieth birthday. He would make an improbable comeback almost eighteen years later, at the age of forty-eight, and won four bouts before losing for the last time in 1998. By then, his father had succumbed to cancer, unleashing emotions he had kept bottled for years. "Everybody was telling me that, back when I had the world title, my father was so proud of me and that he was always telling everybody about me," said Palomino in a 1997 interview. "But he never said any of that to me." Unlike the open relationship Palomino had with his mother Maria, his father wasn't one to express his inner feelings.

Duran's status as an honorary New Yorker was confirmed by his fabulous performance. He often hung out in the city with another Panamanian icon, Ruben Blades, the salsa king. "I knew Ruben Blades when he was nobody. I stayed in the Hotel Mayflower in New York and he used to go there every day to play soccer. After the game, he used to go back to my room and there he stayed playing dominoes. After that we would go eat. He would always come looking for me when he moved to New York and knew I had a fight coming up." A salsa fanatic, Duran was also friends with Celia Cruz, Tito Puente and Hector Lavoe.

After training, Duran would often sit in Central Park, where he liked to watch the people and cars go by. One day he was there when he saw his friend Flacco Bala talking to a man with a child on the shoulders. Duran ran over and was introduced to the man – Robert De Niro, the hottest male lead in Hollywood. They shook hands.

"Robert invited me to go to his room. He lived in the same hotel where I was staying. He said, 'I want you to come to my room. I am going to hold a party so that you meet my friends. You are my favorite.' Twenty-five minutes later, the telephone rang. It was Robert De Niro, but he talked in English, and I do not talk English. So I called Bala and asked him to come with me. And we went there and started talking. Robert De Niro loves boxing. Then came a little guy, one who liked to make fun. We went on talking and then came a tall, thin woman. He asked me if I wanted champagne or wine but when I trained, I never drank. I would only drink after the fights. So I told him that and he said, 'Sure, sure.'"

Duran invited De Niro and his film friends to play football the next day, and then they went on to a meal at Victor's Café. "Roberto De Niro wanted to pay but we had drunk champagne, so I told him that was not OK. Victor was very happy that De Niro and all the artists were there. And you know what? That little guy who jumped and made fun was and is Roberto De Niro's best friend, Joe Pesci. All the artists that appear in the movie are the ones that were playing football with us. The following day we all got together again and I learned Roberto De Niro was filming a movie at that time." The movie was *Raging Bull*, the story of former boxer Jake LaMotta, which would become one of the most critically acclaimed films of the century.

When he wasn't hanging out in the Big Apple, Duran could go home and choose one of his five cars or three maids. His private cook could put together something to eat. All Duran had to do was call his chauffeur to pick him up at his estimated $250,000 apartment complex in Paitilla and take him to a local club. Duran was finally living the lifestyle that he had dreamt of – but you couldn't take Chorrillo out of the man.

\* \* \*

On 28 September 1979, a spectacular fight bill began in Las Vegas. The venue was Caesar's Palace and the main event saw undefeated heavy-weight champion Larry Holmes against the awesome-punching Earnie Shavers. The undercard featured not only Duran but also Sugar Ray Leonard and the brilliant little Puerto Rican Wilfredo Gomez. One writer called it "a program of boxing that may be more representative of great talent than any other in the modern era of the game."

Sugar Ray Leonard was a star for the armchair generation. "He's made for television," said his trainer, Angelo Dundee. "He's got person-ality, charisma, good lucks. He projects himself right out of the screen." For this reason he could command up to $250,000 a time for even routine learning fights as he rose through the ranks. The influential presenter Howard Cosell had championed Leonard above all the others from the successful U.S. Olympic team of 1976 and helped build him into a star and national television broadcast most of his bouts. He couldn't have looked more devastating as he unleashed a dazzling barrage of punches to flatten seasoned campaigner Andy "The Hawk" Price in the first round. It took several minutes for Price to recover enough to leave the ring.

Leonard then watched from ringside as Duran faced the lightly regarded, six-foot-tall southpaw Zeferino "Speedy" Gonzalez, a former Golden Gloves champion who had nineteen wins, two losses and a draw in twenty-two bouts. Gonzalez, from San Jose, California, had worked with a hypnotherapist before the fight to eradicate fear, memorizing "protective suggestions." His boxing plan was cautious and he would later rue not going toe-to-toe with the smaller man.

Duran appeared rusty and out of sorts, reaching and missing with right-hand leads against an opponent five inches taller and not cutting off the ring. On several occasions he even got nailed with a left hand. His body was smooth and fleshy at 149½ pounds, not honed and hard as it had been against Palomino. Occasionally he dropped his hands and mocked his opponent but if nothing else Gonzalez was quick – "He moves faster than a beef stew in a boarding house," said one writer – and the crowd cheered when Duran was caught with a left hook while arrogantly hitching up his shorts. In the eighth the fighters banged heads, and Duran acknowledged it was an accident by touching gloves with his opponent, but soon blood was running down his face. Gonzalez's trainer exhorted his fighter to take advantage of the cut, but he couldn't or wouldn't. Duran won the unanimous decision by a mile but left the ring with a cut over the left eye, to the sound of booing.

Ray Leonard had clearly made the greater impression. Things would have to change.

★ ★ ★

On November 30, 1979, a television audience of millions watched two undefeated prodigies meet in a battle for the WBC welterweight crown and to decide, in effect, who would be Duran's next great challenge. The preparations of unpredictable genius Wilfred Benitez had hardly been helped when his fiery father, Gregorio, no longer his manager but still his trainer, gave an interview to *Ring En Espanol* before the bout, saying, "He can't win this fight … has not listened to anything I have told him and meanwhile Leonard has fought a lot. But Wilfred is a boy who just refuses to listen." His mother, Clara, also chipped in. "Look at how my son has turned out," she bewailed. "All he thinks about now are women. And this is no good during fights."

Some say Benitez had put in only nine full days of preparation before he lost his title to Sugar Ray Leonard when the referee stopped their fifteen-round bout with just six seconds remaining at Caesar's Palace, Las Vegas. Leonard had been ahead on all of the judges' cards, his harder hitting giving him the edge in a tense battle.

Two months later, twenty-four-year Josef Nsubuga, trained by the veteran Eddie Futch, met the serious version of Duran in Las Vegas. A Ugandan fighting out of Norway, Nsubuga was ranked ninth by the WBC and was considered a dangerous left-hooker. He was announced as the "Ugandan Powerhouse" but later admitted making a major error when he tried to brawl with Duran.

Nsubuga kept cool under pressure in the first round, jabbing and moving, and at one point a frustrated Duran pushed him to the canvas. But by the third the shorter, stockier Hands of Stone was taking charge and rocking back Nsubuga's head with hooks and uppercuts. The referee took a close look at the inexperienced Ugandan, but he showed grit and composure to fight back in the closing stages of the round.

In the next round Duran simply walked through his opponent's fading resistance, sometimes grunting as he slammed in shots. With seconds remaining in the fourth round, Duran caught Nsubuga down with a short right hook, and as the Ugandan sagged, Duran shouldered him over, causing him to fall heavily on his back. Nsubuga managed to rise at "eight" and was saved by the bell. He stumbled back to his corner, where the compassionate Eddie Futch pleaded with the fighter's Norwegian manager to retire his man. After consultation with referee Richard Greene, Nsubuga retired on his stool. "I'm the real world champ," Duran told reporters afterwards in his Spanish-accented English. "I want Leonard now, and I'll knock him out."

It was reported shortly afterwards that Bob Arum had offered Duran $1 million to challenge Ray Leonard that summer. Leonard was said to lean towards Arum while Duran was in the camp of his promotional arch-rival Don King. One magazine reported that an Arum acolyte made a secret mission to Carlos Eleta in Panama City to woo Duran away from Don King to face the winner of Benitez-Leonard. King was tipped off and dispatched his own emissary from JFK Airport to make a counter offer. Leonard, never one to undersell himself, wanted $5 million. "That's a bad joke," remarked Don King. "You scare people with talk like that."

The mind games began. Leonard's trainer Angelo Dundee made a point of telling reporters that "three things trouble Duran – speed, a left hand and a calculated fight. You need a well regimented fighter to lick him and that's my guy." Ray Arcel, however, believed Duran's experience would be the deciding factor. Duran, well versed in street pyschology, was already winding himself up for the encounter. When he knew that Leonard was watching him work out in the gym one day, he skipped rope in a squatting position.

Nearly a month after the win over Nsubuga, Duran watched helplessly as his record of ten straight knockout title defenses was broken by Puerto Rican featherweight and bantamweight legend Wilfredo Gomez. On February 3, 1980, Gomez knocked out Colombia's Ruben Valdes. Gomez had been trained by Plomo when he began his professional career in Panama.

Three weeks later, Duran scored his fifty-fifth inside-the-distance win when he punished Wellington Wheatley of Ecuador with two early knockdowns before dropping him for keeps with a right forty-four seconds into the sixth round. "Wheatley countered quite well at times and seemed to jolt Duran a couple of times in the first round with rights," reported *Boxing News*, "but Duran took charge in the second when a cracking right hand lead to the chin put Wheatley down on the seat of his trunks against the ropes." Wheatley got up at four and survived the round but by the fifth he was wilting and took another count from a right-hander to the back of the neck. Duran lowered the boom in the sixth, nailing his foe with a right and then a cruel short left hook, forcing the referee to step in without bothering to count.

"The monster's loose and on his way to the welterweight title," said NBC-TV boxing adviser Dr Ferdie Pacheco, at ringside in Las Vegas.

# 13

# EL MACHO

*A dictionary translation of the Spanish word macho captures the essence of Latin American masculinity. Besides male and masculine, the word means tough, strong, stupid, big, huge, splendid, terrific and doubles as a slang term for a sledgehammer.*

Duncan Green, *Faces of Latin America*

IT STARTED OUT as a leisurely stroll through the streets of Montreal. Ray Leonard, his wife and childhood sweetheart Juanita, trainer Angelo Dundee and his wife were taking a break from the pressure cooker atmosphere before a fight. The weeks leading up to a big bout lie heavy with anxiety, sickness and tension and this was a brief afternoon escape from the hype. But in the summer of 1980, nobody could touch Ray Leonard. He was young, rich and approachable, and had all the talent he could handle.

So when Leonard saw Roberto Duran coming towards him, he smiled that world-seeping-through-his-white-teeth smile and waited for a friendly, or at least civil, response. Instead Duran, who was once described as cursing better in English than most Americans, unleashed a ferocious volley of abuse. He then gave Leonard the finger. "Duran comes around and starts really giving it to Ray and Juanita, talking about 'I'm going to kill your husband' and stuff like that," remembered Dundee. "That got to Ray. He couldn't believe that Duran could be so crude in front of his wife. He was a family man and father." Leonard later told the *Los Angeles Times*, "He taunted me. He cursed my mother, my children, my wife. He said unbelievable things and I let them get to me."

No punches were exchanged but Duran had left his mark. Leonard may have been a supremely talented boxer, but his antagonist was a streetfighter who walked around Panama with a 680-pound lion named Walla strapped to his arm (a present from Rigoberto Paredes, the former head of the Panama racetrack). Perhaps Leonard was already beginning to wonder whether this fight was a mistake.

His first choice of opponent had been WBA champion Pipino Cuevas in a unification match, but this would have left Don King facing "a severe cold in the wallet," according to *Boxing News*. King, an arch-manipulator, contacted WBC president Jose Sulaiman, who in turn called the Panamanian Government. His pitch was that Leonard was doing the dirty to a son of Panama and that the WBA was conniving to allow Cuevas to fight Leonard. The Government then leaned on the Panama-based WBA, which in turn put the squeeze on its own champion, Cuevas. Cuevas was suddenly forced to pull out with an "injury" and Duran, King's fighter, was back in the picture.

Having originally prepared for the Mexican bomber, Leonard was already in shape. Indeed some felt Cuevas would have been a more dangerous opponent. In eight contests at 147 pounds, Duran had scored only four knockouts. "I think a few boxers lost respect for me," Duran told *Sports Illustrated*'s William Nack before the Montreal show-down. "Some said I lost my ability to punch with power. But let me tell you something: if a man is born with a good punch, a change in weight makes no difference."

The bout was finally signed on April 13, but not without immense backstage horse-trading. Bob Arum and Don King, who could barely stand the sight of each other, were forced to form a brief, unholy alliance to co-promote the fight, sharing the dais for the first time. "It was the first time in history that Arum and King worked together," said Eleta. "I brought them to Panama so we could all work this out." Arum at the time had twenty fighters on his books, led by Marvin Hagler, while King had thirteen fighters, with Duran and Larry Holmes at the top. As if to endorse the encounter and its significance, the New York Boxing Writers' Association met in May and selected Sugar Ray Leonard as their 1979 Fighter of the Year, Leonard's trainer Angelo Dundee as Manager of the Year, and Duran and Muhammad Ali as their Fighters of the Decade.

By then, Leonard was beginning to get an idea of the man he would face. He had done his best to respond with a half-hearted "I'll kill you" when the fighters met on April 23 at a press conference in the New York Waldorf Astoria, but the threat sounded not only out of character but

Duran's great rivalry with Puerto Rican opponents spilled over into a punch-up before his contest with the arrogant prodigy Wilfred Benitez (left). Don King acts as referee.

Outboxed by The Radar. Duran looked lethargic against the defensive genius and accurate hitting of Benitez in their WBC light-middleweight title fight in 1982.
*Photo: Linda Platt.*

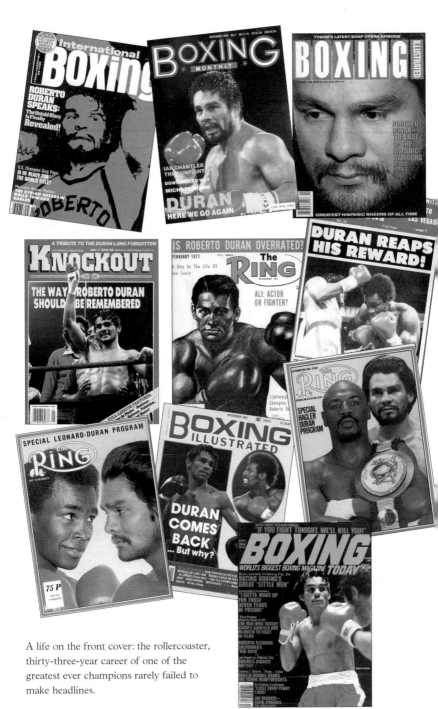

A life on the front cover: the rollercoaster, thirty-three-year career of one of the greatest ever champions rarely failed to make headlines.

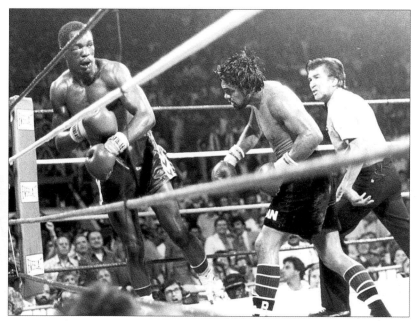

Davey Moore is battered to defeat in eight rounds on an emotion-charged night in New York in June 1983. *Photo: Linda Platt.*

Redemption: The Madison Square Garden crowd sing "Happy Birthday" as Duran holds his arms aloft after beating Moore for the light-middleweight crown.

The formidable Marvin Hagler looks relaxed, Duran looks pensive, and Luis Spada, who took over from Carlos Eleta as his manager, works out the sums before their middleweight title fight in 1983.

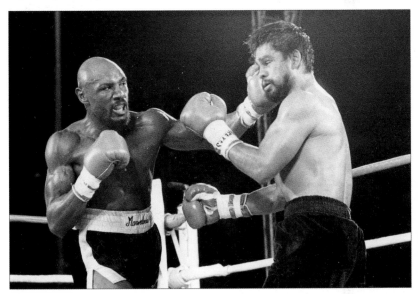

Though Hagler landed the harder, cleaner blows to retain his crown on points, Duran fought magnificently against one of the all-time great middleweights. *Photo: Empics.*

Duran at bay: A classic study of Hands of Stone on his corner stool between rounds.

Size does matter: The disparity in height between Duran and Thomas "Hit Man" Hearns. *Photo: Arturo LeConte.*

Hearns inflicts the most crushing defeat of Duran's career, setting him up with long lefts before dropping him on his face to be stopped in round two in June 1984. *Photo: Jack Goodman.*

Carlos Eleta, business tycoon, politician, athlete, songwriter and one-time manager of Duran, in his office in 2000.

Clara Samaniego with her first son, Duran's older brother Toti.

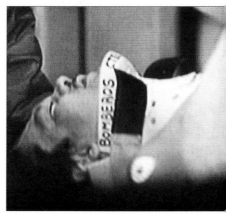

Duran is wheeled into hospital with his neck in a brace after the car crash in Argentina that finally ended his boxing career. *Photo: Reuters.*

Duran with wife Felicidad, surrounded by well-wishers, at the funeral of boxer Pedro Rockero Alcazar in Chorrillo.

Roberto Duran as he is today with the author (middle) and fellow boxing legend Ismael Laguna.

hollow. Minutes before, Duran had held center stage at the podium. He had brought his personal jeweler along for the ride and was kitted out like a ghetto daddy, with over $37,000 of bling on his person – not including his expensive clothes. He looked and acted like he owned the world. In one account of what followed, Duran "cuffed" Leonard after a scuffle broke out while both men tried on a souvenir boxing glove. "He got into my head," said Leonard. "He pissed me off and challenged my head."

Duran, brilliant in the pre-fight mind games, promised that his contempt for Leonard was no gimmick. He didn't hate the American idol so much as what he stood for. "My father was so happy because that fight represented so much," said his son Chavo, who was only six at the time. "It showed all the fans, especially the people in Panama, the people that know boxing, that he was not just one of the crowd. My father had many fights but Leonard was very special because he had won a gold medal at the Olympic Games and was the golden kid in the U.S. at the time."

Duran reviled the kid who grew up with a "golden spoon" in his mouth. He saw Leonard as the product of a privileged childhood. He knew he lacked Leonard's telegenic charisma, but he suspected that Leonard lacked the toughness that one can only earn through battle. He considered the American not a man but a commodity, a glossy figure enhanced by the media. He wanted to expose this counterfeit.

Duran might not have been the favorite, but the Canadians took him to their hearts. To them, there was nothing fake about the man. His outbursts came from his soul. Duran could mingle with the people without first making sure there was a camera close by, while Leonard smiled the smile of a stranger who *expected* to be the chosen one. While Duran wore a T-shirt that read "BonJour" to woo the Montreal French, Leonard, who had won his gold medal in Montreal, couldn't understand the colder reception he received. "That took me for a loop," said Leonard. "I thought that I was the adopted son because of the Olympics and the exposure. But man, when I got there, went into the ring and they were booing me and embraced Duran, it threw me for a loop."

Through the papers, Leonard expressed his concerns, claiming that Duran's tough guy act worked in the ring, but "he should leave it there." It was obvious that he didn't know where Duran was coming from. He made the mistake of treating Duran as a normal human being and expected he would act like one, but this was not someone who was going to heed advice about acting in a civil manner. When people spoke of hungry fighters, in Duran's case it was literally true.

Every time Leonard reacted to an insult, he was becoming a prop in the Panamanian's show. He had never been confronted by an opponent so tactless and virile, but who still combined malevolence with a touch of charm. Duran didn't live by any guidelines. He acted without thought for the repercussions. His boorishness shocked Leonard because this wildman could back up his words. One fan encapsulated the phenomenon when he said, "Duran was just simpler than Leonard." Duran had made him lose his composure without throwing a punch. This was no longer a multi-million-dollar sports event; it was a behind-the-bike-racks fistfight.

Angelo Dundee understood what was happening to his fighter mentally but couldn't stop it. Mentally, he had lost Leonard. Dundee and Duran had known each other since Roberto was a raw young terror at the Fifth Street Gym in Miami. With his jet-black hair, baby smile and a right hand that would push your mouthpiece back into your teeth, Duran terrorized sparring partners. "I've known Roberto since he was a youngster and he was one of the sharpest guys out there," said Dundee. "He could con you just by giving a look. He used to psych out a lot of guys before they got into the ring. Just like Ali, he was good at getting the psychological edge. He was this macho guy, so charismatic, and overshadowed all these guys by putting on an act for each opponent." As for Ray Arcel and Freddie Brown, men he had watched and admired for years, Dundee came up with the classic line, "Those guys, they're older than water."

In the gym, Duran was often pitted against bigger men yet referred to anyone willing to challenge him as a *maricon*, or homosexual. He was used to hitting guys twenty pounds heavier. The ring was his space, where there was no room for mercy or pity. Stepping through the ropes after a fight to the cold concrete, his hatred subsided and even Leonard would remark at what a gentleman Duran was when they squared up for a Sprite commercial with their sons.

At the Fifth Street Gym, Dundee was also privy to his weaknesses. By this time it was no secret that Duran enjoyed his drink and his women, but when he faced a serious challenge the bullshit subsided. Inside the Fifth Street Gym, Duran was pitted against Dundee's Cuban fighter Douglass Valliant. Valliant had once challenged Carlos Ortiz for the lightweight title. He was a showman, the one type of boxer that didn't agree with Duran. Good fighters emphasizing angle, speed and movement could frustrate him. "My guy gave Roberto fits in the ring," said Dundee. "He was a sticker-mover type guy, a good fighter who was in the ring with some great champions, and Duran didn't know what to do with him." Surely Leonard would box him the same way.

The fact Canadians supported Duran also baffled the Leonard camp. "Duran captured the crowd, and they were all pulling for him," said Dundee. "Never in my wildest dreams did I think those people would be pulling for Duran. Ray was a nice kid, good-looking guy, but in certain places they like certain fighters. I thought we had an edge going in there but they were rooting and hustling for Duran like they were doing for Ali in Zaire." Ali had turned an entire country against George Foreman in Zaire and Duran was building a cult following in Canada.

While he liked to talk tough, others saw it as something the media overplayed. For Eleta, the glitch in translation was a bit bothersome. Did Duran really want to "kill" Leonard? "He didn't mean anything by it," said Eleta. "It was taken out of context by the American fans. Every round, as we say in Spanish and it doesn't mean the same in translation, they tried to kill each other. They put everything they had into that fight." Leonard responded in kind because he did not want to be seen to back down. "Duran was very antagonistic and had a bully mentality," said Leonard. "He challenged you and if you didn't stand up, he knew he had you."

But Duran wasn't listening. "Whatever Leonard had to say, I didn't give a damn," he said.

Leonard and Duran needed each other. With every great sports figure comes another individual able to extract the pockets of bravery on reserve for the moments that test the will unlike any other. For Ali, it came in the form of a walking tree trunk named Joe Frazier. There were thousands of other rivals like Tony Zale and Rocky Graziano, Sugar Ray Robinson and Jake LaMotta, or Sandy Saddler and Willie Pep who forced each other to locate such reserves.

Boxing provides the ultimate stage for pre-event hype because the public can hear every word. It is intense and in-your-face and the boxer can't back down. In other sports it is often performed on the field out of earshot. In boxing, the press conferences allow the frustrations, whether real or contrived, to surface. When Leonard had his masculinity challenged, he felt the need to respond. Ignoring it would be akin to being labeled a punk. His problem was that he couldn't release the emotions; they followed him to the opening bell. Duran needed hate to brew in his corner, while Leonard exuded calm awareness. Duran turned his opponents into voodoo dolls before fights. Leonard could be ruthless and arrogant but preferred calculation.

"I had seen Duran on a number of occasions, and I was in Las Vegas … and I think it was the Esteban DeJesus fight," remembers Leonard. "At the time I was a professional fighter. I was sitting behind Jackie Gleason, who I loved because I loved *The Honeymooners*. I told him that I wanted to fight [Duran]. Gleason turned around and said, 'Son, do yourself a favor and don't even think about it because he will kill you.' I stopped watching *The Honeymooners*. He burst my bubble man."

Duran promised war. He had knocked down a horse with a single right hand. How do you hurt a man so possessed? Sugar Ray thought he had an answer. With his christian names taken from one of the world's greatest entertainers, Ray Charles, and his nickname from the greatest-ever boxer, Sugar Ray Robinson, he was to many the savior of the sport. That didn't always make him popular. "Ray Charles Leonard was a prodigy, and no one in boxing really likes a prodigy," wrote one biographer. "For most old-timers, who were made to pay their dues by even older-timers, approval for young fighters is bestowed reluctantly and in inverse proportion to the amount of punishment they've taken. In this ultimate school of hard knocks, all natural talent is suspect."

Despite the belief in some quarters that he had had it easy, growing up in Wilmington, North Carolina, wasn't exactly the high life. According to Leonard, everything the family had "we shared." As one of seven children born to Cicero and Getha, he moved to Washington, D.C., when he was four and his mother, a nursing assistant, and father, who worked in a produce market, put in long hours. "There was a feeling of inferiority from not having anything," Leonard told the *New York Times* in 1979. "There were never clothes to wear or money for things as simple as school field trips. Even lunch money was a problem."

When Leonard won the gold medal in the 1976 Olympics in Montreal with a victory over Cuba's Andres Aldama, he seemed destined for riches in every aspect of his life. His publicity campaign heralded what was to come with boxer Oscar De La Hoya and Michael Jordan in basketball and he displayed an even temperament and good manners. In 1979, Leonard took a magnificent boxer in Wilfred Benitez and stopped him with six seconds remaining in the fifteenth round. The young fighter proved that he could bang with the world's best.

Leonard was on the verge of superstardom. He learned from the Benitez bout that it took more than just great physical attributes to be and beat the best. "It required psychological warfare and mental stability," he said. "It required more heart than you can ever imagine ... I mean when the going gets tough and your lungs are burning, when your arms are tired and they feel like weights, you push for that hidden reservoir of strength. That's when I realized it was far more than being physical or having raw talent."

In 1980, at twenty-nine years old, Duran was taking on the biggest draw since Ali. To Duran, every fight was a one-dollar brawl in Chorrillo. Fighting was survival. Boxing was his only option, while Leonard could have been a success in anything. The truth about Leonard's childhood didn't matter to Duran. He despised Leonard and his image because in his mind, the American hadn't achieved anything. Many years later, on his couch at his home in Cangrejo, Duran traveled back to the man who brought him to the brink of fame, then failure. "Leonard was shitting his pants from the fear he had," Duran said. "I didn't like Leonard because he was the pretty boy for the Americans and I didn't care less about him. I used to tell myself that I was going to beat the shit out of that American so he will respect us Latin Americans."

"Actually there was nothing that could prepare you for Duran," said Leonard. "Duran was a fight within itself. Duran was a crazed, talented, technical boxer. He was a better boxer than people gave him credit for and a devastating puncher ... an extremely good defensive fighter who was very elusive. He was not a stationary target."

Leonard had been schooled in the business side of the sport from the day he met his influential lawyer, Mike Trainer, a University of Maryland law school graduate. Many boxing journalists and promoters would marvel at his ability to make wallet-busting deals for his fighter. After Leonard's post-Olympics college scholarship at the University of Maryland, Trainer also found him a job at the school's Parks and Planning Department. He and twenty associates lent Leonard $1,000 each to sponsor Sugar Ray Leonard Inc., with Leonard being its sole stockholder. Having seen a laughable contract sent to Leonard by Don King, Trainer made a counter offer. "It's the dumbest document I ever saw in my entire life," said Trainer about King's offer. "So I said to Ray, 'If you're really thinking about doing it and if you really think you can box, why do you want to sell part of yourself? Why don't we just set it up like when I went into business? You go to the bank and borrow some money then pay off your loan and everything is fine.'"

Within two years of his debut, Leonard was selling both 7-Up and Dr. Pepper and had a contract with ABC to televise his first six fights. With Trainer behind him, he was more marketable than any fighter in memory. With brains, good looks and great skills, the Trainer-Leonard partnership kicked off the creation of a matinee idol that would exceed anyone's expectations. However, along the way many observers believed that Leonard overstretched his boundaries and began to make champion's demands before he had paid his dues. No one could deny his ability, but the image still outshone his performances. "His appeal is that he's not a stereotyped boxer," Trainer told Bert Sugar. "If you go down the street and ask anybody what a boxer is, most would say, 'He's got a cauliflower ear, a nose all over his face, is missing his front teeth and he can't speak very well.' In short, not very nice people to be around." Leonard, in contrast, appealed to "the guy up on the thirtieth floor on Madison Avenue," according to Trainer. "Forget he's black, forget he's a boxer and remember he's a personality, he's intelligent and he's never going to embarrass anybody."

Those words "forget he's black" would not endear him to his own community or to the blue-collar crowd that rooted for Duran. Not only did the fans forget he was black, but the new image overwhelmed not only race but the boxer himself. Those who thought Trainer was joking when he claimed his fighter would be a better actor than fighter were mistaken. Leonard was an anomaly, a fighter who thought before he spoke, cared about what people thought about him and displayed a keen knowledge of how to play the media. Those qualities simultaneously made him wealthy and distant.

Duran, on the other hand, had no marketing campaign, acted on impulse, rarely thought before he spoke, but was uncommonly sensitive when it came to his family and friends. While Leonard had a say in all of his future opponents, Duran had no problems with who – or what – was placed in front of him. Eleta took care of that; Duran just wanted to fight. And while many fighters padded their records with third-rate opponents, Duran had sixty-nine fights to his name and sixty-eight wins. The only man to beat him had been savaged twice in return, making Eleta reiterate, "When Roberto trained like he knew he should, he was unbeatable."

Many figured the cornermen on each side would play a significant role in the outcome. Here was a trio of trainers who had reached the pinnacle of their profession. Because of his long association with Ali, Dundee was the best-known cornerman in boxing. Steeped in craftiness and a fine spotter of talent, Dundee could have been born next to a turnbuckle. In his most glorious moments, he persuaded a near-blinded Ali, then Cassius Clay, to keep fighting against Sonny Liston, and had "discovered" – some say exacerbated – a tear in his fighter's glove that gave Ali precious moments to recover after being knocked down by Henry Cooper. In a fight with Marcos Geraldo, Leonard was hit so hard – either by a headbutt or punch – that he claimed to have seen three Geraldos. "Hit the one in the middle," quipped Dundee. Leonard did, and won. "That fight showed me how strong Ray really was," said Dundee. "Ray knocked out a middleweight in that fight."

Dundee knew how to dissect a fighter. Having worked commentary for several of Duran's fights, he knew the Panamanian's strengths and weaknesses. Looking back years later, he confirmed he would have loved to have worked Duran's corner. "Roberto had so much ammunition," he said. "I respected the hell out of him. The guy was a complete fighter." Yet he questioned Duran's power at this level, remarking that Leonard, "my guy," was the real puncher in this fight.

While Eleta stressed Brown's value as a babysitter and watchdog in the camp, he realized early on that Duran needed that extra motivation that Plomo, a close friend, couldn't provide. "Arcel was like, how do you say it in English, cabana boy," said Duran. "He used to come a couple days before a fight. Plomo and Brown were always with me."

Plomo reiterated: "I was with Duran from the very beginning. Arcel would just show up weeks before the fight."

Still, as many in Duran's camp would attest, it wasn't always easy motivating Duran. Against Leonard, he motivated himself.

"Gloves, gloves, gloves. You just get bored. Imagine going a month without a rest. Monday, Tuesday, Wednesday, Thursday, Friday, Saturday, Sunday, Monday, Tuesday – damn, you don't have the desire to throw punches anymore. They never give me a day off. I'm taking everything with calmness – at my pace. Everything is being saved for the day of the fight. If I do things with ferociousness now, I won't have any sparring partners," Duran told *Sports Illustrated*.

"What then? I do what my trainers tell me, but I also put in something of my own. Understand? Sometimes the body wants to work and sometimes it doesn't. I have not yet started to throw hard. I should be in much better condition the day of the fight – not now. On June 20th, I should be double what I am now – double."

Despite weight fluctuation and occasionally lax training habits, Duran wasn't delusional. Against Zeferino Gonzalez he admitted to looking terrible, and reportedly he left the ring telling Leonard that next time he would see a different fighter. "I would stop partying and only train for two or three weeks before a fight," said Duran. Leonard, in contrast, found solace amid the punchbags. "I just loved the conditioning, just one of the guys that loved to be in the gym."

In Palmer Park in spring 1980, Leonard began training at a hotel exhibition hall and stayed at the Sheraton Lanham near his home. While some boxers liked to set themselves away from family, Leonard trained near his loved ones. He sparred with then middleweight contender and brother Roger as well as cousin Odell. The daily training sessions began with five miles around the track every morning. "I'd lose them every time when we got to the hills," boasted Sugar. To work on his balance, he took dance lessons with Juanita. Spectators paid $1 to watch him train, while sparring partners were paid $150 for daily beatings. By the time Leonard broke camp on June 6, 1980, he had sparred roughly 200 rounds.

Duran arrived in New York on April 13 to begin training at Grossinger's. People knew he was serious when he was nowhere to be found on the club circuit. When his mind was on the job, his training sessions, including a spectacular rope-jumping routine, could be eerily intense. "And all throughout the workout, in the ring and on the bag and rope, he emitted strange shrill cries," wrote John Schulian. "They were not snorts and grunts many boxers make when punching. They were oohs and aahs, wailed in a sharp, high-pitched staccato, like cries of birds, and seemed to strike an emphasis, set a rhythm or express exuberance."

Still, the training regimen came with the usual minor crises. "I was running up a hill with boots and when I stretched out I messed up my back," said Duran. "I'm still suffering from that pain today. Eleta sent a doctor from Panama because he thought I was lying. I couldn't even sit down. The doctor is observing me and he would look at me with the corner of his eye, but my back really hurt. When we go to Montreal, they take me to a clinic and it was the first time they ever took the pain away with lasers. They take me into an operating room and there's a thing that looks like a barrel and they shoot this laser. The pain is gone, but I ended up feeling very weak. When I started to train very hard, Leonard and all his people were very afraid."

Days before the fight, a routine medical indicated that Duran had an irregular heartbeat and might not be allowed in the ring. The media went into a minor frenzy of speculation. Duran, who thought the whole thing was a conspiracy, had to undergo further electrocardiogram tests at Montreal's Institute of Cardiology before he was cleared to fight. "Everybody there liked me and I won the public over when I trained really hard, and I went on the microphone and said, 'Bonjour madam, bonjour,'" said Duran. "They all fell in love with me, especially when I started jumping rope. The Leonard team got scared and wanted to bring the fight back to New York and made up a story about me having heart conditions. They said that three of the chambers of my heart were bad and they said that they pulled two tumors out of my head and that's how sick I was."

Despite the suspicion in Duran's camp, they had to be cautious. "I sent my own physician down there when I heard about the problem," said Eleta. "There was nothing wrong with Roberto. When the doctor looked at him they said he was strong as a horse." Ray Arcel, always good for a quote, quipped, "They took him to the hospital to check out his heart. But everyone knows that Roberto Duran hasn't got a heart."

"His weight fluctuates so much," said Dundee in a *New York Times* interview before the fight. "Who knows what he's going to be like next year? He gets as big as a house between fights." The war of words had begun. Arcel understood the ramifications of each insult and action but didn't let it worry his guy. From the first time he saw the Panamanian against Lloyd Marshall, Arcel was adamant about not changing his style. It was a sign of his deep knowledge of boxers, of what worked and what didn't. Throughout the eight years they'd been side by side, Duran had gone from a wild puncher to a patient stalker, but Arcel and Brown had never sought to temper his naked aggression.

"In the past, Duran has developed a dislike for a guy and when that happened, he really became intent on destroying him and always did," Arcel told the *New York Times* reporter on the day of the fight. "The one thing I fear and dread is if the ref doesn't let Duran fight inside. If that happens, Duran won't be able to fight his fight. But as long as Duran can fight his fight, he's going to hit Leonard and he's going to drain him … the big question then will be Leonard's stamina and endurance after the sixth and seventh round. That's when Duran gets his second wind and he's all over the other guy." Duran's camp bemoaned the choice of Filipino referee Carlos Padilla, who had an undeserved reputation for not allowing in-fighting.

The universal mantra was that Manos de Piedra could be undone with movement, hand speed and psychology. "I am not going to be standing still and letting Duran hit me with right hands," Leonard told the *Washington Post* almost a month before the fight. "I'm going to upset him with my tactics; he's very temperamental. I'm going to drive him crazy."

In Montreal's Olympic Stadium, known to locals as the "Big O," the combatants fought in a twenty-foot ring, which many felt would give Leonard a decided advantage. The only thing missing that night was the presence of General and Duran confidante Omar Torrijos. Due to a heart condition, Torrijos was advised against attending the bout. They would speak by phone immediately after the fight. Yet, Margarito Duran surfaced again, and told a local Spanish radio station that his son would win a decision if he wasn't knocked out in the first five rounds.

Calculations prior to the fight – which was billed by the French Canadians as Le Face-a-Face Historique – were mind-boggling. It would be shown on closed-circuit in the U.S. in over 340 locations. ABC affiliates bought the TV rights for $500,000 but couldn't show the fight for twenty-nine days after the fight. Arum and King sold the live gate for $3.5 million, and if they sold all 77,000 seats, the Montreal organizers could take in $8.6 million. By June 17, three days away from the fight there were 23,000 sold and they needed 41,000 buyers to break even.

Duran would earn $1.65 million for the fight, Leonard nearly $8.5 million, from a package that included parts of the closed-circuit revenues, upfront money from the Olympic Installations Board and a lion's share of the delayed home TV broadcast rights, as well as sales from the foreign broadcast rights. By eclipsing the $6.5 million that Ali earned for his 1976 bout with Ken Norton, Leonard was the highest-paid boxer in history.

★ ★ ★

In the second preliminary bout, lightweight Cleveland Denny took some heavy punches from Canada's Gaetan Hart and was carried from the ring, his body ominously limp. Most of the crowd, however, was unconcerned or oblivious. They had come for the main event only.

The 46,317 spectators gave Duran a rousing reception as he bounced into the ring on the toes of his white boxing shoes. He sported lily-white trunks and long red, white and blue striped athletic socks. They were quieter for Leonard's arrival, though his own followers tried to pump up the volume. "Leonard held his arms aloft, bent at the elbows," wrote Ralph Wiley in *Serenity*. "He was unconvincing. His face betrayed doubts. He was fighting Roberto Duran, and for the first time, he really didn't know what might happen. Duran, on the other hand, seemed all business, jangling his arms to the sound of blood-stirring, amplified drumbeats."

In truth, Leonard was overawed. "That fight was so big. It far exceeded the Benitez fight," he said. "I was in awe of the whole thing. I recall walking toward the ring and looking up into the huge screen and I remember thinking that this was bigger than life. I was like, wow, let's enjoy this. But Duran was like, 'I will kill you.'"

As referee Carlos Padilla gave the instructions, the crafty Ray Arcel stood with his back to Leonard and pleaded with Padilla not to "take the inside away" from his fighter; in other words, not to break the clinches too soon. Leonard shook out his shoulders, looking slight in his build next to Duran. Then it was time.

From the first bell, Duran attacked, his belligerence matching his speed and movement. He grabbed the momentum and set the pace. Leonard, for once, was not in control. As Duran landed combinations and then smothered the champion, it was obvious that he was honed to a peak and raring to go.

The first big moment came in round two. Duran grazed Leonard with a right, then landed a left hook to the neck that wobbled him. Leonard was suddenly in a place he had never been as a pro, and followed his instincts to clinch for dear life. Pushed against the ropes, his crab-grip was broken by referee Padilla, and the fight continued, to the roars of the crowd. Leonard was forced to backpedal to escape further punishment.

"When I hit him with the left hook, he felt it," said Duran. "I had to demonstrate that I was smarter, faster, and that I could put up with a lot more than him. He committed an error. He put too much Vaseline on his body, so that my punches would slide off him. He would hug me and that's the mistake he committed because I could take my hands off him much faster. When he would tie my hands, my hands would come out much easier to pull out and uppercut him or hook him because all the Vaseline on his body would drip onto my gloves."

Having analyzed Duran mentally and physically for years, Angelo Dundee knew what was happening. "Duran will throw punches, one, two, three, but then he'll put his head in your chest; one, two, three and he'll try to lock you up with his left hand. He likes to wave at you with his left hand. That hand-waving motion throws some guys off their rhythm." Dundee stared into Sugar's eyes before sending him out for the third round. His worst fears were coming true but there was little he could say or do to help his fighter. Duran was fighting with an animal intensity and it was all the American could do to stay with him. The first minute of round three confirmed the worst as Duran blasted in body shots, banged in a hard uppercut and continued to maul Leonard in close. "He had that look on his face and it was so surreal," said Leonard. "I was being transformed from doing what I normally do. I had no control at that point."

Midway through the fourth, Duran made the champion cover up again when he landed a right cross over a feeble jab. Another left hook landed on Leonard's throat and a straight right jolted his head. He tried to use Duran's own tricks during clinches, hooking his arms, but Duran was too strong. To shouts of "arriba, arriba, arriba" from his corner, Duran contemptuously spun Leonard away as the round ended.

Leonard finally unloaded on Duran for the first time with thirty seconds left in the fifth round. Duran was caught off balance as the hooks came wide and fast, the pick of the shots being a peach of a left. "Oh, he hurt me to the body for sure once or twice," said Leonard. "But I hurt him too, whether he admits it or not." Leonard had not wilted and was now clawing his way back – but he was fighting the wrong fight, slugging it out with Duran instead of jabbing, moving and using his longer reach.

By the sixth round (some reports had the eighth), Juanita Leonard had fainted onto her sister's lap. She came to just as her husband was getting back into the fight. Duran sneered and shook his head after taking a left but the punch had hurt. He tried to keep the exchanges close to nullify Leonard's leverage and found an ally in Padilla who, conscious of the pre-fight criticism, was slow to break them. At times it was like a wrestling match as Duran continued to work over Leonard, capping a barrage at the end of the eight with a solid right that sank his foe into the ropes.

Duran jammed his head into Leonard's chin early in the ninth and followed it by raking his head into his eyes. A concerned Leonard checked his forehead for blood before Duran surged into him again, hooking off a jab. Leonard fought back with trademark flurries but Duran pawed at him with that annoying jab, waiting for the fourth one to deliver an overhand right that caught Sugar flush on the chin. After nearly half an hour of combat, Leonard still hadn't learned his lesson and continued to stand directly in front of his assailant.

Yet Leonard fired back with a stunning overhand right thrown in a downward motion midway in the tenth round, his best punch of the night. For the remainder of the round, he speared Duran with body shots and for the first time had recovered his cocksure nature. He even sent Duran back to his corner at the bell with a lightning right cross.

Leonard fired out of the corner for the next round and landed yet another overhand right. It was the cue for a toe-to-toe, blood and guts exchange. For fully forty-five seconds they clawed, clinched, hooked, raked eyes and bludgeoned each other at a pace that hadn't slackened since the first round. Leonard seemed to be landing the harder shots but Duran drove him into a corner for more punishment as the round ended. He carried on where he had left off after the interval, storming forward with the light of battle in his eyes.

As the fighters again returned to their corners between rounds, both had bumps under their eyes, with Duran's blackening slightly. Yet Leonard just couldn't snatch the momentum. A pattern had developed. Even when Leonard pot-shotted Duran from distance in the thirteenth, he couldn't stop the Panamanian from bouncing off the ropes with a furious return rally. Leonard returned fire and landed a flurry in the final ten seconds of the round, an eye-catching tactic that would sneak him rounds throughout his career. Yet even when Leonard won rounds, it *felt* like Duran's show.

On his stool before the start of the fourteenth round, Duran saw Angelo Dundee point over at him and whisper in Leonard's ear. Duran responded with a wave of a glove, urging Leonard to come forward. "Ray was fighting the wrong fight," said Dundee. "When he was coming back to the corner, I pleaded with him to stick and move more. But Duran would get him into a corner and trap him."

After a relatively quiet fourteenth round, Padilla brought them together for the most important three minutes of their boxing lives. Neither fighter could afford to coast, yet Duran did not charge out as he had for most the fight. He now fired punches not in combination but individually, as if he owned the fight, content to make Leonard miss. He must have felt he had the decision in the bag.

As the final bell sounded, Leonard raised his arms, but instead of the customary embrace Duran spurned him with a shove. "When he went to shake my hand, I told him to 'get the hell out of here, you shit. You know you're shit.' I demonstrated to the American public that their idol wasn't worth five cents," said Duran. Was it the best moment of his career? "Of course. He was the man. He was the greatest thing that America had. He was an idol, a hero. To beat a hero, I became a bigger hero."

Duran whirled around the ring like a con released from solitary confinement, then jumped high in the air. *I did it. You, Ray Leonard, are mierda.*

Before he headed back to wait for the final decision, Duran remembered something one of his enemies had said to him. Wilfred Benitez had been screaming obscentities at him the entire match. He broke free from Ray Arcel's arms, pointed at the watching Benitez and grabbed his crotch. His cornerman picked him up and held him high in the air. Even with a welt purpling under his left eye, Duran knew there was only one outcome. The half smile on Leonard's face suggested he knew too. The judges concurred.

Although the bout was originally scored a split decision in several newspaper reports the next day, it was later reversed: Judge Harry Gibbs of England had it 145-144 for Duran, Angelo Poletti (Italy) scored it a draw at 147-all, and Raymond Baldeyrou (France) had Duran 146-144. Poletti came under considerable scrutiny after it was learned that he scored ten rounds even.

Leonard knew it was extremely close but he also knew "just by the ambience of the evening" that the decision would not go his way. Duran had called out Leonard in front of La Casa de Piedra, and had won. "Eleta gave me about a million to fight Leonard but I just went and fought," said Duran. "That's all I ever did. People even said that Leonard was made by the television. I made myself by myself inside the ring. That's why Leonard was afraid."

Duran later unbuckled his WBC belt, a green plastic affair made by Adidas, and handed it to gnarled old Freddie Brown. "Es tuya, te la has ganado." "This is yours. I won this for you."

In Panama, a party began. In Guarare, a whole town rejoiced.

Throughout the bout, Clara Samaniego had closed her eyes, wished away the *brujos*, clung to her faith like a child's blanket and waited for the result. She sat with a reporter from *La Critica* and her daughter in the home her son had bought for her in the Los Andes neighborhood, clutching a mini-crucifix and a bible called "El Magnifico." Tears streamed down her face as she heard the verdict. "I asked the Virgin del Carmen to help him because my son is good," she said. "I remember when Roberto brought me $1.50 so that we could eat. It was a tough life. When I looked sad, Roberto would come to me and say, 'Mama don't you worry. When I am big, you're going to see that everything will change.'"

Leonard conceded to Panamanian journalist Juan Carlos Tapia the next morning at breakfast, in the company of Dundee, Arum and Elias Cordoba of the WBA that "Duran made me react like a man. Next time would be different." Tapia believed that while Leonard knew he *could* win, Duran knew he *would* win. "After Leonard came back from the hospital, he told me that he lost the fight because he wanted to be more of a man than Duran," said Tapia.

Most other observers agreed. "Duran was a classic example of the importance of thinking in boxing," said boxing sage and acclaimed author Budd Schulberg. "I covered the first Leonard fight and Leonard was a great fighter who was in there fighting Duran's fight, punching with him. He was doing everything wrong."

A photo in *Sports Illustrated* encompassed the mood of adulation, jubilation and reward. Stuck in between Duran's thumb, middle and index fingers, a wad of thick bills stood straight up as a wave of followers surrounded him at the press conference. Felicidad's face was partially cut by the perforated edge of the photo, but her eyes were nestled somewhere in her lover's slicked back hair. The couple had not yet married, but Duran had finally earned the respect of her family. She supported her future husband and understood a wife's role in the process. Felicidad knew when to stay away before a fight and when to intervene in Roberto's business.

"She came to almost all of the fights," said Plomo. "She would always come by the end, when there was only one week left. She was a very nervous person. She used to sit on the last row, for she did not like to watch the fight. Once she realized he had won the fight, she would return. She was a very nervous person, and preferred not to be present when he was fighting. She used to remain at the gym until the moment they would announce the fight was about to start. Then she would leave without watching the fight itself."

No doubt money would be spent recklessly in the coming hours, but the shirtless Duran was free, secure and wealthy. Leonard mourned in a grey and red Franklin warm-up, still a doe-eyed kid with his wife resting her head on his shoulder. Around him, his handlers talked prematurely about retirement.

"One Mother, One Tear, One Champion," ran the headline in *La Critica* the next day.

Sixteen days later, Cleveland Denny, who had never recovered from being knocked unconscious on the undercard, died in hospital. He was twenty-four years old.

# 14

## "No Peleo"

*"Anyone told me Duran would quit, I'd spit in his eye."*

Ray Arcel, aged eighty-one

RAY LEONARD FIGURED it out while he was running on a beach in Hawaii. Pounding over the strip of soft sand between lapping waves and palm trees, he arranged his thoughts and came to terms with defeat.

Instead of heading home to heal after the Montreal war, Leonard had taken his family on vacation to Hawaii for two weeks' thinking time. He took inventory of his life. So much had happened before, during and after the fight that he needed to let it all soak in. Only then would he make the decisions that mattered most. His family "was devastated," he said. "My wife fainted. No one has ever seen me get hit like that or lose, so it was very traumatic. If you go back and watch the tapes you see people crying. My sister … they were all devastated."

As his feet sank into the sand on his morning run, confusion, self-doubt and anger turned to burning desire. Duran had beaten him, insulted his wife, derided his masculinity, dashed his aura of invincibility and battered his ego. Yet Leonard had also emerged stronger. By brawling with Duran, by going into the pit with him, Leonard had become not just a boxer but a *fighter*. He had satiated many who feared that he couldn't *take it*. "They saw that I wasn't just another network or Wide World of Sports figurine," he said. "I was legit, and I could fight. I could give back as well as I could take it."

Before the fight, Duran had asked a reporter, what is a kid born yesterday going to teach me? But it was more about what Leonard had learned from Duran. He had learned that he couldn't allow another fighter to intimidate or anger him before a fight, and that he couldn't beat a streetfighter in a slugfest. Hawaii allowed Leonard to face reality. He returned from his vacation set on revenge – but on his own terms.

"When I was running on the beach in Hawaii everyone was telling me, 'Man, that fight was close. Man, if you fight him the other way you'll beat him.' I got such support from fans that I told Mike [Trainer], 'Let's go back and fight him. Now, right away.'"

On June 24, meanwhile, the new welterweight champion had landed in Panama to an estimated 700,000 fans jostling for a glimpse of him. It was declared Roberto Duran Day in Panama. "I want you to know this," he told the crowd, pointing to his championship belt. "This does not really belong to me, but belongs to you, my people, my people who supported me and whom I love." The crowd, misunderstanding where he was pointing, burst into laughter. "The Panamanian public always thinks the wrong thing. I grab the belt and say, this that is hanging here is for you guys," said Duran. "I'm talking about the belt, and the Panamanians thought I was talking about a little further 'down south.' And after a while it became a big joke."

Fittingly, given how he would celebrate over the next few weeks, a new beer, Manos De Piedra, was brewed in his honor. No more dropping horses in Guarare to pay for liquor tabs, or shining lawyers' shoes for pittance; now he had the money to buy the bar and the horse. Young, handsome and draped in the Armani that he and Chaflan used to admire in store windows, Duran had everything he could have dreamed of. With months of hard training and abstinence behind him, he embarked on an unending party, surrounded by a mass of sponging friends and family.

Duran went back to New York to continue the party with his friends Abuela Lopez and Chivo Sagur. "Duran took them both to New York together with his own wife after he won in June," said Plomo. "They remained there until September, and they would go out a lot together. He confessed having spent about $100,000 during that time in New York. He would pay for all the expenses."

Carlos Eleta, whose grip on his boxer had inevitably loosened as he became older, wealthier and more independent, faced a crucial decision. An extraordinarily lucrative offer was on the table for an immediate rematch with Leonard. Should he take it? The rich landowner worried about his fighter's lifestyle. The way Duran was running off the rails it was not impossible that he could lose his next fight even if they selected a patsy.

Ever since the day Eleta had caught Duran stealing coconuts in his backyard, he had felt a bond with the young tearaway. They had made millions together and their business relationship had turned into a familial closeness. But money had also evened the playing field and gave Duran freedom – or license. It was perhaps a sign of how Eleta's control was slipping that he felt compelled to tie up a rematch with Leonard quickly, before Duran self-destructed; for he already suspected he could do little to stop him. "I made that rematch in three months because he started drinking," said Eleta. "I said if he will fight again, he would lose to a second-rate fighter."

To this day, people are critical of Eleta's decision. "I was surprised that he made the rematch that quickly," said Luis DeCubas, who would manage Duran towards the end of his career. "If you know you have a fighter who's going to celebrate for a while, then wait to make a rematch." It was a decision that would come to haunt both fighter and manager. Angelo Dundee, however, knew that money was the most powerful incentive in boxing. "No, it wasn't a surprise at all," he said. "What the heck, the fight was meant to be." By August, negotiations were underway, and the figures being suggested were mind-boggling: Duran was expected to make around $10 million and Leonard $7 million as pay-per-view TV continued to cause massive inflation in fighters' purses. For Leonard, the rematch was inevitable. "It's all about bragging rights," he said. "To prove that you're the best you fight the best. Even if you have to fight him again to prove it wasn't a fluke. I knew the history of Duran and that's why I asked for the rematch so soon because I knew he was in a celebratory mode. I caught him in the middle of that. This all goes back to tactics."

Judging by the mass of backslappers and party people surrounding him, Duran had no intention of staying in shape, or of fighting again any time soon. "I got back to Panama and I felt like the king of the world," he said. "I start drinking and get fat, I am with women up and down. I go to New York and it's the same thing there. I get up to two hundred and twenty-five pounds. Eleta should have never taken that fight that soon. He should have given me time to prepare myself. They said that they offered Eleta ten million dollars to accept the fight, but the truth is that I don't know how much they gave him."

The rematch was officially signed by early September and scheduled for November 25, 1980 in the vast New Orleans Superdome. Duran started training late and had only about two months to lose what he claimed was seventy-eight pounds, though other reports claimed it was more likely that he had to reduce from 185 pounds rather than 225. Certainly he looked decidedly pudgy when he sat at ringside for the pitiful Larry Holmes-Muhammad Ali title fight in Vegas on October 2, a travesty which saw the most famous and charismatic sportsman on the planet reduced to a stumbling punchbag. As soon as the beaten Ali's retirement was announced, the Panamanian leapt into the press bench shouting in Spanish, "Now I'm the Greatest!" He was egged on by Latin commentators, who reached their microphones towards him, but others were embarrassed by his display and he was eventually asked, politely, to sit. Duran was reported as "flabby, scaling at least middleweight" by *Boxing News* editor Harry Mullan. Yet at that moment in boxing history, he was indeed the greatest.

His preparation, in Miami Beach, continued badly and from the moment he and his posse eventually arrived in New Orleans, Eleta felt he could lose. "He committed so many mistakes in training without anybody knowing," said the white-haired patrician years later. "I took him to New Orleans in plenty of time. They say he drank beer and ate too much. There were all these *manzanillos* hanging around. I told him to get all these people out of here but he said they were his friends and he needed them around. Some of them were mixed up in drugs. Some claimed Roberto was also, but I don't think so.

"His friends were bringing him food late at night. Ray Arcel came to me and said, 'Carlos, something is wrong. I am training Roberto and he is not losing the weight. He's gaining weight.' I find out that someone in Panama, they call him Abuela, was taking food to his room, beer and this and that. He was telling Duran that the handlers don't know what they are doing. Fifteen days before the fight he was twenty pounds over the weight. Arcel told me that I had to postpone the fight but when I told my friend the promoter, he told me it was impossible because he put a lot of money into that fight. I made him sign a contract where he has to put all the money fifteen days before the fight in Panama. When Duran entered the ring, that money came to us. I saved his purse in that fight.

"That's why I made the rematch with Leonard in a couple months. Roberto was out of control. I said if I don't go and sign that fight he will go and lose with nobody. I tried to put everybody out, but he said, 'I need these people. They are my people of Panama and I need those people to surround me.' That was the worst thing that he could do. When you have forty or fifty people surrounding your fighter, to sleep with him, eat with him, talk to him and train, it's impossible. After Montreal, he wouldn't listen to Brown, Arcel or myself, he was on top of the world."

Things were not all well in the Leonard camp either. His long-time trainer Dave Jacobs quit after complaining that Leonard should have fought a tune-up bout first. "That sort of fight takes its toll on your body," Jacobs said, referring to the grueling brawl in Montreal. "You need a tune-up to get the timing back. I love Sugar Ray but I don't think it's healthy for him to be fighting Duran right away." An indifferent Leonard shrugged off the split.

The Canadian tax department also weighed in with a claim for $2 million from Leonard's purse for the first fight. The Olympic Installations Board, who organized the fight, had claimed they had been given an exemption from federal taxes, but the Government begged to differ. The Board reported a loss of $900,000 on the promotion when everyone else involved made a massive profit. Despite this, Angelo Dundee knew his man was focused as never before. "I was very pleased with the way Ray prepared for that fight," said Dundee. "I told him not to let this guy psych him out. He was mad enough about the abuse Duran gave to his wife and he used it as motivation."

Duran did his best to play the part expected of him. "You're going to see blood in this fight," he told a New York press conference attended by both boxers three weeks before the event. "I don't like to see clowns in the ring. I like to see boxers. To beat me, you have to come into the ring and fight me. He goes into the ring and tries to imitate Ali, but an imitator is a loser." He then pushed his face close to Leonard's and said, "I'm going to knock you out. I don't like you." Leonard kept his cool, praising Duran's strength, toughness and intelligence and predicting only that it would be a great fight. A few days later, at another presser in New Orleans, he even joked, "He's a lovable guy. I want my son to be just like him."

The Panamanian reporters who made the trip to New Orleans could read Duran better than anybody. They also reported that Flacco Bala had been dancing with young girls from Leonard's camp. That only added to the intrigue. "Two foreign girls (who had been with Flacco Bala) arrived at Duran's suite the morning before the confrontation," wrote journalist Ricardo Borbua. "And it made us think and suspect that many disturbing things had passed before the fight because Duran either was not in optimal point of his physical conditioning or he had been traveling New Orleans in a bad state and little preparation. To say to the contrary would be dishonest."

With three days to go, the *New York Times* reported that only about 15,000 tickets had been sold in the 80,000-seat stadium. King sold the fight package to the Hyatt for $17.5 million and held the Latin American rights with Neil Gunn from Facility Enterprises. Ringside seats ranged from $500 to $1,000 apiece, while prices for the 345 closed-circuit theaters went from $35-$50. Not only had the promotional activities got a late start but also the bout would fall on Thanksgiving weekend, a very busy time to travel. Many fans decided the trip was not worth the hassle. Also ABC had reserved the rights to show the fight thirty days after the bout, leaving some to wait for the replay. While the first Montreal fight amassed close to $30 million, the rematch remained a chilly sell.

Duran's paternal grandmother, Clara, came to New Orleans and put a crucifix around Duran's neck for protection the day of the fight. He would need more that that.

* * *

It may be the most notorious pre-fight meal in history. At 1 p.m. the day of the fight, having made the weight, Duran gorged. The exact combination of foods, and the amounts, would be debated for years to come. Newspapers differed on the quantities but each agreed it included a warm and cold cycle of steak and orange juice. Steak was one food that made boxers feel as strong as a bull; they could piss nails after a protein-packed meal. Duran wolfed his as though back in a Chorrillo *cantina* scavenging leftovers.

Angelo Dundee had been secretly delighted to see Duran gulp down a beef broth as soon as he stepped off the scale at the weigh-in, a sure sign that he had gone through hell to lose weight. According to various reports, Duran then consumed two eggs, grits, peaches, toast, an orange, two T-bone steaks, peas, French fries and fried chicken. He rounded off the meal with beef consommé, hot tea, water, Kool-Aid and four large glasses of orange juice.

"I had a steak and a baked potato," recounted Duran. "You know, boxer's food. I think the major problem was drinking the hot cup of tea, then the cold glass of water, plus the shots I was given to lose the weight fast. I drank a real hot cup of hot tea because I was very thirsty.

But I committed an error because I then drank a real cold glass of water. That's when the pain felt even worse. And then I started to eat too much because I was dying; I was starving. I felt very weak, and my stomach was hurting me." The mysterious weight-losing shots were probably diuretics. "Everybody inside my dressing room, including Eleta, all knew what was wrong. But my mindset ... I thought the doctor was going to give me a shot to make me strong, but he didn't do anything."

Plomo, Duran's longtime trainer, could read all the angles. They had met when Duran was a child and Plomo had watched intently as the fighter gravitated from small-town hero to universal icon. "Duran was acting like a bohemian," he said. "He would sleep all day and party all night. Duran got up to 190 and had to get back down to 147. He ate three steaks and had five glasses of orange juice. Before the fight he complained about stomach pains to me. His stomach was stretching out."

Leonard, for the record, ate two eggs and grits, two pieces of toast, peaches and Kool-Aid for breakfast, then fried chicken, green peas, a glass of water and Kool-Aid for his pre-fight meal. Before the bout, Duran saw him jogging around the Superdome to warm up and thought he looked drawn. "I told myself that I was going to kill him," said Duran. But suddenly he felt even worse than Leonard had looked. "I start shadowboxing in the dressing room and Plomo comes in and I tell him that my liver was starting to hurt." His quick-fix training regime had taken its toll.

In fact when Leonard entered the ring he looked anything but weak. Wearing black trunks, shoes and socks for the first time in his professional career, he was making a statement: Now *I'm* the badass. "Even before the fight started and the referee was giving instructions, Duran was in La-La Land like I was the first fight," said Leonard. "During the referee's instructions, in the first fight I'm looking up at the screen and all around and Duran is looking at me like, 'Man I'm going to tear you up.' In the second fight, I'm just calm and Duran is in a whole other world. It was a different ballgame."

"I got this feeling when Ray Charles came out to sing, it was right up Sugar Ray's alley," said Duran publicist Bobby Goodman. "And I got an eerie, chilly feeling because it was one of the most stirring pieces before a sporting event that I'd ever heard. I just got goosebumps when Ray did it. It set the tone for the evening."

* ★ ★

The night had arrived. Ray Charles, after whom Leonard was named, chose to sing not the National Anthem but a highly charged rendition of "America The Beautiful." He then hugged his namesake and whispered encouragement in his ear. "If that rendition didn't touch, didn't move, didn't cause a chill along your spine," said Howard Cosell, "I don't suppose anything could."

For a man who put faith in the *brujos*, the vibe that night in New Orleans had to concern Duran. There wasn't that animalistic anxiety present that had Duran jumping out of his skin in Montreal; he was listless, appearing almost sedated during the now-customary staredown.

As the two boxers moved together at the opening bell, Duran held out his glove for a respectful tap. Leonard, all business, ignored him. It was a clear reversal of their expected roles. Leonard danced like a young Ali as Duran held the center of the ring. He flitted from side to side, refusing to let the Panamanian crowd him. Inside he played to his own jazz tune as he juked and jived in and out. Duran was baited and then nailed at the bell with a straight right to end the first round.

It was still early as Leonard uncoiled a right hand that stunned Duran, and sent him into a brief frenzy a minute into the second round. Duran charged and flailed at his nemesis against the ropes and walked into another Leonard right hand. Duran was landing also but the punches that stung Leonard in Montreal now lacked bite. At the round's end, Leonard sat in his corner admiring his work. For the first time in seventeen rounds against Duran, he looked content.

If Duran's mind seemed elsewhere, he wasn't hurt. He even managed to control the tempo and win the third with a late two-punch flurry to make up for a left hook that jarred him. But the more Ray Arcel cajoled his fighter to "be the boss," the less he complied. Neither fighter was throwing much leather as the challenger stuck to his safety-first plan of lateral movement and Duran seemed content to stalk – or plod – rather than charge. Leonard found openings for his uppercut to take the fourth, but in the fifth Duran continued to press, slipped punches and pinned Leonard for the first time. Both men had their moments, with Duran landing a clean left-right combination in a round that he won.

Leonard continued to move laterally at speed, and landed a left-right that shook Duran in the sixth round. Looking frustrated, Duran could only stand in the middle of the ring and follow, his jab now harmless.

The climax of Leonard's strategy came in the seventh round. After continuing to dance for the first minute or so, the Sugar Show began halfway through the round. He teed off on a flailing Duran with a startlingly fast five-punch combination while his back was to the ropes, and nearly repeated the same machine-gun flurry seconds later. He then came down onto his heels and went into an extraordinary exhibition. Leonard stuck his face out, baited Duran with an 'Ali shuffle', shrugged his shoulders like a body-popper and made Duran miss twelve punches in a row. As a display of public mockery it was both embarrassing and wondrous to watch, but not everyone was enamored. Even Howard Cosell, a big Sugar Ray booster, commented: "Leonard is showing his confidence but he is doing it in the wrong way."

With twenty-five seconds left in the round, Leonard stood in the middle of the ring and playfully wound up his right hand. Duran went for him with a jab, but Leonard then beat him to the punch with a snapping left. Spectators gasped. That audacious punch would become a metaphor for the whole fight. At the bell, Duran angrily and dismissively waved his glove at Leonard. Had he already given up?

It was the most significant round in both men's lives to that point.

Heading into the eighth, the judges had Leonard winning by gaps of only one or two points. Judge James Brimmel of Wales had it 67-66, while Britain's Mike Jacobs and Belgium's Jean Deswert scored it 68-66. The rounds were 4-2-1 twice and 4-3. It wasn't unusual for there to be disparity between the media and the officials, but Brimmel's score seemed way off the mark to most reporters. Leonard was fighting *his* fight, while Duran couldn't seem to get untracked.

Leonard performed his masterclass on top of a bum canvas, complaining and pointing from the first round on about a soft spot in the ring. Supporting bolts underneath the canvas had snapped, causing it to drop a few inches. "Rather than stop the fight at that point, I told all the guards from local colleges underneath to hold the ring," said Goodman. "It just seemed that night that everything went wrong."

For the first half of round eight, Leonard barely threw a punch as he moved around the ring, sneaking the odd single shot past Duran's guard. A spectator entering the arena at that point would have been unable to tell who was winning – neither was marked, neither was hurt and neither seemed dominant. But Duran seemed to have lost interest completely.

Leonard continued to sneak in punches, a left and short right to Duran's jaw. Seconds before the stoppage a befuddled Duran speared Leonard into the ropes with his head. With thirty seconds left Duran pawed at Leonard. Despite not taking much punishment, Duran put up his right fist to signal enough. Leonard saw Duran's guard down and hit him with a two-punch combination to the body that didn't seem to affect Duran before referee Octavio Meyran stepped between them. Duran turned his back on them both.

The bemused referee urged him to continue.

"Pelea, pelea." Box, box.

Duran walked away and raised and waved his glove again, a sign of surrender. He then looked back towards Leonard, who had moved away to the other side of the ring, and gestured towards him as if simulating masturbation. Leonard, unable to understand Spanish and suspecting a trick to lure him in, came over with his fists up, ready to continue. With twenty-three seconds left in the round, Meyran made a karate-chopping motion to urge the fighters to come together and resume. Instead he received another shake of the right fist from Duran.

"No quiero pelear con el payaso," said Duran. *I do not want to fight with this clown.* According to Meyran, Duran also said in broken English, "I don't box anymore."

"When I asked why," the referee said later, "Duran said, 'No más, no más.'"

Then Leonard heard his brother, Roger, yelling, "He quit on you Ray. He quit." Leonard ran and jumped on a ringpost and applauded himself. Roger stormed into the ring and went to punch Duran in the face; the fighter put his fists up and stepped back.

As Duran's cornermen climbed onto the ring apron, Hands of Stone trudged toward them. The venerable Arcel and Brown, men who had seen everything, were as stunned as the thousands of Panamanians who had bet their paychecks on Duran. "I almost fainted," Arcel told *Ring* magazine. "I thought maybe he broke his arm or something. I don't have the vocabulary to explain it. All I know is I'm quitting boxing. After sixty-three years, and now this? I've had enough. I have never seen anything like this. A big fight like this, and all the money."

Somewhere Duran's mother, Clara Samaniego, lit a candle and prayed for her son. No one was listening anymore.

★ ★ ★

Outside the ring, confusion reigned. "We didn't know what happened," said ringside reporter Bert Sugar. "The referee didn't know what was happening. It didn't calibrate. They said he was quitting and someone next to me said, 'Bullshit.' I didn't hear 'no más' but I saw him go like that [wave his glove]. Leonard hit him with a bodacious uppercut to the body and he didn't blink. And they're going to tell me it's stomach pains? He wasn't even looking at Leonard."

Steve Farhood was sitting a few seats away from Bert Sugar. "The *New York Times* business bureau had a function for the fortieth anniversary of JFK's death. They had great guests who were all in Dallas the day of Kennedy's death. One of them was talking about how he never [before] saw a rumor literally move through a room," said Farhood. "And you don't know what the rumor is, but you can see it turning. It was the same in New Orleans, except we saw it actually happen but we didn't believe it happened. I remember a head turning to me and saying something and me turning my head to the right to tell someone else. And we were all looking for confirmation that we just saw what we saw."

The simple, awful truth was that Duran had broken the unwritten contract he made the day he stepped in the boxing ring: To punch till the end. There was no need for translation, he had surrendered, demolishing the Latin notion of valor that he had helped build. Speculation raged as everyone in the arena searched for an explanation. Some were already starting to call Duran a coward, a fake, a phony.

One person had a closer view than anyone else. "He was in total frustration," said Ray Leonard. "It was like going to work and you can't get your car started. Then there's traffic and it's like, what do I do now?"

As Duran sat with his handlers and answered questions about the stoppage, his eyes drooped, but veteran TV broadcaster Howard Cosell let him down easy, unwilling to apply the knockout punch. Duran immediately retired, "No peleo más," and told Cosell that he would never fight again. Even at that point, too many pieces didn't fit. Duran didn't have any clue as to how the boxing world, his people, the fans who snuck into training sessions to see him, would react. Draped in superficial *manzanillo* flattery, the people who claimed to be his true friends had already vanished. "I think when he quit, he didn't realize the repercussions it would have on the world, his legacy," Leonard said.

Cosell, however, had already been instrumental in creating the central myth of the fight, with two words that will dog Duran for the rest of his life. The words had come out of Duran's mouth as, "I will not fight with this clown anymore." While broadcasting the fight, Cosell picked up only on the words "no más" and the phrase would live in sporting infamy. Referee Meyran also said he heard those two fateful words.

Carlos Eleta, however, insists they were never spoken. "I was right there and he never said no más," said Eleta. "Leonard was dancing around and making fun of him, mocking him. No, he just said he wasn't going to fight with this clown anymore. Leonard was circling in and trying to tire him because he knew Duran wasn't in good shape. Then Duran got mad and said, 'He's running, I'm not fighting with this clown.' I ran up to the ring and said, 'You have to fight.' It was too late."

Others ringsiders tried to reason with the seeming aberration.

"I was right there sitting with Eleta. Eleta kept a score of the fight on a yellow piece of paper," said Hall-of-Fame boxing historian Hank Kaplan. "We were both completely shocked. He didn't say anything to me. He just jumped up to the ring. I couldn't figure out why he turned his back. But I know he was in lousy shape and he depended on voodoo. He hired witchdoctors and he would bring chickens up to his room and slit their throats in the bathtub. You know that santeria stuff. He hired some guys from Latin America to do voodoo. He didn't train and when he did it was just to amuse his followers. He was disrespectful to Freddie Brown and only concerned with making his friends laugh. He thought he was invincible."

*Payaso*, or clown, was the Spanish word that Duran used to describe any opponent who refused to mix it with him. Duran curses in a cool Spanish argot that makes words like *maricon* and *puta* slither off his tongue: *Maaa-rrr—eeee-cahone*. Even watching a replay of the fight twenty years later in his home, the word buzzed off his lips. He would claim that Leonard didn't want to fight and he didn't want to chase him. It was hardly a good enough reason to quit in one of the biggest fights of all time, at least not on its own.

It was later reported that Duran had told Plomo in Spanish about stomach pains around the fifth round, the suggestion being that the message wasn't passed on to Arcel. It was an unlikely story that Duran would refute. They had never had much trouble with the language barrier in the corner. "I didn't say anything to my cornermen," said Duran. "When I stopped the fight, Eleta jumps up into the ring and says, 'Cholo, what happened?' I tell him that 'my stomach hurts, man. I got a pain right here, I feel really bad, I can't continue.' I told Eleta to just give me the rematch and I'll train better. I could have finished that round and not come out to fight. But I didn't want that, I wanted to end it right there. I couldn't move anymore. Every time I moved it was really difficult to breathe and I felt really weak."

It was apparently Freddie Brown who made up a story about stomach cramps. "He said he had a stomach ache," Brown told reporters. "I said, 'So what, youse get over it, get out and fight.'"

Said Leonard, "You couldn't fathom any fighter quitting, but Duran? No, how could you imagine that? That's a sensationalized dream. Duran quitting, no way." Leonard had made the bravest of men walk away. Before their first fight, he had promised to "upset Duran with my tactics; he's very temperamental. I'm going to drive him crazy." In their second fight, he made good.

Did the controversial ending detract from Leonard's superb performance? "No, it didn't," said Angelo Dundee. "They say he quit, but Duran was being knocked out by Leonard. He was this macho man. He couldn't take being kayoed. Ray was hitting him with tremendous shots to the body. You don't take those types of shots and survive. And I resent that people say that Duran was a quitter. Ray changed and Roberto couldn't cope with it. He was so much better this time around. Ray wanted it so bad he could taste it."

Not everyone, however, admired Leonard's antics. Thomas Hearns, sitting ringside, said how disappointed he was to see Leonard resort to taunting. And the formidable Iran Barkley would later say, "One thing I have to say about Duran is that when he went to fight, Leonard wouldn't fight him. And Duran always said Leonard was a faggot or *puta* in Spanish cause he wouldn't fight."

Eleta hadn't had the time to invent any feeble excuses. "If I knew that would happen," he said, "I would have told Ray [Arcel] to say something was wrong with his hand." Still, he tried his best to divert the criticism. First, he put an end to a party back at Duran's hotel. On the eighteenth floor of the Hyatt Regency in Room Number 1843, a gaggle of hangers-on were soon drinking and carousing with Duran. Journalist Ricardo Borbua wrote that the people yelled, "In the good times and the bad." He saw Duran singing and playing the juiro.

"He was with his friends, all these colonels from Panama, drinking, dancing," recalled Minito Navarro, a radio presenter and friend of the boxer. "They had no shame." Stephanie Arcel, looking for her husband, walked in on Roberto and Felicidad singing a duet. "You'd think he won the fight," said a despondent Freddie Brown. It was only when Eleta barged into the room to find Duran drinking too that the party broke up.

"It hurt me more when I went back to the hotel and there was a fiesta," said a frustrated Eleta two decades later. "After that I sent every-body out. I took him to the hospital." In the car with Papa Eleta, Duran began to cry. He realized what he had done.

Eleta still insists that the medical staff confirmed that Duran's stomach cramps were genuine and were the result of over-eating. Certainly Dr Orlando Nunez, after seeing the fighter, reported that he suffered from acute abdominal pains and would have fainted if he kept fighting. Nunez was Duran's special physician, and also claimed in a TV interview that Duran never took or was prescribed diuretics. Two other physicians looked at him. The Louisiana Athletic Commission had Dr A.J. Italiano test Duran for possible symptoms that would have forced a stoppage. Italiano said the stomach pains could have come from overeating during the afternoon hours before the fight. Dr Jack Ruli, who checked out Duran from the Southern Baptist Hospital at 3 a.m. the morning of the fight, said that he was "fine," but did admit a possible inflammation of the stomach.

Shep Pleasants was at the time the Vice-President for Development and Public Affairs for the hospital. He said Duran entered with an entourage and was taken to a $255-a-night suite on the fifth floor. "I didn't know Duran was in the hospital until I arrived the next day for my shift," recalled Pleasants. "I was deluged with calls from the media, friends, family. The phone was ringing off the hook. I just told everyone that he was fine. The one call that I remember vividly was from Duran's father in Arizona. I told him his son was fine and I thought to myself why Duran hadn't called his father himself.

"When I walked in, he had his whole entourage surrounding him. He was bright as a bullet. There was no distress hovering over the man. I said, 'Buenos dias, campeon,' but nothing more. He was sitting on the bed and he wasn't in hospital garb. At that time the sucker was fine, but I … if he had had a gastric problem, it could have been gone by the time I saw him. I think he went to the hospital as a public relations move. And most everyone in the hospital and the town figured that out. You can't just quit a fight and head back to the hotel and then decide to come to the hospital."

It was widely circulated among Panama reporters that Duran had told his closest confidantes at the Hyatt that there was no validity to the story about the stomach ache. "There was nothing wrong with him and the proof of that, he goes to celebrate with his friends in his hotel room," said journalist Juan Carlos Tapia. "Eleta arrives to go to hospital to justify that there would not be a more serious problem. But Duran didn't have anything wrong. There were no stomach cramps. He was simply not prepared for that fight. Leonard was beating him bad and Duran said that nobody will knock me out."

Of all the things that Duran lost that evening, from pride to the respect of his fans, he was able to keep his purse. As long as the opening bell rang and Duran entered the ring, his money was safe. By getting the money paid in a letter of credit, Eleta ensured that Duran would receive his share. It was that share that the Louisiana Ordinance Commission felt they were owed due to the "dishonest act."

Don King publicist Bobby Goodman went back to a meeting with the Louisiana Commission to clarify the terms of the agreement made before the fight even started. "The commission wanted to hold up his purse. I had to run back for a meeting with the commission and I told them that the purse was already paid in a letter of credit," said Goodman. "And the condition of the letter of credit was that we had to show them a newspaper article that the fight had happened. And it certainly happened. As soon as the bell rings, it was good. That was the terms of the contract, not that he fought badly, poorly or quit or whatever."

Although the commission fined Duran a nominal amount of $7,500, Goodman quickly cut a check and paid the fine. There were still some explanations to be heard. "I made an appeal to the commission that Duran had stomach cramps and how do you know what went on in the mind of this great champ to the point that he just couldn't continue," Goodman said. "I had mentioned the ring snapped and a lot of things were going on. And they accepted that."

Goodman had been close to Duran in the build-up to the fight and had noticed a change in him. "I didn't get the sense that he was as intense for the training. Knowing Roberto, the macho part of being Roberto Duran where he had achieved such legendary status was part of his being. He was Duran and you didn't have to say anything else. He was very proud of that and became quite a celebrity. Even up at the camp … I think he was so full of what everybody had written about him. I don't think he got a big head, but I just think he eased up."

* * *

The boxing world struggled to comprehend the incomprehensible. Roberto Duran, the man with hands of stone and a heart to match, who had never been stopped, knocked out or even badly hurt, had apparently given up. Most could not believe it; everyone had an opinion. "It would require a deal of convincing to shake the conviction here that Duran had to be sick or injured," wrote Red Smith, America's greatest sports columnist and winner of the Pulitzer Prize, "because Roberto Duran was not, is not, and never could be a quitter."

Forty-eight hours later, the man himself had changed his mind about retiring. "After what happened I've done some thinking and I've spoken to my wife and told her I'm going back to the ring. I had thought of retiring, but I'm not going to retire because Sugar Ray Leonard is not a man to beat me," he told a reporter.

But when asked about the promotion of a third bout between them, Don King told reporters, "The next time I promote a Leonard-Duran fight, it will be on the planet Pluto."

Duran, a sensitive man, cared deeply about the way Panamanians thought about him. Now a cloud hung over his proud little nation. "We drove all day and all night from the hotel to Miami," he recalled. "My wife and my kids and Danny Castro, and two Dominican friends of mine: Fabio Matos, his girlfriend, and a friend named Abuela Lopez and his wife. They all stayed with me. That was it. Everybody else abandoned me. I told Eleta to give me the rematch, but he said that Leonard doesn't want to fight with me. I said, 'Why not, we're one-and-one?'"

Duran offered to donate his purse in a third fight to charity, but later reneged. "I read all the stuff in the papers about claiming to fight for charity and my response to that is, 'Give the last one back; that's the one you didn't earn. I'll pay for the next one if you go the distance,'" said Trainer in an interview with *The Ring* in 1981. "But there's a problem. Duran has to go out and prove to the American public that he's not going to quit again. And he has to go out and fight somebody very significant to show them. Until he does that, another fight with Leonard is unthinkable."

Duran hid out in Miami as speculation raged. "Nobody knew exactly what happened," said boxing analyst Gil Clancy. "They were thinking all kinds of things. Everybody was saying, 'No más, no más.' He was sick to his stomach, and that's what it was. He couldn't help himself. He was going to go in his pants. That was the truth. Leonard fought a good fight and Duran was not ready for him. He gorged himself before the fight with food and malted milks and got hit in the belly and he just fell apart."

Plomo thought he had the answer to the no más riddle. "Duran has always been an extraordinary boxer, a monster as you say. On many occasions he has fought feeling not well, but no one knew about it. He would not tell. But this time it was the stomach, and besides, this rival had not come to box; he had come to behave like a buffoon. This conduct much angered Duran, who wanted him to fight. This is why he told him he could be the winner. Leonard had not really hit him, it was Duran who actually abandoned the fight."

But many were unwilling to believe that a man who once threatened to knock out God if he entered the ring had surrendered without even being hurt. Few events in sports history have been more controversial. "I don't think that was him that night," said veteran trainer Lou Duva. "When a guy has been fighting all his life, he would fight a tiger. But when he gets in and does that, that wasn't him that night. Something was wrong. I don't think it was so much Leonard but I think he was beat before he got into the ring. Something was wrong."

Bobby Goodman: "The no más was more of him not being as prepared as he was the first time. He was showing his macho and was mad because Leonard didn't want to fight. I didn't accept that talk about stomach cramps, and I didn't know why he did it, but I knew his macho and the fact that this guy wouldn't meet him toe-to-toe was upsetting to him. You don't want to fight, forget it. Sticking his nose out and his tongue out, and Duran was like, 'Fuck you, I'm not fighting anymore.' It was emotional. Maybe he was misguided but that was his feeling. And I've never known him to not do what he felt."

Bert Sugar: "He's never fully explained it, but if I can be a ringside psychiatrist practicing without a license, which we all do, it was the schoolyard bully syndrome. If you run from him he'll catch you; if you hit him he'll beat you. He said he wasn't going to fuck around with clowns. The first fight Leonard had the worst game plan since Goliath tried to come forward dead."

Emanuel Steward: "He just got frustrated by Ray. Ray was so sharp that night and he wouldn't fight Duran like he wanted to. He was using all of these annoying tactics. So Duran was like, 'The hell with this. I'm leaving.' With his mindset it wasn't like he was quitting; it was a macho thing. He was called a coward but it wasn't that way. He just wasn't going to be bothered with all that stuff. With Duran you were dealing with a high-strung emotional person and what he did wasn't a way of surrendering. This highly instantaneous personality helped make him a great fighter. You can't knock him for that."

Ismael Laguna: "We have never talked about that no más fight. Duran had a lot of pride and wouldn't allow Sugar Ray Leonard to put him on the canvas. He'd rather walk away than see himself get knocked out. He was different when he got money," added the former champ. "Once he became a millionaire, he felt that he could do anything that he wanted. When Duran lost to Leonard I told him to retire, but he told me no and that he could keep fighting. I explained to him that it was better to retire young and healthy."

Luis DeCubas: "There's a lot of theories about no más that only Roberto can answer. Some people pushed all the right buttons and Mike Trainer was one of those guys. He knew that Duran was going to keep partying right after that fight and had the sense to make the rematch right away. Leonard was back in the gym right after that fight. Ray fought a good fight but Ray's people won that fight. Back then the weigh-in was the day of the fight and he ate a big steak and it gave him stomach problems. That's what happened."

Juan Carlos Tapia: "There were no stomach aches, cramps or problems. Simply Duran was not prepared and had to lose a lot of weight. Leonard was beating him real bad and Duran said, 'No one is going to knock me out.' He turned his back and he left. It was total frustration."

Journalist Hank Kaplan: "The morning after no más, I was eating breakfast at the Meridien hotel with my wife and Willie Pastrano. Duran was two tables away eating the biggest breakfast I have ever seen in my life. He had just gone to see a doctor to run a test about his stomach. It was about 9:30 AM and he was eating this huge breakfast with a plate half the size of the table. It didn't speak well of his upset stomach. The way he looked it was as if he was completely oblivious to what he created. Maybe he was harboring the pain and stupidity of the fight. But he was getting whacked in the mush that night and he probably just said the hell with it. I don't think it was much more than that."

Others believed the overriding factor was Duran's lack of condition. "In the second fight, Duran was out of shape and that's why he pulled the *no más* stuff," said former opponent Lou Bizzarro. "The boxing people couldn't believe it. I knew he was out of shape for him to quit like that. Even when he put his arm up, Leonard hit him to the body but it didn't faze him. Still, he knew he couldn't handle a pace like that. Duran would have destroyed Leonard if they fought at lightweight. Leonard couldn't shine Duran's shoes. Leonard was a welterweight who had a lot of things going for him, if you know what I mean. But people pay money to see a good fight and you just can't do stuff like that. If you get knocked out they accept it but if you make a U-turn and walk out, to me that's not right. It's something that a fighter should never do."

J. Russell Peltz: "Whenever I think of a guy quitting, I think of Carmen Basilio. Here was a guy who would walk through Hell. I saw him attack a referee in the second Fullmer fight for stopping the fight. He was getting his ass kicked. So when I see these guys quit, and I'm not knocking fighters because they all have stones just to be a fighter, but relatively speaking that's how I feel about that stuff."

Within the boxing fraternity, fighters and trainers alike searched for answers. Only those who had faced such a situation in the ring could hope to understand it. "I think a lot of fight people saw it as Duran just being frustrated," said Carlos Palomino. "He was a street guy and just acted without even considering the repercussions. He was probably like, 'Fuck it. No más.' I could see it when he took the robe off that he wasn't the same fighter as the first fight. He didn't look cut like he had before.

"But that was Duran's rep, he would blow up so quickly between fights. Even as a lightweight I heard about how he would go back to Panama and get up to 180 pounds. He would just get into shape for the fights that he wanted. He even went up to 200 pounds when he was fighting at 147. He didn't have the energy against Leonard. He couldn't push up against the ropes like he did in previous bouts. He couldn't close on Ray."

Budd Schulberg: "Duran was a classic example of the importance of thinking in boxing. I covered the first Leonard fight and Leonard was a great fighter who was in there fighting Duran's fight, punching with him. You realized in that fight he was doing everything wrong. Then, in the second fight, he took Duran apart. But he didn't do it physically;

he did it with his mind. He absolutely frustrated Duran by being so evasive and driving him so crazy, but no punches were being landed. Really nobody was hurt in that fight, but when Leonard stuck out his tongue – which I couldn't entirely admire him for – at maybe the greatest lightweight that I've ever seen, poor Duran threw up his hands and said, 'No más.'

"Throughout the fight there was a growing frustration with Duran. He would say, 'C'mon, let's fight.' He came out of the streets of Panama, and all he knows is the fight. And he is all of a sudden confronted by someone who says, 'I'm not really going to fight you, I'm going to destroy you by not fighting.' It blew his mind. I've always said that boxing is a chess match. The chessboard is the body and the face of the opponent. I never saw that proved more than when Duran was outchessed that night."

One boxing magazine mooted several theories, including the Duran Was Behind And Knew He Wasn't Going To Beat Sugar Ray No Matter What Theory, the Duran Didn't Feel Like Fighting And Took The $8 Million And Ran Theory, and the Duran Downed Enough Food The Day Of The Fight To Feed A Family Of Four For A Week Theory. It concluded, however, that Duran's walkout was "strictly an instinctive act that he almost immediately regretted," a reaction to his own lack of fitness and Leonard's taunting. It remains the most plausible explanation.

Hundreds of times since, Duran has reiterated that his stomach wouldn't let him continue. "I would do it again if I had the pain," he says in his scratchy voice in his house in the Cangrejo district as his son, Fulo, climbs on him. "Let's put it this way, when I got up into the ring I couldn't even move. I was fighting to breathe and by the third round the pain was really sharp, and I thought to myself that I had to go fifteen rounds of this."

When Duran finally returned to Panama several weeks later, after his sojourn in Miami, his reception was hostile. People called him a coward. They wrote "Duran is a Traitor" on murals. It was reported in several publications that people vandalized his mother's home in Los Andes. While her son claimed, "I don't believe in witches, only in God," Clara would blame the *brujos* for his loss, and remembers how the crowds wailed, "Cholo, perdio," and lamented outside her home. "The saddest moment for me is when we saw Roberto give his back to Leonard," she said. "That was very, very sad. I knew that Roberto was not well prepared."

Despite the reaction of many of his countrymen, journalists supported him. "All the country was against Duran," said Juan Carlos Tapia. "They were very angry. Duran took about three weeks before he came back to Panama. He was ashamed. I made a program when Duran arrived of all the big victories of Duran's career. In the end I talked about the *no más* fight and I asked the public to put everything in a balance, his successes and *no más*. The public understood they had to support Duran in that moment. They forgot about it very quickly. The positives he had done were much more than he had done in one fight."

Duran refused to leave his house. Locked in like a caged animal, hiding from the world, he slumped into a depression and railed bitterly at his critics. "Hypocrites, all of them," he said. "I came home and I wouldn't leave. My wife was telling me to go out and have fun with my friends. I just didn't feel like going out because people were going to start talking stuff and throwing cheap shots at me. I didn't feel like hearing that.

"What most affected me was that my people turned their backs on me. I was always in the house. I wouldn't even go outside. I would stay three weeks up to a month right here and I wouldn't go anywhere. I told Eleta to give me the rematch. My birthday was coming up and my wife had a party for me. I got drunk but I never left the house."

Duran had a lot of time to enjoy the toys that his new life afforded. Already a millionaire, the huge payday in New Orleans had given him money to burn. Exempt from paying taxes in Panama, he already owned eleven cars, including a pair of Pontiac Trans-Ams, a Lincoln Continental, a Fiat, a Mercedes from Eleta, and a $25,000 van equipped with a stereo, TV and telephone. General Torrijos gave him the van after he knocked out DeJesus in 1978.

According to Eleta, Duran's share of the purses, after taxes, was $6 million, and this had been put in an account in Panama. At least one-third of the money was ring-fenced for Duran's future. "When I came back to Panama, I put two million dollars in the bank. He has ten per cent interest on that money. I knew that he would spend all that money quickly so I made him sign with his wife a document so that all the money goes to the bank and he couldn't touch it for ten years," Eleta told this author years later in Panama. "What happened was, [Colonel] Paredes went to the bank with Felicidad and the bank handed over the millions of dollars. His wife bet thousands and thousands of dollars daily. His friends took money away from him. I just lost control of him. With all those people around all the time, I couldn't control him anymore and that was it." Ruben Paredes was a high-ranking National Guard officer who came to power in a coup in March 1982.

Duran found some sympathizers. "I felt sorry for him," said Budd Schulberg, author of *On The Waterfront* and *The Harder They Fall*, who was in the press row at the fight. "The whole culture of Latin fighters and Mexican fighters is to come to fight. They don't come to dodge and miss and duck, they just come to fight. And so it was sort of a culture clash that night between a predator who only knows one way to go, one gear, and Leonard who had discovered a whole set of gears. Some cars have five gears and some cars have three, and Sugar Ray had five that night."

Schulberg's soft spot for Duran is evident. One of the few writers who saw both Benny Leonard and Duran fight live, Schulberg always put the fighter first. "I felt sorry for him because I understood him and it simply underscored for me one more time what a mental game boxing was. In spite of that night, I will remember him as one of the greatest lightweights that ever lived. Duran never had the power at welterweight that he did as a lightweight, and he never had that power as a middleweight that he did as a welter."

*No más* became a universal phrase. Do you want anything else with dinner? *No más.* So you don't want to stay at this job any longer? *No más.* Hey, it's funny, you don't even have to know who or what a Roberto Duran is. "The no más thing? It's like being in love with a girl then being betrayed and devastated, but you can't get her out of your system," said Las Vegas oddsmaker Herbie Lambeck.

"I didn't speak with Duran about no más," said Leonard. "He has to deal with that and live with that. I'm sure there's not a day that goes by when he's out in public that someone doesn't say, 'No Más.' It also became the butt of jokes for a while. I didn't sympathize directly. But looking back on it, naturally I wouldn't wish that on anyone, to make a decision in the ring that is going to make you the butt of jokes throughout your life."

Duran wouldn't return to Panama for weeks after the fight. Judging by the anger and even looting that followed the result, it was a wise decision. However, before he left the parking lot that evening in New Orleans, Duran was waiting in the passenger's seat of his van. As Leonard walked through the lot he noticed a Panamanian with a blank stare. After getting Duran's attention, he gave him a quick wave.

A reluctant wave where a middle finger used to be.

# 15

## KING OF THE BARS

*"Sometimes I look like a dragon, sometimes I'm radar."*

Wilfred Benitez

NO ONE TOOK the debacle harder than Ray Arcel and Freddie Brown. Arcel would be asked about it for the rest of his life, but even the man who had seen almost everything in boxing and in life was at a loss to explain it. "I almost had a nervous breakdown," he later told an interviewer. "Something happened, and we don't know why he did it. To this day I don't know and the kid himself doesn't know. You know, we're all human beings. Unless you've boxed, you don't know the physical and mental torture. I mean it's *torture*. It's like a guy waiting to be electrocuted."

According to the author Ronald K. Fried, in his book *Cornermen*, Freddie Brown fell into a lasting depression. Randy Gordon, editor of *The Ring*, told Fried he returned to New York on a plane with Brown. "Freddie cried like a baby on my shoulder," said Gordon. "Because he had seen them all. Jack Johnson and Benny Leonard. And Harry Greb. And he was always saying Roberto Duran could probably beat any one of them in his prime ... And then he went out and quit – something that Freddie Brown really could not understand any real fighter doing, much less Roberto Duran." The old cutman locked himself away at home, refused to take calls, stopped even watching fights.

Brown and Arcel also fell out. There had been tension between the two for some time over who did the most work in the camp. Arcel, an articulate and considered interviewee, tended to draw press attention while Brown felt that he was Duran's true conditioner, dealing with the fighter's tantrums and moods until Arcel swanned in a week or so before a fight from his day job to "oversee" things and run the corner. Brown also felt Arcel was wrong to tell reporters he had no idea why Duran quit; to Brown, you covered for your fighter no matter what. That was why he had put out the story about stomach cramps. "If they knew in Panama he'd quit, they'd have murdered him when he got back," Brown told Dick Young of the *New York Post* in 1984. "So I made the alibi."

Eleta went back to Panama, and berated his fighter through the press. Never one to hold back, he pleaded with Duran to lose the hangers-on. Another of Duran's mentors, Omar Torrijos, also took *no más* badly. "After Roberto did that, Torrijos never talked to him again," claimed Eleta. Duran claimed that he and Torrijos had resolved their differences concerning the bout. "The General said that many Panamanians are hypocrites, and he knows the people better than I do," Duran told reporters in Panama. "The General had considered this case like that of Judas. These people, that were with Duran before the fight, had abandoned him after it."

The country's mood of gloom deepened when Torrijos died in a mysterious airplane crash on 30 July 1981, on a flight to the town of Colecito. The tragedy was related in the book *Our Man in Panama* by John Dinges. "It was said that Torrijos had no sense of danger and forced his pilots to fly no matter what the weather. That day, he chose to fly despite the storm front shrouding the mountains around Colecito, and heedless of the relative inexperience of the pilot. The plane struck the top of a hill while the pilot was maneuvering for a landing. All aboard were killed." It ended a twelve-year reign in which compassion for the poor had made him the most revered figure in Panama since independence in 1903. The country had lost the head of the National Guard but also a calming figure who acted as a rational mediator between other Latin American countries. It affected Duran as deeply as the death of Chaflan.

It would also mark a decline in Panama's fortunes. Inevitably a military power struggle followed the President's death. Many thought the crash had actually been engineered by his understudy, Manuel Noriega. The country fell into a political quagmire as various factions competed for supremacy. Colonel Ruben Paredes, who had promoted himself to head of the National Guard, forced out the incumbent President Aristides Royo and set his sights on the 1984 presidential elections. However, Noriega, who took over as National Guard leader in 1983, had other plans. He undermined his colleague, and after a period of factional strife emerged as the most powerful figure in the country. With the violent Noriega at the helm, Panama was soon tagged internationally as a drug-trafficking, corruption-filled country that was both politically and financially unstable.

Duran, meanwhile, wallowed in self-pity. Moves were made to match him with undefeated junior welterweight sensation Aaron Pryor, and Pryor told a *New York Times* reporter in late February 1981 that he had signed a contract for $750,000 to face Duran in New York, but the fight was pushed aside for the heavyweight contest between Gerry Cooney and Ken Norton. A ferocious prospect who few wanted to face, Pryor offered to spot Duran ten pounds in weight. "Duran needs me," Pryor said. "I think he's got to prove to a lot of people that he's not a quitter and what better way to do it than fight an undefeated world champion."

Finally, nine months after holing up in his palatial home, Duran ended his exile and took a fight against a much easier opponent, his former sparring partner Mike "Nino" Gonzalez. The bout was staged by Don King in the promoter's hometown of Cleveland, Ohio. Duran's public workouts in Cleveland's Union Terminal drew large crowds and surprisingly they cheered his every move. His optimism began to return.

"The Comeback," as King inevitably billed it, took place on 9 August 1981. Gonzalez, from Bayonne, New Jersey, was for some reason dubbed the "Storm Cutter" and came in with a 24-1 record. He had traveled with some other Jersey fighters to work with Duran before he faced Leonard in Montreal and felt confident enough to stand and trade punches. Duran's body looked soft, not taut, and he fought like a man who had been locked in his home for months, coming in at 155 pounds. He won clearly on the scorecards but Gonzalez showed bravery, especially in a grueling ninth round, and cut Duran's eye. "I haven't fought in nine months," Duran said afterwards. "I felt strong with the weight, but I got a little tired near the end. That was because of the layoff. I couldn't make my body do certain things."

People expected more. On September 26, Duran took on European light-middleweight champion Luigi Minchillo, who had won thirty-five of his thirty-six bouts. They fought in Vegas in bright sunlight and near-ninety-degree temperatures before a crowd of about 2,000. Duran suffered a cut over his right eye in the third round but it was staunched by veteran cutman Bill Prezant, renowned for his patchwork with heavyweight Chuck "the Bleeder" Wepner. Minchillo bored in and tried to pressure Duran but the Panamanian bossed the fight from the start, slamming in the harder punches, especially to the body, and rocking the moustachioed Italian several times. Minchillo finished the bout with his left eye almost shut, his right eye swollen and blood coming from his nose. Duran, who weighed in on the light-middleweight limit of eleven stone, said afterwards he felt strong and was punching harder then ever.

★ ★ ★

In 1982, Wilfred Benitez was The Radar. He could slip punches with his senses and made opponents feel lonely in the ring, jutting out his chin then retracting it before a glove could touch skin, standing within punching range yet avoiding shots by fractions. On March 6, 1976, he made the great Antonio Cervantes miss for fifteen rounds to win the WBA junior welterweight crown and confirm his precocious genius. At just seventeen, he was the youngest boxer ever to win a world title.

"People went crazy in Puerto Rico when Benitez became champion," said Jose Torres. "I was there and that fight was spectacular. Punch and move, punch and move, body and head, he never got tired. What he had was impossible to learn, nobody could teach you that. He was so perfect. He was so young to understand that; he just did it instinctively. He didn't say, 'I was smart, that's why I win.' He was not aware. He just knows that he punches when he has to punch."

Benitez was the youngest of eight children born in the Bronx, New York City, where his father and mother, Gregorio and Clara, had moved in the early Forties to work. When Wilfred was seven they moved back to St George, seven miles from San Juan. Two of his brothers, Gregory and Frankie, became boxers and young Wilfred followed. He was easily the best and his rare talent saw him included in the Puerto Rican team for the Central American and Caribbean Games at the age of just fourteen. Pitted against men, he had the misfortune to draw Olympic champion Orlando Martinez of Cuba, one of the best amateurs in the world. Astonishingly, he lost only by split decision. After more than 100 amateur contests, with just six losses, he turned pro at fifteen, with his father doctoring his application form to disguise his real age.

Benitez made his debut in 1973 and took down Hall of Famer Cervantes three years later. Nobody was supposed to be so good, so soon. Cervantes had seemed unbeatable; indeed Duran's manager had apparently avoided him. "Back in 1974 when Duran was lightweight champion there was a good opportunity for him to fight Antonio Cervantes," said former manager Luis Spada. "It would have been a very, very good fight in Latin America. But Carlos Eleta thought that it was a dangerous fight because Cervantes, who was a great fighter, was bigger. I am sure, though, that Roberto would have had no trouble beating him."

Benitez, who beat Carlos Palomino to win his second title, liked to call himself "the Dragon," but the Radar tag was far more apt. Matchmaker Teddy Brenner called him "at one time the best fighter in the world." Yet the young prodigy with the veteran mind was still a child outside the ring. He womanized, skipped training, partied hard and generally gave his authoritarian father fits. Before he was stopped with six seconds left in the fifteenth round against Leonard in 1979, he lost his way to the gym. The lack of discipline forced his father to take a stand. "Even if they gave me $200,000 to work in his corner, I would not," the elder Benitez told a *Ring* journalist. "I refuse to be in his corner … I am not a hypocrite. There is no fighter who can be inactive for seven or eight months and then compete in a fight such as this one and hope to be sharp. It is not important that he is starting to train well now. He has not listened to anything I have told him. But Wilfred is a boy who just refuses to listen."

It was common knowledge in the fight game that Benitez trained a little over a week for Leonard. Yet his brilliance was undeniable. "Benitez is a ghost," Leonard said. "He anticipates your moves and almost makes himself invisible. I never met a better defensive fighter."

Benitez jumped up to light-middleweight. He was too good to remain contender for long, and in May 1981 challenged Britain's Maurice Hope for the WBC title. Hope was a decent champion, but Benitez was in a different class and cold-cocked him with a blistering right hook in round twelve, knocking out two of his teeth. "He can put his teeth under his pillow," remarked Benitez later. "Duran is dead. He is afraid of me. He knows me. When somebody talks about me to Duran, Roberto tells them don't talk to me about Benitez, I am afraid of him."

Benitez had been winding up Duran for several years. The Puerto Rican often sat ringside at his contests and shouted abuse, something to which Duran would respond with crude gesture and threats of his own. Their animosity spilled over at the post-fight Duran-Leonard press conference in Montreal. "I just told Roberto, give me a chance, give me a chance," Benitez said. "He said, 'Get out, I'll kill you.' I said to him, 'Let's do it right now, right here.'"

With Duran now campaigning at light-middle too, and both men promoted by Don King, a bout between two Latin kings was a cinch, especially given Duran's oft-declared antipathy to all things Puerto Rican. Contracts were signed for a title contest to take place at Caesar's Palace, Las Vegas, on 30 January 1982. In the pre-fight interviews, Benitez showed more of a willingness to speak in English, while Duran used Luis Henriquez and other translators as his mouthpieces. Duran understood most of what was being said in English but did not feel confident enough to speak it; he was never going to sit still long enough to perfect a foreign language. Benitez's co-manager Jimmy Jacobs – who bought his contract for $75,000 from Gregorio – admitted that his boxer also unintentionally alienated the American audience by not conversing in English "but when he tries to express himself in English, so many thoughts are misunderstood and misrepresented. But it's a calculated risk to communicate in English when he's infinitely more superior in another language." The refusal of Duran to learn English meant he was unable to market himself effectively to the U.S. public and probably cost him millions in endorsements.

To make certain that his fighter arrived in prime fighting condition, Eleta sent him to training camp on the penal island of Coiba, off the coast of Panama. A kind of open Alcatraz, Coiba housed Panama's worst criminals, on a godforsaken island surrounded by strong currents and shark-infested waters. Duran was permitted only to fish, eat, train and rest. "Wow," Duran told *Sports Illustrated*. "I was a prisoner among prisoners. To make a telephone call you had to climb a mountain. You called by shortwave radio. There were many murderers there; not many thieves, mostly pure murderers. I was scared. The prisoners walked around with machetes because they used them for work in the mountains. Whenever I went into the streets, I had a guard with me. At three a.m. roosters would be crowing. I couldn't get any sleep. I was pulling my hair out. That was a disgrace. It was a big mistake, a bad decision to go there."

Eleta wanted Duran's trip to be so dull and lonely that all he had to think about was destroying the young Puerto Rican who had often badmouthed him. It was also the only way to ensure that the hangers-on would stay away and Duran would stay faithful to his training regimen. No women, no beer, just steak, water and sweat. Eleta wouldn't let Duran and new trainer Panama Lewis off the island until he got down from 167 pounds to 156. The strategy seemed to work as Duran had no trouble getting to the 154-pound limit by fight time.

Even Ray Arcel, drafted in by Eleta as an "adviser" for the bout, claimed, "He's in the best shape, physically and mentally, that I've seen him since he knocked out DeJesus four years ago." Arcel also complimented Benitez, whom he said knew everything there was to know about the ring.

Before traveling to Vegas, Duran visited the grave of Torrijos, pledging to bring back the WBC junior middleweight for the late dictator. But Benitez, who was set to make nearly $1.5 million to Duran's $750,000, was the 9–5 favorite, The Puerto Rican favorite. Duran was now thirty, seven years older than Benitez. Benitez was coming in at 43-1-1, with 26 knockouts, while Duran was 74-2, with losses to Leonard and DeJesus. Benitez stepped off the scale at 152¼ pounds to Duran's 152½. Despite how hard Duran had trained, he couldn't change the reality that the bigger Benitez was coming down in weight and that he would be punching up at the five-foot-ten Puerto Rican. How would Duran handle the counterpuncher when he sat on the ropes and waited? Would he come at him or cut off the ring? Would Benitez be able to take a punch from Hands of Stone?

There were hints on the eve of the showdown that Benitez had matured. His father talked before the bout about his son's focus and even praised his training methods. Benitez admitted that he couldn't return to his country without the belt. "It's not so much the title that is motivating Wilfred," said Jim Jacobs. "He knows about Duran as a legend, and now Wilfred wants the glory and the recognition as the greatest Latin fighter."

Although Gregorio and Jacobs (co-manager with Bill Cayton) knew the tendencies of the unpredictable Benitez, they didn't allow room for speculation during the tense minutes before the young prodigy entered the ring. "Nobody talks tactics to Wilfred during the weeks he is training for the fight," said Jacobs to the *Washington Post*. "He is his own man; he has his own mind. But around fight time, he does listen to his father. Wilfred has been fighting since he was eight years old, and all those years when he went back to his corner, his father was always there. Let's just say that he trusts his father on fight night."

Before the fight began, traditional rivalry spilled over. At a New York press conference, Duran took a swing at Benitez and was clipped by a right hand in return. Duran also taunted Gregorio Benitez, under the false impression that he would be capable of backing up his words later in the ring. It was Papa Benitez who noted that his son had never taken a fight so seriously. "If I lose this one I will not be able to come back home to my country," Wilfred told himself. "I have to win this one."

In January 1982, the judges watched intently as, nearly two minutes into the bout, Duran's head was jolted backwards by a right-hand lead in an otherwise even first round. Soon the truth emerged: Duran was a very good 154-pounder, while Benitez was a more natural, magnificent one. Some fighters go into a fight with the belief that they had done everything right in training, from ringwork to conditioning. This was no flabby Duran; he was 152 pounds weeks before the fight, and truly believed he was prepared for fifteen rounds. But this was vintage Benitez, and as the referee Richard Green stepped between the combatants at the conclusion of each round, the ugly truth emerged. For each punch Duran landed, his opponent stuck two or three back in his face.

Realizing that he had to push Benitez against the ropes and bully him, Duran took the initiative in the third round and plunged toward the Puerto Rican with the intensity of a boy who had just seen his own blood in a streetfight. However, Duran's strategy of throwing punches hoping that a lucky one would land left him vulnerable. Every time Duran rushed the ropes, he ran into fists, and as the round closed out he took a huge straight right that completely threw off his equilibrium.

Balance was an art perfected by Benitez, ring magician. Benitez used his supreme reflexes and balance to land a gorgeous triple-hook to the body and head in the fourth round. His performance was as riveting as Leonard's in New Orleans, and this time Duran was being punished more. It was in this round that Duran connected on his first worthwhile punch of the evening, a sorry stat which was more revealing than all of the punches Benitez had landed to that point. The excuse that Duran had overtrained had already hit the airwaves.

If there was one punch in Benitez's arsenal that found the range as the fight progressed, it was his right uppercut. He showcased it in the seventh round. While playing his risky hide-and-seek game along the ropes, Benitez landed the ferocious uppercut directly on Duran's left eye. Blood seeped from the eye immediately.

Duran's handlers managed to keep the bleeding under control, but Duran was now being punished every time he stepped in range. Benitez landed big one-punch shots in the ninth and tenth rounds as Duran showed his usual aggression with little thought behind his actions. Instead of trying to enter and fight on the inside with the jab, he walked directly into the gunfire. At times, it appeared he was worn out as he shook his arms out on several occasions. Tired and unable to throw punches in rapid succession, Duran continued to plead with his arms.

Before the fourteenth round began, Arcel for the last time implored his fighter, "You can still win this fight." Benitez proceeded to bang Duran to the body as if he had heard the comment. Duran was pushed around by the bigger fighter, which was a rarity, and spent too much time against the ropes. Every time Duran looked to quicken the pace, Benitez would stop him with smart jabs and superior defense.

As both fighters came out at the start of the fifteenth round, there was little doubt that Benitez had taken this one personally. And with less than a minute remaining Benitez went to the ropes and motioned Duran to come to him one more time as if to remind him, *this is my night*. It was his way of closing off his virtuoso performance. It was Benitez's bolo punch, his Ali shuffle, and not only did he taunt Duran, but he called for Duran and then punished him. Few fighters would have exuded such bravado. Duran resisted one last time and brushed Benitez off as the final bell sounded.

There would be no late-night quarrels over a pitcher of beer as to who was the better fighter that night in Vegas; Benitez won by a mile. Even staunch Duran fans had to acknowledge defeat. Ringside scribes struggled to find a round, let alone rounds for Duran. Scoring on the ten-point must system, Lou Tabbat had it 145-141, Dave Moretti, 144-141, and Hal Miller scored it 143-142 with a straight face.

"It was great to watch Benitez fight," said boxing personality Bert Sugar. "He could duck so much that all you could get was an ear. Later he lost his timing and they hit him and he got brain damage. But he was brilliant. I remember sitting at ringside of that fight in Vegas and I was heard audibly and it was quoted in the papers by the Brits. I gave Duran the fifth round and he asked me why and I said, 'I have to give him something.'" Jose Torres thought that Benitez had not even had to extend himself to win, and saw "qualities Wilfred displayed in this match that only a conscious quest for perfection could produce ... His control was absolute." Steve Farhood of *KO* magazine wrote that when Benitez was motivated he was "the sweetest, slickest, smartest, most natural, the best boxer in the 'sweet science.'" It was this Benitez who Duran faced in Las Vegas. Yet, it was also his last hurrah, as he, a current shell of himself, currently lives with his mother in Carolina, suffering dearly from the aftereffects of the brutal sport.

Quizzed again about retirement, Duran said he would do what his manager told him to do. Eleta responded, "The time has come. I think I will retire him." If he wanted to do things his way it would be without Eleta calling the shots. In fact, a chasm began to open between the two men, especially when Duran learned through the media that Eleta intended to renounce his managerial services.

Eight months later, Duran would be back in the ring and Eleta would be back to his horses. "I liked the horses better because they didn't talk back," said the manager.

★ ★ ★

Duran again ballooned, to almost thirteen stone, but he resumed his career, intending to box on at light-middleweight. "The American press is always saying I'm fat," he said, "but I see Tony Ayala fight and he looks fat but no one says anything." Ayala was a stocky but rip-roaring junior middleweight who was tearing through the division. Unfortunately he found himself in and out of trouble with the law. "Just keep me out of jail long enough to knock out Duran," he said.

Duran found himself in the middle of a power struggle between the two most important promoters in boxing. Don King and Bob Arum hated each other with a passion. King had held exclusive rights to Duran during his prime years, though he and Arum had grudgingly buried their differences to co-promote Duran in the past. With Eleta now seemingly uninterested in his charge, Duran agreed to box for Arum in a title challenge to WBA light-middleweight champion Davey Moore. King, however, declared Duran was already bound by a three-bout agreement leading to a prime-time TV mega-bout with the unbeaten Ayala that November. With a view to building up the Ayala bout, King found Duran what he assumed would be a relatively easy tune-up against England's Kirkland Laing. Arum hit back, claiming that Duran was only under contract with King for the Laing fight. He declared that the row was merely a pretext by King to grab a piece of his Duran-Moore title promotion in November. "Duran Just a Pawn in the Arum-King Chess Match," declared the *Miami Herald*.

King won out. Duran admitted that he had made a hasty decision, sheepishly apologized to King, returned a $25,000 payment from Arum and planned to meet Ayala after he beat Laing – which all parties assumed was a foregone conclusion. On September 4, however, a 155-pound Duran, now trained by Bill Prezant and handled by Luis

Henriquez, traveled to the Cobo Arena in Detroit and subjected himself to utter humiliation, fighting and acting like a journeyman. The Jamaican-born Laing meant nothing in America but was known in the UK as an unpredictable maverick who could outbox most welterweights when his mind was on the job. He started hesitantly but grew in confidence as he found Duran easy to hit, and jolted the former champion several times. In contrast, Duran's punches carried little kick. The beer-bloated Panamanian lost a split, ten-round decision, two judges voting for Laing and one for Duran. "You a very smart sonofabitch," he told Laing afterwards in his broken English. It was the fourth loss of his career and the first to a fighter regarded as less than top-notch. *Ring* magazine's 1982 Upset of the Year left Duran in career limbo.

"Eleta turned his back on me and that hurt me. After that fight with Benitez, he wasn't interested in me at all," said Duran. "They all thought I was burned out. Eleta leaves me with Don King and King gets this fight for me." Duran had trained for Laing in Easton, Pennsylvania, the hometown of heavyweight champion Larry Holmes. "Holmes takes me to his bar, and I used to go every night there and I never trained. I tried but I couldn't make the weight and some deadbeat beats me. I go to the hotel with Plomo and I start laughing. 'This deadbeat beats me,' I say. Plomo tells me that my career is finished and what I needed to do was quit screwing around and get back on track.

"I didn't take care of myself. I was so fool-crazy with women that Eleta called me into his office and said, 'Cholo, Cholo, come here.' And I'd go and Eleta would ask if I wanted a fight with whoever and say, 'Do you want to take it or not?' I'd ask how long before the fight. 'Three weeks,' he would say and I told him to give it to me. Give me ten thousand dollars ahead and I would take the fight. I would take the money and I would go drink with a bunch of whores. I would feel like the King of the Bars."

Despite the language barrier, Holmes and Duran were friends. "I knew Roberto Duran before he started to train in Easton," said Holmes. "I trained at Bobby Gleason's Gym in New York. Roberto Duran was all they talked about. My trainer Ernie Butler took me to meet him and we've always been friends.

"When he was at my place in Easton, I told him, 'You got to get ready for a fight.' But he said, 'I ready. I ready. I fight. I beat him. I knock him out.' He was drinking 150-proof out of my bar and I was hollering at him. He didn't want to hear that. He did what he wanted. I cannot tell a multi-millionaire that is champion of the world what to do.

"I got into an argument with some of his crew … because all they wanted was the money. There's more to boxing than, 'Give me the money.' It's about the guy's health and well-being and make sure he's not doing the wrong things. It's so easy to get caught up into that. I know. What can you say? I wasn't with him all day and all night long. He had a following, women from all over. They'd come to Easton where he was training. There was like 16,000 people in the city. When Duran came, there was like 40,000. Nobody had control over Duran."

Duran had used up his boxing lifelines. Don King, never a man to stick with a loser, berated him in the locker room after the fight for not trying and for having too many people around him. Not only had Duran embarrassed himself, he had also ruined the possibility of a lucrative bout with Tony Ayala. The scolding prompted Duran to tell a *Miami Herald* reporter, "I won't fight any more for Don King. Never again. Even if he begs me."

Abandoned by Arcel and Brown, deserted by Eleta and now shunned by King, Duran cut a forlorn figure as he trekked to Bob Arum's New York office in search of a payday. If Arum rejected him, it really would be over. He would retire with a whimper, his genius forever overshadowed by the ignominy of his decline. "He wasn't worth a plugged quarter," said Arum.

The Harvard-educated lawyer was distinctly unimpressed but someone whose judgment he respected spoke up for Duran. Teddy Brenner, for years the matchmaker at Madison Square Garden, had booked Duran for his first ever US bout. In 1980, Brenner had joined Top Rank, Inc. Now he told Arum, "There's nothing wrong with this guy, physically. He's never taken a beating. Whether or not he wants to fight again is a question mark." Brenner later told *The Ring*, "King chased him. Duran was waiting for one kind word. He came to us, we sat him down. We gave him a chance. If we hadn't, it might have been the end for him." Arum admitted, "I don't know about boxing, but I've got a man who knows as much about fighters as anybody, and Teddy said there was nothing wrong with Duran that being in good physical and mental condition wouldn't solve. Teddy said that if you get him mentally right, he'd probably beat anybody around."

To see what he had left, Arum and Brenner found Duran a match with another former British champion, Jimmy Batten, who had moved Stateside to further his career. The bout was negotiated on Duran's behalf, not by Carlos Eleta, but by his former matchmaker Luis Spada, an old and loyal friend. It marked the final rift between one of the great partnerships in boxing.

In the bad times after Montreal, when crowds threw stones at Duran's house and ripped down his mural on Avenida Balboa, Luis Spada had gone to see him and said, "Anytime you need me, even to carry the spit bucket in your corner, you could call me." Duran had not forgotten. Quiet and reserved, yet respected for his boxing acumen, Spada would be content to stay in the background.

He was born in Buenos Aires, Argentina, and caught the boxing bug and fed an early boxing fix when he visited boxing gyms while stationed in New York as a member of the Argentine Navy during his twenties. In the early Seventies, he built a reputation in boxing in Los Angeles. In 1971, he was invited to dinner with "some boxing people" from Panama. They turned out to be Carlos Eleta and his lawyer, Jorge Ruben Rosas. Eleta talked about his desire for a world champ and Spada said he could get a title fight with Nicolino "The Untouchable" Locche for Eleta's fighter Peppermint Frazer. "He was very enthusiastic," recalled Spada. "He told me to make the fight with Locche through his manager Tito Lectoure. Eleta invited me to Panama and we dicussed the terms of the fight. I went to Argentina, and closed the deal with Lectoure for March 1972."

Frazer won, and Eleta talked Spada into working as his matchmaker and boxing advisor while making Panama his permanent home. He became a fixture in Duran's entourage and went with him around the world. Spada broke off with Eleta in 1975, and started his own promotional company in Panama City. He developd his own stable of world champions, including Panamanians Rigoberto Riasco and Hilario Zapata and Nicaraguan Eddie Gazo.

In September 1982, in the depths of his doldrums, Duran called Spada and asked him to handle him for the Batten fight. "I tell Spada, 'I don't want you to carry my bucket for me; I want you to be my manager,'" recalled Duran. "After that, Spada goes back to Eleta and tells him that I asked him to be my manager. He asks Eleta if he still has some formal contract with him. Spada tells Eleta, 'I'm going to help Duran.' Eleta says, 'Keep him, keep him.' I'm in the gym; the Rock is back."

Spada recalled the episode: "I always had a good appreciation for Roberto. He called me one day and asked me to be his manager and I said that I would be over at five p.m. the next day because I needed to talk to Mr Eleta first to be sure that Duran didn't have any commitments with Eleta. I didn't want to take a fighter from anybody. Before I got him,

Duran was losing to guys like Laing in Michigan. Laing used to be a sparring partner for Duran. Eleta said that he no longer worked with Duran. He wished me luck and that afternoon I went to Duran's house."

Spada asked for only one-tenth of Duran's purse money rather than the normal one-third. "So I tell Eleta I go my way, you go your way," Duran recalled. "Then I start training again. I still feel good. Spada comes into play. I fired Eleta. I tell those guys, now I'm going to become champion again. I started to prepare myself."

Any improvement in form, however, was not immediately apparent. The Batten fight was on the same bill as the Alexis Arguello–Aaron Pryor headliner at the Orange Bowl, Miami, on November 12. Duran had specifically requested that his bout be the final one of the evening, in the so-called "walk-off" slot when most people were on their way home, so that few people would be around to see him. Considering his showing, it might have been better if he'd waited till the arena had cleared. Arguello-Pryor was a classic, Duran-Batten a stinker. "At 157 pounds, Duran waddled his way toward a fearful Batten and scored with one harmless punch at a time," according to reporter Steve Farhood. "Even though the Pryor-Arguello press conference was over by the sixth round, few writers had returned to their seats to witness the once-great Duran. With strangers in his corner and loose skin hanging obscenely over his muscles, this was a different fighter, a *finished* fighter." The crowd booed as the scores were tallied and Duran took the unanimous decision and $25,000.

In what really was his last chance, Top Rank plunged Duran into a Latin showdown with the fearsome Pipino Cuevas.

* * *

If ever a fighter wasn't going to back up against Duran, it was the man they called "The Assassin." Pipino Cuevas was the embodiment of *encender*, a Spanish word meaning to strike a match or to incinerate. In Mexican boxing, it denoted an explosive combination of power, charisma and volatility. "He makes Rocky Marciano look like a sissy," said Ernie Fuentes, a San Diego promoter. His dark, brooding eyes and impassive face added to an aura of imminent danger. "Most fighters don't even have a face like this," wrote *New York Times* reporter Dave Anderson about Cuevas.

He was born Isidro Pipino Cuevas Gonzalez, one of five boys and six girls to a small-time butcher in Hidalgo, Mexico. Young Pipino was a loner and often picked fights in school. His despairing father, Geraldo, took him to a boxing gym at thirteen and he became hooked. Trained by Lupe Sanchez, Cuevas would turn pro at fourteen after just nineteen amateur bouts. He was stopped in two rounds in his debut, and lost another four of his first twelve bouts, but when he hit people they stayed hit, and his wins almost always came inside the distance. Cuevas punched his way up the rankings and won the WBA welterweight title at just eighteen when he knocked down champion Angel Espada three times in the second round the summer of 1976.

"That night in Mexico where I won the title was a beautiful thing," said Cuevas. "It was a dream come true for me. I had three fights with Espada. The second fight was the toughest of my career. I had three jaw fractures, two fractured ribs and three or four cuts on my face."

As champion, Cuevas came into his own. He flattened or stopped ten out of eleven challengers and was talked about as potentially one of the division's all-time greats. Pipino had learned the puncher's secret of punching not *at* the target but *through* it and he didn't just beat his challengers, he beat them up. Shoji Tsujimoto was still unconscious twenty seconds after being counted out. Billy Backus suffered an orbital fracture of the eye socket and had headaches and double vision weeks after their fight. Harold Weston's jaw was dislocated. Angel Espada's jaw was broken. Even a fighter who outpointed him, Andy Price, remarked with awe, "Cuevas could knock down walls with his punching."

"Pipino has always been different," said Chargin. "He has never been real flamboyant. He was always that you-win-some-and-lose-some type of guy. When I see him he is still that same down-to-earth type of guy."

Cuevas became a huge hit among the Mexicans of the West Coast of the USA. They loved him for his *fuerza* and crowds filled the Olympic Auditorium to glimpse his vaunted left hook. "He drew such tremendous gates," remembered promoter Don Chargin. "He was so hot. Nobody was drawing like that during that time. There was a huge population of Mexicans in Los Angeles, and he was such an idol with Mexicans. That left hook was it. When he would hit guys with that he would really stretch them."

The welterweight division was not for the meek and the test of a fighter's greatness was how he fared against the other greats then storming the division. Cuevas was lined up for what would have been easily the biggest purse of his career, a so-called superfight with Ray Leonard, but backstage machinations saw him edged out in favor of the better-connected Duran. Instead, he faced the fast-rising Tommy

Hearns. Styles make fights, and for all his frightening power, the short-armed Cuevas was made for the rangy Detroit Hit Man, especially in the challenger's hometown. In September 1980, Hearns burst Cuevas's bubble when he took him out in sensational fashion in two rounds at the Joe Louis Arena. The Mexican assassin seemed psyched out by his laser-eyed opponent and Hearns would later say that the punch he hit Cuevas with was the hardest he'd ever thrown.

By the time he met Duran in 1983, Cuevas was also coming off a decision loss to Roger Stafford in *Ring* magazine's Upset of the Year. Like Stone Hands, he was desperate to resurrect a flagging career. Though he was still only twenty-five, this would be his last shot. His skills had diminished, but his punch remained and no one was betting that it would go the distance. "Cuevas would fight Duran the same way he fights everybody else," his adviser Rafael Mendoza told *The Ring* when the match-up was still speculative. "He'd make Duran back up. And if Duran didn't back up, Cuevas would run him over. Duran could never beat Cuevas. Not on his best night, he couldn't."

In fact there were rumors on both sides that neither fighter wanted to get in the ring and that Cuevas wanted too much money. Also, there were rumblings that Cuevas only wanted to fight in Mexico City, with a guaranteed title shot for the winner. Cuevas responded with a telegram that was published in *Ring* magazine.

I have never ducked a challenge from Duran. Will sign any time to fight him. Will even fly to New York. To sign right in the offices of RING Magazine. Don't care when or where we fight. The money is not that important. Let's just fight.
Signed, Pipino Cuevas

Having worked in Duran's corner for ten years, Ray Arcel had such reservations about his former fighter getting in the ring with Pipino Cuevas that he wrote a letter that was published in the *New York Times* on 15 January 1983.

Dear Roberto,
Life is like a book. There is a beginning, there is a middle, and there has to be an end to the story. And so must a career come to an end. I hope that you will see fit to end your career.
Ray Arcel

After consulting with Duran about Cuevas, Luis Spada closed the deal with Bob Arum for January 29, 1983, in the Sports Arena in Los Angeles. Duran had fought in LA twice before on cards promoted by Don Chargin and had his own following there. He promised discipline in his training regimen. "After the loss to Leonard, I was starting to drink, fooling around, going to nightclubs, and was in very bad shape," Duran told a reporter in 1983. "Then one day I say, 'I have to do something if I am going to continue boxing.' I start to change when I fought Pipino Cuevas."

Duran's wife, Felicidad, saw his enthusiasm return when they told him he was going to fight Cuevas. "From that point on, I began to see the same Roberto as before – happy, joyful, the one that liked to joke around. I recovered him. He was back. He was the same Roberto I once knew."

"I told him that if he wants to come back, he'd have to work very hard because I didn't want to waste my time and his time," said Luis Spada. "He promised to work hard, not to worry that he would do whatever I say. And when Roberto was training, he would work very, very hard. Of course when he was on vacation, he liked to eat a lot. But coming to train, he was very dedicated with me."

Tension was tangible at the Sports Arena as the two black-haired, heavy-handed hitters faced off for a punch-out that would see one of them face career oblivion. Duran, who was actually the heavier man at 152 and looked stocky but strong, circled to his left, away from Cuevas's left hook, and jabbed, then landed the first telling blow with a right to the jaw. Utilizing his six-inch reach advantage, the rail-thin Cuevas, 149, went after Duran and landed three of his signature wide shots to the body, and later rammed home a shot to Duran's chin. The Mexican looked sharp and accurate. Just to secure his territory, Cuevas sent a left hook Duran's way after the bell sounded.

Then came a key adjustment. "One thing that happened before that fight was very important," said Luis Spada. "Duran was the only boxer to ever tell me, 'Viejo, if you see that I am doing something wrong, please let me know and I will change it.' In the first round with Cuevas, Roberto was ahead, but was in front of Cuevas, who was a good puncher. I told him that he needed to box. If not, maybe Cuevas will hit him with one of those big punches. He said, 'Okay, Viejo.' In the second round, Roberto started boxing."

Duran came out for round two with fierce intensity and stuck a pole-like jab in the face of the Mexican. This wasn't the lethargic and tense Duran of the first round, he was sharp, menacing and focused, looking to break down Cuevas. Duran went toe-to-toe with the Mexican, looking for the left hook to the body. Both gave and took big shots, but Duran was quicker, and working harder.

In the third round, the upright Cuevas began to let the big bombs go. He wasn't the most accurate of hitters – Carlos Palomino once said Cuevas missed opponents even when they stood still – but he nailed Duran with three uppercuts on the inside. A left hook from Cuevas further stirred the Mexican contingent as it landed flush on Duran's chin. But Duran, unfazed, fired back with two clean hooks and mocked his opponent, pointing to his chin. Duran set up Cuevas with a right to his neck, and then a left hook that momentarily jerked Cuevas's head and body completely around. Although Cuevas answered back with his uppercuts, Duran's punches were clearly draining him. Cuevas kept punching; it was all he knew. There was no strategy; he threw bombs in desperation. If Duran decided to move his head in front of one of them, so be it. Pipino landed a left hook that would have felled lesser men; Duran just stood there swinging. Duran was quickly back in his corner at the end of the round, anxious to get back out there to end the fight.

Duran was now hot in pursuit. He circled to his left at the outset of the fourth round, jabbing and moving as Spada had asked. A straight right from Duran sent Cuevas down for the first time and brought a standing eight-count from referee James Jen Kin. A moment later, Duran lodged Cuevas against the ropes for another fusillade. Cuevas backpedaled out of danger, but couldn't shake his pursuer. A right jolted back his head.

Latin pride was at stake and as stoic and brave as Cuevas was, in his prime he couldn't have prevented the incoming onslaught in the fourth round. He barely moved as Duran nailed him with a right hand in the middle of the ring, and then began to backup as if survival was the only thing on his mind. He had nowhere to go. An exhausted Pipino sat on the ropes, threw desperate rebuttals, and then suffered a right cross that had him looking directly at the canvas; a follow-up left hook had him reeling. Duran connected with another right forcing Cuevas to grasp Duran for safety, but was quickly rebuffed with three uppercuts. He would not surrender. A disjointed and weary Cuevas flew against the ropes like a pinball and squatted as the referee jumped in to start the eight-count. Cuevas looked to his corner for help; he was the portrait of a beaten fighter.

Both of Cuevas's eyes were blackened, and his mouth was wide open in anticipation as he prepared for the inevitable ending. He could no longer turn to his power for backup. With over a minute remaining, Duran cornered Cuevas and landed almost a dozen uppercuts and hooks that bounced the Mexican into the ringpost. Cuevas hung on and refused to let go of Duran until Kin broke them apart. It was his only respite, as Duran moved him against the ropes for another ambush. He banged a right hook to the body and then to the head. Another uppercut had Cuevas wobbling to the other side of the ring. No longer was he throwing punches. A straight right jolted the head of Cuevas, forcing many in the crowd to wonder, how much more can he take?

It was a sad sight as Cuevas couldn't defend himself anymore. Duran wailed away with five punches, the left hook to the ribs did the most damage as Cuevas slumped to his knees and grasped the ropes. He had risen by nine, and signaled with his glove for manager Lupe Sanchez to stay put, but it was too late. As Cuevas began to walk toward Duran to continue, Sanchez had already thrown in the towel. The fight was stopped at 2:24 of the round; the twenty-five-year-old had aged ten years in as many minutes.

Having never mastered the classic bob-and-weave, Cuevas tended to move toward punches, not away from them. He would lose six more bouts to inferior opposition before leaving the game in 1989. "I am a good friend of the Duran family and I think of him as a brother," said Cuevas. "I remember the punch Duran hit me with. It was a bad fight for me."

Duran looked ahead. As for the letter from Arcel, he had responded with his fists in a manner his words couldn't express:

*Dear Ray, I appreciate your concern, but I'm not done just yet. I have only begun.*

*Regards, Cholo.*

# 16

## RETURN OF THE KING

*It was a slow, deliberate pounding. And Davey Moore, because of his youth and because of his heart, took a lot more punishment than he should have. It was a massacre. You had a sense watching it, that this was it for Davey Moore, and sure enough it was.*

Steve Farhood

IN THREE YEARS, Roberto Duran had traveled the gamut from hero to hopeless, beloved to despised. The crushing of Pipino Cuevas had restored at least some of his lustre. Duran had made a promise at Torrijos's graveside to bring home one more world championship in his honor. Whether his next move would fulfill that vow or send Duran closer to his retirement speech was up to an undefeated junior middleweight from New York's toughest neighborhood.

It could have been billed as the Vet vs. the Rookie. Davey Moore was a young stud from the Bronx, a WBC junior middleweight champion of limited experience but great potential. Muscles sprouted on his frame; his was the kind of body that despised fat. He had challenged unbeaten world champion Tadashi Mihara with a number ten ranking and only eight pro fights to his name but had won in six rounds and many fight insiders had him on the trail to greatness. Moore had watched the Cuevas fight on TV from an Atlantic City hotel where he'd been celebrating victory of his own over challenger Gary Guiden. He had been impressed but not overawed.

The fight was scheduled for Duran's thirty-second birthday, June 16, 1983, and was originally supposed to be held in Johannesburg, South Africa, but promoter Bob Arum moved it to Madison Square Garden when undercard fighter Ray "Boom Boom" Mancini was injured. "We decided to train in Buenos Aires because we had a direct flight to Johannesburg," said Luis Spada. "On the same show, Mancini was going to fight, but he got a broken hand. I got a call and Arum had to change the spot of the fight. Then I heard it was Madison Square Garden. Roberto was happy because that's where he wanted to fight. He said, 'Okay, let's stop in Panama first.' It was natural for Roberto because he always wanted to see his family and his children. But I knew better and told him that we would go straight to the training camp in New Jersey."

Something early on told Duran that this wasn't going to be as difficult as everyone thought. "Many people felt I had nothing left to give," said Duran. "People always think in what they see but people don't think in what I have in here [his heart]. When I saw Davey Moore fight, I said, 'This isn't shit. I'm going to make him eat that shit.'"

Duran set up training camp at Great Gorge in McAfee, New Jersey, and then moved to Gleason's Gym. A couple days before the bout, Duran found his opponent preparing for morning roadwork in New York and leapt at the chance to intimidate him. "One day I'm finishing running at the park and Moore was about to start running," said Duran. "I keep staring at him. He tried to impress me with his body. I laugh in his face. I tell Plomo after this guy passed by that I'm going to beat the shit out of him. He looks back and I look back at him and laugh at him. I tell Plomo I'm going to rip him apart."

With the weigh-in at 11 a.m. on the day of the fight, Spada checked Duran's weight at 8 a.m and he was easily under the 154-pound limit. However, Moore wasn't in the same shape. "The day of the weigh-in this guy couldn't make weight," said Duran. "I told everyone, you go send out for my dinner and what not, but I'm not moving until he makes weight. I stood there and he's watching me eat in front of him."

Spada recalled the scene: "The people of Davey Moore made a big mistake because they believed that Duran was too old and Moore was a good, young champion. Moore came in overweight at 156 pounds and Roberto made 152. After making weight Roberto went to eat, he loves that. Moore had two hours to make weight. I stayed with them until they made the weight."

The weigh-in also gave the first inkling of the extraordinary support Duran would call on that night. "It was the most amazing thing in the world," said boxing editor Bert Sugar. "I'm at the weigh-in and they have flags. If you placed a call to Panama that night, no one would have answered: They were all in NY." Even Carlos Eleta would show up. "We went in the dressing room," said Duran. "A godfather of mine comes in and tells me he has a message from Eleta. 'What does he want?' I ask. 'He wants to come to the fight and be in your corner.' I tell him that I don't want him to come to the fight or be in my corner or anything."

It seemed like an odd time for Eleta to try to get back into Duran's life. "My godfather Tito Iglesias said, 'We respect him but we don't want him here.' Spada started crying and I ask him what's wrong," said Duran. "I tell him I don't want Eleta here and a bunch of things. I get my godfather and I tell him that I don't even want to see Eleta here in a can of paint. Tell him to look through the TV and I'm going to be champ. And when I go back to Panama, I tell him not even to say hello to me. I told him that that night I would become a champion again. And I did." Eleta disputes that such a conversation ever occurred.

No matter how physically gifted and perfectly sculpted, Davey Moore was a youth compared to Duran. The Arum-promoted fighter turned twenty-four just a week before the bout. He had started boxing not long after leaving high school and as an amateur won four Golden Gloves titles and compiled a record of 96-6-4. He had won the world title in only his ninth bout and had defended it three times.

Although Clara Samaniego believed in the power of sorcerers and witches and would blame them for cursing her son when he lost, Duran claimed to be a Catholic who put his faith in the saints Virgin del Carmen and Saint Lazarus. However, he also believed in a *Babalu aye*, a *santeria* (the Afro-Cuban faith with roots in the Yoruba region of Nigeria) god of health and healing who concerns himself with the poor. Identified with St Lazarus, *Babalu* is also the wrath of the earth and will punish those that disrespect it. Duran would call upon these mystical sources for strength against Moore.

The brash young fighter referred to Duran as over the hill, and predicted a first-round knockout the day before the fight. Duran told a *Boston Globe* reporter that he was beginning a "new stage" in the career.

The numbers from the fight proved astounding. Moore-Duran fight brought the biggest crowd – 20,061, of which 19,000 were paid admissions – since Ali-Frazier II in 1974. Duran was on a $100,000 purse, with the possibility of $500,000 in incentives, while Moore was guaranteed $300,000.

More than 20,000 packed the Garden that June evening. Coming in to the fight, Duran was a 2-1 underdog. Boxing experts such as Michael Katz, Shelly Finkel and Jim Jacobs all sided with Moore. In fact, very few thought Duran would win. Although Moore was a Bronx native, the momentum shifted as the majority of the fans flocked to see their own Latin legend. "This is my town, my city, I'm the all-American, and everybody was for Duran," Moore would complain later. "Everybody was Panamanian." Not quite everyone, however. Before Duran stole the spotlight, another icon stole his thunder. "All of a sudden Muhammad Ali walks into the building and you hear nineteen thousand people start chanting his name," said Steve Farhood. "And remember he's only three years removed from boxing."

During referee Ernesto Magana's pre-fight instructions, Moore took the notion of staredown literally as he tucked his head in his powerful chest and thought about the coming battle. With Moore's chin on chest and Duran swiveling his head like a speed bag, Magana addressed both fighters as a son would his children. Duran looked over at Moore's bowed head with a glare. Moore was a kid who could be great, but *Cholo* had been there already.

The first minute saw barely a punch landed as the combatants circled the ring. The key moment came just before the bell. Duran threw a jab and seemed to thumb Moore in the right eye at the same time. Moore lifted his glove to the eye and pawed at it, a giveaway that he was hurt. The move was more than a distraction, but was emblematic of the ensuing violence, as Moore was in with an opponent for whom rules meant little.

The injured eye was already closing when Moore came out for the second. For the next two rounds Duran, the veteran, embarked on a controlled but brutal assault, his hooks pounding the champion's ribs, his jabs finding that damaged eye. Moore fired back, but at ringside Ray Leonard noted that Duran was "going with" the punches, rolling his head to mitigate their impact.

Duran poured it on, insulting Moore in the clinches, slipping his counters, jerking his head back with uppercuts, splitting his bottom lip. Moore had never been privy to such savagery, and had no idea how to cope. He started at Moore's chest, then led to his head, confusing the younger man. "Is he hurting you?" Moore's worried trainer asked between rounds. "Are you all right?" Moore didn't need to answer: the shock and pain was written on his bruised face. In round five, the challenger landed two crunching rights, then was warned for a low blow. He showed no mercy, never did. By round six, Moore's eye was closed so tightly that his corner no longer worked on it. With Moore blind in one eye, Duran was now picking his shots, while the champion tried to work inside where his lack of vision was less of a hindrance.

In the seventh round, it became massacre. Moore was still throwing punches but Duran's short left hooks found his jaw with sickening repetition. After one short flurry from Moore, Duran gave him a classic shit-eating grin. Puss and sweat flew off Moore's right eye. Ringsiders cringed or hid their eyes behind fingers. Moore's girlfriend and mother passed out. Journalist and Athletic Commission boxing representative Jose Torres, who had seen men die in the ring, was on his feet screaming, "Stop the fight, stop the fight."

The massacre hit its hideous peak as Duran finally threw a straight right off a hook and Moore was blown off his feet and hurled to the canvas near the ropes. Nobody would have objected to stopping the fight as a brave Moore pushed himself up on his feet. There was little left in the fighter, but heroically he rose to his feet at the count of eight and was saved by the bell. Duran was so pumped that he sat down on Moore's stool before Plomo rushed in and grabbed him. As he crossed Moore's path, he cocked his right glove menacingly. Despite his destructive path and Moore's unyielding spirit, Duran had never bludgeoned an opponent so convincingly. Every emotion from confusion to sorrow to complete exasperation formed on Moore's face.

Bumps contoured Moore's face, yet for some reason the normally competent Magana let the slaughter continue. He seemed to be the only person in the Garden happy for the bout to go on. "Davey Moore was terribly beaten," remembered Bert Sugar. "The generic ringside writers thought that Duran had stuck a thumb in his eye, myself not included, because his eye had ballooned. He was getting the shit kicked out of him. That was Duran at his greatest because he was through, or at least that was the thinking."

The referee visited Moore's corner but still the bout continued. Round eight was torture. Moore tried to hold on, but was trapped in his corner and terribly beaten, Duran's thumping right landing again and again. A white towel fluttered into the ring, thrown by Moore's corner, but Magana didn't see it, and ignored screams from ringside for it to be stopped. Only when Duran's handlers rushed between the ropes did Magana finally spot the towel and halt the round at 2:02.

Leon Washington, Moore's trainer, would later claim in an interview that, "The only reason [Davey] wasn't defending himself was that he couldn't see." Washington's logic was based on the absurdity that he had no problem allowing a blind fighter back into the ring with a butcher. "Watching that fight, we knew we were watching the end of Davey Moore," said Steve Farhood. "Duran was Duran and took this guy apart," added Gil Clancy. "He did a complete job on him."

Jumping up so that his body would hang over the top rope, Duran searched the crowd through tears of joy. More than twenty thousand fans lifted the Garden roof with a chant of "Doo-ran, Doo-ran" as the fighter, with tears rolling down his bearded cheeks, stepped through the ropes onto the ring apron and extended his arms, chanting with them, "the satanic eyes suddenly so human and weak." Someone held him around the waist to stop him falling into the press section as the fans in the $100 ringside seats strained to touch him. In the cheaper seats, his fans waved banners declaring, "Feliz Cumpleanos, Manos de Piedra" – "Happy Birthday, Hands of Stone" and began to sing "Happy Birthday." Soon the song was taken up by the whole stadium. "It was an amazing moment," said Farhood. "It was like you were watching a rebirth." Even Sugar Ray Leonard, looking on from ringside as a CBS commentator, climbed into the ring and held Duran's arm aloft. The new champion thanked him, then added in English, "Say hello to your wife and your son." Old enmities were blown away in the tide of emotion.

In eight rounds of action, Duran almost knocked the life out of Davey Moore. He also became the seventh fighter in history to win titles in three weight classes, joining the elite fraternity of Bob Fitzsimmons, Tony Canzoneri, Henry Armstrong, Barney Ross, Alexis Arguello and Wilfred Benitez. He cracked open a bottle of Moet and Chandon champagne in his hotel room to celebrate.

Duran had fulfilled the promise he made in the fall of 1982 to win a title in Torrijos's honor. "I can't find words to express how I failed in the past," said Duran after the fight. "There are no excuses. Once I thought I was a man; now I am a man and I know it. In truth, I have such enthusiasm, like it was the first time I came to New York."

"When everybody was thinking I am finished, I am world champion again," said Duran the next day, after partying into the early hours (*Knockout*, Spring 1990). "After last night, I forget what happened in the past. I think only in the present and the future. I was born again last night."

* * *

Those people that had lined up to disparage Duran after Leonard II, were crowding those same streets to share in his return to glory. Duran eventually returned to Panama after making a pit stop in Miami. As Duran exited the plane that was sent to him by President Richard de la Espriella, he cut a glorious figure in his white designer suit and hat. Thousands braved the rain to honor their hero; schoolchildren threw flowers; men tipped their glasses; and Duran was presented a key to the city. The rapturous victory parade traveled along the 10-mile route from the airport to the executive mansion.

To Duran, they were all hypocrites as he would remember the familiar faces that he hadn't seen in years. "When Duran was fighting and the fight was on TV, his fight had the greatest rating, everybody's watching all over Panama," said Spada. "When we came back from Moore fight, they send Duran in Miami in the President's own plane. They brought us here to Paitilla, there was thousands of fans waiting for him. We went to the president's house and Duran is one man who has made more Panamanians happy than anybody else. We will have other champions, but not like Roberto."

There was a reunion of sorts in Panama. There had been lingering rumors that Eleta had stolen money from Duran. "Time passes on and I go to eat at a restaurant where I was going to have a press conference. What a coincidence, when the conference is over, politics begins," said Duran. "One of the waiters tells me that Eleta is in the other room. In my mind, this bastard is in here. I go to where he is and I say, 'How are you Eleta? Champion of the world, did you see this?' He's with a friend and you could see the tears in his eyes. His friend tells me that he needs me for political reasons. I don't care about politics or Carlos Eleta. I'm the new champion and you doubted me. And I left."

Eleta refuted the charge on many occasions. "All those people say what they want and Duran would believe them," he said. "I never took anything from him. He was a man so worried about what the people around him said and thought of him."

Although the common belief in Panama is that Eleta did skim from Duran's purses, there were those who sided with Eleta.

"When I found out that Eleta took fifty grand from me, I made a big commotion about it," Duran said. "Before I make the story any longer, he paid my money back piece by piece. He wanted me to sign a piece of paper that said I didn't owe him anything else and everything was settled. It wasn't Eleta himself, he sent a lawyer to sign the thing. My father-in-law tells the lawyer, 'No, Duran can't sign that paper because we don't know if Eleta still owes him any more money.' At some point he screws me out of my money but I can't elaborate on a lot of the specifics."

"I've heard all of the stories," said LA-based promoter Don Chargin. "At the time I met Roberto he was young, and they change. They're willing to do anything. I remember how close he and Eleta were. So I was really surprised at the break-up."

Chargin saw firsthand how money destroyed many relationships. Having been close to several fighters throughout his career, he also had been privy to the combustibility of dealing with high-strung, spontaneous personalities like Duran. Often, with Don King as its pioneer, the sport dictated that promoters receive a bad rap and boxers always are the victims.

"After Leonard, [Duran] was the boss," recalled Chargin. "It was pretty hard back then. Nobody could tell him what to do. I think he hurt himself. You always have to be careful because fighters blame people … they say, 'It was my manager.' The real good managers look out for the fighter's welfare all the time."

After the win over Moore, Eleta was a stranger to Duran, who must have felt a twinge of sadness watching another male figure check out of his life. First his real father left, then Chaflan and father figure Jose Manuel Gomez died, now the man who Duran once called Papa had turned on him. Or that's how Duran perceived it. Consolation came from the adulation of his supporters. "An outpouring of acceptance and appreciation of Duran was never at a higher pitch," said Sugar. "He wasn't supposed to beat Davey Moore and yet all of a sudden 19,000 people were chasing the pigeons out of the Garden to see him; they didn't come to see Davey Moore."

Meanwhile the inquest continued over referee Magana's belated stoppage of the bout. Watching Moore drown at the Garden, it had been obvious that boxing was the one sport where a bad night could pluck years off a fighter's shelf life. Moore's armor was peeled off piece by piece. In nearly twenty-four boxing minutes, Davey Moore was stripped of the exuberant, cocksure nature. Those who witnessed the bout tried to make sense of it all.

"And then when they threw the towel, he stops the fight," said Juan

Carlos Tapia. "It was one of the most cowardly moments ever by a referee. He could have done a great loss to Davey Moore." Writer Jack Newfield referred to Magana as a "voyeur of masochism" and noted that it was like "death entering the arena."

"I watched it with dread," said author Budd Schulberg. "There are nights like that that make you feel guilty about boxing. I think the commissions are very culpable. I don't know if they check enough on the previous condition of a boxer. Thank God it doesn't happen too often. It made me sick. It was one of those terrible nights that makes you nervous about boxing. It was a sensitive group around ringside and the more sensitive were increasingly apprehensive because there was a sense that the poor kid had no armor against Duran. And oh, he was relentless that night. You had an awful sense that something terrible was going to happen. I didn't know if he was going to die but I knew it was the end of him." *Sports Illustrated* writer William Nack summed up the referee's performance when he declared, "Leave it to the WBA to hire a turkey to run a cockfight."

In March 1984, Moore told a *New York Times* writer the true implication of what happened to him the night he ran into Roberto Duran: "Oh man, that fight broke my heart."

# 17

# REDEMPTION

*"Roberto's story is like a religious story. The glory, the fall and the redemption."*

Luis Spada before the Hagler bout

THE SCENT OF millions followed Marvelous Marvin Hagler up into the ring moments after Roberto Duran had mugged Davey Moore in Madison Square Garden. The shaven-skulled middleweight king reached out and held up the hand of the new three-time champ as photographers boxed each other out for position. A contest between the two of them, which would once have seemed absurd, was now a serious proposition.

A month later, it was announced that the two champions would meet for Hagler's middleweight crown in Las Vegas (initially it was announced for the Dunes casino-hotel outdoor arena but it would eventually take place at Caesar's Palace). A crowd of 1,500 mostly Duran fans, turned up just for the press conference at the Felt Forum in New York. "It will be the biggest closed circuit fight in history," declared Bob Arum. "I believe this is the greatest fight in our lifetime." He suggested the boxers could earn as much as $10 million each from all possible revenue sources, though they were believed to have been guaranteed $5 million. Speaking through his interpreter, Duran said he would train even harder than for the Moore bout and Hagler would "go down for sure."

The menacing middleweight champion was unmoved. "Two things are on my mind," he glowered. "Destruct and destroy." The pro-Duran crowd booed but few among them could help feeling uneasy. Hagler was the toughest proposition Duran had ever faced. "There's a monster that comes out of me in the ring," he once said. "I think it goes back to the days when I had nothing. They're all trying to take something from me that I've worked long and hard for, years for." He wasn't about to let "them."

Hagler grew up in New Jersey and moved to Brockton, Massachusetts, hometown of the legendary Rocky Marciano, when he was sixteen years old. Before turning pro in May 1973, he won the National A.A.U championship at 165 pounds. He was guided by the Petronellis: Guerino Petronelli had boxed (as Goodie Peters) and his brother and sidekick Tony developed fighters in a small Brockton gym. When Marvin wasn't training, he worked at the Petronelli Construction site.

A southpaw who could adroitly switch to conventional style, Hagler paid his professional dues. He won his first seventeen, fourteen inside the distance, with a victory over Olympic gold medalist Sugar Ray Seales establishing him as a potential contender. The Petronellis showed tough love for their young prospect, refusing to take the easy route of set-up fighters as early opponents. A steady diet of feared Philadelphia middleweights, then toughest around, didn't shrink Hagler's star: wars with the likes of Bobby "Boogaloo" Watts, Willie "The Worm" Monroe, Eugene "Cyclone" Hart and "Bad" Bennie Briscoe only enhanced his reputation. He would avenge his only two losses by stopping Watts and Monroe.

Hagler, who soon took to calling himself "Marvelous Marvin," won the WBC and WBA middleweight belts from Alan Minter in September 1980 on a riotous night in London. He took out IBF champ Wilfred Scypion three years later to reign undisputed. No challenger came close to beating him in seven defenses. Indeed, with no worthy challenger to truly test him, against whom to confirm his greatness, people began to question Hagler's greatness and criticize his style because he was so much better than anyone else. Yet, if he didn't confirm that greatness on every occasion with brutality and precision, the people would slowly yank him from the pedestal. Perhaps he was getting bored. Since those early setbacks to Watts and Monroe, draws to Sugar Ray Seales and Vito Antuofermo were the only other blemishes on his record. While Duran ranked with the best lightweights ever, Hagler was one of the greatest middleweights to grace the sport. He could outbox the best boxers, outpunch the hardest punchers, trained obsessively and had a chin of iron. He treated his body like a temple while Duran rarely scoffed at the extra buffet trip. Would it even be a fair fight?

Yet in the ring after his defeat of Davey Moore, it must have become evident to Duran that Hagler was not much bigger than he was. Though he had a five-inch longer reach and was three years younger, he stood only five feet nine. Conversely, while there was nothing about Roberto Duran that should have concerned Hagler, something did. It might have been the history of violence and comebacks, or the effrontery of the man, Duran's air of unpredictability and danger. It might have been the mystique, the eyes, whatever, but Duran did something to Hagler that nobody thought he could do in or out of the ring. People wondered what a stubby 160-pounder who started the profession at 118-pounds was going to do to a powerful middleweight whose resume consisted of lopsided victories in a division devoid of top-flight contenders.

While Duran was loud, bodacious in his movements, tactless in his mannerisms, Hagler was the silent stalker, content to shuffle, move, jab, all the while taking a piece of his opponent with each round. His style was tactical, exact. No one left a Hagler fight dazzled by his footwork or even his one-punch power, but they marveled at his toughness, technique and generalship. Hagler fought to win, not to impress, and that didn't always appease fight fans. Former Duran trainers Brown and Arcel knew his capabilities, and either out of a respect for Roberto's ring genius or a belief that Hagler was overrated, both trainers gave the Panamanian an edge.

Duran was his first truly great opponent. *People would remember this,* he thought, the day he took down the legend and shoved him so far into retirement that they would only let him back for a Hall of Fame induction. To increase the incentive, Duran was going for records this time around. If he defeated Hagler, he would be the first boxer to win four titles in different weight classes.

Duran's entourage, with a few new faces including training physician Dr Robert Paladino, arrived in Palm Springs, California, on November 1. While training for the bout, Duran found himself in the sights of a famous Hollywood sex symbol, who came to his training session and would sit ringside on fight night. The pneumatic blonde actress snapped photo after photo of Duran but apparently the actress wanted more than pictures. "She was there with a camera but she definitely wanted to fuck him," said former manager Mike Acri. "When I told Roberto, he looked at her and said, 'She too skinny.' I was thinking, look at this girl, too skinny? But those Latins love big asses. Roberto loved big asses, and black girls."

Duran was solid with Felicidad but he could have easily ended up with someone else. "In Las Vegas, he met a very pretty Cuban woman who loved him very much," recalled his mother Clara. "She was called Silvia Garcia. She worked in a hotel. I do not know what happened to Duran, why he did not return to her later. She was a very good woman. She used to send me pretty presents from the States. They lived together for some time, but then they separated. After that, Roberto met Felicidad." Mireya added: "He has a daughter called Dalia, and had also one with a Cuban woman."

A story made waves in local papers that Duran and Hagler had a less than cordial introduction days before the fight. Both camps met by chance on the Dunes Hotel golf course and Hagler apparently put up his arms and made a point not to look Duran's way as they crossed paths. To Duran's followers, the gesture was a clear sign that Hagler was intimidated. Hagler seemed to hold a respect for Duran that belied his usual contempt for his opponents. "I think Duran's already starting to get to Hagler psychologically," said Angelo Dundee a week before the fight. "He knows how to psych guys out before the fight."

Having himself nixed a mega-fight with Hagler, Ray Leonard weighed in on the subject: "I expect Duran to fight Hagler the same way I would have fought Hagler, the same way I fought Duran in our second fight," he told a reporter. "Box him, go to the body. Not toe-to-toe, but test him at times. If he makes a mistake, jump on him, stand there and punch, then get out. You can't be one-dimensional against Hagler, your mind must be a sophisticated computer. Just react. You can't stop and think or he'll be all over you."

The thirty-two-year-old Duran may have been the WBA junior middleweight champion but Hagler, twenty-nine, had cleaned out the competition in his divison. Hagler was fighting the first of his two-fight contract with Top Rank Inc. The fight was held in a sold-out crowd of 15,200 in the outside arena at Caesar's Palace in Las Vegas, and shown in close to 400 closed-circuit locations in fifty countries. *Ring* magazine polled twenty-five boxing insiders and not one predicted a Duran victory.

During the official press conference, Duran offered to fight Hagler "right now, why wait?" To which Hagler responded, "I thought the man couldn't speak English." Though both seemed confident, Duran looked in charge. One reporter covering the pre-fight hype noted that Hagler had become a guest at Roberto's fight.

"I think beating Davey Moore proved to people and proved to me that I still have all my skills," Duran told a reporter. "I still have my power and my speed and most of all, my experience. I think the key to beating Hagler is to get inside and I'm smart enough to know how to do it. With someone with his height and reach, you have to get to his body. He'll try to work his jab but he can't keep me off. I'll get inside and once I do, I'll prove to Marvin Hagler that I can punch with the middleweights. Hagler hasn't been tested in years. Nobody's hit him. I'm going to hit him. We'll find out if he can take a real punch."

Marvin countered, "He likes to brawl and maul but I don't intend letting him get close to me. I can box, I've proved that to people, and I'm going to box Roberto Duran. I'm going to pop away at him and keep him off balance. I'll be sticking him with the jab and when I see the opportunity, I'm going to nail him with combinations. I really want to bust him up. The more his people talk and the more they call me names, the more I get up, the more damage I want to do. The thing about Roberto Duran is that he's not afraid to get hit and that will be his downfall. I plan on busting him up so bad he won't be able to go back to his division and defend his title. I want to retire Roberto Duran."

The 3-1 betting line in Hagler's favor before the fight moved to 7-2 on fight night, November 10, 1983. The champion had won fifty-seven and drawn two of his sixty-one bouts, with forty-eight stoppages. A stellar line-up of former champs were introduced before the bout: Jake LaMotta, Kid Gavilan, Gene Fullmer, Carmen Basilio, Joey Maxim. The judges chosen by the WBA committee and Elias Cordoba were Guy Jutras of Canada, Ove Oveson of Denmark, and Yasuku Yoshida of Japan. The crowd dripped in wealth. Fifteen-dollar Duran T-shirts easily outsold Hagler shirts. Buglers blared the entry of the boxers, Duran to the *Rocky* theme tune, Hagler to "Stars And Stripes Forever."

The preliminaries were drawn out, with the boxers waiting in the ring for over twenty minutes in cool evening air, but Duran seemed to savor the atmosphere, bouncing around the ring and smiling. The combatants jawed at each other during pre-fight introductions, but seconds later they quickly touched gloves, a rarity for Hagler.

The chess match commenced at the opening bell. Even the casual fight fan could have predicted that the taller Hagler would use his reach advantage to good effect. Duran came in prepared, without the roll of body fat that occasionally surrounded his midsection. Hagler, one of the hardest trainers in the game, had his usual rocklike look.

Coming off thirty-two straight victories, Hagler landed the first significant punch when he sneaked an uppercut under Duran's guard in the second round. Hagler landed it when he needed to. Often, Hagler set it up by placing his left glove on top of Duran's head, and then sticking the right uppercut into the base of Duran's beard. At the end of the initial stanza, Duran landed a straight right on Hagler's temple, creating a response from the crowd as if it were performing the wave.

The bell ended the second round, and both fighters stopped throwing punches. In an unnatural move, Hagler curled up both gloves against his head to protect himself as the fighters separated. Instead of turning around and heading back to the corner or even throwing a punch after the bell to send a message, Hagler was more concerned with keeping his guard up. It became a theme of the evening.

Duran stepped around a huge Hagler left to start the third round, and delivered a compact left hook to the champ's midsection. It didn't hurt Hagler, but reminded the southpaw that he had everything to lose in the fight. Since Hagler wasn't pressing, Duran was able to conserve his energy, and that was never a good sign for any of his opponents. Both fighters would tease the crowd with a brief middle-of-the-ring duel toward the end of the third, but then Hagler responded to his inner clock.

In the fifth, Duran injured his right hand, which began to swell between the first and second knuckles down to his wrist. Yet he never once gave away his injury, not even grimacing as he continued to land full-blooded rights to Hagler's shaven skull. Gutsing it out, he dismissed the pain to open up in the final fifteen seconds of the fifth. First, he nailed Hagler with a straight right as the southpaw was throwing a jab. Then in one beautiful sequence, Duran closed the gap and landed a right to the body and left hook to the head.

Perhaps because booing had started around the arena, Hagler came alive in the sixth. He shot his jab into Duran's face, switched from southpaw to orthodox and back again – he could box equally as well in either stance – and landed a hard left hook. After a Duran right harmlessly bounced off his shaven skull, Hagler shot an effective right cross. Moving now with purpose, Hagler sunk in three left hooks to the body, pushed Duran against the ropes, reverted to southpaw, moved to the middle of the ring, turned conventional again and then banged Duran with a right cross that stunned him for the first time. It was the best punch of the fight. After motioning Duran to the ropes and feeling the wheeze of his breaths on his shoulders in a clinch, Hagler landed a final right uppercut before the bell sounded. No longer was this Hagler covering up as he spun to the corner. Hagler placed his bald head in Duran's chest, landed a clean right hook, followed by a left hook to close out the seventh round. Duran ended the round in classic gunslinger pose but his courage hadn't been enough to win him the round.

Those close to the middleweight champ knew he had to go after Duran and he finally complied. Staring at Hagler with exhaustion pasted on his face in the ninth, Duran, mouth agape, took three straight jabs. Duran had started fast but was tiring. At his age, it was impossible to keep up the pace. He continually shook his arms as if pleading with them to comply. No discernible response came as Hagler reverted back to his technical dismantling rather than follow-up the previous battering.

Commentator Al Bernstein noted in the eleventh that "something might be going on in Hagler's mind" as he questioned the hesitant nature of the champion. Hagler moved inside in the twelfth, where he'd been dominant despite his long reach, and bullied Duran. With his hands down by his side, Duran put on his first real scowl of the night in attempt to mock Hagler. It was bravado from a man who managed to provide brief sparks but little more. Moments later they were finally in the trenches again and squaring off as Hagler motioned Duran forward after nailing him with a right hand. Duran landed a straight right followed by a nice uppercut as Hagler motioned to his face for more. A cut, which was swelling, appeared underneath Hagler's left eye from absorbing straight right hands. Dipping into his broad repertoire, Hagler displayed a straight left, right jab and another of his pinpoint right uppercuts to best Duran in the thirteenth. As the round closed, Hagler wagged his tongue at Duran, a sign that even the serious stalker could have a little fun.

Yet sensationally the official scores had Duran ahead. Going into the fourteenth round, judge Jutras had it 124-all, Yoshida scored it 127-126 for Duran, and Oveson also had it by a point, 125-124, for Duran. He had to win only one of the remaining two rounds to pull off one of the greatest upsets in history.

Hagler showed his mettle. After landing six consecutive shots to start the fourteenth, he then obliged the WBA judges with short, pulverizing right hooks to Duran's hanging head, and continued to press in a work-manlike manner. By outpunching Duran in the final stanzas, Hagler would leave the judges no choice. It was clear at that point why Duran only occasionally took the risks that defined him in previous bouts. As timid as Hagler was in certain spots, he was just too big and strong.

Duran came out for the final round pounding his chest and sticking out his chin. Nevertheless, Hagler now had a slight lead: one point, one point, and two points on the three scorecards. He padded the lead with an assortment of punches, which included three uppercuts along the ropes, a straight left, and a short right hook, laughing inside as Duran couldn't come close to turning any of his punches. The fight ended with Hagler bundling Duran against the ropes. As the bell sounded, Duran squatted and glared menacingly at Hagler, as he had after his first fight with Leonard. He spat glorious defiance to the end, while Hagler brooded, blood seeping from a cut around his swollen left eye.

As the men waited in the ring, Duran walked over to Hagler, put his fist in the air and berated him. Hagler, who picked up a purse between $8 and $9 million, answered with his hands toward the sky as the scores were read in his favor: Jutras, 144-142, Yoshida, 146-145, and Oveson, 144-143. Had Duran stolen just one of the last two rounds, he would have won. It would have been a bad call, for all the courage and skill of his performance. Many believed Duran's aura swayed the judges to make the fight much closer than it was. "I give Duran a lot of credit but you got to give me credit, too," Hagler said afterwards. "Come on man, you gotta give it to me. That man's a legend."

Judge Yoshida had six rounds even, prompting Bert Sugar to quip, "The Jap thinks this guy 'Even' is now champion of the world." British writer Hugh McIlvaney suggested he "might have scored Pearl Harbour a draw." There was a huge disparity between the judges' scorecards and the overall feeling of the sportswriters: Jerry Lisker, *New York Post*, 11-4; Dick Young, *New York Post*, 10-4-1; Pete Axthelm, *Newsweek*, 9-5-1; Phil Pepe, *New York Daily News*, 11-3-1; Stan Hochman, *Philadelphia Daily News*, 8-5-2; John Schulian, *Chicago Sun-Times*, 8-5-2; Joe Gergen, *Newsday*, 10-4-1; Bob Verdi, *Chicago Tribune*, 9-4-2; Will Grimsley, Associated Press, 8-7, all for Hagler. The morning headlines ranged from "Hagler is still champ, but invincible no more," to "Mere Survival Isn't a Revival for Duran," to "Hagler Survives Duran."

Radio analyst Gil Clancy managed to grab the loser afterwards. "I was the only guy he would talk to after the fight. He said, 'Popi, muy cansado.' He said he was very tired. I had him ahead going into the thirteenth round and then Hagler came back to win the last couple rounds."

The consensus seemed to be that Hagler deserved to win but Duran was a moral victor. "Hagler was intimidated by Duran," said trainer Emanuel Steward. "I don't know why, but he just was. Duran got to him." Had he stolen one of the last two rounds, the challenger would have become the first man in history to rule four divisions. "Duran Steals All The Glory" was the headline in the British trade magazine *Boxing News*. "The stigma of the '*no más*' fiasco in New Orleans in the Ray Leonard rematch is erased forever, and his place with the ring's immortals is assured," wrote its editor, Harry Mullan. "Hagler's post-fight comment, that 'If I'd had one more round I could have knocked him out, but all I wanted to do was to win, and I did' provided a precise illustration of the difference between these two modern greats. Hagler, the bleak professional, had been to work: but Duran, wonderful, unconquerable, fiery Duran, had been to war."

A lot of spectators felt Hagler let Duran off the hook by thinking and not acting. He was too methodical in his approach. Against Duran, he rarely made a move without calculating the repercussions. "If Marvin had put more pressure on early," admitted Pat Petronelli, "it wouldn't have gone fifteen." Adding insult to the criticisms of his performance, the WBC withdrew its recognition of Hagler as champion because the bout had been fought over fifteen rounds rather than the new WBC maximum of twelve. It was a typically churlish action on the part of one of the governing bodies, who often seemed less concerned with governance than with making money from sanctioning fees and exercising their dubious authority.

"A lot of people think his best fight was with Leonard, and I was there in Montreal. But that is a personal opinion. I thought that was his best fight, right there," said Luis Spada of the Hagler fight. "After the thirteenth round, he was one point ahead. You need to take into consideration that Roberto had the body of a lightweight. To fight with middleweights that was something else. Duran was outboxing him even though Hagler was taller and had a longer reach. He learned over the years with Ray Arcel and Freddie Brown to be a complete boxer. In that fight he was like a helicopter. You watch that fight and sometimes he was over-boxing, but he was punching to the body then moving to the side beautifully."

Hagler tried to justify his risk-free strategy after the bout. "I fought him at half-distance," he told a boxing writer. "I was waiting for him to unload so I could score on him. Whichever hand he unloaded with I was ready to counter. I was beating him without mixing it up too much. You don't barrel in on a guy like Duran." A commentator reiterated what many believed to be true: Hagler won the fight, but Duran won the night. "I was a little tight. It wasn't the atmosphere. It was inside. It was between Roberto and myself," said Hagler. Still, the Marvelous One would have a chance to win back the fans against Thomas Hearns.

"Everyone was saying he was a destroyer," Duran said. "But when he hit me it didn't do a thing to me. But I was scared to throw my right hand." He was still ebullient at a press conference the morning after. Facially unmarked and sporting a yachting cap, he rubbed together the fingers on his swollen right hand and joked, "No good punching, plenty good counting money." Hearing of a Hagler complaint that he had been thumbed, Duran burst out laughing.

"He win, I lose, he complaining," he quipped.

# 18

## TOMMY GUN

*"A lot of people came to me and said to watch him because he was a legend, but I already knew this, and he could do anything he truly wanted to do in that ring. But I felt like my skills and my abilities were greater. More than me watching him, he had to watch me."*

Thomas Hearns on Duran

IT WAS, IN hindsight, a mistake. To fight the world's best middleweight, take a seven-month layoff, then step straight into a war with the world's best light-middleweight without so much as a tune-up bordered on madness. But money has a way of barging aside all other considerations in boxing. In the latest in a series of massive bouts, Duran agreed to fight Thomas "Hit Man" Hearns on June 15, 1984, in the arena outside a Caesar's Palace parking lot in Las Vegas. Hearns's WBC junior middleweight title belt, which he had won from Wilfred Benitez in December 1982, would be on the line.

Duran should have defended his own 154-pound WBA title against number one contender Mike "Body Snatcher" McCallum, but abdicated his belt for the money bout with Hearns rather than face the mandatory challenger. The skilled McCallum showed up at the Duran-Hearns press conference to protest the decision to push him aside but no one was listening. "Originally Duran was going to fight a rematch with Hagler because he fought him so tough the first time around," said Emanuel Steward, who managed both McCallum and Hearns. "The WBA told me that Duran was not going to fight McCallum. It was either Duran fight Mike for $500,000 or Hagler for $5 million. Due to Rule Nineteen or something like that, something about the betterment of boxing, it would be Hagler and Duran again. I told Mike that we

254 HANDS OF STONE

couldn't stop the WBA. I said, 'I tell you what, Mike. Duran can fight Tommy and you could fight the winner for the title.'"

Although McCallum agreed to Steward's proposition and was put on the undercard of the Hearns-Duran fight, he was angry. "Mike was supposed to fight on the undercard for $250,000, which was the most he'd made to that point," said Steward. "I wasn't going to take a penny of that, I told him. Then Mike said that he wasn't going through with the fight because he was supposed to fight Duran instead of Tommy. So he fell off the card."

Duran had lapsed back into his old routine and was more interested in making music than training. Some reports had him coming down from as much as 196 pounds. "He was not in the best shape," said Luis Spada. "The time before that fight, he was involved in his music orchestra. When we signed the contract in the Dominican Republic to fight Hearns, he went to play in the orchestra. Roberto wanted me to stay with him and the orchestra. I said, 'No, I'm not here for the music. I am going back to Panama.' After that he was taking too much time with the orchestra. When he needed to train, there was no time left for training." Duran struggled to focus on the bout at hand. His ultimate aim was a return bout with Leonard but it didn't pay to underrate the Hit Man.

Tommy Hearns was an elongated stalker of frightening power. His hooks landed like whiplashes and his straight right was one of the hardest in boxing. Hearns also felt Duran was made for him: too small, too old, no longer dangerous. From the fashion in which Duran picked off punches, probed with his left to land the right, pulled his head back, searched for the left hook to the body and even to his defensive tactics, Hearns knew how to respond. Steward taught Hearns to shoot jabs to Duran's chest to bring down his guard and the pair analyzed every attribute about the man. While Duran had grown into his role as more erudite than powerful in the ring, Hearns had to prove to himself that the right hand he injured against Wilfred Benitez was back to form. During training sessions, Hearns sparred with Olympic hopeful Mark Breland, Milton McCrory and Duane Thomas. Breland was so quick that Duran would appear in slow motion by comparison. There were days in training that Hearns wouldn't even win a round and it became an inside joke at camp.

"Duran wasn't a spent fighter at that time," said Steward. "He was coming off a great fight with Marvin. I always liked to work with speed and it was Tommy's speed that was too much for Roberto. When we prepared for Duran we didn't have any short guys for Tommy to work with. But we worked on many little tricks for Duran. It was all about speed and Tommy would say, 'Duran won't be as quick as these guys I'm training with.'"

In contrast, little went right for the Duran camp. "When we left Panama we went to Nassau in the Bahamas," said Plomo. "He had been drinking and was throwing up, which lowers his defenses. We spent two months there but he was not able to train there even once. He was sick all the time. After two months there that Duran had not been able to train even one full day, he was not in good condition to fight against Tommy Hearns. If Duran ran, then he would not be able to do anything else, and if he trained, then he could not run. When we arrived in Las Vegas, Duran had still six pounds to lose. He had to run in the morning and then go to a sauna before getting on the scale. After this Duran thanked God because he had arrived to the required weight. He said he did not know what would happen during the fight but he could not cancel it, for he would have to face a claim in such a case and that would be too expensive." Duran admitted to this author that he trained only two weeks in the Bahamas and one in Hollywood for the bout.

Two days before the bout, Duran told a *New York Times* reporter, "More than anything else, I wanted a rematch with Leonard. He was the best I ever fought, and I wanted to show him that I could beat him when I was at my best." It suggested his mind was not on the job in hand, even though his opponent was every bit as formidable as Leonard. Hearns's goal, meanwhile, was an assault on Marvin Hagler's middleweight crown.

Before the bout, a story made the rounds that Hearns burned Duran mentally without trying. If true, it marked the first time that Duran was intimidated before a bout. Duran was a past master at pre-fight intimidation. With some it worked, with others it didn't. Thus, Duran expressed his fears and insecurities through intimidation. When it didn't work, he lost an edge. For years he had been typecast as a maniacal fighter with little control. Now, Hearns had switched the roles. At one point before the bout, Hearns pulled Duran's hat down over his eyes, a sure-fire mistake in any setting.

"That happened, sure," said Hearns's trainer Emanuel Steward. "Roberto just ran away when Tommy pulled his hat down. I don't know what it was, but Tommy always intimidated Roberto. Even when

Tommy was like twenty years old and he was at a fight with Roberto in Las Vegas. I'll never forget because Roberto was talking to someone and Tommy went up and tapped him on the shoulder. Roberto quickly backed away when he saw Tommy. It was like he saw a ghost or an evil spirit. That was Duran's role; he was the intimidator. But Tommy always possessed something, like a spiritual thing over Roberto. Roberto was always passive around him whether it was at the press conference or on the street. It was very unlike Roberto."

To Hearns, whose memory is sketchy, the hat incident seemed harmless. "It could have been true," said Hearns. "Me and Roberto were playing around and I pulled his hat down. I thought it was just build-up for the fight. I didn't look at it like it could have been something to make a man change his heart. Just playing around." Hearns would later add, "It was always a must for me to take control before a fight. You never let a man dictate what that you're supposed to be doing. I must be in charge and if I'm not then there's something wrong."

Juan Carlos Tapia concurred, "I would go running with him every morning. He was not in shape. He was intimidated by Hearns and I could tell he was not ready for that fight." Carlos Eleta recalled, "I saw him training by the TV before the Hearns fight. I said, 'My God he is going to fight him like that. He cannot even fight with me.' He didn't train at all."

Others leapt to Duran's defense. "That fight should have never been made," said ex-manager Luis DeCubas. "Duran took it for the money, and he didn't train like he should have. Duran told me personally that making weight for that fight was one of the hardest experiences of his life, but intimidated, *never!* That guy don't get intimidated by nobody."

Whether Duran had fallen under Hearns's spell or not, all indications showed that he had begun to mellow. Plomo Quinones recalled other problems. "There was an American man who used to say he was a friend of ours but he was actually Hearns's spy. We only found this out after the fight, when we realized he was happy with the results and celebrating with the people surrounding Hearns. Duran is such a good person that he thought this was a real friend."

Both men suffered to an extent from the Leonard Syndrome. Hearns had their 1981 fight to win, but got tagged and stopped in round fourteen. "I hurt myself against Leonard three years ago," said Hearns. "I've been proving myself ever since, but the Leonard fight is in the past. It should be kept there. I resent it when people keep putting it up to me."

The promoters of the fight were Shelteron, headed by Shelly Saltman, and Gold Circle, run by Bill Kozerski and Walter Alvarez, who would deal with a worrying financial ebb and flow before the fighters met in the ring. Days before the event, the boxers still weren't sure if or when it would happen. "Even up to the day before, it was a question of financing, the promotions, the whole thing was built out of a house of cards," said Bert Sugar, who broadcast the bout. Emanuel Steward made sure a letter of credit was in the bank weeks before the scheduled date or he was taking his fighter back to Detroit. "I was packed and ready to go home," he said. "Tommy would never fight unless we had a letter of credit a week and sometimes two before the fight. But the promoters hadn't given us the money. So Henry Wald, the President of Caesar's, came to me and promised me that Caesar's would stand by a guarantee. Wald stopped me from packing and I went on with the fight. I had even reduced Tommy's, whose WBC title was the only one on the line, purse so that Duran was making more money than he was."

Duran might have benefited from a postponement. He was reportedly making $1.6 million to Hearns' $1.8, significantly more than if he had fought McCallum, but the move was tantamount to boxing suicide. People criticized Hearns's chin but nobody, legend or not, was going to best him in a shootout – not at 154 pounds. "Hearns could intimidate but he could also hit," said Bert Sugar.

They called it "Malice in the Palace" and 14,824 people waited for the entrants. Duran came in at 154 pounds, bang on the limit, with Hearns nearly a pound lighter yet looking twice as big. While Duran had five losses in eighty-two bouts, Hearns's only blemish in thirty-nine bouts was the Leonard loss. More important than the records, Duran was giving up five inches in height and eleven in reach. "No one has ever really tried to hurt Duran," said Steward before the bout, "but Tommy will."

The theme to *Rocky II* blared from the speakers as Duran, who had officially relinquished his WBA light-middleweight title shortly before, followed a cadre of handlers into the ring. Spada, in a tight-fitting blue jumpsuit with DURAN stitched on the back, nudged the ropes so that Duran could climb through. He looked sharp, replete in a jet-black robe and a thick beard that perfectly fit his face. Hearns, in a red robe with gold trim, seemed almost to gleam as he moved slowly behind a mass of soldiers resembling Roman gladiators. Twisting his arms and then shaking them out to the end of his fists, he breathed intensity. Reaching the ring, he disrobed to show a wiry but sculpted body. Hearns had been sparring in the Kronk Gym with some of the quickest and most talented boxers in the world. He bounced around the ring and shot blur-fast jabs. The Hit Man had never looked in better shape.

In contrast, a strangely subdued Duran sat on his stool before the introductions. The Panamanian didn't stick his fist in Hearns' face like he had done to DeJesus seconds before their battles, nor did he swagger past, throwing a glare or a punch in the direction of the opposing corner. Instead he sat in his corner with shallow eyes. "I wasn't with Duran in that fight," said former manager Luis DeCubas, "but I remember hearing about how he used to go into the shower after work-outs and just lay down on the shower floor for hours because he was so weak. When he got into the ring, he was just sitting there."

Such a small detail might have been missed in an ordinary fighter, but it was easy to look into Duran's eyes and notice emptiness. Even if Duran wasn't scared of Hearns, the popular opinion was that he had not prepared sufficiently to be in that ring that evening. "There were only a few fighters in the history of boxing who could not be intimidated at all. And Duran was one of them," said Jose Torres. "If it's true that he didn't train properly at times, then of course he hurt himself. He was such a mental fighter that he had to be aware if he was in condition or not. Even if you are not in condition but you are aware that you didn't train properly, it affects you. If he didn't train, then he knew he didn't train and that's the thing about smart fighters. They use their heads for every-thing, even unconsciously."

Under a darkening night sky in the temporary outdoor arena, Duran tentatively circled to his left, seeking an opening. To land a shot, he had first to reach Hearns, but the American's jaw looked like he'd need a ladder to hit it. A jab bounced harmlessly off Hearns's washboard stomach. The Hit Man looked supremely confident, flicking out his left to set up the missile in his right glove. Duran appeared concerned about getting hit. Pushed against the ropes with a strong right hand, he flailed back.

In the middle of a combination that sent him falling through the ropes, it appeared that Duran was bravely calling for more punish-ment. A clipping Hearns uppercut opened a cut over his left eye. It was the least of his concerns. There was confusion, which brought a tempo-rary halt to the action, and Duran put his hands up matador style and turned his head as if to ask Padilla for an explanation. A split second later, another uppercut sent him reeling around the ring. "Hearns moved in, purposeful and unhurried, feinted with a left jab to the body and quick as a flash brought over a right to the chin that put Duran down heavily," reported *Boxing News*. "Duran propped himself up on his left elbow, got to his knees and made it to his feet at the count of five. But he looked unsteady." Despite this, he waved Hearns in with his glove, ready to take what was coming, in desperate trouble but the King of Macho once more.

Hearns blitzed him against the ropes with both hands, then dropped him again with a short left hook with a few seconds left in the round. Padilla gave him a standing eight-count and Duran, visibly shaken, headed toward the wrong corner between rounds, something he often did. As if chasing a drunken buddy walking into traffic, Plomo sprinted over to redirect him, a dripping sponge in his hand ready to rinse Duran's blood-smeared face.

At the start of the second Duran appeared to have recovered and the two fighters touched gloves respectfully before resuming. Hearns, sharp and focused, quickly exerted pressure. Duran did land some punches, but not hard enough to even dent the Detroit slugger. Hearns ripped away, tagging Duran flush on the chin with terrible rights. The challenger was in deep trouble and fought back on instinct in a final show of defiance. Then came the end. "Hearns missed with a big right but Duran was backing up again and in disarray," said *Boxing News*. "Hearns shot out a quick double jab to the body, more feints than serious punches, and then struck with a pulverizing right hand to the chin that ended the fight."

The punch landed with such force that Duran was out before he hit the ground, face-first. Referee Padilla stepped in and declared a technical knockout at 1:07 of the second round. There was no need to count. "After that last knockdown it was like he was dead, gone," said Emanuel Steward. "It wasn't just a right hand he hit him with but what we call a 'running' right hand. He was sliding in fast when he hit him with it. Tommy was looking at his chest and Duran never saw the punch."

In the middle of the ring, Hearns – who was aware that a Hagler fight was all but guaranteed – said he knew that Duran was hurt in the first round. "It's the Hit Man coming back again," said Hearns, who fulfilled a second round prediction he made in the papers before the fight. Then he hugged Duran and picked him up like he was a little kid.

As Plomo and Spada rushed Duran out of the ring as if fleeing a bad dream, a crimson stain marked the spot where Duran had landed. If the exit in New Orleans left a bad taste, the head-first collapse that Duran took was more uncomfortable to watch on many levels. In New Orleans there was confusion and it took time for people to understand what had occurred. At first nobody, including Leonard, had an idea that Duran had surrendered. And although the boxing community might never come to terms with Duran's shocking exit, it wasn't painful to watch. Hearns left him flat out, his face on the canvas in a fusion of blood, slobber and sweat. "The final curtain falls on a legend," lamented *Boxing News*.

No one had ever knocked out Duran, a man whose solid chin was even harder than his fists. Anyone with an interest in him – friend, opponent, family member, associate – would have difficulty dealing with it. "Thomas Hearns really beat him up. It was a sad day for Panamanian boxing," said Ismael Laguna. "Hearns had all the advantages against Duran, more reach, he could hit hard and was taller. The way he caught Duran with that one-two punch and the way Duran fell without even putting his hands on the floor, the way he hit the floor head-first, I would not forget that moment. Duran would trust his punching power too much, especially his right hand. My wife was a very big fan of Roberto and I had to take her to the hospital after the fight. She almost fainted. She was so mad about what happened that she thought Duran was dead."

Money, a lot of it, had softened his edge, his belly. Even the anger that so defined his ring presence seemed to have disappeared, and with it his threat. "I do know that he didn't train properly," said Bert Sugar. "Yes he got the shit kicked out of him brutally with overhand rights right on the jaw but I got the impression from not training and not knowing it was going to happen, he just wasn't prepared. These were guys who could intimidate and not back it up. Hearns could hit. When Duran went down in the second round, nose bounced on the canvas, it was like a plane landing."

"That was one of the harder punches that I threw," Hearns said years later. "But also one I hit Pipino Cuevas with. I think that punch was harder than the one I hit Roberto with…but I had to be superb that night. If I didn't go in and knock Roberto out like I did, I probably wouldn't have won the fight because Duran was a legend in the boxing world. It had to be decisive." Reflecting on the fight, Hearns had forgotten little from that Vegas evening. "I was training real hard, so hard because I knew I was fighting a legend. A man that had done a whole lot for boxing, that at an early age he was already a champion. But I had in my heart and my mind that I could win, that I wanted to be successful, and that I was going to do all it took for me to be successful. I was expecting a very tough fight and that's what I trained for. When I saw the opportunity to change that that was a big release of all my heart, of my mind and my soul. I knew my ability, but I wanted to impress the people who came to watch the fight and [thought] that I was going to lose."

Steward was not one of those individuals. Ever since he started working with Hearns, he knew there was something extraordinary about this prizefighter. Although he had come up short against Leonard in 1981, Hearns faced a fighter in Duran, who would stand right in front of him, and no longer had the head movement or reflexes of his fabulous Seventies incarnation.

"I wasn't surprised how quick he got to him because when Tommy was right, and he was a great boxer, he could beat any top fighter in the world," said Steward. "When two great fighters get in the ring, you never see one great fighter destroy another one. Marvin or Ray couldn't do that but Tommy could. When he was right he could go in and make a world-class fighter look like nothing. If you didn't know who Roberto was you'd think he was a slow kid from Panama."

As Duran was led out from the outdoor arena, onlookers wondered if they just saw the last of him. "If Benitez proved that Duran could no longer cut off the ring on a slick boxer, and Hagler showed that the Panamanian could never beat a middleweight," wrote *KO* magazine's Jeff Ryan, "then Hearns stripped Duran of his ability to take a punch and his pride, the only two qualities that he still retained." (Nov 1986) There was nowhere left for him to go.

Duran announced he was retiring and flew home to Panama, where he was promptly honored by the appearance of his head on a postage stamp – and was thrown in a jail cell. According to a story he told author Peter Heller, Duran was seized when he reached Panama City, for reasons not explained. "Then I got rebellious and aggressive and I started to argue with the guards," he said. "They wanted to hit me. They called the colonel, Colonel Paredes, and the captain said we have Duran here and no one can hold him, he says he'll hit anyone who tries and we'll have to kill him … They just grabbed me and detained me. I don't know why. So Paredes said, 'Just let him go.'" The reasons for his arrest are still unclear, even to Duran, but it may have been an angry reaction by the military authorities to his poor showing.

Hearns and Duran retained a special fondness for each other. "I love the man and I have nothing but respect for him still," said Hearns. Both fighters later got to spend time together in Panama. "We were in Panama for a WBO Convention and as soon as Duran sees Tommy he starts screaming, 'Tommy Hearns, Tommy Hearns,' and hugs him," said Manny Steward. "He grabs Tommy and takes him all over town. They were like little kids."

The boxing reporters, once again, wrote Duran's career obituaries but this time it really did seem all over. "It was a sad way for Duran to go," said *Boxing News*, "but at least he fell to a superb champion, and not a man from the lower orders. That would have been tragic. We'll remember Duran as the snorting, scowling, grinning fighter who destroyed the best lightweights of a generation and then moved up in his later years to become a triple champion." His seventeen-year, eighty-three fight career, with just a handful of losses, had been one of the greatest ever. He had equaled the record for lightweight title defenses, won world championships at three weights and was the only man to beat Ray Leonard. Now the rollercoaster ride was finally over.

Old Stone Hands was finished.

## 19

# "I'm Duran"

*"It was like watching Rembrandt paint a picture."*

Irving Rudd, Publicist

FOR OVER A year and a half, Duran loafed and enjoyed his millionaire status. He ballooned to over 200 pounds. He played music. He drank. But the poverty of his past continued to haunt him. "When I was penniless, Christmas and New Year's Eve were the saddest days not only for me but for my mother and family because while others celebrated we had to go to bed early because there was not even enough to buy gumballs," he told author Peter Heller in an interview in the mid-Eighties. "Now every time it's New Year's Eve and I'm home drinking and celebrating with friends I'm happy but only on the outside. On the inside I'm sad thinking of my mother and thinking of those times when I was penniless."

Indeed, by May 1985 rumors were spreading that Duran was much closer to broke than rich. There was speculative talk of an enforced comeback. Trying to fend off the stories that her gambling and her husband's spending on cars, motorcycles and even a plane had forced them to sell some of their assests, Felicidad Duran spoke to a Radio Mia reporter that summer. "We have sold what we wanted to because we have the right to do as we want and it is private. We are in a good financial situation that assures our children's future." Felicidad admitted that her husband had returned to the gym to try to retain his boxing passion but said there was no guarantee of an immediate comeback.

It was no huge surprise, then, when in January 1986 Bob Arum of Top Rank announced that Roberto Duran *would* be returning to action. Arum even played for reporters a tape of Duran insisting that he could beat both Hagler and Hearns. No one was laughing; it wasn't even funny any more.

On 31 January 1986, he took on Colombian novice Manuel Zambrano in the Nuevo Panama Gymnasium. Duran trained at the Rodrigo Colon Sanchez Gym in San Miguelito for the bout. Twelve thousand fans gave their national hero a roaring ovation and despite weighing his heaviest ever at 165lbs – having shed an alleged fifty-five pounds – he didn't disappoint. A left hook put Zambrano down for the full count at the end of round two, with his jaw broken in three places. Zambrano would never win another bout. Three months later in Panama, Duran moved on to the unknown Jorge Suero from the Dominican Republic. It was another mismatch, with the 162-pound Duran knocking out Suero at 1:45 of the second round. These "fights" rated little blips even in the boxing papers, but observers noted Duran was looking sleeker.

On June 23, 1986, the thirty-five-year-old Duran stepped into the ring in Las Vegas to face Marvin Hagler's half-brother Robbie Sims, a tough middleweight with a solid record. Sims was a live one, ten years younger and ranked fourth by the WBA. He had several fine victories to his credit, most notably a sixth-round KO of a young prospect named Iran Barkley. It had been two and a half years since Duran engaged Hagler and now Sims wanted to finish what his brother couldn't.

"Robbie Sims says he's the policeman who will stop anyone trying to get to Hagler," Duran told a UPI reporter. "Well, I'm the general who is going to put him in jail. He'll have to call his brother to get him out." He continued, "I should have never gone ahead with the Hearns fight. I just never got myself into shape. I got a late start in training and then I had some problems along the way. It turned out that I had to lose too much weight in too short a period of time. I felt totally drained when I went into the ring. I had nothing left to hold Hearns off. I was a defenseless fighter. This time, I won't be so stupid. I'll be training the right way now. I know what's at stake this time. Robbie Sims had better be ready. I'm coming to fight."

In the scorching desert heat in the open air at Caesar's Palace, Sims came out throwing bombs, but near the end of the first round Duran stunned him with a left hook and sent him back to his corner with blood trickling down his left cheek. He had learned that it still didn't pay to take Duran for granted. For the next few rounds, Sims racked up points and even opened a cut inside Duran's mouth, and by the fourth the veteran was gasping for air.

But in the sixth, Duran took charge. He held the centre of the ring, jabbed sharply, then made Sims hold on after a left hook and a big right. A sizeable egg formed under Sims's left eye and by the seventh, Duran was in full cry, banging in punches and bloodying Sims's nose as the crowd chanted his name. One ringside reporter called it "the best round he had fought in nearly three years.".

With a few rounds remaining, both men had swelling around their eyes and Duran was spitting blood from a cut inside his mouth. If Duran hustled the eighth from Sims, he was nearly as fatigued in the ninth. Despite battling in the tenth, Duran couldn't maintain the pace, and in the end youth and strength prevailed, though only just. At the end of a grueling ten-rounder, the split-decision went to the rugged, unspectacular Sims. If a point had not been taken from Duran for low blows in the eighth round, he would have managed a draw. Duran earned $100,000 for his work. Judge Art Lurie scored it 96-94 for Duran, while Bill Graham, 97-92, and Jerry Roth, 96-94, favored Sims, who finished looking like the loser, with his left eye almost closed and his mouth bleeding.

"Duran sure has a lot left," Sims told a reporter after the bout. "I made a mistake by letting down in the middle rounds. I knew that Duran was always dangerous and he shook me up a couple times. I got a little weary and paid for it. But I knew I was the clear-cut winner and this was just one hell of a fight."

The loss was a setback but Duran had been in the fight all the way. "If this was Roberto's Duran's last stand," said *Boxing News*, "at least he went out the way we all hoped he would, spitting defiance to the end." *KO* magazine called it "Roberto Duran's Last Night In The Spotlight." As usual, however, Duran had not been reading the script. "If the people, if the press want me to come back, I come back," he said. "If you want to see Duran fight, he will fight."

He was out of miracles, or so it seemed. The nostalgic reunion with Luis Spada had run its course, and now Duran concentrated on his salsa, following in the steps of his brother Armando, who had formed the popular group Arena Blanco. The boxer began to tour with his own band, yet he still didn't feel his fight career was over. That December he met a cab driver and part-time herbalist named Carlos Hibbard at a music gig in New York. Hibbard, a Panamanian Jew living in Brooklyn, had no boxing education, placed his faith in the mezuzah he hung around his neck, and drove a cab without a license. Duran, who was always attracted to mystics and quacks, was amused at his chutzpah and intrigued by his ideas on diet and weight loss. Somehow a man with no steady job and whose motto was "you can't be a loser if you got the mezuzah" gained his ear, and months later, Hibbard joined the Duran team as a nutrition guru. By 1989, he was reportedly earning one-quarter of Duran's purses, by which time speculation was also widespread that Duran had exhausted most of his money and even had dipped into his children's trust funds.

Now under the management of Miami-based Cuban Luis DeCubas, he would fight five times over the next two years. "I got Duran after the Robbie Sims loss. I was living in Miami at the time," said DeCubas. "I got him the fight with Victor Claudio. I was working as his manager, and pretty much doing, everything like finding sparring partners, getting opponents, and locating a place for camp. When I saw him at the airport in Miami, he was 227 pounds. He looked me in the eyes and told me he would become champion again, and I believed him. I was a young guy and here was Roberto Duran telling me he was going to be champion. Of course I believed him."

Moving away from his Vegas stomping grounds, the Duran camp headed to the East Coast to Miami and the Atlantic City casino stage. On 16 May 1987, he earned a unanimous decision over Victor Claudio, a former Olympic boxer from Puerto Rico, in front of 3,500 fans at the Convention Center, Miami. Duran ripped open a cut over Claudio's eye in the third, and knocked him down in the ninth round with a left hook, but couldn't put him away. His hand troubles also flared again, and he headed straight to Mount Sinai Hospital for X-rays after the fight.

He returned to Miami that September to take on Paraguay's Juan Carlos Gimenez, and trained with Carlos Hibbard at Caron's Gym in Miami. Known as "El Toro," Gimenez was 27-3-2 and was the WBC's number eight middleweight contender. It was his first bout outside of Latin America. Duran appeared to be in trouble in the first round after Gimenez crashed in a right hand over the top, and the bearded veteran had to call on all his experience to survive the follow-up barrage of hooks. But he then took over the fight and boxed beautifully, using his underrated jab and occasional thudding rights to finish a clear points winner after ten rounds. "The ex-champ's often under-appreciated defensive skills were very much in evidence," wrote Graham Houston in *Boxing News*. "He feinted, slipped punches, made Gimenez miss by pulling his head back and then countered. Duran used his left jab like a master boxer, sometimes just flicking to keep Gimenez occupied, then suddenly following with a jarring right-hander in a classic one-two sequence."

In January 1988, Duran was hit by a claim for $4.3 million from the American Internal Revenue Service. The IRS said he had understated his taxable income from 1977 to 1984 by $3.8 million, with an additional $618,000 in penalties. His Miami lawyer claimed the assessment was "greatly incorrect."

Still on the comeback trail and hoping for a final big payday with Ray Leonard, in February a pudgy Duran – "like a little beer barrel" according to US trainer Gil Clancy – outpointed Ricky Stackhouse at 162 pounds in the Atlantic City Convention Center. He showed flashes of his greatness. In round two, he sidestepped a jab and dislodged Stackhouse's mouthpiece with a straight right. In round six, he sent Stackhouse to the canvas. In round eight, he dropped him again with a beautiful combination. He was getting back to where he wanted to be, though he claimed he'd had to lose two stone in a month to make the weight.

DeCubas had partnered with Jeff Levine and Mike Acri, a booking agent from Erie, Pennsylvania. Levine paid Duran a $30,000 retainer for promotional rights, and set up the Stackhouse bout. "What was amazing was the fan appeal," said manager Mike Acri. "When he went back to the dressing room after the Stackhouse fight and walked back out and there were hundreds of people … it was like he was Mick Jagger, just hundreds of people chasing him. These people left the stands and started to run after him. He was the king of macho and was as big as Ali for the Latinos. We used to tell him, 'You're fucking Roberto Duran!' And he would be like, 'You're right.' And we would motivate him."

At the Tropicana Resort in Atlantic City on March 14, Duran stopped Paul Thorne at the end of six rounds with a badly cut lip, though he suffered a cut eye himself from a clash of heads. Duran knocked Thorne down in the second and split his lip nearly to his nose. "The punches began to rain down," Thorne, a recording artist, later remembered in a song. "He hit me with a dozen hard uppercuts and my corner threw in the towel. I asked him why he had to knock me out, and he summed it up real well. He said, "I'd rather be a hammer than a nail.""

"Now the champions will want to give me a fight because they are sure it is easy to beat me," Duran told *KO* magazine. He had long since learned to play the media. "Making conversations with him are studies in frustration," wrote's *KO's* Jeff Ryan. "Just as soon as Duran learns that he is speaking to a reporter, he utilizes the only defensive skills that Father Time hasn't yet stolen from him. Up goes the guard. Out goes any touch with reality." Yet Ryan and other writers had written off Duran so many times, he had a right to be annoyed at them. "Who is anyone to say I can't?" said Duran angrily. "If I want to fight, and I get hurt, that's my problem, not yours. Everybody keeps saying I *was*, I *was*. I still *am!* How can I hurt my image? The name I built up cannot be torn down. I'm *Duran*."

It was not only the writers who were deeply skeptical of his latest comeback, however. Even the most knowledgeable fight observers felt Duran was finished, washed up. His heart made promises his knuckles couldn't keep. "Deep down, I think he's still fighting because he's broke," said Ray Arcel, who by then was eighty-seven. "And if he's broke, I know how he got that way. He always misused his money. He has a heart that is bigger than he is. He once told me that Panama is a very poor contry and that he felt he had to take care of everyone there because he was the only one with money."

Duran beat the unheralded Jeff Lanas on a split decision in Chicago on 1 October 1988. Far from looking good, he seemed to be behind by the middle of the fight and only an aggressive finish secured the win. Once again he had struggled to make weight and had to go running the day before the fight in a bid to shed a final six pounds. In the last round, he had stuck out his chin to taunt Lanas but was too slow to pull it away and was caught by several blows. It was a humiliation that augured badly for his challenge against the powerful, aggressive Barkley. "Roberto's an old man," declared one headline. Still, his camp believed this fight was the impetus for his showdown with the Blade.

The Lanas bout almost hadn't come off, as Duran ran into a problem outside the ring. He had a daughter, Dalia, to Silvia Garcia, who lived in Miami. "Roberto was sitting on the couch with his arm around his pregnant 'wife' and in walks, guess who, Felicidad," said Acri. "All hell broke loose. Felicidad went nuts. I almost had to postpone the fight because of it."

As much as Duran loved to party and have a good time, few talk about him solely as a womanizer. Felicidad allegedly blew millions at casinos but she and Roberto also had an extremely loving, and to some extent open, relationship typical of many Panamanian couples. "He told me this story about this girl in Chile," said Acri. "She smoked marijuana and then they had sex. She starts breathing real heavy and Roberto was like, 'Is that from the marijuana or from our passion?' She looks at him and goes, 'I have asthma.' He told that story in front of Felicidad.

"He wasn't always into the women that much. He knew how to take advantage of celebrity but all fighters do. He wouldn't have sex with Felicidad three or four weeks before a fight. He was too disciplined. Don't get me wrong, a lot of women wanted to have sex with him but they weren't flocking to him like he was Oscar De La Hoya or even Hector Camacho."

★ ★ ★

Had the two met at night in a New York ghetto, it would have been the streetfight of all time. The Stone and the Blade. No guns or knives. Just a black gangbanger from the South Bronx and a ferocious *Cholo* who once beat five men in a brawl.

For all the talk about how badass Duran had once been, no one intimidated like Iran Barkley. Six feet and 160 pounds of pent-up rage, he was Ronnie Lott coming over the middle on an unsuspected wideout; he was Fred Williamson without the 'fro, with Jim Brown's scowl. Barkley didn't defeat people; he fucked them up royally. He was a ghetto nightmare who had run with the Black Spades, a ferocious street gang that numbered hiphop pioneer Afrika Bambaataa among its former recruits. When bored of watching the local drug dealers, Barkley and his crew would "go around beating people up, stabbing them and hitting people with lead pipes." Barkley was so menacing he might have forced some of Duran's backup in Chorrillo to get backup.

He had finished a job on Thomas Hearns that Duran couldn't even start. Cut badly above both eyes and behind on points, Barkley had blazed back in round three to floor Hearns twice and stop him in a sensational war in June 1988 to take the WBC middleweight title. "I don't care about the cuts because I didn't have time to bleed," said Barkley afterwards. His destruction of the Hit Man was a reminder that slowly the great fighters of the Eighties were falling to combustible young talents. As Barkley watched Hearns topple from a left hook, he stood over him and banged him with another right hand, as if trying to send him through the canvas. One legend was down, another was next. The people who once feared Duran could now look across the ring and see a bigger, meaner version in black trunks.

And then there was Davey Moore. Moore was like a brother to Barkley. They had grown up together in the South Bronx, boxed as amateurs together, sparred with and supported each other as pros. But Duran had ruined Davey's promising career. He was never the same after that brutal beating in New York, had gone into a decline, lost fights he should have won. In June 1988, in a freak accident, Moore left his car idling in reverse when he stepped out to open his garage door; the car backed up and crushed him to death in the driveway. He was twenty-eight years old.

Iran Barkley became Davey's avenging angel. "If he thumbs me like he did to Davey, I'll thumb him," vowed Barkley. "If he bites me, I'll bite him. If he kicks me, I'll kick him. I'm gonna clear Davey's name. This is a personal vendetta."

Based on recent performances, Duran didn't deserve a title fight, especially against a warrior as formidable as Barkley. But he still had marquee value and also the backing of WBC president Jose Sulaiman, who had often helped him in the past. Barkley's management had also been convinced by Duran's lacklustre showing against Jeff Lanas that while the veteran might stick around for a few rounds and make a fight of it, he had little chance of winning. They agreed to a defense of the title on February 24, 1989, in Atlantic City. Coming from the viscid heat of Panama, Duran would be forced to see his breath in the frigid New Jersey night.

Yet Duran could sense something, as he had with Hagler, Cuevas, and so many other hard men. He appeared not the least bit intimidated. "Barkley's the one who's going to have to worry," he said calmly. "I'm going to prove I'm not finished." Barkley's wide-open, wade-in style was made for the older Duran, who now liked men to come to him rather than having to chase as he did in his youth. Barkley could be tagged and hurt, had taken punishment in the past and was technically clumsy. "The wind is old but it keeps blowing" was an old proverb Duran was fond of quoting. He believed that he knew too much for Barkley. He had been boxing professionally for twenty-one years. The consensus, however, was that Barkley was too big, too young, too tough and too strong.

Duran came into camp at a whopping 220 pounds, having put back on all the weight he had lost for the Lanas fight. Now handled by promoter Luis DeCubas, advisers Mike Acri and Jeff Levine, he went through hell in his Miami training camp. "He had to get back down to a hundred and fifty-six," said DeCubas. "In sparring sessions he was getting the shit kicked out of him on a regular basis. Then, as he got down in weight, he would do the kicking. The reason we got the Barkley fight was because of the Jeff Lanas fight. Barkley saw Duran in that fight and thought it was going to be an easy fight for him." Added Acri, "We were tough on him and I think he respected us for that reason. We would tell him he looked like shit when other people wouldn't. But you had to stand up to the guy or he would run right over you."

It had been close to two decades since Duran had overwhelmed Ken Buchanan and a long time since he had been the favorite in a title fight. Boxers of his magnitude rarely threw up so many contradictions. Arguably the greatest fighters of the Eighties were Leonard, Hearns, and Hagler. Hagler didn't always fight with passion; Leonard had his detractors, who despised his showboating; Hearns could be hurt and knocked down. All three had their deficiencies but their careers did not have the extreme highs and lows of Duran's. There were no Kirkland Laings or Robbie Sims on their records and they never neglected training. None had such a gap between their zenith and nadir. However, when Duran entered the ring, the audience knew they "were going to see a fight," whether it was a good one or not. It wasn't going to be a dance or a sideshow.

If Duran hadn't sunk low in previous fights it wouldn't have been what Gil Clancy called "a miracle" when Duran pasted Moore. To his credit, the fact that Duran made his debut in 1968 and still had it in the ring was a miracle of sorts. He could have retired a legend after the first Leonard fight nine years earlier. As he kept on fighting, the audience kept guessing, not because they wanted to but because Duran prefaced every comeback with failure. But Duran didn't see it as failure. To him, each loss was just another fight where he hadn't trained properly and he'd make it up somewhere down the line. There would always be another fight. It was like he enjoyed creating doubt so he could dissolve it.

Duran was at home in Miami, similar in climate and atmosphere to Panama City but without the endless throng of fans. He had a house there and friends, and he trained hard. Among his sparring partners was cruiserweight Leroy Heavens. According to childhood friend

"Chapparro" Pinzon, who described himself as Duran's valet, Heavens refused to step back into the ring after one brutal four-round session, complaining of pains all over his body.

Certainly his passion, and anger, seemed to have returned. By earning $350,000 to Barkley's $500,000, Duran felt he wasn't getting the respect he deserved. "Another rumor spread that I was burned out and finished," said Duran. "I started again to train, and I was going to teach all these Panamanians and shut the press up that talks a lot of shit here in Panama. I inspired myself. I had a fight with Spada [and] I left and found a new manager in Carl Hibbard. Then I get the fight with Iran Barkley, that's the toughest man to show the Panamanian public. When I fought with Davey Moore, the people weren't on my side. I'm sitting there thinking I had to be champion again."

The people's doubts fired up Duran. The less supportive they were, the more determined he became. Yet what Duran called the "rumor" of him being burned out was, as far as anyone could tell, reality. Ray Arcel said that the Panamanian people didn't like losers. Barkley could be his final vindication.

Members of Duran's camp needed to spice things up. Was it possible that the death of Moore could work as motivation for both fighters? "There were a lot of things said like this was payback for Davey Moore, who had just died before the bout," said DeCubas. "It got personal and we tried to get Duran psyched up." It worked. Duran was pumped. "I heard what Barkley said, he said he was going to avenge the defeat of Davey Moore. I tell Plomo, 'This motherfucker acts as if I killed Davey Moore. But this one I am going to kill. Wait.'"

In the locker room before the fight, Duran burned. "You should have seen him," said Mike Acri. "He was just sitting there, rocking back and forth chanting Barkley's name. He was so focused. The morning of the fight, Duran was eating breakfast and he just kept saying, 'I feel like fighting tonight. I feel like fighting tonight.'"

A 3-1 underdog by fight time, Duran couldn't go in there and brawl with Barkley. At least, that wasn't the strategy. Three punches had served Duran especially well in his career: the straight right, the left hook (often thrown after faking the right and sliding over) and the uppercut, a devastating weapon on the inside and he could throw it from all angles. He would have to land all of those patented shots while avoiding Barkley's booming hooks. Speed and stealth would blunt the Blade. "I was sparring with this guy who was really fast and tried to pummel me. His name was Carlos Montero and he later fought with me," recalled Duran. "He was really fast, didn't know nothing but I couldn't keep my eyes off him because he would hit me. He was really quick. I'm ready now when I see Iran Barkley. I just look at him and I just tell Plomo, 'This black guy is really big dude. But don't worry Plomo. *No te preocupes*. I'm going to make him eat punches.' And that's what I did. I beat him. I shut the Panamanian public's mouth."

Years later Barkley would downplay the claim of exacting revenge for Moore's defeat. "Everybody built that fight up like it was a grudge match for my best friend Davey Moore, who got destroyed by Duran," said Barkley. "Sure, I was revenging his thing, but also for me. It was for him, but it was more that he was inside of my spirit fighting with me."

While Duran (84-7, 64 KOs) came in at 156¼ pounds, Barkley (25-4, 16 KOs) weighed at 164 on his first try, then returned moments later to make 160. Rumors had a member of the Duran camp playing games with the scale as Barkley somehow dropped four pounds in a minute. Barkley noted that his goal was to finish off the legends. "This is personal," he said. "His people have no respect for me so I have no respect for him."

The fight was the same weekend that Frank Bruno challenged Mike Tyson in Las Vegas and many of the leading sportswriters were forced to choose between the still-great Tyson or the once-great Duran. Most chose Vegas. Then a sudden snowstorm on the eve of the Atlantic City fight buried the Boardwalk under a foot of snow and closed down the city, as the frigid New Jersey shore in winter housed locals in casinos and bars. It lent a funereal atmosphere to the build-up. Even the Greyhound buses ferrying in the daily slots players were cancelled. Many fight fans sat it out in the popular Irish Pub, the only bar open twenty-four hours, where fight debates dragged on over lager and the famous crabcake sandwiches.

"Barkley was a tough kid, but he wasn't great by any sense of the imagination. I gave Roberto a shot going into that fight," said Bert Sugar. "I had a choice of going to the Saturday night fight Bruno-Tyson or the Friday night here, and I chose Vegas. We sat in a tent watching it and I thought I just made the wrong plane. I particularly thought that when Bruno came into the ring crossing himself twenty times. [Duran] was an echo of boxing past."

If stature meant anything, Barkley had all but won the bout before Panama's National Anthem. He stood six feet one, weighed 159 pounds to Duran's 156¼ and had a six-inch advantage in reach. Duran was unlikely to beat him from the outside and to get inside meant risking Barkley's pounding hooks. And then there was age: Duran was thirty-seven, with the wear and tear of twenty-one years as a boxer.

It was the kind of night where the inside of a boxing event actually guaranteed warmth. The only reason to be outside was to get to your car or a cab. High-rollers took their comp'd tickets to see Duran one more time; others who knew nothing about the sport could at least recognize the name and the reputation.

As Duran walked to the ring, many felt it was the last time they would see this great champion. Even his son Chavo was scared. Barkley looked bigger than ever as the combatants faced each other, bathed in sweat, for the pre-fight instructions. Referee Joe Cortez called for a reluctant Barkley to touch gloves.

"Iran, c'mon. Shake hands."

Duran stood and waited.

Starting the fight, Duran moved to his left, and felt his way around the twenty-foot ring. Barkley loomed forward like a nightclub bouncer keeping a troublemaker out of his club. Despite controlling a good portion of the three minutes, Barkley was shaken at the end of the round when Duran landed an overhand right that forced him to back-pedal to safety. Not in serious danger, Barkley smiled to the crowd, the grin of a boxer who got hit with a punch that he knew he shouldn't have. What should have been *his* New York crowd started chanting "Doo-ran" after the bell, but Barkley didn't seem fazed. He had his supporters too. "Duran was a legend so you could expect half of Panama to show up," Barkley said. "Half of the Dominican Republic and blacks from everywhere came to see me and we sold this place out."

Duran found his faithful short left hook off the ropes, overhand right, then clinch, to be effective. The right hand, held high for protection, slowly dropped down by his chest as the fight progressed. Duran's mouthpiece showed early in the fight, a worrying sign that a boxer is gasping, but he knew how to pace himself. He came off the ropes in a fury in the fourth round and hit back with ferocity for the first time. The sudden ambush elicited a brief return to his youth. *There is someone in front of me who will push me one last time. In him, I see myself, my power.*

Duran tripled up his right hands in the fifth and appeared invigorated in the sixth, while the Blade concentrated on a consistent body attack. Between rounds white healing cream was smeared on Barkley's eye. In the opposite corner, Plomo sponged Duran's face hard. Another man massaged his stomach. Duran was already looking through them, listening to his own instincts rather than his cornermen. "The big thing was how Duran changed his game plan during the fight," said DeCubas. "The original plan was to turn Barkley, make him move and never let him get set. But the canvas was so thick that Duran had to stay in the trenches with him and go into the eye of the tornado."

Barkley doubled up on a left hook and stunned Roberto late in the seventh round. Duran stuck his chest out as Cortez jumped between the fighters at the bell, then Plomo entered and nudged him back to the corner. Neither boxer was backing down.

*This one is for Davey.* Barkley nearly laid to rest Davey Moore's ghost with a brilliant left hook in the eighth round. It caught Duran walking in and spun him around like a shotputter, his glove brushing the canvas, then his body contorted away from his opponent. Duran's army of fans fell silent. Barkley stood for a moment, astonished his foe was still on his feet, then stormed in throwing right uppercuts and left hooks to the body. He raised his hand as the round ended. The crowd booed him but he had won the round and was gaining the edge.

"Barkley threw a punch at my chin, and I moved so Barkley would miss. I slipped and I ended up looking at the ring," recalled Duran. "When I looked up Barkley hit me in the neck. He thought that he had me in a bad state but he didn't have me dizzy. When I got back to the corner, Plomo said, 'What the hell's wrong?' I said, 'No Plomo, I went to go maneuver around and he hits me square in the throat.' He asked if I was dizzy and I told him what the hell dizzy was. 'Clean these gloves, I'm going to beat this black guy.' I inspired myself from within. I told him, 'You're too strong for me; you're too tall for me; but I know more than you.'"

Barkley's left eye was by now a slit covered by bumps. Still, as the tenth closed Barkley's left hook had proven to be just as effective as Duran's right hand. Then Duran came back. Having tasted a left hook early in round eleven, Barkley got nailed late in the round with a right hand that froze him for a glancing left hook and another solid right that sent him to the canvas. Referee Cortez was over him counting away as he stared into Barkley's squinting eyes. Rolling on his back, Barkley pushed himself up by the count of five as Roberto waited patiently to begin his celebration. With twenty-five seconds left for Duran to finish him off, the shots didn't come fluidly enough and Barkley hung on, though partially blinded and stumbling.

The legions of fans who had made the snowy trek were on their feet. It had been a caustic eleven rounds of give-and-take. The final stanza began with a Duran left hook on the inside; Barkley responded with an uppercut. Both knew that they needed a strong finish, and with no charades they fought till the end. As the bell rang, Duran in typical style jutted his jaw in the middle of the ring as if to ask for more.

Plomo embraced him at the bell, then Duran hugged Barkley and told him in broken English, "Man, you very good, very strong." Propelling himself closer to the crowd from the top rope, Duran signaled for approval. "Next time I fight Leonard I will be in a lot better shape. I love you Panama! I like you Miami. I like you United States." He looked up and pointed his fist to the sky in relief and exultation. And as the scores were about to be read to the crowd, there was no indication that this was the last time Duran would truly be young again.

As the hubbub fell silent, the verdict was announced. The official scorecards showed a split decision: 118-112 and 116-112 for Duran, against 116-113 for Barkley. At thirty-seven years and eight months, Duran was the oldest fighter to win a world title since Bob Fitzsimmons in 1903.

"People thought I was crazy to put Duran in there," said DeCubas. "When he won that fight, I had put him with the greatest warriors of all time. Barkley told me that the left hook he hit Duran with would have knocked down a wall. People look at me crazy when I say that at thirty-seven years old … and fighting a full-fledged middleweight was the greatest sports accomplishment of all time."

Duran had taken a puncher and made him come after him. "I could have knocked Barkley out in the first round," he claimed later. "I got him into a really bad state. But Plomo said, 'No, stay calm, it's twelve rounds and this guy is big and heavy. It's going to be a long bout and you're going to need the extra strength down the road.' I started studying him and I saw short arms. When he would defend himself, I was too far from him. I had to think a lot to come into him. How would I make him miss to throw mine? What beat him was the necessity I felt to become champion and the fortitude I had to be a champion again. When he would hit me, he would knock me off balance. I would stand there and he would throw his punches so hard that he would throw me to the side. So I could never really hit him as hard as I wanted to."

When both men would see each other years later they would hug, knowing that their fists had created an unbreakable bond, brothers in blood. "Duran is a great fighter and I am a great fighter and we made one of the greatest fights in our time in Trump Plaza in 1987 in the snow," Barkley would say years later. But he never accepted that he had lost the fight. "You can't win a fight on one knockdown," said Barkley. "It should have went to me. I knew he was a crafty guy. I knew he was dangerous and did dirty things in the ring. He kept a clean fight, and sadly to say it was a great fight that I knew that I won. In spite of the situation, I had to take it on the chin. But that fight made me and Duran best friends. I didn't get bitter because I knew I won, and I walked away as a champion and that's what a champion is all about. You walk away with your head up and don't worry about what is what. Duran didn't cause that fight for me; it was … the promoters. I got cheated out of it."

Barkley would subsequently hint darkly that the boxing powers had conspired against him because a Duran-Leonard rubber match was on the cards. He felt he had been sacrificed to build up Duran. Others also had Barkley winning the fight. "I was the scapegoat for him to make that fight with Sugar Ray Leonard," he said. "They needed my belt to do that fight and that's what happened. The deck was stacked against me. [Arum] frankly lied and I knew he was lying because he said to me, 'After you fight Duran you're going to fight Leonard for the big money.' I knew that was a lie and I knew that at that point in my career I couldn't say no because they would have stripped me of my title. Back then Arum had control … and Sulaiman was great marketing for Duran because Duran was Latino. I just went on with the fight."

Duran headed to New York City and Victor's for a free dinner for everyone. It would be the last significant victory feast he would have there. "Victor's kids used to hate it when Duran came because he never paid a cent and he brought all of these people with him," said Acri. "They never paid for anything."

The doyens gave their approval. "Duran is a marvel who's still got head action he always had," Angelo Dundee told the *Washington Post*. "He stands on a dime and makes you miss, like Willie Pep did. Don't count on landing a punch against Roberto."

The ninety-year-old Ray Arcel exclaimed, "That was the way I knew him." Another great trainer, Emanuel Steward, was amazed. "I'll never forget when he beat Barkley, who was so much bigger physically than

Roberto. Not only did he beat Barkley, but he also dropped him. He stood toe-to-toe with him in a slugfest."

Daughter Irichelle concurred: "I know that Buchanan and Sugar Ray Leonard were very important fights, but I was too little to enjoy them. It was Barkley; I was fourteen and it was the greatest fight for me. Here in Panama everyone was going crazy. The people lost faith in my dad and that kind of restored faith. My dad teaches us to give people a second chance in life. And that was a good example for me."

Ismael Laguna, who in 2001 would be inducted into the Boxing Hall of Fame, agreed. "I think Duran redeemed himself with the win over Barkley. I saw him in the gym before that fight and I told the people, 'Hey, Duran is really coming to train.' When Duran trains, I know the result. I told him before that fight exactly what would happen and everything I said came true. He trained so hard, when he works that hard, I don't think anyone could beat him."

One of his four sons, Roberto Junior, or "Chavo," had a front row seat for his father's last great fight. "Iran Barkley was a monster. I was afraid because I saw that guy and he was tall and he beat Tommy Hearns twice. My father demonstrated he was the best."

Mike Acri added a fitting postscript: "I'll never forget, at about three a.m. I get on the elevator and I see two guys carrying Barkley upstairs. Barkley just kept saying, 'The man just got too much heart. Too much heart.' And he was beat up. Duran didn't have a scratch on him."

# 20

# THE NEVER-ENDING COMEBACK

*"There's only one legend. That's me."*

Roberto Duran

DURAN WOULD FIGHT twenty-seven more times on his I-need-money tour, losing almost as many as he won. His last bout of any historical significance would be the final showdown of his trilogy with Ray Leonard, at super-middleweight, on December 7, 1989. It was billed as *Uno Más*: One More. Nine years had passed since their last meeting and neither man could conjure up much false bravado during the pre-fight hype. The truth was they were two pugs way past their prime, looking for a final payday.

Leonard had quit the ring with an eye injury in his prime and remained inactive in the mid-Eighties. He abused cocaine and drank heavily, missing the highs of his boxing career. But in 1987 he had returned with cropped hair and a bulked-up frame and had sensationally taken the middleweight title in a controversial decision from Marvin Hagler. The following year he won the WBC super middleweight and light-heavyweight titles, making him a champ in five weight divisions, and in June 1989 retained his super middleweight crown with a disputed draw against Thomas Hearns. Duran, who by now had fought ninety-two times, winning eighty-five and losing seven, was still the only main to have beaten him in thirty-seven bouts.

"I never said I was going to retire during my career. Nunca. I might have said that I might retire, but that was not a fact. I never made it official. One time I'm drinking with these women. I love whores. The hookers told me, 'You need to screw with us and then go out and beat the living shit out of that black man.' They start kissing on me and I told them, 'You're right.' I come home and tell my woman that it's the last time I drink. Then I start to sharpen myself, and by now I'm praying for the rematch."

The fight was made, strangely, at 162 pounds, six pounds inside the division limit, something Duran did not seem to realize until it was raised at the pre-fight press conference. As ever, Leonard seemed to be calling the tune. "He wanted to fight with me four or five years later, but he doesn't want to fight with me in the 168-pound division because he knows I'm going to rip him apart. If he fought me at 168 I would have ripped him apart. At 162, I couldn't. He almost didn't make the weight himself. He also didn't catch me in condition. At the time I had a really big problem that was eating away at my brain. I owed some money to the IRS. But I was happy because I paid everything I owed to them."

Duran was said to be getting $7.6 million and Leonard closer to $15 million. His IRS debt of $1.7 million had come about through an accounting error after the second Leonard bout, according to adviser Mike Acri. "He got a sixteen-thousand-dollar refund coming from 4.2 million. The withholding taxes in Canada and those places, King held onto it and never paid the government, I believe," said Acri. "When they checked it, he was supposed to get a refund of sixteen grand in the late fall of 1988 before Barkley. He gets one check for sixteen grand and cashes it, no big deal. Next week he gets a hundred and sixty grand, cashes it and a couple weeks later, 1.6 million. The government fucks up. That's why he had to pay back $1.7 million after the third Leonard fight. He took eight hundred grand of the 1.6 back to Panama in cash and put in on his whole family, carrying cases all over them. He lost one hundred grand in cash one time when he checked it on board. It never got back."

As he had in Montreal, Duran made sure to include "the people" again. He held daily workouts in the hotel atrium open to hundreds of fans. Leonard kept to himself in locked workouts in the warehouse district. The press hounded Duran about *no más*, but the angst and disdain had subsided with time. Neither fighter yearned to revisit the baggage that carried over from New Orleans. Duran made the right noises before the bout, saying how he had waited nine years, but the "fight" itself was instantly forgettable. On December 7, 1989 a crowd of 16,305 showed up at the outdoor arena at The Mirage in Las Vegas.

Duran, at thirty-eight, showed all the aggression of a sloth in a coma, while the thirty-three-year-old Leonard was a muscular shadow of his glorious pomp, though he still danced and strutted his stuff. Duran did land a glancing right hand in the first round; his next real punch came ten rounds later. By the second round, Leonard was already show-boating and seemed in complete control. He hit on the break, stared down the Panamanian at the end of rounds and even threw low blows. In round three, Leonard side-stepped a Duran rush and rubbed his head against the top rope out of view of referee Richard Steele. Then he let him up and thrashed him with a left hook. The tactics that Duran taught other fighters were being painfully recycled on him.

By the middle of the fight the fans were booing and by the tenth round they chanted, "Bullshit! Bullshit!" The safety-first Duran seemed to be waiting for inspiration or motivation that never came. Before the eleventh, Plomo stood in front of his fighter and pleaded with him to throw punches, but even when Leonard then suffered a bad cut above his left eye, Duran didn't capitalize on it. Despite his injury, Leonard won a wide twelve-round decision.

Leonard would need more than sixty stitches from the cuts in his mouth and above his eyes, but there was never any doubt about the outcome. Duran had barely even gone through the motions. "The war becomes a bore" and "Leonard beats hapless Duran" declared the papers the following day. Bizarrely, Duran claimed he should have won the decision. "He never could get off," said Duran's manager Mike Acri. "It was freezing, his corner wasn't prepared. There was no blanket in the corner. The next day he was embarrassed and very nervous. We went back to the airport and when he started to hear that Leonard didn't fight good either, he felt a little better. Someone said it was, 'One wouldn't and one couldn't.'" Duran told a *Miami Herald* reporter, "Leonard didn't beat me. The IRS did."

Leonard would fight twice more in the next eight years, losing both, but like Duran his place in the boxing canon was assured. They will forever be intertwined. While Duran couldn't balance the excesses of fame and sport for one tragic evening, Leonard shone. However, while Duran lived for the moment, Leonard never took the time to enjoy the jewels of his success. "The thing about life itself is that once you're in the limelight you're too deep into it to really appreciate and smell the roses," said Leonard. "But once you get out of it and see some of the things you could have corrected or taken advantage of. But all in all, I'm healthy; I'm happy; I have a family and a career. I have a vision and life is good."

Duran ballooned again. "We saw him five, six months after Leonard and he was fat as a pig," said Acri. "He had just bought a pair of $400,000 diamond earrings. I don't know if he was ever that extravagant, but these people spend like they had rock-star money. I think his kids and his wife for a long time used to live off the hog. They never thought the money would run out and that's why he kept fighting: fifty grand here, seventy thousand, he couldn't turn it down.

"As far as leeches, he never gave them anything. They just followed him and got to eat free and got fat. It wasn't like he gave people close to him or his family money, no. He'd give a stranger money before he gave his good friend money. That's just how he was." Accounts to the contrary belie Acri's convictions about the fighter not helping those close to him. They would later have a falling out.

The famed Peruvian writer Mario Vargas Llosa once wrote about a nomadic friend who felt that "getting rid of everything he had as quickly as possible was, for him, something of a religion." That could have been Duran. While his handouts helped him connect to the people, and distance him from the star label that so many athletes clung to, his generosity tag factored in to his current fluctuating financial state. This state was defined by an ebb and flow of income that contradicted any real consistency.

"Duran always liked to be admired and he actually had an escort of followers," said Augustin Jaramillo, a Panama City resident. "Whatever he would tell them, they would accept. He never had problems with them because they never contradicted him, in particular after receiving the money he used to give them. I believe he used to do that in order to feel stronger and that he needed people to be constantly flattering him. This made him feel well. It was kind of a necessary expense for him. All these admirers would only tell him good things, and would hide the bad ones, in order not to contradict him. They would always tell him that everything he did was correct and maybe this is what brought Duran bad luck, because they never told him the whole truth."

Spada added: "The man had such a big heart. But maybe it was too big. He closed my mouth once. I used to ask him why he gave all his money away. He said, 'Because those people are my friends.' He closed my mouth."

Though the performance against Barkley gave Duran the juice for the final showdown with Leonard, his bag of miracles was empty. Those who watched the celebration dinner at Victor's were privy to the last page of a legend, the last bite of the steak. Barkley represented the last sip of champagne, the final standing ovation for a man steeped in the brutal epithets of fame.

\* \* \*

At 1 a.m. on December 20, 1989, 27,000 U.S. troops, backed up by Stealth fighters and Apache helicopters, invaded Panama. Operation Just Cause was launched to depose and capture the irascible despot Manuel Noriega, who was wanted for drug smuggling and money laundering. The might of Uncle Sam quickly overwhelmed the 3,000-strong Panama Defense Force, though the military operation continued for several days, mainly against small bands of loyalists. An attack on the central headquarters of the PDF touched off several fires, one of which destroyed most of the heavily populated El Chorrillo neighborhood in downtown Panama City. Most of the homes there, meant originally for laborers building the Canal, were wooden. The little houses Roberto Duran moved in and out of as a child burned to ashes. Chorrillo was laid waste.

The invasion followed a failed attempt by the George Bush administration to oust Noriega in a general election that May. For all its visible poverty, Panama had for many years enjoyed economic success thanks to revenues from the Canal and its position as one of the world's major crossroads. But opposition to Noriega, who was strongly suspected of drug running and money laundering, led to American financial pressure that had left the tiny state a shadow if its former self. Many of the banks on Central Avenue closed; people couldn't cash cheques and every day seemed like a Sunday on the once busy streets.

The Central Intelligence Agency (CIA) was given $10 million to funnel clandestinely to the election campaign of Noriega's main rival, Guillermo Endara, in the hope that the pockmarked military strongman they called "Pineapple Face" would be overthrown. The plot did not work out as planned. Not only did Noriega immediately annul the election result, but the "bagman" entrusted with laundering the money into Endara's campaign was arrested in the United States and charged with conspiracy to import vast amounts of cocaine. The bagman was none other than Carlos Eleta Almaran, tycoon, political patron, sportsman, songwriter and one-time manager of Roberto Duran. Endara, a wealthy corporate attorney, had worked with Eleta for twenty-five years and was a stockholder in one of his companies. Eleta was arraigned in Bibb County, Georgia, by Drug Enforcement Agency officials who also accused him of setting up dummy corporations to launder projected drug profits.

Questions arose from the very beginning about Eleta's arrest. Many in Panama have always believed that he was set up by his enemy, Noriega. "Middle Georgia's biggest drug case ever – involving an alleged plan to import 1,320 pounds of cocaine a month into the state – has given an ironic boost to General Noriega's fortunes and added new intrigue to Panamanian politics," reported the *Atlanta Journal and Constitution.* "This has played beautifully into Noriega's hands," said an expert on the political situation in Panama, who spoke to the *Journal* on condition of anonymity. "It has given him an opportunity to connect the opposition to drug trafficking."

Noriega-backed newspapers railed at the seventy-year-old businessman and efforts were made to close down his Channel 4 television station. "The general feeling I perceive from everybody I talk to in Panama is that this could be a setup," said Roberto Eisenmann, editor of the opposition newspaper *La Prensa.* Eisenmann's paper had been closed by the Noriega regime and he fled to Miami for his safety.

While Eleta sat in a Georgia prison – with partners Manuel Castillo Bourcy, Panama's former ambassador to Belize, and Juan Karaminides – protesting his innocence, Noriega was enjoying the last months of his rule. Born in a neighborhood called Terraplen, not far from the Canal and home to many port workers, he had grown up fatherless and hawked newspapers at an early age. In his biography, it was noted that Noriega had lived a troubled upbringing. "Growing up among foreign sailors and prostitutes and with a daily life punctuated with drunkenness and violence, Noriega became street smart without becoming a tough. He was small for his age and tended to be the one the rougher kids picked on." He and Duran became Panama's most famous, or infamous, sons. Both had a passion for women and drink. Duran loved whiskey and milk; Noriega's choice was Scotch. Both loved designer clothes, both had wives named Felicidad and both occasionally traveled with personal jewelers.

A Department of Defense Intelligence Report in the Seventies described Noriega: "Intelligent, aggressive, ambitious, and ultra nationalistic, a shrewd and calculating person." Sycophantic to his superiors, he was tyrannical to subordinates. Noriega knew power and how to use it. Like his predecessors, Noriega exploited Duran's fame for his own ends. "Duran always was used by the president or military as a figure to promote themselves," said boxing journalist Juan Carlos Tapia. "The one exception was Omar Torrijos. Torrijos really loved Duran and supported him but most of the others used Duran for publicity because he was an idol. Noriega was the one who used him the most for his own benefit."

Noriega was also wracked by paranoia, hate and fear and was suspected of decapitating his political rival Hugo Spadafora, whose headless body was found stuffed in a post office bag in 1985. Duran's former adviser Mike Acri said, "I think that they wanted Duran to get political and he wouldn't. Duran didn't want to be political [Duran would run for Senate in 1994, but his grasp of politics was shaky at best]. Even when Ruben Blades ran for president, they were trying to get Duran to do some things and he wouldn't do that. I think he was smart enough to realize that if he pissed off one party, what happens if the other people get in power?"

Evading capture in the initial hours of the invasion, Noriega hid out and eventually sought sanctuary in the Vatican embassy. He spent Christmas and New Year's there, surrounded by U.S. troops who baited him by blasting out rock music like "I Fought The Law" and "Working On A Chain Gang." (Despite the attention on Noriega, it was still Duran's country: the boxer was mobbed when he walked into a Holiday Inn across the street from the embassy to speak with reporters one day in late December.) After nineteen days, the Papal Nuncio convinced him that enough was enough and he marched out to his captors in military uniform, a bible in his hand. Endara was installed as the new president.

The incarcerated Eleta, meanwhile, had befriended his fellow inmates and become a sort of cult hero in the slammer. Despite being a millionaire, Eleta was no snob. His ability to mix with anyone served him well in prison, where for the first time in his life he was stripped of his status. "We would play cards all the time. The people inside the prison loved me," said Eleta. "When I left the jail in Macon, the guards even gave me a watch as a present."

"Noriega was a criminal and a sonofabitch, he ran like a rat," added Eleta years after the event. "When they came after him, he didn't defend himself. But I knew that if I ever got back there I would take care of him. I saw a killer in Noriega but I was not afraid of anything." By then he could afford to talk tough. Noriega would be tried and sentenced to forty years (later reduced to thirty) in jail for drug trafficking and racketeering. Carlos Eleta was freed on $8 million bail. After the U.S. invasion of Panama, all charges against him were dropped.

* * *

Fifteen months after Leonard, Duran returned to the ring against "Irish" Pat Lawlor on 18 March 1991, at the Mirage in Las Vegas. Lawlor had only fourteen wins and one loss in his brief career, but after five rounds was ahead on points. Duran had hurt his shoulder during training, and after getting hit in the bicep in the sixth the pain returned. Referee Carlos Padilla took the injured veteran over to ringside doctor Flip Homansky and the fight was called off in Lawlor's favour at 1:50 of the round. A second *no más*, some called it. "I'm going to ask Don King for a rematch," said a weary Duran. "This was practice."

He next hit the ring in October 1992, at the age of forty-one, to score a wide ten-round decision over American Tony Biglen. Duran, now trained by the Martinez brothers, Hector and Freddie, actually looked in shape and had Biglen down in the first and fourth rounds but couldn't finish him off. Duran was by now a master at playing to the gallery. In the fourth, as Biglen's father screamed instructions to his son, Duran moved Biglen into his own corner, stuck his head through the ropes and shook his head "no" at Biglen's father.

He closed out 1992 with a string of wins against second-rate opponents. He fought three times at Casino Magic in Bay, Mississippi. Small casino towns had now become his home, out-of-the-way gyms his temporary havens. People wondered why the man was still fighting, but for Duran boxing was his way to keep afloat financially and mentally. In December 1993, Duran went into his hundredth bout, against an opponent half his age. "Not many make it to one hundred fights," he said. "I want to be known as the greatest fighter of all time. I've been rated number two behind Sugar Ray Robinson. I think I deserve to be number one."

Originally the bout was set for early November and coincided with the Day of the Dead, a tradition common throughout Central America and developed from a mixture of local religious practices and Christianity. Families congregate in cemeteries and around altars in the home, accompanied by music and song. Those who gather in cemeteries take picnics, making sure to put some food aside for deceased relatives. The superstitious Duran refused to box on that day. "Because it was Duran, we postponed it six weeks," said Mike Acri.

During the postponement, Duran ran for political office for the Arnulfista Party, which was traditionally strong in the rural interior. Elections were being held that summer. "My mother asked me to run for the Senate, to run for the people of Panama," said Duran to a local reporter, a former boxing champion in four weight classes. "I know the people, know what it is to be poor. The people need me, they need somebody just like them." Duran would miss being elected in a close race.

Despite the fact that corruption was still rife in Panamanian society and politics, the environment was noticeably less hostile. "Indisputably the country is better off," wrote reporter Alma Guillermoprieto in *The Heart That Bleeds: Latin America Now.* "With occasional lapses, there is press freedom, in which any number of dreadful tabloids revel. The National Assembly has approved, in record time, a package of sensible changes in the Constitution. The oppressive atmosphere of the final days of the Noriega era is gone …"

Training in Diamondhead, Mississippi, Duran had his usual entourage of friends, hangers-on and backslappers, but was now a very different person to the wired teenager who bragged about putting people in hospital. On December 14, Duran (90-9) knocked down the twenty-one-year-old Tony Menefee in round five with a straight right over a weak jab and dominated his brave opponent until the bout was stopped in the eighth. When the end came, with Menefee struggling to rise after another knockdown, Duran actually gestured to referee Elmo Adolph to stop the fight. "I didn't want to kill him," he said later. "I signaled to the referee because he's a young fighter, an up-and-coming guy, and I didn't want to hurt him." How times had changed.

A month after the Menefee beating, Duran stopped Terry Thomas at Casino Magic. Duran broke Thomas's nose midway through the third, the popping sound being heard by ringsiders. Thomas courageously continued but the fight was stopped in the fourth round.

Next was his most meaningful opponent since Leonard. On June 25,

1994, Duran dropped former champion Vinny Pazienza in the fifth round on his way to a close twelve-round decision loss for something called the IBC super middleweight title. The IBC, or International Boxing Council, was yet another unnecessary "governing body" in a sport already plagued by confusion and politics. But Duran and the colorful Pazienza, known as the "Pazmanian Devil," were still a draw and over 10,000 spectators packed the MGM Grand Garden in Vegas to see the former champs battle it out at a contracted 165 pounds.

Before the fight Duran sneered at Pazienza's usual outrageous macho act: "He thinks he's the mother of Tarzan." And the sight of Pazienza on the canvas in the fifth round from a perfectly executed right-hand counter sent the crowd into a frenzy. The three judges, astonishingly, were much less impressed and all scored the round a 10-10 draw. A clash of heads brought blood flowing and Duran continued to punish Pazienza, opening a cut on his face and denting his pride. He couldn't keep up the pace, though, and let Pazienza back into the fight. The Pazman won the last five rounds on every scorecard and the unanimous decision. "I outpunched him," Duran claimed afterwards. "If this kid is so tough, look at his face and look at mine. What did he do? He slapped the whole night. Everybody thought I was old but it was the other guy who fought like an old man. I didn't lose the fight."

He set his sights on a rematch with Pazienza, first stopping Heath Todd in what amounted to a tune-up at Casino Magic. But when he met Pazienza again for the same title on January 14, 1995, in the Atlantic City Convention Hall, he was never in it and lost a lopsided decision. On some cards, Pazienza won every round. Duran took his best shots and remained standing but couldn't shake off the rust of the years.

In February 1996, a flabby old man outpointed Ray Domenge over ten tepid rounds in front of 1,800 at the Mahi Shrine Temple in Miami. "Once upon a time, Duran generated fear and awe," said *Boxing News*. "Now it's pity … He looked like a 'weekend' athlete who should not have been doing anything more demanding than riding an exercise bike." Vinny Pazienza, at ringside, remarked, "I like Duran, now that we ain't fighting, but he ought to retire." Hector "Macho" Camacho, who lined up to fight Duran that summer, was equally scathing.

The decision win over Domenge, and a couple of stoppages of similarly weak opponents, helped prepare Duran for a showdown with Hector "Macho" Camacho, the flashy, loudmouth Puerto Rican southpaw, for the vacant and lightly regarded IBC middleweight title –

well above both their natural weights. They fought on 22 June 1996, at the Trump Taj Mahal in Atlantic City, and it was an indication of their continuing appeal that the bout was screened on US pay-per-view television. Both men traded insults and threw punches at the press conference after Camacho repeatedly made jibes about the *no más* fight. The promoter, who stood between them, came off worst, though Camacho cut his hand on a ring on Duran's finger.

Both fighters would have put on a fine display of speed and power in their lightweight primes; now it was a case of who had more left. As 5,200 witnessed in the sold-out Mark Etess Arena in the fight billed "Legend to Legend," the question would be answered in a surprisingly entertaining twelve-rounder. The bout featured many vintage Duran exchanges. He had gotten down to 157, his lowest weight in seven years, his stamina held up and his punches were crisp and definite. The posturing Camacho brought out the competiitve fire in him, and each right hand that bounced off the Macho Man's temple brought a glow of satisfaction to the old warhorse.

Camacho created an early lead with his jab but Duran came back at him and in the middle rounds his more accurate and harder shots cut the light-hitting Puerto Rican. Duran talked to Camacho during infighting, let him know who was the boss. He targeted a cut under the Macho Man's right eye in the fourth and had him desperately clinching in the fifth. For all of Camacho's flash and braggadocio, his swagger had waned and ability to avoid punches had eluded him over the first half of the fight. That classic right hand was often deposited from various angles, and Duran looked to build an early lead. Would the judges reward speed or strength? Even though Duran had matched Camacho and even bested him during several trade-offs, he had lost steam in the late rounds and couldn't win over the judges. Camacho ended up winning an unpopular yet unanimous decision. "Why should I quit?" Duran told reporters at the post-fight press conference.

Back in Panama, Duran was pitted in a horribly overmatched bout with Ariel Cruz, who hadn't won a fight in thirteen contests, that August. Duran disposed of the journeyman in one round, and would head back stateside. Less than a month later at the Mountaineer Race Track in Chester, West Virginia, Duran faced Mike Culbert, a southpaw from Brockton, in front of a crowd of 2,800. He knocked Culbert down three times, opened a sizable gash on the side of his left eye and eventually stopped him in the sixth round. Duran earned

$50,000. "'Old Man' Scores a TKO" was the headline in the *Charleston Daily Mail*.

In June 1997, Duran scored his hundredth win and gained revenge over Argentina's Jorge Castro, the former WBA middleweight champion who had controversially outpointed him in February. On the evening before his forty-sixth birthday, he survived a fierce pummeling from Castro early in round three to take a narrow ten-round decision – 97-95 on all cards – before close to 10,000 spectators in Panama City. Castro's strong start had petered out in the intense heat and Duran earned a top-ten ranking in the super-middleweight division with the win. Years later, this author sat with Duran watching a tape of one of the Castro fights and he declared what he would have done to the man if he were in shape. By now he was boxing with little, if any, training.

Two days later, he was interviewed by Joe Cross of *International Boxing Digest* in Ralph's, an "upscale poolroom-bar" on Via Espana in Panama City. "He was celebrating with both hands," recorded Oliver, "a drink in one, a pool cue in the other. Two days after scaling 168 for the fight, he weighed 180. Duran gets fat by breathing smoke and looking at food." He was surrounded by young women, and friends, and seemed happy, talking about another big payday against Leonard or Camacho.

Duran kept plugging away but the deterioration that he had hidden so well in the Camacho bout was now undisguisable. It showed on November 15 when he traveled to South Africa to fight. Replacement David Radford was flown in from England at two days' notice to fight him and managed to rock Duran on two occasions before losing the eight-round decision. Duran went down in a storm with the South African crowds and was presented with a photograph of himself and Nelson Mandela, who reportedly described him as the most charismatic fighter he had ever met.

Duran met the canvas in his next fight. Fighting at a gross 170 pounds, he went down in the first round to Felix Jose Hernandez, a 10-5-1 "tomato can," but came back to fell Hernandez in the fifth and twice in the eighth round. He won an eight-round decision and kept alive his streak of never having lost a pro bout in Panama. It was something to cling to.

Those who called for Duran's retirement were placated by the fact that he still had his mind, his experience and a residue of his skills. Against inferior opponents, these were enough, and no one on his seemingly never-ending comeback tour had hurt him – until he signed to fight the WBA middleweight champ. Roberto Duran had nothing left to teach WBA middleweight champ William Joppy. They were set to fight

August 28 at the Las Vegas Hilton on a Don King production. Well aware that he was sending Duran to slaughter, King was more concerned about his still-evident ticket-selling potential. Joppy was strong and close to his prime, with twenty-five victories to one loss, and the little tricks and tactics Duran had perfected in the clinches and off the ropes were not enough. Press conference talk of him springing a surprise on the young fighter was drowned out by laughter.

Joppy punished the Panamanian for two rounds before referee Joe Cortez stopped the bout at 2:54 of the third. The sight of Joppy pummeling a helpless Duran – after a blistering right hand midway through the round had forced him to cover up – should have been enough. Even Duran promised, "I'm finished." The Nevada Boxing Commission suspended him while his back-up team, which consisted of Acri, DeCubas, and attorney Tony Gonzalez bickered. "Gonzalez made the Joppy fight," said Luis DeCubas. "That was the worst thing I ever saw in boxing. It was criminal." The IRS reportedly took $225,000 of his $250,000 purse money to pay back taxes.

Duran followed up the Joppy catastrophe with a ten-round loss to Omar Eduardo Gonzalez in Argentina. On his forty-ninth birthday Duran waited in Panama to take on journeyman Pat Lawlor in a rematch. He trained in a San Miguelito Gym with Plomo and female trainer Maria Toto. The fight was titled "The Battle of Five Decades" as Duran, almost incredibly, had fought in every decade since the Sixties. In 1960, he was running the streets with Chaflan, learning to survive. In 1970, he was assaulting the lightweight division. In 1980, he conquered the indomitable Leonard by forcing him into an alley brawl. In 1990, he was coming off a victory over Iran Barkley. In 2000, the fame and nearly $45 million has vanished through investments and the belief that it would never end.

Before the fight Duran told the press, "Lawlor is fatter and crazier. Sadly, he came to Panama to get a beating." He then went out and celebrated his birthday with a points win, avenging that earlier stoppage loss to Lawlor when an injured shoulder had forced him to quit.

The show puttered on. Two months later Duran faced P.J. Goosen at the Legends Casino in somewhere called Toppenish, Washington. The unheralded Goosen came in with a 19-2 record. Duran, in his 119th bout, railed against his naysayers. "I ignore all the people who say I shouldn't do this. I don't care what they say," he told reporters. "The commissioners in Las Vegas should worry about their own boxers. I've seen ten-times worse boxers down there and they're still able to box when they shouldn't have a license. I've taken every test, and besides, I know what my body's able to do. I listen to my body, and I will know when my body tells me it's time to quit. The decision will be made by me. When I step into the ring I'm just doing my business." After promising reporters, "you will see if my hands are still made of stone," Duran banged out a ten-round decision.

"The problem is that the only thing he can do is to fight, and all he's done is fight; he doesn't know anything else," said Juan Carlos Tapia. "He'll risk his life to fight just to get money for his family." Eleta urged him to quit, "I told him, 'Before you hit them and they went down. Now you push them and then embrace them. What happened to you?' He didn't like that."

Duran was only fighting to pay back debts that he claimed his wife accrued and money Carlos Eleta stole from him. It was never his fault. After a loss, he never took any blame, and in life, it was always someone else who made him broke. All of the money had disappeared with his skills. The man had fought since 1968, and he felt he had earned the right to spend his money accordingly. "We went to Panama once to see his house and where he was born," said promoter Butch Lewis. "This guy would go down the streets of Panama and dig into his pockets and give money to people, kids in the streets. It didn't matter how much he made in the fight because he would split it amongst the kids in the neighborhood. There's no coincidence he's a hero and it's not about the money. After every fight he always came back and never forgot. And that's the way things are."

As he traveled to Denver, Colorado, to fight Hector Camacho on 14 July 2001, the man was stuck in a vacuum. The cold reception of only 6,597 fans in the 19,000 Pepsi Center revealed the truth that he wasn't marketable anymore. His boxing daughter, Irichelle, backed her father's decision to continue fighting. "How can you ask a man who has boxed all his life to do something else?" The truth was you couldn't. Duran was going to box; it was his life. Even at fifty. Camacho pounded out a unanimous decision to win the National Boxing Association super-middleweight belt in a quickly forgettable twelve-round fight. "I was affected by the altitude in Denver," said Duran. "If Camacho can't knock me out, then who can?"

Salsa legend Ruben Blades said before the first Duran-Leonard that the American was "not fighting a man … he is fighting an emotion." Now Duran was fighting in slow motion. It was time to leave the sport. But would he do it on his own terms?

# 21

## THE LAST SONG

*"The end is going to be exactly how it started, in Chorrillo."*

Juan Carlos Tapia

IN THE BACK of every ex-boxer's mind lurks a belief that he can still fight. He watches bouts on television and mentally breaks down the competitors, finding their faults, thinking how he could beat them, kidding himself. It is a dangerous illusion.

Even at the age of fifty-four, Duran still wished he was in the ring. "I would have no problem with the young guys today," he told *Sports Illustrated*. "None." But by then it was, finally, all over. He would always be *Manos de Piedra* to his people, Duran to the boxing fanatics, the *no más* guy to the casual sports fan. But he would never be a boxer again; never lean over the top rope to salute the fans, never breathe the sweet scent of success, never watch a man fall to the canvas before him. He did not go without a fight.

On 3 October 2001, he was in Argentina to promote a salsa CD and was traveling with his son Chavo and two reporters when their car crashed. Duran suffered several broken ribs and a collapsed lung. Slowly he would recover from the injuries, but his boxing career was finished. For those who cared about him, the accident came not a moment too soon. Finally something would stop him ever getting in the ring again. On January 27, 2002, Roberto Duran officially called an end to a glorious, memorable career that stretched back five decades.

"I did not want him to fight any more, I wanted him to retire," said Clara. "Then the accident took place. So then he said, 'Mama, I am going to stop fighting, I am going to retire.' I went to thank God for this decision. While I was opening my arms to thank God, I saw a cloud close to me, and I said, 'God, I want to thank you again because my son has retired now and he is going to be a good man now.' Then I saw the cloud was leaving."

Ismael Laguna knew it was time. "I left at twenty-eight but Duran stayed around until he was fifty-one," said the former champ. "Duran came on TV and said that maybe the accident and what happened to him in Argentina was a message from God that he couldn't keep himself in the ring at that age. It was definitely a message from the man up there to not fight anymore."

He looked instead to his salsa, his motorcycle (which would again land him in a hospital bed in March 2005), boxing promotions and his family to replace the game he had ravaged since the late Sixties. He split his time between appearances at boxing matches, autograph shows in the US and Europe and singing in his own band. He even retained the five championship belts that were previously stolen from his home in September 1993 by his brother-in-law Bolivar Iglesias. "I've spent three or four million dollars on music," he told *Sports Illustrated*. "I am never home." He helped Luis DeCubas, his former manager, promote shows for his Florida-based Team Freedom Promotions, became a partner with DeCubas and Dan Wise in another promotional concern called DRL, and talks often about making a movie on his life, although he thinks there would have to be two: "One where you laugh, one where you cry."

At times during his boxing career, Duran had put more focus on his music. He played in a salsa band called Tres Robertos (with Roberto Ledesma and Roberto Torres) and played bongos and sang for his Orquestra Felicidad, named after his wife. As early as 1985, he made a recording, *Dos Campeones*, with the Colon-born "King of Salsa," Azuquita. The songs he sang included "La Casa de Piedra," an ode to his childhood in Chorrillo.

When Roberto Duran walks into a room, people no longer gape. Women don't swoon or check themselves in the nearest mirror. Men don't step aside or back. Reporters don't fumble over their notebooks or recorders for a juicy quote. The autograph lines have shortened. There is no longer a Marvelous One, a Sugar or a Hit Man to recreate the pre-fight hysteria reserved for men of grandeur. The muscles, no longer taut, now hold a belly full from fine Panamanian meals in his Cangrejo home or complimentary casino steaks.

Yet he is not heavy like a man who has let himself go. Duran's belly may be round, but it is still solid and you still wouldn't want to take one of his punches. When he is angry his Spanish comes in bursts, he waves his hands and gets inches away from his target's face. Such moments are rare. He is more likely to grab any person within range and hug or make fun of them. If a reporter asks him a question in English that he doesn't want to answer, he flexes his muscles and smiles into the distance as if to say, "I am still Duran."

He makes people feel wanted, a trait he inherited from his mother. His cherubic smile is that of a man who can laugh at himself and at others. It illuminates his face and makes everyone around him enjoy whatever he is happy about at the moment. Nor is it affected. For this reason alone, people love to be around him, much more than they would Leonard, Hagler or Hearns. He has the Ali aura of warmth and fun. Yet he still has a fighter's face. While the anger has subsided, Duran with all the signature creases and jet-black hair still looks like a man who once ruled with his fists.

The fun, the spontaneity and the smile mean that Duran can still draw a crowd no matter where he goes. One thing that separates him from most of his greatest opponents is that he has no problem being part of the crowd. Fitting in has always been a Duran strength. When he became a world champion, he didn't *have* to go back and play dominoes with his friends from Chorrillo. He didn't have to go back to the old haunts to gorge on beans and rice. He didn't have to walk around Panama handing out his purse money. And he didn't have to stay put in Panama, a downtrodden country where a lot of the world-class athletes have escaped with the fame. But he did.

One can see the real Duran when he is home with his family. He has four sons, known as Chavo, Robbie, Branbi and Fulo, and three daughters, Irichelle, Jovanna and Dalia, and has recently adopted another son. Chavo and the pretty Irichelle both briefly became boxers themselves, though neither showed even a sliver of their father's genius for the ring. In Panama, one can find him sorting through his huge DVD collection – Al Pacino and Robert DeNiro are his favorites – playing pool with a friend or joking with his sons. If he is not home, he could be shooting pool and drinking a beer at one of his local haunts, Magnum Eventos. Wherever he is in Panama, he is always accessible, and Felicidad is not far behind. "My dad would die for us," says Irichelle.

There were times that Duran feared for his own life. In the Eighties, he was flying a plane over Panama without a pilot's license. He was enjoying the view when the plane started to plummet toward the ocean. He started to tell himself, *I can't die now. What will they say about Roberto Duran?* The plane crashed in the water, Duran got out of the cockpit, and then swam the two miles to shore. "I knew I was not supposed to die this way," he said.

Duran believes that he will be rich again and millions will come his way. He has said this many times. If fate has it, he will. Always he is waiting for insurance money from his accident or a business deal that never comes. Impulsive in the ring, he is worse with cash in his hands. There never has been a plan because as anyone associated with him knows, "Roberto does what he wants with his money." In that sense, nothing has changed. He made between $45 and $50 million in the ring. Everyone associated with Duran has a story to tell about his generosity: walking through the streets of Panama with a bag full of money or giving an opponent an expensive wristwatch. "He liked to give away presents," said Plomo Quinones. "When he won the championship and he already had money, lots of people used to come up to him for unpaid bills they had, and they would ask him to help them cancel their debts for electricity, water, etc. And he would help them all, one after the other. I remember one Saturday when after finishing giving away the money he had been asked for he looked at me and said, 'I have given away ten thousand dollars this week.'"

"One time him and his friends stayed for a few days in a hotel in New York," said his former promoter Walter Alvarez. "People were signing his name for meals and bar tabs and gifts. The bill came to something like $60,000. I've seen him go in restaurants, pay everyone's bill, and end up spending $4,000."

Duran's true gratification during his spending sprees came from allowing poor people from Chorrillo and other low-income areas to eat prime rib and sip the best champagne in fine hotels for the first and last time in their lives. It was no exaggeration; he tried to bring Chorrillo with him. "I remember when there were 500-600 people waiting outside in the freezing cold to meet Roberto," said his lawyer Tony Gonzalez. "A young guy in his 20s had brought his father to meet Roberto as a surprise and kept his back turned until his father reached the front of the line. When the guy turned around to see Roberto, he immediately broke down in tears."

The stories never ceased: "My dad was a mason and one time he went to do a job for Roberto Duran. Duran was the world champion at the time," said two-time world champion Hilario Zapata. "All the boys looked up to him. One day Duran tells my father, 'I hear you have a son who is always fighting.' He said, 'He fights so much that I don't know what to do with him.' Duran says, 'Take these gloves and give them to your son so he can practice.' The gloves were sixteen-ounce and they were yellow. I was so happy to receive the gloves but I was more happy because they were the world champ's gloves. I still have the same boxing gear that I began with back then."

Many benefited from Duran's spectacular Robin Hood complex. "A close friend of Duran's once told me that Duran would bring $14,000 every time he went back to his old neighborhood," said local promoter and manager Carlos Gonzalez. "And those people never forgot. They loved him. He would just go through the streets handing out money. It was amazing."

Many also say Felicidad gambled away much of their fortune. "She lost much money," said Plomo. "There were times when the National Police, the Comandos, the highest rank officers, would go to the casinos where she used to gamble. He would sometimes mention this but his love for her is so big. She was spending lots of money, twenty-five thousand dollars, fifteen thousand dollars, a lot of money. But he learned to cope with this. She took advantage of his love for her because she could get hold of the money in the bank. She would withdraw money and spend it freely."

People in Panama love to speculate how much Felicidad lost at the tables. The responses range from "a lot" to the Panamanian term for broke, "limpio." When Duran was making $8 million for eight rounds in the Leonard rematch, he never expected the cash flow to stop. When Duran had a Panamanian bigwig break into an account worth $2 million that Eleta had opened for him after the Leonard debacle, he figured he could double that in the third fight that came a decade later. Athletes rarely think that their time will wind down and their gifts will slowly disappear. According to many associated with the family, when Felicidad had money, it was a good guess where she was heading.

"She spends a lot of money," said Mike Acri. "She likes to shop. I don't know if that affected Duran. They are still together and it is some form of relationship that has strength and endurance. At times they would fight and if he tried to interfere or get into something, they would have a problem. She didn't interfere in the boxing. I like her.

"Once I said to her and Plomo, because I was pissed off at Duran, the insurance policy was seven million and I said we should shoot him when he's doing roadwork. Then we could split the money. After two seconds, I was like, 'I'm just kidding.' But Plomo looks over and says, 'That's not enough.'"

Fight doctor Ferdie Pacheco, who remembered the up-and-coming prospect at the Fifth Street Gym in Miami, was less forgiving of what many considered Duran's ultimate fault. "People like him are either broke or have got a lot of money. They can't hold a dime. He was a puma inside the ring and a manchild outside of it. He couldn't hold money and whatever he had his wife gambled away."

Carlos Eleta didn't blame the gambling. "All the family tried to intervene in the financial affairs. It wasn't just Felicidad. Even without her, he would have lost that money anyway. Even before he was champ, he wanted to be like Robin Hood and give his money to the poor. [Felicidad] was in the picture from the beginning. She was a good influence and was good to try to keep him away from other women."

However in an August 1988 *Ring* interview, Eleta had a different perception. "When Duran got married to Felicidad, that was the beginning of all the problems. The father of Felicidad was always difficult. I used to control all the money that Duran earned but as Felicidad couldn't touch any money, they forced Duran to turn against me. The father started to take care of the rent of the house. Then Felicidad started businesses. She also began gambling every night."

Duran didn't deny it. When interviewed by a Panama reporter about his money woes, Duran told the reporter that he better ask Eleta or Felicidad where the money went. But he knew that being his wife was no easy job. "To be married to Roberto Duran for thirty-five years is not possible," Duran told a reporter. "She is a saint."

In 2000, Duran was winding down and the purses had vanished through bad investments and unrestrained spending. He had in fact hit rock bottom in 1997, when his family was nearly forced out of its home in Cangrejo. There were rumblings that Mike Tyson, whose hero was Duran, had planned to step in and foot the bill. "He was going to lose his house because he owed a lot of money and he put his house up as collateral," said Tapia. "He never paid that money. When Ernesto Endara was President, he asked me personally to resolve

Duran's problem with the house. I talked to the men who Duran owed the money and told him that the interest rates were high and I made the loan go down from five hundred to three hundred thousand dollars. And then I met with several people to resolve Duran's problems. I had a meeting with Duran's bank manager, so he would give a twenty-year mortgage and give Duran twenty years to pay for his house, not immediately.

"We were a hundred grand off and I told Duran that I could make a campaign with my friends. Four people that could give twenty-five grand each and the problem would be solved. But I needed his authorization. He said no and that he had money. The problem was not resolved. He's very proud. For many years Duran has hidden his true economic situation. He tells everyone he's a millionaire but he's not."

Duran claimed that when he needed help, Panama turned its back. "If the Government really wanted to help me when I was down on my luck they would have helped me pay for it," he said. "Any one of the past presidents like Endara could have helped. When I paid for this house, they should have helped me because I really needed this house. When I pay my house off I'm going to put it into the paper, 'I paid my house with no help.' What a shame for the Panamanian Government."

Although some remark on his stubborn ways and refusal to take handouts, Duran has asked for and accepted help on many occasions. He has also been forced to adapt his lifestyle. He used to drink Chivas Regal from the bottle after fights, now it is Seco and orange juice or an Atlas beer, his favorite. Of the eleven cars that he once owned, only a motorcycle and a couple of cars remain in his driveway. There are no chefs or hired help, just a man and a dog hiding in the shadows to keep away fans or reporters. Duran is not alone; many boxers fail to manage their money wisely. Duran had the leeches, the women who spent freely, and a lack of education. All contributed to his current plight.

"There's a lot of people who want to see him well but he thinks because we tell him the truth that we're the enemy," said Tapia. "Duran is not prepared to make sacrifices, he wants the easy life. You have to remember … there were many negative times during his career. He has lost all his money and three times he has gone bankrupt. He spends it. They take it from him. They give it away. He does everything. In his mind he thought that he had gone through a lot of effort to earn that money. Since he's a great boxer, he thought it would be easy to keep making money."

Duran has claimed in the past that he has no need for material things. The white Armani suits, often worn with a driving cap, are gone. He no longer flashes $1,000 earrings and his gold jewelry has been auctioned off. Having been so enamored of the outfits of the wealthy, it is possible to conceive that Duran misses these items the most.

Eleta is one of a select few left from the good old days. Duran said Flacco Bala died of AIDS and in the end was two-faced. He also has the same disgust for Molo, a close friend and confidant from Chorrillo. Arcel and Brown passed away years ago, but Plomo can still be found toiling away at the Jesus Master Gomez Gym in Barrazza.

"The poor people from where he comes from, they don't care that they abused Duran," said Panamanian boxing personality Daniel Alonso. "They interpret it as the possibility of having something of all that Duran has earned, someone from their own family. To me, Duran has one of the noblest hearts. He always trying to go out and help people. When you put everything he's done in a balance, the satisfactions that Duran gave us against his bankruptcy, mistakes, failures, the result is very favorable for Duran."

A common theory that some hold as absolute truth is that Eleta skimmed a lot of money from his fighter. After I interviewed Eleta for this book, several individuals sent warnings of his motives. With white, receding hair, and a stylish dress shirt, Eleta, eighty-six, came across as a classy gentleman who didn't let age stop him from continuing to work. Yet he kept retelling the same stories, as if he were convincing himself of his innocence during Duran's career. "I want this to be known. I tried to preserve his money," he said. "They say that Eleta is stealing Duran's money. Duran believed everything that the people told him. I wanted to save his money. The people here are against anybody who makes money. They are not hypocrites but are envious."

Although Eleta seemed to care more about his own image than Duran's ultimate fate, he has an insight into the man that few people have. With the autograph signings dwindling and the flow of money having stopped, there was a ubiquitous feeling in Panama that Duran would end up right where he started. "I was in a restaurant and he came and embraced me," said Eleta in 2004. "He said, 'I know that you are mad with me. I will not talk bad about you anymore.' I said, 'It's about time.' Some people have lost respect for him but they pardon him. They know that he is crazy and he talks too much. What he says, they don't pay any attention to. But they know what he did for Panama.

"He will end with nothing; he will end up worse than that. He tells me that he will come to my office but he will not ask me for money. I will help him in my way when he has nothing left. I don't know if it will have a sad ending. I don't know how sad. I know that he'll never lack to eat or to sleep because I'll be after him."

★ ★ ★

Duran's family finds it easier to look back to happier times than face the present. The beer flowed at parties; women were everywhere; cash was abundant and everyone dipped into the money pot for any need or want – some more than others. Now, for most of the extended Duran family the gleam of the glory days has turned to rust.

A man once told Clara Samaniego, "There has not been another woman here in Panama that has given birth to a man like Roberto Duran." From almost since he was old enough to walk, she relied on her son. Now La Casa de Piedra is a memory, replaced by a crumbling apartment building. Chorrillo is a dark place, an epicenter of drugs and crime, and there is no sign that Duran ever lived there. A vast army of unemployed wander the streets. Scarred children with sunken eyes hang out of broken windows draped with washing, staring down on empty futures. It will perhaps never be as dangerous as the appalling Colon, but violent death is a constant threat.

During his adolescence, Duran often turned to his stepfather Victorino Vargas for advice. However, by the time Duran had reached his mid-twenties, Vargas and his mother had split. Today it is only possible to reach Vargas's home in Guarare Alto by traveling along several winding dirt roads. There he sits on his porch, cornered by filth. A flattened barbed wire fence lies on the ground, almost inviting one of the several small children running around the yard to step on it. Neglect is a feature of his home. Broken glass substitutes for a window. Clothes are scattered around the yard.

Victor was once slim and powerful; now his full belly rests on his thighs. He has trouble remembering all his five children's names, and he no longer speaks with Clara or any of her offspring. When he asks an interviewer to tape a recorded message for his daughters Anabelle and Isabelle, he purposely leaves out Clara. But he strongly defends Roberto's wife.

When he was earning millions in the early Eighties, Duran helped his family. Whether paying their electric bills or helping to buy a house for grandmother Ceferina, he knew that he was in a special position and felt responsible to spread the wealth. However, many have noted that the fighter would buy drinks and steaks for the *manzanillos* before he would consider helping his family and close friends.

"After winning the championship, he started opening some businesses. A grocery store, then a boutique, and he then bought a couple of buildings. He did not buy any more, he just kept these things," said Vargas. "He did not want to go on with this. He bought a car, a big screen for movies because he likes movies very much, and that is about all. He also bought a piece of land with cows around here. He contacted me and asked me to go and take care of those cows. But in the meantime he got me a job at INTEL, the telephone company, so I did not go there. He talked personally with the manager there and succeeded in getting me a job. I worked there twenty-two years. Till today I am thankful to him for this job. I retired after working there."

Vargas is one of the few family members who didn't charge Duran with not doing more with his money. Although Vargas left his mother, Duran continued to help his stepfather. "One day Justiniano [Vargas's son] was stabbed. Fula was around, and he was taken to hospital," Vargas recalled. "They had a kiosk and a couple of criminals tried to rob him and stabbed him. He had to be urgently operated on because his stomach was badly damaged. And Duran paid for it all. I was once in the hospital myself and Duran paid for the operation. I had to be operated on several times because of a cyst but the operations had not been properly done. So Duran talked to Eleta in order to find a place where I could be operated on properly. I was sent to San Fernando. I got in on a Sunday, and on Monday I had already undergone surgery. He paid five hundred dollars for my stay there. So I can say nothing bad about him, for he always helped me out whenever I was in trouble."

Vargas also staunchly defends Felicidad. He claims he would sometimes go to casinos with her and "she would never lose. On the contrary, she would always win two or three hundred dollars. People used to say she was wasting his money at the casino but since I would go with her and be present, I saw she did not waste the money as people liked to say. I do not believe it was her who spent the money. After winning her money, she would say, 'Let's go home.' And we would go back home."

Toti Samaniego, Roberto's older brother, also defends Felicidad. "If he is married to his wife and he decides to give her money, then she may spend it on whatever she likes, right?" he said. "If he knew that she would go to the casino, did he give her money? This is the way he was. He did not care about the money. He would just give it away for her to do whatever she pleased. And since she lacked nothing at all, what could she do with the money? She would just go into the casino and use it all there."

Living with a woman in Nuevo Arreglan, in a house that Roberto bought for him twenty-five years ago, Toti has had little contact with his family over the years. He has the impish quality of a cartoon character and emotion resonates on his large face. He doesn't look like his brother and the world seems already to have passed him by. His smile is sad and his wrinkles suggest a lifelong struggle. He survives with an energy touched by exasperation.

Duran's uncle Moises was an accomplished folk singer, but it is Toti's voice that the family raves about. While money flashed signs of freedom and autonomy for Roberto, it didn't affect his brother. Although Toti currently lives a twenty-five-minute cab ride from Duran's home, it is in a community way off the beaten path. He has no phone and to find him visitors travel through a thick forested area and ask for "the house of the brother of Duran." Toti sits nervously in a café off the main highway in Nuevo Arreglan and speaks about his love for his brother. Little seems to connect the brothers anymore. While Roberto constantly travels abroad, Toti rarely leaves the small town he calls home.

"Whenever I asked for money, it was because I was in real need of it. He would always give us money, his family," said Toti. "His friends would also ask for money but they would end up taking his things away, stealing the money from him. He once held a party in his house and he had a wallet with six hundred dollars in it that he left on the table. The wallet got lost in the middle of the party and since those were all hundred-dollar bills he could have asked to search everyone in the party for the money. But Duran said he did not care about the money, he only wanted to get back his ID and the other documents. And the wallet turned up, without the money, which meant the thief was still there at the party. Those were the *manzanillos*.

"Yes, they did take everything. Whatever was left there: things, money, shoes, anything. They would take whatever they found. They were his friends and he would not hear a word against his own friends, even more when it was not possible to point at one of them in particular. Besides, it was his home. I cannot tell him what to do. It is his house and he is the one to decide."

Before Toti moved to his current house to live a more primitive lifestyle, he shared in his brother's financial success. Nor has he been pushed aside. Roberto and Felicidad have tried to accommodate a move back to Panama City.

Toti fidgets with his matches as he lights a cigarette. There is work to be done at his home, he says and motions to leave. Like Clara and Victorino, he lives in near poverty. Still he doesn't complain about his lot. He doesn't blame Roberto for anything and lauds him for being a great brother. "I must admit that we used to be a lot closer in the past. At present we are not that close. It is nothing like it was at those times when we were together all the time. I do not go to Panama now. He still treats me well when I go to visit him, but it is not the same. He used to be nicer with us then. When I go there we do talk. He always advises me to come where he is and to stop drinking. But I am not used to luxury places. I do not like this."

Moises Samaniego lives several miles from Toti. Moises is Duran's uncle on his mother's side. Back in the Seventies, when life was good, Moises had a minor following as a folk musician. Stylish and good-looking in old photos, Moises, whose wife Rosina has passed away since then, seems content. Back in the 1950s, he spent time working with Margarito Duran in the Panama Canal Zone and still reserves a special place for his friend. Moises looked after young Roberto for long periods of time when Clara needed to get away. However, Samaniego doesn't hold Roberto in the same regard as he used to. There is a sense that Moises is even angered by Duran's careless nature with money.

"Sesenta millones, sesenta millones or sixty millions," Moises repeated over and over again as if he couldn't believe what he was saying. Although it might be an exaggerated sum, Moises holds Duran responsible for the state of the immediate family. "Something happened to my sister Clara. Now she is too poor."

When Moises needed Duran to get his son out of jail for gun possession, he was left waiting. There was no money at the time. "My son was in jail for having a gun without a permit," said Moises. "I asked Roberto to help me get him out of jail, but he was waiting for a million dollars that was coming from Argentina. He never got it, and my son is still in jail [in April 2004]. I can't get him out.

"[Roberto] hardly did anything for his family. He never cared as much about helping his family as he did for the chombos, or blacks. I was trying to help my friend get a business started and he needed some money to start it up. Roberto didn't want to help. He never did anything for this family. I want this to be told."

Jairo Ivan Garcia is another who sounds a critical note. Tears come down his face, the tears of a man who felt spurned by a member of his own family, of a man who wants to be part of something again and not be treated as a stranger. Garcia lives on 4th Street in Guarare, next to the green house where Ceferina lived. He says that he is Duran's uncle, though that is disputed amongst family members. In the tangled genealogies of Panama, anything is possible. Certainly he *is* related to the boxer and did play a role in raising Roberto.

"Roberto used to come here when he was little. That boy would eat anything," said Garcia. "He would even eat iguanas. My brother Socrates was very good with him and taught him how to box. Socrates was a very big man and was always with Roberto. That is where Roberto inherited his power from. My brother challenged Ali to a fight one time but he said no."

Garcia was at La Cantina Choco Choco when Roberto flattened the horse. Choco Choco is still in Guarare across from the park. "When he used to come to stay here, I would get out of my bed and sleep on the floor," said Garcia. "I would give Roberto my bed to sleep in. He loved to watch cartoons and wrestling. Even back then he would fight anyone in the streets." Although Garcia claims to never have seen Duran lose his temper, there was always the threat. "He talks very loud and strong when he got mad."

One time, when Duran was famous, Garcia went to his house to drop off something, and some money disappeared. "He accused me of stealing five thousand dollars," said Garcia, "and he wouldn't talk to me after that. We haven't spoken in twenty-two years. When he comes here to Guarare, he never stops here." Garcia uses the back of his hand to dry his tears and looks next door for more evidence of Duran's hard-heartedness. There is a huge crack in the concrete and the house looks abandoned, a small toy car the only hint that anyone has been there in years. Decades ago, Ceferina ruled that same house with a strong fist.

"Look at that house," said Garcia. "He never even helped repair that broken down house. That is the house that he grew up in. I would have liked that house to be open for people to see the help Duran would give his family. Duran used to help strangers but not his own family. When people would ask him about the needs of his family in Panama, he would always pride himself on the help he would offer. But that was a lie. He only helps his friends, not his family. Please write this because it is the truth about Roberto. He did not help his family to live."

To stress his own generosity, Garcia points to the floor, "This is where I slept when Roberto came to stay, right here."

"All families have differences," shrugged Mireya Samaniego, Clara's sister and Roberto's aunt, "Jairo says that he is Roberto's uncle, but he is only a cousin because he isn't a brother to Margarito or Clara. No one in the family talks to Jairo because he talked rudely to my mother. Also, Roberto bought a lot of things for Jairo to help him at his house."

Jairo did spend some time with Roberto during his career. Like always, the money flowed. "He had seven cars, seven. But he only needed one. Why seven?" The sadness turned to anger.

Mireya Samaniego is unlike many of her relatives. She is married to a doctor and lives in a well-kept, one-story home in Guarare, across from the Escuela Juana Vernaza school where young Roberto and his sister Marina were briefly enrolled nearly four decades ago. Mireya has two sons, one named after Roberto, and quickly shows her fist and recalls the time when her mother, Ceferina, knocked out husband Chavelo with one punch and then helped deliver Duran hours later. She also recalls a time when Duran argued in the street with Ceferina and threw a $100 bill at her.

Mireya has a round face and an engaging laugh. "Many people became rich taking advantage of Duran. Many indeed," she said. "And Roberto knows it. But he says, 'I owe to God all I have.' He has not been an ambitious person. I believe this is because he knew what it is like to be poor. And he will also die in poverty. This is what Roberto is like. He has always had an enormous heart and has never been ambitious. He did not like to show off either. He would come to visit us in his BMW and he would give away the keys for others to drive it. If he had been different he would not have let others touch his car. But he is a person with very good feelings. He loves his kids very much, and has never abandoned them."

\* \* \*

There has always been an affinity for Duran in Guarare, his mother's birthplace in the Los Santos province, bordered by the Pacific Ocean on one side and the Bahia de Panama on the other. Everyone there who was alive at that time can remember where they were or how much they won when Duran won the lightweight title in 1972 or dethroned Leonard in 1980. "I was watching that fight on a big screen that they set up in a field here in Guarare," says resident Daniel Peres, sat in a local bar. "All the lights were on in the town and when they announced that Duran was the winner, a man next to me flung a child very high in the air. That's all I can remember from that night." And when he lost to Leonard? "The city was dark that evening."

Traveling through Guarare to the several apartments and homes that Clara used to rent near La Plasita del Toros, along with Duran's old hangouts, it is clear that the people recall him with great affection. "I remember he used to steal coconuts from El Rio. He used to come around here to the house as a young boy," said Lesbia Diaz, who lives a block off the Carretera National. "He would walk in and ask my mother, 'Mama, mama, tengo hambre?' She used to feed him rice, beans, patacones and anything she put on the table he would eat. The whole town would be lit when Duran won." Lesbia's late father, Arquimedes, was Duran's biggest fan, and would travel from Guarare to Panama City to congratulate him after victories. Diaz can pull out an entire photo album from a parade the town had after Duran won the lightweight title. Duran was their hope.

Clara Samaniego still lives in the house that her son bought her in the Seventies. It is in Los Andes No. 2, a district in the town of San Miguelito. When Duran bought the house, Los Andes was a safe place to live. It no longer is. Cab drivers refer to it as a red-light district, another name for a low-income housing project. It is the same house where Clara sat with a local reporter to watch her son defeat Sugar Ray Leonard in 1980. She was also there for the rematch, and she remembers hearing people yell, "Cholo, perdio, Cholo perdio," after he walked out. Euphoria and joy encompassed the house when Clara's son was still great.

Young, half-dressed children spread around the house in chaotic disharmony. Dirty dishes are stacked in the small sink to the left. Random phone numbers are scribbled in frat-house comprehension. It has been decades since Clara Samaniego was young but the hard years have not dissolved her kindness. She waits outside her home on a chair for nothing in particular. People pass and exchange glances or small talk. We drive up in a cab, and the driver asks her for "La mama de Duran."

"Soy yo," said Clara softly.

Twenty-five years earlier, things were better. Roberto took care of her. He bought this home for her, one that time has ravaged. Now, with the exception of Roberto, all her sons struggle to make a good living. "I was sad because I fought really hard so as not to fail to my children," she said. "I never failed them. When I say you fail your children, I mean you abandon them. I never did that. I started working to buy their food. Roberto was born with a weight of eleven-and-a-half pounds but he always had his milk ready because I worked. There is a form where you write month after month your baby's weight, and he grew pretty well. His milk bottles were always ready for him when I went to work and my *compadre* took care of him. Upon my returning, I would bring some more money to buy extra food. They never knew what to be hungry was.

"One day there was a party at home, and Roberto asked me to sing a ranchera for him, 'Volver, Volver.' When he was a child he liked a ranchera called 'Ya No Llores Más.' He used to be very happy whenever I would sing that song for him. I had a rocking chair where I used to sit and he liked to come to me when I was sitting there and to ask me for that song."

Duran's sisters Anna and Isabelle live with Clara at the home in Los Andes. They are obviously fond of their brother and credit him, not Victornino Vargas, with being the father they needed. They talk about Duran's jealous streak and how every boyfriend feared their brother. However, Anna does not like the attention that she gets for being related to a famous boxer. Everywhere she goes people say, "There's Duran's sister." She has stayed with her mother for support but yearns to travel. There are no chairs in the house, just empty space. Family members and friends filter in and out throughout the day. Ripped photos of Duran's career adorn the walls. All of this is a sign that life has changed and might never be the same.

"It was a painful moment when Roberto was boxing," said Clara. "It was a great pain to know he was receiving punches. I would always just wait until it was over and then I would ask him if he won. I don't know what happened [to my son]," said Clara. "Sometimes this idea makes me very sad, and so I start singing a song, a popular song, and then I feel like crying…

"I go to his house because he does not come to my house. He always behaves very well with me. He kisses me and asks me to take care of myself. I always tell him not to worry about me. So I leave and come back home. He asks me not to marry again and I tell him I won't. I do not know how does he feel now … It just makes me sad to see my son like this, for he was a very good son. That is why I sometimes feel like singing the song that goes, 'Mano de Piedra Duran …' [she starts singing a song in which she prays to the Virgen del Carmen for her son, and another one which also tells about Duran's life, 'No Llores Más,' a *bolero*]. This is a song Roberto likes very much. I heard this last song when they were singing it on the radio, and I learned it."

Tears form as she sings the final song for her son.

★ ★ ★

Journalist Daniel Alonso, who has known Duran for many years, calls his life "a story with a sad ending." But it is not over, and who can say how it will end? Sadness and poignancy there is, but also hope and a defiant kind of joy. "He has that house and many expenses and many problems," said his brother Toti, "but he remains the same person. He has not lost his high spirits. He is never sad. You can see him here in the Chorrillo on Sundays, always laughing and having fun. He goes to the beach. If he sees someone who needs money, he will always give him some. He does not care about money."

Salsa superstar Ruben Blades once told a reporter, "You go to his house and there he'll be in his shorts. It is not a plastic thing, Roberto's life. It is amazing. The more attention he gets, the less complicated he gets. He is very, very close with all of his relatives. He doesn't travel with people who want to make him feel great by saying, 'Yes, Yes, Roberto,' all the time building up his ego. He doesn't need them or want them."

Roberto Duran's hands are soft, fleshy maps of a life of fighting in streets and rings. His knuckles are ghastly bumps, narratives of the men who confronted him. The man – father, friend and son – has lived in extremes. He has stood with presidents, dined with world figures, danced with goddesses, defeated poverty, partied with celebrities, sipped the world's best champagne, driven expensive cars, draped himself in rare jewelry, and brawled and bested the world's toughest men. He thrived among crowds. When his people turned away, he turned inward; when the world called out, he soaked in its luxuries. When he fought, he punched to kill. When the sport passed him by, he still heard its addictive call. All fighters do. As his reflexes and skills slowly left him, he tilted at ghosts that no longer existed.

Yet when someone was in need, he emptied his pockets and expected nothing in return. His children adore him; his wife has never left his side. He treats his sons like royalty, his daughters like queens. They live for him. His people affectionately chide him, "Duran is loco, but we love him and always will." He found happiness with friends and family, in small things like sitting down to black beans and fried plantains at Victor's Cafe, playing dominoes or billiards, listening to Celia Cruz or Willie Colon, playing the bongos till dawn, drinking a whiskey with milk, eating an ice cream dessert, or heading to the beach on a Sunday afternoon. At his lowest, he settled for lonely makeshift gyms and club sandwiches in far-away forgotten casino towns. Those who love him won't remember that Duran. They will remember the fighter that made war on life.

The man himself remains optimistic: always a fighter but perhaps, above all, a survivor. He will never change. "The Panamanian public loves me now, now that I'm old," he said. "They've recognized now that the greatest thing that Panama ever had was Roberto Duran. They have to accept that. I was born poor in Chorrillo, never smoked marijuana, don't do drugs, have beautiful kids, good education ... never stole from anyone, give money to others when I have it. I could be starving but if I see another man starving I would take my food and give it to him."

Then he flexed his muscles like the Duran of old.

# NOTES

Unless otherwise stated, all quotes come from interviews with the author.

## Chapter 5

"Don't you dare ... he's in shape," Dave Anderson, *Ringmasters* (Robson Books, 1991). "He was dangerous ... you know a lot,'" quoted at www.cyberboxingzone.com

## Chapter 6

Popular opinion ... Buchanan seemed to fit the bill, quoted in Harry Mullan, *Heroes and Hard Men* (Hutchinson, 1990). "If Duran wants ... the book," he promised, quoted in *Boxing News*, 14 July 1972.

## Chapter 7

"The second oldest trade ... which they pronounce 'Bookanar,'" *Boxing News*, 7 July 1972.

## Chapter 9

"A woman came ... throw a punch," *Boxing International*, October 1975. "Edwin frustrated ... stood there and fought me?'" *Knockout*, Spring 1990. "I was supposed to be ... apologized to me," *Boxing News*, 21 March 1980.

## Chapter 10

"Holy Christ!" said ... a Puerto Rican gym, *Boxing News*, 5 November 1976. "I told Duran not to worry ... It worked," *The Ring*, January 1977.

## Chapter 12

"A programme of boxing ... modern era of the game," Hugh McIlvanney, *The Observer*, 15 June 1980. "He moves faster ... in a boarding house," *Boxing Illustrated*, May 1980. One magazine reported ... to make a counter offer, *Boxing Illustrated*, March 80.

## Chapter 13

"Ray Charles Leonard was a prodigy ... all natural talent is suspect," Sam Toperoff, *Sugar Ray Leonard and Other Noble Warriors* (Simon & Schuster 1988). "And all throughout the workout ... or express exuberance," John Schulian, *Inside Sports*, 31 August 1980.

## Chapter 14

"He was with ... had no shame," *Miami New Times*, 5 October 1995. "It would require a deal ... never could be a quitter," Red Smith, reprinted in *The Red Smith Reader* (Random House, 1982). One boxing magazine ... and Leonard's taunting, *KO*, April 1981.

## Chapter 15

"I almost had a nervous breakdown ... to be electrocuted," *World Boxing*, July 1982. "At 157 pounds ... a *finished* fighter," *Knockout*, Summer 1993.

## Chapter 16

"The satanic eyes ... so human and weak," *Knockout*, Summer 93.

## Chapter 18

"Then I got rebellious ... 'just let him go,'" Peter Heller, *In This Corner* (Da Capo Press 1994).

## Chapter 19

"When I was penniless ... those times when I was penniless," quoted in Peter Heller, *In This Corner* (Da Capo Press, 1994). "The best round ... in nearly three years," *KO*, November 1986. "Roberto's an old man," declared one headline, *Boxing News*, 14 October 1988.

## Chapter 20

"I didn't want to kill him ... didn't want to hurt him," quoted in Arlene Schulman, *The Prizefighters* (Lyons and Burford, 1994).

## Chapter 21

"One time him and his friends ... end up spending $4,000," quoted in *KO*, July 88.

# ACKNOWLEDGMENTS

I conjure up strikingly vivid images every time I think of Panama City. I remember dodging the incoming punches of the prince of Panamanian boxing, Ismael Laguna, in the middle of the night, and will forever treasure the pride on his face as he relived, at a restaurant, every second of his 1965 victory over Carlos Ortiz.

In Chorrillo, I saw the sorrow sad, slow descent into the ground of former world champ Pedro "El Rockero" Alcazar, as thousands of fans said goodbye. I remember the surreal scene of his casket being first driven through the streets while a fellow boxer followed in a slow jog. Alcazar was twenty-two years old.

I remember walking into the Jesus Master Gomez Boxing Gym in Barrazza to see a trainer stitching back together the remnants of a boxing glove. The speed bag was wrapped in tape. The protective headgear was falling apart. In a Curundu Gym, the roof couldn't contain rainwater from a storm and would flood often. The back bathroom was gutted and dirty. The locker rooms doubled as bathrooms. Yet, the fighters found solace in the disorder. Hope grew in small pockets of the gym, while the Government looked away.

In the Papi Mendez Gym in San Miguelito, boxer "Chemito" Moreno's glove flapped in the wind as he pounded away at his trainer's hand pads. His stablemate Ricardo Cordoba was busy lifting rusty weights, while preparing to spar in a ring that had potholes under the canvas. There was no running water and the electricity was about to be turned off. The wires were duct-taped together. Another stablemate, Pambele Ceballos, walked around with holes in his sneakers. Fighters slept in a bedroom in the gym. They never complained. Each one treated me like family.

The amateur boxing program barely stayed afloat. In fact, during an evening of bouts in the Rommel Fernandez Stadium, the fighters depended solely on handouts from parents and coaches for proper equipment and food. It didn't change the mood of the evening, as the little kids belted away. The lack of security at fights was forever a concern, as anyone in the crowd could run up to the ring apron unopposed. In one instance, a mother ran into the ring to get avenge her knocked-out daughter, yet to many it only added to the collective chaos. That was Panama.

Trainer and close friend Celso Chavez Sr. passed away, but provided a presence and a smile for any kid who wanted to dedicate himself to the sport. Pedro Alcazar left too soon, and journalist Alfonso Castillo also died during this research. And as I look back, I will think of the fighters who knew there was no future, but who had to keep fighting to pay bills or support their families. There were those who were ravaged in the ring, yet returned out of necessity. This book was written for those fighters.

This journey would not have been possible without the unwavering help of friends, my entire family and the people of Panama. Without them, this would still be nothing more than an ambition. I can never forget the Panamanian people who took me in and supported me, a stranger. When I think of Panama, it was the legacy of Duran for which I searched, but I found the love of the Bravo family of Poppa Juan, Edilma "Mimma", Romellin, Itzel and the rest of the family who introduced me to *patacones* in Sabana Grande.

I would not have completed this biography without the support and lifelong friendship of Carlos Gonzalez. It is essential that he knows how much he means to me. It would take me years to properly thank Greg, my best friend, for his devotion to this book, and endless one-on-one games. Amy and Ali always supported me, and I love you for it. Tair was my heart and soul throughout. Nora Davila gave me advice, *platanos* and Barillito rum. Ildemaro and Munchi gave me life in Panama, and educated me on the baseball rivalry between Chitre and Chiriqui. Hector Villareal, Ludo Saenz, Fredy Moreno, Celso Chavez Jr. and his wife were always there for a meal or to steer me the right way. Guarare resident and friend Daniel Peres led me to places I never would have reached, and gave me somewhere to stay. Every Panamanian taxi driver kept me entertained with endless conversation.

I want to thank Monica Krebs for her flawless translation and generosity. Lee Groves provided me with countless videos, while Rick Scharmberg never lost hope. Jose Torres met me in a deli in New York and changed the face of this book with his knowledge. I never met

Chon Romero in person, but this book has felt his impact and I am deeply grateful for his kind and generous donation of photographs. The people at *Fightnews* and *Gloucester County Times* were indispensable resources throughout.

Panama consul and friend Georgia Athanasopulos always made time for a visit, and it was greatly appreciated. Dale Carson put up with me through this project, while Steve Farhood, my first real interview, provided countless connections and feedback. Miguelito Callist took me under his wing and protected me in the worst gyms, while translators and friends Alexandra Newbold, Margorie and George saved me in times of need. I can't repay Clara for all her class and dignity, while Toti, Ana, Isabel Moises, Jairo, Mireya, and Victorino welcomed me into their lives. Lesbia Diaz invited me in and I felt her passion for Duran. Boxers and trainers Peppermint Frazer, Pambele, Yanez, Soto, Victor Cordoba, Antonio Campbell, Franklin Bedoya, Chavo and Carlos Eleta gave me a history lesson on boxing in Panama. The enthusiasm of the students in the Haddonfield school district, and more specifically Bob Bickel, Chuck Klaus, Mike Busarello and Stafford, was an inspiration. Behind the scenes, Mike Willmann and John Yurkow did extensive PR work. Ed Koenig has been and always was there for me. Dan, Cory, Brian, Kevin and Matt had faith in the book. Peter Walsh deserves my utmost respect for believing in my ability and tracking me down. Lou Papa, a great man, shared a love for travel and boxing with me. Buddy Nask told me never to back down from this challenge when it seemed hopeless. To Angel Romero, my thanks for teaching me how to box.

I will never understand the generosity and love of the Panamanian people who took me in, treated me like family, and never expected anything in return. This journey is my gift to them.

# ROBERTO DURAN'S
# PROFESSIONAL RECORD

Birthplace: El Chorrillo, Panama
Hometown: Panama City
Birthdate: 16 June 1951
Record: 104-16 (70 KOs)

**W = won on points. KO = knockout. TKO = stoppage. L = lost on points.**

| Date | Opponent | Site | Result |
|------|----------|------|--------|
| **1968** | | | |
| Feb 23 | Carlos Mendoza | Colon | W 4 |
| Apr 4 | Manuel Jimenez | Colon | KO 1 |
| May 14 | Juan Gondola | Colon | KO 1 |
| Jun 30 | Eduardo Morales | Panama City | KO 1 |
| Aug 10 | Enrique Jacobo | Panama City | KO 1 |
| Aug 25 | Leroy Cargill | Panama City | KO 1 |
| Sep 22 | Cesar De Leon | Panama City | KO 1 |
| Nov 16 | Juan Gondola | Colon | KO 2 |
| Dec 7 | Carlos Howard | Panama City | TKO 1 |
| **1969** | | | |
| Jan 19 | Alberto Brand | Panama City | TKO 4 |
| Feb 1 | Eduardo Frutos | Panama City | W 6 |
| May 18 | Jacinto Garcia | Panama City | TKO 4 |
| Jun 22 | Adolfo Osses | Panama City | TKO 7 |
| Sep 21 | Serafin Garcia | Panama City | TKO 5 |
| Nov 23 | Luis Patino | Panama City | TKO 8 |
| **1970** | | | |
| Mar 28 | Felipe Torres | Mexico City | W 10 |
| May 16 | Ernesto Marcel | Panama City | TKO 10 |
| Jul 10 | Clemente Mucino | Colon | KO 6 |
| Sep 5 | Marvin Castanedas | Chiriqui | KO 1 |
| Oct 18 | Ignacio Castaneda | Panama City | TKO 3 |
| **1971** | | | |
| Jan 10 | Jose Angel Herrera | Mexico City | KO 6 |
| Mar 21 | Jose Acosta | Panama City | KO 1 |
| May 29 | Lloyd Marshall | Panama City | TKO 5 |
| Jul 18 | Fermin Soto | Monterrey | TKO 3 |
| Sep 13 | Benny Huertas | New York | TKO 1 |
| Oct 16 | Hiroshi Kobayashi | Panama City | KO 7 |
| **1972** | | | |
| Jan 15 | Angel Robinson Garcia | Panama City | W 10 |
| Mar 10 | Francisco Munoz | Panama City | KO 1 |
| Jun 26 | Ken Buchanan | New York | TKO 13 |
| | (Won WBA Lightweight Title) | | |

| | | | |
|---|---|---|---|
| Sep 2 | Greg Potter | Panama City | KO 1 |
| Oct 28 | Lupe Ramirez | Panama City | KO 1 |
| Nov 17 | Esteban DeJesus | New York | L 10 |

**1973**

| | | | |
|---|---|---|---|
| Jan 20 | Jimmy Robertson | Panama City | KO 5 |
| | *(Retained WBA Lightweight Title)* | | |
| Feb 22 | Juan Medina | Los Angeles | TKO 7 |
| Mar 17 | Javler Ayala | Los Angeles | W 10 |
| Apr 14 | Gerardo Ferrat | Panama City | TKO 2 |
| Jun 2 | Hector Thompson | Panama City | TKO 8 |
| | *(Retained WBA Lightweight Title)* | | |
| Aug 4 | Doc McClendon | Puerto Rico | W 10 |
| Sep 8 | Ishimatsu Suzuki | Panama City | TKO 10 |
| | *(Retained WBA Lightweight Title)* | | |
| Dec 1 | Tony Garcia | Panama City | KO 3 |

**1974**

| | | | |
|---|---|---|---|
| Jan 21 | Leonard Tavarez | Paris | TKO4 |
| Feb 16 | Armando Mendoza | Panama City | TKO3 |
| Mar 16 | Esteban DeJesus | Panama City | KO11 |
| | *(Retained WBA Lightweight Title)* | | |
| Jul 6 | Flash Gallego | Panama City | TKO5 |
| Sep 2 | Hector Matta | San Juan | W10 |
| Oct 31 | Jose Vasquez | Costa Rica | KO 2 |
| Nov 16 | Adalberto Vanegas | Panama City | KO 1 |
| Dec 21 | Masataka Takayama | San Jose | KO 1 |
| | *(Retained WBA Lightweight Title)* | | |

**1975**

| | | | |
|---|---|---|---|
| Feb 15 | Andres Salgado | Panama City | KO 1 |
| Mar 2 | Ray Lampkin | Panama City | KO 14 |
| | *(Retained WBA Lightweight Title)* | | |
| Jun 3 | Jose Peterson | Florida | TKO 1 |
| Aug 2 | Pedro Mendoza | Managua | KO 1 |
| Sep 13 | Alirio Acuna | Chitre | KO 3 |
| Sep 30 | Edwin Viruet | Uniondale, NY | W 10 |
| Dec 20 | Leoncio Ortiz | Puerto Rico | KO15 |
| | *(Retained WBA Lightweight Title)* | | |

**1976**

| | | | |
|---|---|---|---|
| May 4 | Saoul Mamby | Florida | W 10 |
| May 23 | Lou Bizzarro | Erie | KO 14 |
| | *(Retained WBA Lightweight Title)* | | |
| Jul 31 | Emiliano Villa | Panama City | TKO 7 |
| Oct 15 | Alvaro Rojas | Florida | KO 1 |
| | *(Retained WBA Lightweight Title)* | | |

**1977**

| | | | |
|---|---|---|---|
| Jan 29 | Vilomar Fernandez | Florida | KO 13 |
| | *(Retained WBA Lightweight Title)* | | |
| May 16 | Javier Muniz | Landover, MD | W 10 |
| Aug 6 | Bernardo Diaz | Panama City | KO 1 |
| Sep 17 | Edwin Viruet | Philadelphia | W 15 |
| | *(Retained WBA Lightweight Title)* | | |

**1978**

| Jan 21 | Esteban DeJesus | Las Vegas | TKO 12 |
| | (*Unified World Lightweight Title*) | | |
| Apr 27 | Adolfo Viruet | New York | W 10 |
| Sep 1 | Ezequiel Obando | Panama City | KO 2 |
| Dec 8 | Monroe Brooks | New York | KO 8 |

**1979**

| Apr 8 | Jimmy Heair | Las Vegas | W 10 |
| Jun 22 | Carlos Palomino | New York | W 10 |
| Sep 28 | Zeferino Gonzalez | Las Vegas | W 10 |

**1980**

| Jan 13 | Joseph Nsubuga | Las Vegas | TKO 4 |
| Feb 24 | Wellington Wheatley | Las Vegas | TKO 6 |
| Jun 20 | Sugar Ray Leonard | Montreal | W 15 |
| | (*Won WBC Welterweight Title*) | | |
| Nov 25 | Sugar Ray Leonard | New Orleans | TKO by 8 |
| | (*Lost WBC Welterweight Title*) | | |

**1981**

| Aug 9 | Nino Gonzalez | Cleveland | W 10 |
| Sep 26 | Luigi Minchillo | Las Vegas | W 10 |

**1982**

| Jan 30 | Wilfred Benitez | Las Vegas | L 15 |
| | (*For WBC Light-Middleweight Title*) | | |
| Sep 4 | Kirkland Laing | Detroit | L 10 |
| Nov 12 | Jimmy Batten | Miami | W 10 |

**1983**

| Jan 29 | Pipino Cuevas | Los Angeles | TKO 4 |
| Jun 16 | Davey Moore | New York | TKO 8 |
| | (*Won WBA Light-Middleweight Title*) | | |
| Nov 10 | Marvin Hagler | Las Vegas | L 15 |
| | (*For World Middleweight Title*) | | |

**1984**

| Jun 15 | Thomas Hearns | Las Vegas | TKO by 2 |
| | (*For WBC Light-Middleweight Title*) | | |

**1986**

| Jan 31 | Manuel Zambrano | Panama City | KO 2 |
| Apr 18 | Jorge Suero | Panama City | KO 2 |
| Jun 23 | Robbie Sims | Las Vegas | L 10 |

**1987**

| May 16 | Victor Claudio | Miami Beach | W 10 |
| Sep 12 | Juan Carlos Gimenez | Miami Beach | W 10 |

**1988**

| Feb 5 | Ricky Stackhouse | Atlantic City | W 10 |
| Apr 14 | Paul Thorne | Atlantic City | TKO 6 |
| Oct 1 | Jeff Lanas | Chicago | W 10 |

**1989**
Feb 24 Iran Barkley Atlantic City W 12
*(Won WBC Middleweight Title)*
Dec 7 Sugar Ray Leonard Las Vegas L 12
*(For WBC Super Middleweight Title)*

**1991**
Mar 18 Pat Lawlor Las Vegas TKO by 6

**1992**
Sep 30 Tony Biglen Buffalo W 10
Dec 17 Ken Hulsey Cleveland KO 2

**1993**
Jun 29 Jacques Blanc St. Louis W 10
Aug 17 Sean Fitzgerald St. Louis KO 6
Dec 14 Tony Menefee St. Louis TKO 8

**1994**
Feb 22 Carlos Montero Marseilles W 10
Mar 29 Terry Thomas St. Louis TKO 4
Jun 25 Vinny Pazienza Las Vegas L 12
*(For IBC Super Middleweight Title)*
Oct 18 Heath Todd St. Louis TKO 7

**1995**
Jan 14 Vinny Pazienza Atlantic City L 12
*(For IBC Super Middleweight Title)*
Jun 10 Roni Martinez Kansas City TKO 7
Dec 21 Wilbur Garst Fort Lauderdale TKO 4

**1996**
Feb 20 Ray Domenge Miami W 10
Jun 22 Hector Camacho Atlantic City L 12
*(For IBC Middleweight Title)*
Aug 31 Ariel Cruz Panama City KO 1
Sep 27 Mike Culbert Chester, WV TKO 6

**1997**
Feb 15 Jorge Castro Buenos Aires L 10
Jun 14 Jorge Castro Panama City W 10
Nov 15 David Radford South Africa W 10

**1998**
Jan 31 Felix Jose Fernandez Panama City W 10
Aug 28 William Joppy Las Vegas TKO by 3
*(For WBA Middleweight Title)*

**1999**
Mar 6 Omar Eduardo Gonzalez Buenos Aires L 10

**2000**
Jun 16 Pat Lawlor Panama City W 12
*(Won NBA Super Middleweight Title)*
Aug 12 Patrick Goossen Toppenish, WA W 10

**2001**
Jul 14 Hector Camacho Denver L 12
*(For NBA Super Middleweight Title)*